GOD BLESS THE CHILD
THAT'S GOT ITS OWN

American Academy of Religion
Academy Series

edited by
Susan B. Thistlethwaite

Number 89

GOD BLESS THE CHILD
THAT'S GOT ITS OWN
The Economic Rights Debate

by
Darryl M. Trimicw

Darryl M. Trimiew

GOD BLESS THE CHILD
THAT'S GOT ITS OWN
The Economic Rights Debate

Scholars Press
Atlanta, Georgia

GOD BLESS THE CHILD
THAT'S GOT ITS OWN
The Economic Rights Debate

by
Darryl M. Trimiew

Library of Congress Cataloging in Publication Data
Trimiew, Darryl M., 1952–
    God bless the child that's got its own : the economic rights
debate / by Darryl M. Trimiew.
        p.   cm. — (American Academy of Religion academy series ;
no. 89)
    Includes bibliographical references and index.
    ISBN 0-7885-0356-1 (cloth : alk. paper). — ISBN 0-7885-0357-X
(pbk. : alk. paper)
    1. Human rights. 2. Human rights—United States. 3. Distributive
justice. 4. Economics—Moral and ethical aspects. 5. Christian
ethics. I. Title. II. Series.
JC571.T743 1997
331'.01'1—dc21   97-9981
                                                  CIP

Printed in the United States of America
on acid-free paper

To my mother,
Oner Mae Trimiew
and to the memory of my father,
Oliver Lee Trimiew, Sr.

CONTENTS

ACKNOWLEDGMENTS

I am grateful to many people, some living, some dead. All live in my memory and in my heart. To my nonliving ancestors, that holy cloud of witnesses I am particularly humbled by the opportunity given me to express, in some partial way, the wisdom of our clan. This work could not have been written without the hard work of my director, Theodore Weber, whose attention to detail is nonpareil. Special thanks must also go to members of my dissertation committee at Emory University: Stephen Tipton, Robert Michael Franklin, and Jon Gunnemann. The Fund for Theological Education is also deeply appreciated for their financial support, intelligent criticism and expert mentoring. Susan Thistlethwaite, as editor of this series was very generous and patient as well as Dennis Ford and Robert Hauck of Scholars Press. My deepest gratitude goes to the late Romney Moseley who mentored me as a graduate student and whose absence is sorely missed. Last, I am grateful to the anonymous referees of the American Academy of Religion whose selfless work and helpful criticisms enabled me to improve this text over the years.

CHAPTER ONE

THE ECONOMIC RIGHTS DEBATE

Them that's got shall get, them that's not shall lose
so the Bible says and it still is news,
Momma may have and Papa may have,
But God bless the child that's got its own,
that's got its own.[1]

This haunting refrain reminds us that basic human needs permit
human flourishing. People use whatever resources they have in
order to maximize their holdings or those of their superiors.
The underlying biblical source for these lyrics is the parable of
talents.[2] In this passage a fearful cautious servant buries his
master's money in the ground. He is unceremoniously demoted
by the acquisitive master as soon as his error is discovered. The
most productive servant is given more to invest and,
presumably, further benefits the master and himself. The
parable emphasizes crafty responsibility over fearful security.
The song emphasizes the blessedness of children who have their
needs met and hints at the wretchedness of the children of want,
children of the dust, children whose parents are not shrewd, or

---

[1] *God Bless the Child that's Got its Own*, A. Herzog, 1955.
[2] Matthew 25: 14-30.

fortunate or industrious. Neither the parable nor the song tell us, however, what constitutes basic necessities and what makes up one's "own." Accordingly, we are compelled to investigate these issues and to argue over the nature and scope of basic needs, basic rights, and what constitutes human flourishing.

This is an extremely important discourse and these are crucial arguments. In remembrance of the sentiments of the late John Courtney Murray, David Hollenbach, S.J., noted moral theologian, writes, " . . . important arguments are never finished. They always have a 'growing end.'"[3] With this shared sentiment, Hollenbach and Murray recognized the nature of modern moral discourse, namely, its decided inability to achieve a satisfying closure or consensus. Yet this lack of finality did not distress them. In contrast, Alasdair MacIntyre is deeply distressed by modern moral debates, which in his opinion are interminable.[4] This work rejects the pessimism of MacIntyre and embraces the cautious optimism of Hollenbach and Murray, which maintains, despite widespread moral pluralism in modern discourse, some arguments at least, appear to be headed toward a "growing end." Indeed, like Hollenbach, this author posits that the economic rights debate is one such concluding debate.

The purpose of this dissertation is to explore the contours, colors and contexts of an ongoing debate in Western liberalism as to the moral nature and functioning of economic rights in the dynamic interaction of moral relationships and systems. What will be explored are the moral foundations of economic rights as well as their authority and appropriateness for formulating and implementing United States public policy, including foreign policy.

---

[3] David Hollenbach, "The Growing End of An Argument," *America*, November 30, 1985, Volume 153, no. 16.

[4] MacIntyre writes, "It is precisely because there is in our society no established way of deciding between these claims that moral argument appears to be necessarily interminable. From our rival conclusions we can argue back to our rival premises; . . ." *After Virtue* (Notre Dame: University of Notre Dame Press, 1984,), 9. MacIntyre concludes, of course, that the arguments do not grow toward an end, but stalemate in incommensurable premises. Ibid.

Accordingly, this study will identify and analyze the major issues in the ongoing economic rights debate comparing and evaluating contrasting positions. Among other concerns, the study should reveal whether this debate is moving toward some resolution, that is, whether there is a "growing end to the argument."[5]

This study presupposes that there already exists, in America, a deep and broad consensus that political and civil rights are the foundation upon which public policy is constructed. Civil and political rights are also commonly understood by Americans to be valid human rights. Given this consensus, economic rights should win widespread acceptance as human rights *provided* they can be shown to be inherently interconnected and interdependent with civil and political rights.

It is the thesis of this study that economic rights skeptics are wrong, that economic rights are indeed true human rights. They are human rights because they are inherently connected to civil and political rights. Accordingly, they are worthy of the same recognition and honor accorded to civil and political rights. What are economic rights? For reasons that will become apparent in this chapter, only a provisional answer can be given at this time. Economic rights are rights that have as their object what Alan Gewirth has described as basic goods.[6] To enjoy economic rights, claimants must not be prevented from acquiring basic goods, and under certain circumstances must be provided with basic goods. Economic rights are necessary and crucial moral constructs for the maintenance of equality, justice,

---

[5] The "growing end to the argument" is a reference that Hollenbach makes with regard to his debate with Michael Novak. Both are familiar with the work of John Courtney Murray who maintained that important arguments were never finished but simply grew toward an end. David Hollenbach, "The Growing End of An Argument," *America* , 153: 16, November 30, 1985, 366.

[6] Gewirth writes, "Basic goods are the essential prerequisites of action: they include life, physical integrity, health, mental equilibrium, and such specific goods as food, clothing, shelter, and medical care." "Economic Rights" in *Poverty, Justice, and the Law: New Essays on Needs, Rights, and Obligations.* George R. Lucas, Jr., ed. (Lanham: University Press of America), 1986.

freedom, and security in a modern society that recognizes rights claims. However, to prove the correctness of this thesis economic rights must be shown to be inherently interdependent with civil and political rights. Furthermore, the objections that economic rights skeptics raise regarding economic rights will also have to be shown to be erroneous. Testing this thesis will not necessarily demonstrate that civil and political rights are in fact human rights; their status as such is our given, our epistemological starting point. Instead, once economic rights have been convincingly interconnected with civil and political rights, then a strong argument will be made that the actualization of political and civil rights requires the acceptance of economic rights as human rights. This conclusion undercuts the objections of economic rights skeptics and requires logically the recognition and implementation of economic rights in American public policy.

To explain the intricacies of the economic rights debate, several important concerns must be addressed. These concerns constitute the content and structure of this chapter, and proceed in the following order: first, the nature of rights is explained by an exposition highlighting three primary ways that rights have been used and understood. This explanation addresses contested issues such as the processes by which rights are related to duties. It pays particular attention to situations in which the rights are positive rights, creating positive duties. This preparatory step sets the stage for subsequent explanations of the process by which rights have, historically, emerged and evolved in three generational stages. Next, the relations between human rights and economic rights are carefully analyzed. Following this analysis, I present a history of economic rights. My analysis of this material allows me to present subsequently and formally what I believe to be the problem of economic rights. An outline of this study follows this analysis that details the contents and layout of the succeeding chapters. Since I am aware of the enormous body of literature on the subject of rights, out of necessity I then limit the scope of this research and demonstrate its relationship to the pertinent literature. Finally, I sum up the chapter with remarks on the significance of economic rights.

To describe the nature of rights is difficult. It is difficult because "rights" approaches to moral relations constitute a wide variety of moral systems. No consensus exists about what constitutes a right. Currently, though most nations in the modern world bandy about the term rights, the rampant pluralism evident in the system of nation states mirrors the myriad ways of describing or referring to rights. Some societies use the term--rights, most clearly and frequently concerning what the West calls "group rights." Understandings of group rights are clearer in non-Western moral traditions such as Hinduism and Islam. Those traditions are not considered irrelevant to this work, but such interpretations are treated herein as essentially distinct from the Western approach. Thus groups rights are, from a Western perspective, considered "third generation" rights. Their further consideration and discussion will, for now, be postponed as our attention will focus and proceed from a Western perspective.[7] In proceeding in this fashion, as if the Western tradition were more important than others, no claim is being made that our tradition actually is more important. What is being highlighted is the focus on the Western tradition in contradistinction to other traditions. It is only in claiming that this work proceeds out of a Western orientation that the description of rights discourse and its development retains a parochial integrity and accuracy that does not need to expend any time, space, or energy defending its position from other accounts from other traditions. Furthermore the West's very lack of a strong and clear understanding of "group rights" constitutes the distinctiveness of the Western approach and suggests the importance of the economic rights debate for our tradition. Indeed, one might surmise that the vigor with which economic rights are championed and opposed by Westerners is itself an unanticipated manifestation of a conceptual glitch or void in the functioning of the Western approach. In other words, liberalism argues most vociferously over the aspects of rights discourse that imply intergroup obligations and de-emphasize the rights-

---

7   As the taxonomy of rights will show, group rights are a recent development in Western rights discourse although they are featured very significantly and very early in non-Western accounts.

claiming of distinct individuals. Thus it might be said that the economic rights debate was and is conceptually necessary in the West precisely because the West has, historically, denied the validity of group rights.

By Western liberalism I mean a history and tradition of discourse that cannot be described with any easy precision. It is an Anglo-American tradition, but not exclusively so as it also includes the political philosophies of German idealism, French Revolutionary contributions, and Christian contributions from Protestantism and Catholicism. These sub-traditions are, of course, related yet quite distinct and the very rich differences and contributions these sub-traditions emphasize make the economic rights debate both complex and rewarding.[8]

The Nature of Rights

Rights are, if they are not anything else, principles or rules designed to compel the performance of certain human actions, and the forbearance of other specified actions.[9] Much of the economic rights debate is caught up in a conceptual conflict over the definition, content, and use of the term "rights."[10] One

---

[8] By Western democratic liberalism I mean the tradition described as liberalism in: Steven Charles Mott's helpful work, *A Christian Perspective on Political Thought* (New York: Oxford University Press, 1993), Chapter nine, 131-150, and in Ian Shapiro's *The Evolution of Rights in Liberal Theory* (Cambridge: Cambridge University Press, 1986). See also Chapters Three and Four in Max L. Stackhouse's *Creeds, Society, and Human Rights: A Study in Three Cultures* (Grand Rapids, Michigan: Eerdmans Publishing Co., 1984).

[9] Rights are commonly considered inhabitants or exemplars of a deontological approach to ethics. As deontological approaches, rights do not specify the good independently from the "right," or interpret the "right" as maximizing the "good." Whether deontological approaches are the best methodological approaches for addressing ethical concerns is an unsettled issue.

[10] Alison Dunden Renteln observes that, "There is considerable disagreement among theorists about both the nature and legitimacy of rights." "A Conceptual Analysis of International Human Rights" (Ph.D. dissertation, Berkeley: University of California, 1987), 54. Renteln further observes that, "There are as many theories of rights as there are rights theorists," 55.

traditional approach to explaining the nature of rights is to compare and contrast various definitions of rights. Rights have been variously defined as claims, entitlements, advantages, and discretionary powers.[11] The comparisons of rights definitions approaches are no longer useful. There are too many different definitions of the term and no justifiable way of demonstrating the superiority of one definition over another. To give some order and insight into the use of the term rights, three prototypical explanations of rights are offered: claims, interests and trumps.

Three Theories of Rights: Claims, Interests, and Trumps

Alan Gewirth is an influential rights/claims commentator who has an important analysis of the elements that make up a right. He employs a rights-claim usage of the term rights, writing, "A has a right to X against B by virtue of Y."[12] The five components of all rights are explicated as follows:

> There are five main elements here: first, the Subject (A) of the right, the person who has it; second, the Nature of the right; third, the Object (X) of the right, what it is a right to; fourth, the Respondent (B) of the right, the person or

---

[11] For a definition of rights as claims, see Alan Gewirth, *Human Rights: Essays on Justification and Applications* (Chicago: University of Chicago Press), 1. For rights as entitlements-see James Nickle, *Making Sense of Human Rights* (Berkeley: University of California Press, 1987). For rights as advantages-John Kleinig, "Human rights, legal rights and social change," *Human Rights* (St. Martin's Press, 1978) 42. For rights as discretionary powers-H. L. A. Hart, "Are There Any Natural Rights?" in *Philosophical Review* LXIV (1955), 175-91 at 181. Wesley Hohfeld, the legal jurist, provides the standard legal definition of rights in which four specific types are identified-*Fundamental Legal Conceptions* (New Haven: Yale University Press, 1919).

[12] Gewirth, *Human Rights: Essays on Justification and Applications,* 2. Even this definition is somewhat controversial, since it is simply one definition of the term rights. Indeed, both this definition and some elements within it are disputed by other experts.

persons who have the correlative duty; and fifth, the Justifying Basis or Ground (Y) of the right.[13]

This structural analysis of a right is not exhaustive; rather it illustrates one way of taking careful notice of the components of a right.   It also gives us a provisional vocabulary for discussing these components.   Gewirth's fourth element, the Respondent, or (B), calls to our attention the fact that he believes that a right always entails a duty.   Thus, a right is always more than just a claim for an Object; it is (for Gewirth) a claim against someone (a Respondent).   Gewirth's emphasis on the claiming actor (the Subject of the right) also designates him as a representative of the will theory of rights.[14] John Warwick Montgomery has an insightful analysis of this approach.[15] Montgomery writes regarding the will theory, that, "The will theory stresses the place of choice of claims in the nature of all genuine rights."[16] Given this emphasis, it is not surprising that most jurists, such as Hohfeld, H. L. A. Hart, and others, are classified, by Montgomery, as "will theorists."[17] Legal systems are claims-driven systems so that rights as claims is a theory that is quite natural to them.

---

13 Ibid., 2. Though Gewirth uses this structural analysis for special rights, human rights, these elements may also be found in other types of rights.

14 Gewirth does not see himself as primarily a will theorist as he emphasizes both the claiming aspect of rights theory and the entitlement, or interest aspect. I designate him as a will theorist, because his primary justification for his theory of morality (by which he justifies his rights theories) is totally concerned with human agency and human action.   Agency always entails the engagement of the human will, therefore, he should be considered a will theorist. The will theory of rights is a theory that focuses primarily on the Subject of the right and their claiming, in contrast to the interest theory of rights concerned primarily with the possible objects of the rights rather than the subject or beneficiary of the right.   Will theory is a prominent example of rights/claims theory.

15 John Warwick Montgomery, *Human Rights & Human Dignity* (Grand Rapids, Michigan: Zondervan Pub., 1986), 72.

16 Ibid.

17 The views of Hohfeld and Hart will be fully examined later in this chapter.

Opposing Gewirth's "rights-against-someone" position
(which is followed by Hohfeld, H. L. A. Hart and Feinberg) is the
entitlement or interests theory of rights. H. J. McCloskey, a
proponent of this type, prefers to characterize rights as
entitlements rather than claims, because, in his opinion, the
latter characterization is based on the premise that rights". . .
are and must always be rights against some other person or
persons."[18] For him, rights are always rights to, rather than
rights against: this is the way he believes rights function. This
second approach Montgomery calls the interest theory of
rights.[19] Montgomery disputes the correctness of the will theory
by pointing out the cases of entities being accorded rights when
they obviously cannot make claims for them, i.e., children
and/or animals. Although Montgomery has reservations with
regard to the interests theory of rights he eventually adopts it,
following McCloskey, Alan White and Neil MacCormick, two
other major proponents of interest theory.[20] In his adoption of
the interest approach, Montgomery, like McCloskey, is trying to
account for recognized rights in cases where the beneficiary of
the right cannot claim the right (an infant, for example) and no
specific bearer of duty for the right (the correlativity aspect) can
be found.[21] One final important alternative theory of rights is
that of Ronald Dworkin. Dworkin, a legal philosopher, believes
that rights are best understood as trumps used by individuals to

---

[18] H. J. McCloskey, "Rights," *Philosophy Quarterly* 15 (1965), 118.

[19] John Warwick Montgomery, *Human Rights & Human Dignity*,
74.

[20] See Alan White, *Rights* (Oxford: Clarendon, 1984). See also, Neil
MacCormick, "Children's Rights: A Test-case for Theories of Right,"
Legal Right and Social Democracy (Oxford: Clarendon, 1982).

[21] Gewirth shows great insight into the analysis of rights language
when he argues that the two theories, will theory and interest theory,
are not mutually exclusive. From his point of view, the will theory
emphasizes the Subject who acts, and the act itself, which is a claiming.
The interest theory focuses attention on the Object of a right and in a
passive way on the Subject of the right as a would-be recipient of the
Object. For Gewirth, the entitlement theorists (who are really interest
theorists) also emphasize the Justifying reason for the right. Since
Gewirth's understanding of rights has these emphases, and others, he
does not see the two schools, will theorists and interest theorists, as
mutually exclusive.

frustrate the overreaching of the collective demands made by large groups in society.[22]

The Institutionalization of Rights
in Legal Systems

These types of rights do not call one's attention to the institutional systems that recognize and implement rights. The most important system is, of course, the judicial system. That rights language has been understood as having originated in legal settings, suggests that our discussion should continue there. First, however, an important distinction must be made between legal rights and moral rights. Joel Feinberg, a social philosopher, describes legal rights as follows:

> Legal and institutional rights are typically conferred by specific rules recorded in handbooks of regulations that can be observed and studied by the citizens or members subject to the rules. But not all rights are derived from such clearly visible laws and institutional regulations. On many occasions we assert that someone has a right to something even though we know there are no regulations or laws conferring such a right. Such talk clearly makes sense, so any theory of the nature of rights that cannot account for it is radically defective. The term "moral rights" can be applied to all rights that are held to exist prior to, or independently of, any legal or institutional rules. Moral rights so conceived form a genus divisible into various species of rights having little in common except that they are not (necessarily) legal or institutional.[23]

Feinberg's description of the difference between legal rights and moral rights emphasizes the fact that legal rights are always embedded in the law of the land: their existence is grounded in legislation and judicial interpretation. In contrast, moral rights in some instances, may or may not have any legal connections. Although Feinberg does have a distinctive definition of the term "moral right," definitions of that term cannot be given now because of the enormous variations in the

---

22 Ronald Dworkin, *Taking Rights Seriously* (Cambridge, Mass.: Harvard University Press, 1977).

23 Joel Feinberg, *Social Philosophy*, 84.

definitions.[24] A representative definition of a moral right will be given with our discussion of human rights. Early in this century, Wesley Hohfeld classified legal rights in four categories: claims, liberties, powers, and immunities.[25] Of these four categories, the one that is most often used to describe a right in the strict sense of the term is "claim."[26] Joel Feinberg adopts this usage from Hohfeld:

> To have a right is to have a claim to something and against someone, the recognition of which is called for by legal rules or, in the case of moral rights, by the principles of an enlightened conscience.[27]

Legal rights are, therefore, claims that rights holders can take to court for redress. If they are upheld, they can then invoke the power of the state to secure the actual enjoyment of the object of the claimed right.[28] That a purported legal right may not be upheld, calls to our attention the distinction between recognized claims and unrecognized claims. Renteln recognizes this distinction, writing, "What distinguishes a right from a

---

24 There are at least as many definitions of the term "moral rights" as there are for the term "rights." Furthermore there is more opportunity for disagreement, since writers can disagree regarding the meaning of "moral" as well as the meaning of "rights."

25 Wesley Newcomb Hohfeld, *Fundamental Legal Conceptions* (New Haven: Yale University Press, 1919). See also Carl Wellman, *A Theory of Rights* (Totowa, NJ: Rowman and Allanheld Pub., 1985), 9.

26 For a full discussion of other rights, see Joel Feinberg, *Social Philosophy* (Englewood Cliffs: Prentice-Hall, 1973), Chapter Four. See also Carl Wellman, *Theory of Rights*, Chapter Two.

27 Joel Feinberg, *Rights, Justice, and the Bounds of Liberty* (Princeton: Princeton University Press, 1980), 159-60.

28 By object of the right, all that is meant herein is the interest that is the subject of the claim, that is, the "good" that the right is seeking to get, or to keep free from threat or interference: this object is simply (X) in terms of Gewirth's structural analysis, which has been given previously. For example, a right to a fair trial has as its object the right of the individual to be immune from the arbitrary curtailment of his freedom without a prior showing of due process of law: that is, without the employ of a system of justice, in which a good reason for society's removal of his rights is demonstrated, as in a fair showing of guilt.

demand is that it is justified, either by appeal to preexisting legal rules or to morality. Thus a right is a *valid* claim."[29]

Rights mandate that certain actions be performed and certain other actions be refrained from; this last consideration of rights reveals their coercive nature. Rights, as has been pointed out by John Kleinig, are of such seriousness as to invoke the power of the state for their implementation or to prevent their violation.[30] The coercive nature of rights is such that many are reluctant to invoke their power, because state power can easily get out of hand. It should also be recalled that rights have been used, historically, to restrain state power rather than to employ it. I have chosen to closely examine herein, rights-claims; that is a conceptualization of rights that has a Subject who claims and a Respondent who has a duty to recognize and implement rights-claims. This approach is not the only approach, nor, necessarily, even the best approach; it is, however, the one best

---

[29] Renteln, 56. Joel Feinberg concurs with this assessment. He uses as his example, a highwayman's robbery. He writes, "The highwayman, for example, demands his victim's money, but he hardly makes claim to it as rightfully his own." What Feinberg is emphasizing is the fact that the highwayman is making a coercive demand; he knows that when he is demanding loot he is making a claim that is not justified by either law or morality. In his mind, he does not think that he has a right to the loot, or that his victim thinks he has a right to it. For him, the demand for loot is a patently unjustified claim, this is why he resorts to the use of force. *Social Philosophy,* 65, 66.

[30] For a good discussion of the coerciveness of rights, see John Kleinig, "Human rights, legal rights and social change," in *Human Rights*. Kleinig writes, "That second question, I would suggest, is to be answered as follows: human rights represent those minimum conditions under which human beings can flourish (that is as moral agents) and which ought to be secured for them, if necessary by force. The close connection between rights and the justifiable employment of coercion arises from the importance of the interests they are designed to secure namely the welfare interests of individuals. Welfare interests are *minima*, those more or less indispensable preconditions for the pursuit and fulfillment of characteristically human interests, and which constitute human life an object of dignity and respect," 44-45. For example, the Union troops stationed in the South during Reconstruction were there for more than the purpose of keeping order. They were there to protect the newly created and recognized rights of citizens who, before the war, had been slaves.

suited for addressing some important problems presented in the economic rights debate. My examination of rights-claims also necessitates my use of the term itself. This usage should not imply that the rights-claims approach is the only correct way of understanding rights. Our classification of rights into three types merely demonstrates some different ways in which rights have been understood. This classification demonstrates that there is no one, self-evident way of defining or using the term "rights." However, two of the major problems discussed in the economic rights debate are the problem of the correlativity of rights to duties and the distinctions made between "positive" rights and "negative" rights. To address these questions, it is necessary to opt for the understanding of rights that is most closely associated with the term "claim." Rights-claims presuppose (in ways that the term "entitlement" does not) that there are duty-bearers named in a system of rights who may not wish to bear their purported duties (in Gewirth's terminology, respondents).[31] By choosing to use the understanding of rights as related to claims, we can select an understanding of rights that is not arbitrary and that also addresses two of the major problems in this area. Obviously, these problems revolve around the identification of the Respondent of a putative right and the scope and limit of the duties that he or she may encounter. However, to explain this problem, it is necessary to

----

31 Further, the reason that is commonly given as to why these duty-bearers may object, is that they may be forced into performing "positive" in comparison to "negative" duties. However, our discussion of rights will show that the correlativity thesis maintains that for every right, there is a corresponding duty. Our examination of rights will also make clear that a "positive" duty requires a duty-bearer to positively perform some act, or to provide some good, rather then (as with "negative" duties) simply to mind his/her own business. Thus, to say that one has a right is usually to say that one has a claim for something from someone--a claim to rather than a claim from (someone or something). As Alan Gewirth maintains, "claim-rights possess logically implied correlatives. A claim-right of one person entails a correlative duty of some other person or persons to act or to refrain from acting in ways required for the first person's having that to which he has a right." *Human Rights: Essays on Justification and Applications* (Chicago: University of Chicago Press, 1982), 2.

further explicate the nature of rights regarding possible
Respondents and their duties.

Respondents, Correlative Duties
and Positive Rights

One aspect of McCloskey's entitlement, or interest theory
of rights is his de-emphasis of the aspect of claiming against a
respondent.   This de-emphasis minimizes the traditional
concern with rights *in personam* in relationship with rights *in
rem*. Rights *in personam* are commonly understood to be rights
against a specified, identifiable, individual or group of
individuals.   Rights *in rem* are rights directed toward an
unidentified person, or group of persons; as such these rights act
like a manifesto, staking a claim to the performance of certain
deeds, or the noninterference in actions one might want to
perform that should be socially protected from all others in
society.   For example, a worried parent may go to the
department of health to demand that all parents submit their
children to inoculations against deadly diseases on behalf of
herself and/or her child. According to this theory, this parent
would not have to know that other children had not been so
inoculated to state a valid claim. Similarly, the right to privacy
is predicated upon an *in rem* conceptualization: one does not
have to know who is likely to tap one's phone or to engage in
voyeurism to be entitled to society's recognition of one's right to
privacy.[32] McCloskey's understanding of rights calls into view

---

[32] Writing concerning McCloskey's views on entitlement, Feinberg
notes that, "As far as I can tell, the only reason McCloskey gives for
denying that *in rem* rights are against others is that those against whom
they would have to hold make up an enormously multitudinous and
'vague' group, including hypothetical people not yet even in existence.
Many others have found this a paradoxical consequence of the notion of
in rem rights, but I see nothing troublesome in it. If a general rule gives
me a right of noninterference in a certain respect against everybody,
then there are literally hundreds of millions of people who have a duty
toward me in that respect; and if the same general rule gives the same
right to everyone else, then it imposes on me literally hundreds of
millions of duties--or duties toward hundreds of millions of people. I
see nothing paradoxical about this, however. The duties, after all, are
negative; and I can discharge all of them at a stroke simply by minding

the second important consideration that shapes any discussion of rights, that is, the correlativity of rights to duties issue. The "correlativity of rights to duties issue" is important because it has been a major point of dispute among differing views on "newer" understandings of rights. The correlativity of rights to duties theory may be summarized as follows: since every recognized right requires a person or persons to perform some act, or to refrain from performing some act, the recognition of the right inherently entails some duty, at least for the respondents of the right.[33] For example, my right to free speech, protected by the Constitution, has at least two requirements. First, it precludes Congress from passing laws infringing upon my right to free speech. Secondly, it requires the police powers of the state to stand ready to use force against anyone who attempts to violate my right to free speech. Nevertheless, my right to free speech does not require people to listen to me, or to agree with me. Admittedly, I should not slander others; not slandering others is my moral duty. Yet, if I believe that my speech is true and fair, I have the legal right to run the risk that my free speech may slander someone. If my speech proves to constitute slander, I will, most likely, be constrained to provide restitution for my victim. Such a punishment would be merited.[34] What is important, however, in this observation, is the fact that my right to free speech is not predicated upon my success at fulfilling my moral duty to avoid slandering people: by its own force, my right generates duties.

---

my own business. And if all human beings make up one moral community and there are hundreds of millions of human beings, we should expect there to be hundreds of millions of moral relations holding between them." *Rights, Justice, and the Bounds of Liberty*, 155.

[33] Some duties are *in rem* in nature, such as those duties generated by my right to free speech. Everyone else in society has an obligation to refrain from abridging my right to free speech. Some duties, though strict in nature, are limited to specific respondents in society. For example, though it may be heroic for me to rescue a stranger from an armed highwayman, it is not my duty; unless, of course, I happen to be a police officer.

[34] Jack Donnelly's helpful work called this distinction to my attention. *The Concept of Human Rights* (London: Croom Helm Pub., 1985), 79.

For example, the government has its two aforementioned duties, because my rights to free speech demand and create them. The state may not like my using my right of free speech to criticize its actions, but it must (if it is to recognize my right) fulfill its duty in restraining its impulse to silence me. Thus for many writers rights generate duties and not the converse.[35] An additional moral consideration that is inherent in the correlativity thesis concerns duties to recognize the rights of others. If I believe that I am entitled to free speech, simply by virtue of my status as a human being, I am constrained by the laws of logical consistency to refrain from courses of action that may infringe on someone else's free speech rights. Because my right to free speech acts primarily as a restraint on the actions of myself and others, Renteln, following Hohfeld's classification, calls this right an immunity.[36] As Renteln observes, "The view that rights and duties are correlative used to be the dominant one among philosophers."[37] But Renteln insightfully details several recent rejections of this traditional view.[38] While most writers still insist that rights must be correlated to duties, McCloskey, Lyons, Feinberg and others are notable exceptions. Feinberg's rejection of the correlativity thesis is particularly

---

[35] Gewirth, for example, is most emphatic on this point, "Respondents have correlative duties because Subjects have certain rights, and not conversely. This priority of claim-rights over duties in the order of justifying purpose or final causality is not antithetical to their being correlative to each other." *Human Rights: Essays on Justification and Applications* , 14.

[36] Renteln, 59.

[37] Renteln, 57.

[38] Renteln, 57-64. Renteln explains why Lyons and McCloskey are wrong to reject the correlativity thesis. In both writers, she finds that the confusion lies in their inability to grasp the fact that *in rem* rights assign duties to duty-bearers, although the assignment awaits an unknown number of duty-bearers to come into relation to the rights holder for the assignment of duty. For example, Lyons fails to realize that his right to turn on red in traffic is possible only because some duty-bearers, who cannot be identified in advance to his turn, have the actual duty to refrain from stopping his progress or interfering with his turn. Paradoxical to this scenario is the fact that the actual identification of the duty-bearers is never made, unless they fail to carry out their duties and an accident occurs.

interesting in that his argument is based upon a reversal of this thesis.[39] Feinberg identifies duties that do not have corresponding rights, such as the duty to give to charity.[40] Renteln's reply to this line of reasoning is telling and important for this study. Renteln writes:

> There are at least two objections which can be raised to arguments of the kind advanced by the above philosophers [Feinberg, included]. The first is that, in the cases where we would agree that there are such duties, there is also a corresponding right. If society recognizes duties to be kind to animals and babies, for instance, then, indeed, those entities could be said to have rights. The second is that, in those cases in which we are hesitant to assert the existence of a right, it is because the attribution of the duty seems dubious. Unfortunately, many persons do not recognize duties of charity, for example, perhaps because such duties give rise to something resembling economic rights. The reluctance of theorists to acknowledge the existence of rights corresponding to duties held to others, may stem from the fear that to do so would cheapen rights language by a proliferation of less significant rights. But the problem does not lie in the correlation: it rests in the absence of some mechanism for justifying the assertion of particular rights/duties.[41]

Renteln calls to our attention, in this extended quotation, the high degree of disagreement prevalent among various political and philosophical camps concerning their understanding of human nature and morality as a whole and rights in particular.[42] Thus, for some writers, certain kinds of rights are conceptually invalid because their correlative duties appear to promote social policies and/or obligations that are not attractive to them. However, it is this "mechanism for justifying the assertion of particular rights/duties" that Renteln

---

39 Ibid.

40 Joel Feinberg, *Rights, Justice, and the Bounds of Liberty*, 145-46.

41 Renteln, 62.

42 See also Jack Donnelly on this point. Donnelly devotes his postscript to the problem of conflicting taxonomies of rights. *The Concept of Human Rights*, "Postscript: The Problem of Lists."

refers to, which is crucial to this study, which will be examined in depth in Chapters Two and Three.[43]

One last major distinction regarding rights now draws our attention: the aforementioned positive rights/negative rights distinction. A survey of the field reveals that Western philosophers and jurists have traditionally divided rights into two categories: positive and negative.[44] This division has been associated with what we will call "first generation rights," i.e., civil and political rights.[45] This division enabled the correlativity of rights to duties thesis to remain plausible. Simultaneously, commentators have thereby limited the number of duties for which individuals and even the state could be held responsible.[46] The limitation on the morally required number of duties placed on individuals was imposed, ostensibly, to protect the individual from being consumed in a differentiated and pluralistic society by all of the demands such a society could make on him/her. The limitation of the number of duties imposed upon the government was designed to check the power and reach of the state into the affairs of individuals. Since these rights were considered to be sacrosanct by these writers, the chief right being the right to liberty, the duties correlated thereunto had to be duties that were "perfect duties": duties that could be performed by a wave of the hand.[47] Duties that required the state or individuals to provide something, or that might impose on one's liberty, were to be minimized (in the classic construction of rights) if not

---

[43] Renteln's "mechanism for justification" is analogous to Gewirth's Justifying Cause. Chapter Two will examine the Carter Administration's attempt to justify economic rights. Chapter Three will examine the debate over Justifying causes that rages between skeptics and proponents of economic rights.

[44] Chapter Three amply reveals the specific literature that addresses this point.

[45] The meaning of the term "first generation rights" will be given later in this chapter.

[46] The limitation of the duties of individuals and the duties of the state has always been a source of concern in Western political liberal thought.

[47] The best explanation of the distinction between imperfect duties and perfect duties may be found in Henry Shue's "Mediating Duties," *Ethics* , 98, no. 4 (July 1988), 687-704.

eliminated altogether. Thus, the distinction between "positive" duties and "negative" duties helped to shape the distinction between "positive" rights and "negative" rights. Positive rights were rights that required some duty-bearer to perform some positive duties, i.e., the provision of basic goods, or, if necessary, jobs. Negative rights on the other hand, were rights that, at least in classic liberal theory, required mere self-restraint. "True" natural rights were, accordingly, solely negative rights; positive rights were considered a misunderstanding of rights. However, as will be demonstrated in our "generation of rights" section, positive rights did find acceptance with socialists, and with some non-socialists of the Western liberal tradition, while continuing to be rejected by "classic" Western liberal theorists.[48] This discussion of the nature of rights is not exhaustive. Rights, however, have a lengthy historical background and have arrived at their current state by means of an evolutionary process.

The Evolution of Rights in Generational Stages

John Warwick Montgomery calls our attention to "newer" rights, by distinguishing between first generation and second generation rights.[49] These references to rights by their generation demonstrate the chronological appearance and development of rights theory.[50] By first generation rights, Montgomery is referring to those rights that we have termed civil and political rights. These are rights to noninterference, liberties, and immunities, which grew out of Enlightenment social contract theories. These first generation rights are located firmly in the Western notions of justice. These civil and political rights are understood by Montgomery and Cranston as

<hr>

[48] The clearest and most extended work on the issue of positive and negative duties, and rights is the work edited by Eric Mack, *Positive and Negative Duties* (New Orleans: Tulane University, 1985).

[49] John Warwick Montgomery, *Human Rights and Human Dignity* (Grand Rapids, Michigan: Zondervan Pub., 1986), 69.

[50] Karel Vasak is considered to be the originator of the conscious conception of rights as created and carried out in generations. See *The International Dimensions of Human Rights* (Westport, Connecticut: Greenwood Press, 1982).

being positivized by the American Bill of Rights; however, their pedigree is traceable to Enlightenment produced "natural rights." D. D. Raphael, the Edward Caird professor of Political and Social Philosophy at the University of Glasgow, recounts the transition that took place in which natural law theories generated natural rights theories, which in turn changed into modern moral rights. Raphael states that natural rights theory finds its distinguishing movement (from natural law theory) in the writings of John Locke. Raphael maintains:

> The traditional doctrine of natural law does not give any particular prominence to the idea of individual rights. Law implies both duties and rights, and it is no doubt fair to say that the ancient and medieval theories of natural law were more concerned with the foundations of moral, legal, and political duty than with the foundations of rights.[51]

Thus, according to him, natural rights as individual rights were developed by Locke out of the traditional understanding of natural law that regarded itself in relation to Divine Law.[52] Since natural law was concerned primarily with the natural obligations or duties that men owed to each other that impacted upon their freedom, the derivative concept of natural rights was, not surprisingly, primarily rights to liberty, that is, rights that obligated people at large from interfering in the movements of others, and secondly, rights to what we have called in Hohfeldian terms, immunities; that is, rights that restrained the government from interfering in the exercise of certain rights such as their freedom of speech. The primary Law of Nature for Locke was the right to self-preservation; yet his primary natural right was the right to property.[53] Raphael observes that Locke gave ". . . the word 'property' an extended

---

51 D. D. Raphael, ed., "Human Rights, Old and New," 55.

52 Donnelly perceptively writes that, "In fact, for Locke, God is the source of natural law, which is a law of reason not individual interests, and natural law obliges both in the state of nature and society." For this conclusion Donnelly cites Locke's *Two Treatises of Government*, ed. Peter Laslett, (Cambridge: Cambridge University Press, 1967) at paragraphs 6, 12, 16, 57, 59, 60, 118, 124, 135, 172.

53 Donnelly, 70.

meaning so as to cover life and liberty as well as 'estate'".[54]
Nevertheless, in Hohfeldian terms the best description of these
rights is summed up in the words claims and immunities. These
rights were civil and political, because they enabled a citizen to
own property, to engage in political affairs and to be protected
from the State. None of these rights required that the state
specifically perform any action against any one individual. As
such these rights were rights *in rem*, requiring all the world to
restrain itself (except in emergent circumstances) from
interfering with the actions of individuals. These were the
rights of the individual in a way that the old natural law did not
emphasize.

This new emphasis can be attributed to their conceptual
context, the social contract theories of Locke and Paine. These
two Enlightenment writers saw the individual as the chief moral
unit in their accounting of human morality and politics. Thus
the Enlightenment was the birthplace of "new" natural rights.
This first generation of rights legitimated the new socially
contractualized State and the new conception of the human:
first, as an individual, and secondarily as a member of society
and citizen of the State.

Continuing our examination of the history of rights, we
must now consider Montgomery's concern for a second
generation of rights. We can see the genesis of second
generation rights even in the first generation. What are second
generation rights? Montgomery maintains that second
generation rights are "social and economic rights."[55] Raphael
notes that even Cranston is aware of some evidence that the
genesis for these rights has a chronological connection to the
first generation rights, i.e., Enlightenment civil and political
rights. Raphael and Cranston note a reference to a "right to
work" in the work of Turgot in 1776 and Robespierre in 1793.[56]
In addition to these references, Raphael points to the clear
demand for economic rights made by Thomas Paine in his work,
Agrarian Justice.[57] Nevertheless, he concludes that the second

---

54 Raphael, 61.
55 Montgomery, 69.
56 Raphael, 62.
57 Ibid.

generation rights are primarily a product of socialist thought, and that (excepting Babeuf--whom he also finds calling for economic rights) none of the other theorists in question are socialists.

This study need not establish the exact chronological origin of second generation rights before it concludes that their fullest expression came with later socialist thought, toward which we should now turn.[58] Before turning, however, it should be noted that even the first generation rights, the civil and political, were revolutionary in nature.[59] These rights disputed

[58] Before we turn away from Locke, however, we should note a passage in which he seems to entertain some notion of a "right" to subsistence. Locke wrote that, "But we know God hath not left one Man so to the Mercy of another, that he may starve him if he please: God the Lord and Father of all, has given no one of his Children such a Property, in his peculiar Portion of the things of this World, but that he has given his needy Brother a Right to the Surplusage of his Goods; so that it cannot justly be denied him, when his pressing Wants call for it. And therefore no Man could ever have a just Power over the life of another, by Right of property in Land or Possessions; since 'would always be a Sin in any Man of Estate, to let his Brother perish for want of affording him Relief out of his Plenty. As Justice gives every Man a Title to the product of his honest industry, and the fair Acquisitions of his Ancestors descended to him, so Charity gives every Man a Title to so much out of another's Plenty, as will keep him from extreme want, where he has no means to subsist otherwise; and a Man can no more justly make use of another's necessity, to force him to become his Vassal, by withholding that Relief, God requires him to afford to the wants of his Brother, than he that has more strength can seize upon a weaker, master him to his Obedience, and with a Dagger at his Throat offer him Death or Slavery." *Two Treatises of Government* (Cambridge: Cambridge University Press, 1960) First Treatise, Section 42, 205, 206. It would be difficult to claim that Locke makes a clear claim for a legal right to subsistence, given his use of the term "Charity." However, a strong argument could be given for maintaining that Locke is making here a moral claim for subsistence "rights."

[59] C. B. MacPherson observes regarding all human rights that, "We should not be surprised at such division of opinion about human rights. For in any class-divided society and, above all, in a class-divided world--I mean a world divided into the poor nations and the rich nations--the slogan 'human rights' is bound to appear--as it has historically been--something of a threat to the established order. That was certainly the case in the French Revolution, when the 'rights of man' were

the interference in the affairs of individual citizens even by monarchs alleged to rule by divine right.[60]

---

pressed as a weapon against the highly unequal class state of the old regime." *The Rise and Fall of Economic Justice and Other Papers* (New York: Oxford University Press, 1985), 21.

[60] The association of rights with social change, including revolution, has a long history. Maurice Cranston relates that Burke associated certain rights (French Revolution rights, clearly not the customary rights of Englishmen) with revolution, "For Burke the Rights of Man were mere abstractions: the rights of Englishmen were realities . . . Both Burke and Bentham had a political as well as a philosophical interest in this question. Both regarded talk about the Rights of Man as mischievous as well as meaningless. Burke, the conservative, objected to such talk because it stimulated revolutionary sentiments, it injected 'false ideas and vain expectations into men destined to travel the obscure walk of laborious life.'" "Human Rights Real and Supposed," *Political Theory and the Rights of Man* (Bloomington: Indiana University Press, 1967), 44. Eugene Kamenka notes, "The demand for rights in the seventeenth and eighteenth centuries was a demand against the existing state and authorities, against despotism, arbitrariness and the political disfranchisement of those who held different opinions," "The anatomy of an idea," in *Human Rights* (New York: St. Martin's Press, 1978), 5. Jack Donnelly writes in regards to the last resort aspect of rights: "This extralegality implies that the primary use of human rights will be to change existing institutions. For example, Soviet dissidents press their human rights claims in order to alter the standard practice of the Soviet state. Therefore, the close connection between natural rights ideas and, for example, the French Revolution, is characteristic rather than accidental. If systematically unenforced rights are to be enforced and enjoyed, institutions must be transformed. This is true of all rights--consider, for example, the widespread changes brought about by the American civil rights movement--but the higher the right, the greater the likely change." In *The Concept of Human Rights*, 22. John Warwick Montgomery notes, "The 'first generation' of human rights, suggested by the concept of 'liberty,' embraces the civil and political freedoms that were so central to the eighteenth-century French and American revolutions." From *Human Rights and Human Dignity*, 27. Even Abraham Lincoln connected some notion of rights and revolution, writing, "This country, with its institutions, belongs to the people who inhabit it. Whenever they shall grow weary of the existing government, they can exercise their constitutional right of amending, or their revolutionary right to dismember or overthrow it." From Lincoln's "First Inaugural Address" (4 March 1861), in *Lincoln's Stories and Speeches*, ed. Edward F. Allen (New York: Books, Inc., 1920), 212.

Regarding second generation rights, Raphael correctly asserts that, despite their foreshadowing in Babeuf, in Thomas Paines' *The Rights of Man*, and in others, such rights were fully developed only after Karl Marx's criticism of civil and political rights. Marx was critical of the first generation understanding of rights.[61] He felt that such rights were simply the fictions of bourgeois law that supported the capitalist economy and system of private property.[62] Nevertheless, despite this hostility to first generation rights, communists, after Marx, readily adopted the use of rights language.[63] Though they retained their antipathy toward liberal theories of civil and political rights, they emphasized instead economic and social rights.[64]   What is important to notice at this time is the fact that these new rights

---

61 Karl Marx wrote, in 1843, that, "The so-called rights of man, the droits de l'homme as distinct from the droits du citoyen, are nothing but the rights of a member of civil society, that is, the rights of egoistic man, of man separated from other men and from the community." From, "On the Jewish Question," with Frederick Engels, *Collected Works* III (London, 1975), 162.

62 Yet, despite his criticisms of "first generation rights," Marx was not an advocate of their abandonment. Jack Donnelly emphasizes this point, writing, "Marx criticizes the bourgeois character of rights in the early, transitional phase of socialism, from the point of view of the coming higher phase" but as we saw, he does not call for abandoning them at this point. Likewise, 'bourgeois' human rights in bourgeois democratic republics are criticized for being partial, but Marx does not suggest that they simply be abolished, for their abolition would mark a return to an even lower stage of despotism. The early stages of socialism can even be seen as a consistent, impartial and universal extension of the principles of bourgeois right. *The Concept of Human Rights*, 76.

63 Robert Traer, "Human Rights: A Global Faith" (Ph.D. dissertation, Graduate Theological Union, 1988) Chapter III. For a similar reading see Alice Erh-Soon Tay, "Marxism, socialism and human rights," *Human Rights* (N. Y.: St. Martin's Press, 1978), 104-12.

64 Stanislaw Kowalczyk, "The Possibilities of Christian-Marxist Dialogue on Human Rights," *Soundings* LXVII, no. 2 (Summer, 1984), 70.

were addressed to citizens.⁶⁵ And, these citizens' rights were to be located and enjoyed within their planned state economies.⁶⁶

With all of the foregoing discussion, we are almost in a position to discuss formally economic rights and to explore how they relate to other rights. Yet the discussion of economic rights cannot begin with either a definition, or a brief example. A clear discussion of such rights should continue to examine the process of their generation. Since such rights, despite their first generation connections, were fully (but not solely) expressed by socialist thought, our response should probably begin there.

Not surprisingly, for socialists, the right to work was the most important economic right.⁶⁷ Since socialist thought understood conflict to be generated primarily in reference to labor and to ownership of the forces of production, clearly, rights would first and foremost have to protect the proletariat, the working class, from other forces and classes in society. Thus latter-day, post World War Two socialist thought insisted that economic rights be recognized and implemented prior to and in preference to the recognition of civil and political rights.⁶⁸ As we

⁶⁵ Laszlo Makkai, "The Development of Human Rights in Hungary from the Reformation to the Present," *Soundings* LXVII, no. 2 (Summer, 1984) lodges all rights into the control of citizens, specifically the working class.

⁶⁶ Ibid., 68.

⁶⁷ Tom Campbell writes, "Given that the image of productive man is so basic to socialist philosophy, it makes sense to think of the positive right to work as a fundamental or human right in socialist societies . . .." From *The Left and Rights: A Conceptual Analysis of the Idea of Socialist Rights* (London: Routledge & Kegan Paul plc, 1983), 177.

⁶⁸ Campbell also states, "The Social ownership of the means of production is posited on the centrality of labour to human nature. The right to work is therefore constitutive of socialism and could not be made subject to the contingent decisions of social authorities. In a socialist society the right to work is an untouchable right in that the right could not be denied without that society ceasing to be socialist. One technique which such a right would exclude is that of creating or allowing unemployment in order to secure more jobs in the long run. Human rights cannot be traded off against themselves in this way in non-emergency situations." Ibid, 178. This high valuing of the right to work, creates in Campbell's opinion, the correlative duty to work. He admits that the positive duty to work (unless unable) often irritates economic rights skeptics, because they construe the right to work as a

shall soon discuss in depth, these socialist claims (which prioritized economic rights over civil and political rights) posed a fundamental challenge to economic rights skeptics.

These socialist economic rights were, conceptually speaking, still characterized as individual rights. But the protection that is sought for the individual in these economic rights, is sought by means of the state against powerful forces of production in society. This is a marked difference from the first generation civil and political rights tradition. The other major, structural, difference is that these rights require the state to take a positive action, to provide, if necessary, jobs for individuals. Under the first generation of rights theories, the state was understood as primarily restraining itself and acting positively only when necessity required it to restrain others: all for the sake of the individual. Turning back briefly to Feinberg's consideration of negative duties, it is clear that under the first generation's requirements states and individuals might have millions of *in rem* duties, but they could be successfully completed, to paraphrase Feinberg, by simply minding one's own business.[69]

In contrast to first generation rights, second generation rights, i.e., social and economic rights seem to require not just acts of omission and restraint, but also acts of commission. These acts of commission constitute, of course, positive rights and positive duties that immediately put the socialist conception of rights into conflict with most first generation rights theories.

Our discussion of the evolution of rights including the creation of second generation rights brings to our attention the manifestation of the post-World War Two Cold War struggle that was also waged within the United Nations. This ideological struggle was overtaken in a new debate by new voices in the United Nations making claims to a "third generation" of rights. Before turning to this last generation of rights, we should pause to consider one other important fact. The post-World War Two economic rights debate was more

guaranteed right. Such a guaranteed right would obligate government to constantly intervene in the free market by creating jobs. Thus civil and political rights attendant to the management of property and the hiring and firing of workers, might easily be curtailed by the government.

[69] See note 29 herein.

than a simple ideological dispute between two different political camps. It was also a dispute over the "morally correct" conceptualization of rights. As a result of this debate, rights stopped being considered the sole construct of the liberal West, and this change was internationally recognized.[70]

"Third generation" rights must now be considered. According to Montgomery, third generation rights:

> . . . so called "solidarity" rights--are more recent, nebulous, and controversial. . . These rights are an expanding category which at least include national self-determination, the right to economic and social development, the right to benefit from the "common heritage of Mankind" (sharing of the earth's resources and wealth--as embodied in the recent United Nations Law of the Sea Treaty), the right to a healthy environment, the right to peace, and the right to humanitarian disaster relief.[71]

These third generation rights are the products of the rights debate in the United Nations that has been most closely associated with the defeat of Western political imperialism and the emergence of "new" Third World countries.[72] By the time

---

[70] See Adamantia Pollis and Peter Schwab's insightful essay recounting this change, "Human Rights: A Western Construct With Limited Applicability," *Human Rights: Cultural and Ideological Perspectives* (New York: Praeger Pub., 1979). Chapter One.

[71] Montgomery, 28. It is not suggested by Montgomery or myself that the Third World invented the notion of a right to national self-determination. Rather what transpired in these more recent debates is that the claim for national self-determination was conducted alongside claims for economic rights. National self-determination is a concept with a long history, in Europe and elsewhere. For example, this right is included in the Fourteen Points of Woodrow Wilson.

[72] Marnia Lazreg writes, "The contradictory nature of the 1948 Declaration resulted in the very situation which it sought to prevent, namely, 'rebellion against tyranny and oppression.' Since 1948, colonized nations in Asia and Africa have had recourse to rebellion while invoking the terms of the Declaration and subsequent covenants, despite resistance at the United Nations by the colonial powers formerly responsible for the drafting of the Declaration." "Human Rights, State and Ideology," *Human Rights: Cultural and Ideological Perspectives,* ed. Adamantia Pollis and Peter Schwab, (New York: Praeger Publishers, 1979), 32-33.

these last debates emerged in the United Nations, the Universal Declaration for Human Rights had long been signed and ratified. Nevertheless, despite the passage of the Universal Declaration of Human Rights, third generation rights were met with opposition, and generated a good deal of controversy. The Third World, which has been, for the most part, politically and economically unstable, was, despite its problems, fully competent to mount serious moral claims in U.N. debates. By distinguishing itself from the two super powers, the U.S. and the U.S.S.R., it collectively demanded that it be seen as more than just a pool of available converts to the cause of either side of the Cold War: or to their respective understandings of rights. In short, the Third World had another agenda.[73] Poverty-stricken colonies that had only recently thrown off their former colonial masters were suspicious of all of the ideologies of those masters. Since part of the colonization process had been the systematic exploitation of their labor as a group of people, and their natural resources, they wanted yet another recognition of protective rights. Group rights, which were designed to protect whole nations from the depredations of other nations, were an entirely new application of the idea of rights to moral and political problems.[74] Third World nations understood their relationships with their former colonial masters as remaining basically hostile. Nevertheless, despite their suspicions about rights language, they adapted its use in an attempt to protect themselves from further foreign exploitation. This rights oriented approach was fairly new. Traditionally, relief from hostilities between nations has been addressed,

---

[73] A good statement of this different agenda is expressed by José Figueres, "Some Economic Foundations of Human Rights," *The Human Rights Reader*, ed. Walter Laqueur and Barry Rubin (Philadelphia: Temple University Press, 1979), 270.

[74] Traer maintains that, "It is no accident that both the International Covenant on Economic, Social and Cultural Rights and the International Covenant on Civil and Political Rights begin with the same first Article: 'All peoples have the right of self-determination. By virtue of that right they freely determine their political status and freely pursue their economic, social and cultural development.'" "Human Rights: A Global Faith," (Ph.D. dissertation, Graduate Theological Union, 1988) 71.

during peace times, by diplomacy, and during times of war, by just war theories, peace treaties, or humanitarian conventions. Thus new claims that certain nations should be obligated to provide positively for the economic development of other nations was both novel and offensive to most in the West.[75]

What is important to notice is not the issue of neocolonial relationships, but the form of these third generation rights. These rights are not directed at individuals. They are not predominantly negative in their structure; that is to say they make claims for the positive provision of certain goods, as well as restraints on the conduct of economic relations that might take place between have and have not countries. Further, objects of rights, such as "development" in the "right" to self-development, are objects that are open-ended, or indeterminate. By the term indeterminate what is meant is that there is no clear method for determining whether or not these rights have been fulfilled. For example, there does not appear to be any clear method for determining the point of completion of a country's self-development, not even by the country itself. More importantly, there does not appear to be any clear method for determining, in feasibility terms, when the development of a country has arrived at its absolute limits. Thus, the problems that face the third generation of rights are more than the first world's resistance to contributing to the creation of a new economic order, though it is also certainly that. Clearly, however, conceptual problems remain in regards to what may be claimed by third generation rights. Lastly, the structure of these "group" rights must be examined more closely: they are in

---

[75] But George Shepherd sees the claims of the Third generation of rights as transcending traditional categories. In particular, he feels that the distinction between individual rights and group rights may be overstated in a world that is now a global village. Shepherd writes, "This global view sees rights as both inherent in the individual and socially derived by development. Political freedoms are not possible without primary social development and conflicts are resolved in terms of the welfare of society as a whole." "Transnational Development of Human Rights: The Third World Crucible," *Global Human Rights: Public Policies, Comparative Measures, and NGO Strategies*, ed. Ved P. Nanda, James R. Scaritt, and George W. Shepherd, Jr. (Boulder: Westview Press, 1981), 215. This view of Shepherd was called to my attention by Robert A. Traer's helpful work previously cited herein.

fact rights *in rem*. This is to say that they create duties for an undetermined number of foreign nations, for the benefit of an undetermined number of impoverished nations, containing an undetermined number of impoverished individuals.

This brief depiction of rights evolution in generational stages, along with our typology of rights theories, helps us to understand the important disputes in the economic rights debate. These disputes as to what constitutes a right are important because of the close association of rights, in the West, with the political and moral foundation of modern Western nations. Thus, for us, rights disputes invariably involve disputes over questions of social justice and a nation's own understanding of its meaning and mission. As such, these debates are never simply desultory disputes, but are instead important examples of moral reasoning and discourse that permit continued social cooperation and social and national self-respect. What this brief account of the "generations" of rights has disclosed is that the concept of rights is a dynamic one whose meaning is subject to a continuing development. It is also susceptible to the ideological influences of its proponents. Thus, the fight for the right to represent one's views of rights as being the correct one appears to be intense and perpetual. Our discussion must now consider the impact of the status of human rights on the economic rights debate.

Human Rights and the Economic Rights Debate

The economic rights debate is complicated by the present status of human rights. Human rights impact economic rights because economic rights are commonly understood by some to be a form of human rights. The status of human rights is currently problematic, because of the absence of a consensus as to the content and justification of human rights. To see this problem requires us to consider three different approaches to understanding human rights. Louis Henkin, an international jurist, writes in regards to human rights that:

> The end of the war saw wide acceptance of "human rights" reflected in two forms. Human rights appeared in the constitutions and laws of virtually all states. Conquerors wrote them into law for occupied countries; for example,

Germany and Japan. Departing colonial powers sometimes
required them of newborn states as part of the price of
"liberation," and many new states wrote them into their
constitutions as their own commitment. Older states,
responding to the Zeitgeist, also emphasized human rights
in new national documents. The human rights movement
also took a second, transnational form. Human rights were
prominent in the new postwar international order: in
treaties imposed upon vanquished nations . . . in the UN
Charter . . . In the United Nations "human rights" was on
every agenda, and the dedicated efforts of individuals and
some governments resulted in important international
political and legal instruments, beginning with the
Universal Declaration of Universal Rights . . . I stress and
distinguish those two different manifestations of general,
worldwide concern with human rights.
"Universalization" has brought acceptance, at least in
principle and rhetoric, of the concept of individual human
rights by all societies and governments and its reflection in
national constitutions and laws. "Internationalization" has
brought agreement, at least in political-legal principle and
in rhetoric, that individual human rights are of
"international concern" and a proper subject for diplomacy,
international law, and international institutions.[76]

This extended quote from Henkin demonstrates the
triumph of human rights as a necessary construct in
international relations and in international moral discourse.
Almost every country now claims to be upholding human rights,
regardless of whether they are upholding them or not. The
universality of "official" acceptance of human rights is an
empirically verifiable reality--not that human rights are shown
to be morally justified, but that they are taken seriously
internationally. This circumstance only proves, however, that
everyone "acts" as if "human rights" were "true." Thus, what is
undeniably true about human rights is that, regardless of their
objectively "true" status, they are, from this perspective,
important moral constructs. Now this position should be
contrasted to Robert A. Traer's position. Traer writes:

---

[76] Louis Henkin, "International Human Rights as 'Rights,'"
Human Rights, ed. J. Roland Pennock and John W. Chapman (New
York: New York University Press, 1981), 258-59.

To decide then whether faith in human rights is true
involves faith itself: faith that there is a moral universe in
which it is meaningful to affirm human dignity. This is
logically problematic, but makes sense in human
experience. For faith is not founded on reason, but is the
foundation of reason . . . Human Rights are a response to
that which transcends what is known, which is to say that
they are a matter of faith. And human beings find this
truth confirmed in their experience, as they choose to live
out their faith in human dignity and in human rights.
Thus human rights are not merely a matter of political or
ethical concern, but a matter of faith: not "blind faith" but
the faith of courage and commitment to standards of
human dignity, even at risk to one's own life, despite the
inability to probe to the satisfaction of others that such
standards are true.[77]

Here Traer affirms a different understanding of the
"truth" of human rights. For Traer, the central concern is not a
philosophical demonstration that the concept of human rights is
an objective, normative standard, or the simple empirical
manifestation of the international recognition of human rights
in the world. Rather, what is important, for him, is that they are
concepts lived out in faith, on a global scale, that have the
power of revealing a moral universe and guiding one's actions
within it. In contrast to Traer is Alasdair MacIntyre, professor
of philosophy at Vanderbilt University, who writes in regards to
human rights that:

The best reason for asserting so bluntly that there are no
such rights is indeed of precisely the same type as the best
reason which we possess for asserting that there are no
witches and the best reason which we possess for asserting
that there are no unicorns: every attempt to give reasons
for believing that there are such reasons has failed.[78]

MacIntyre maintains therefore that:

Natural or human rights then are fictions--just as is
utility-but fictions with highly specific properties. . . . A

77 Traer, 310.

78 Alasdair MacIntyre, *After Virtue* (Notre Dame: University of
Notre Dame Press, 1984), 69.

central characteristic of moral fictions which comes clearly
into view when we juxtapose the concept of utility to that
of rights is now identifiable: they purport to provide us
with an objective and impersonal criterion, but they do
not.[79]

Human rights are portrayed here in three distinct ways.
The first, Henkin's way, is descriptive; he notes what human
rights have effected in terms of creating certain institutions and
a certain order. Traer's position grounds human rights in a
global faith that is obviously not philosophically justifiable.
MacIntyre, the philosopher, sees human rights as defective
moral constructs--deceptive because they require certain
curtailments on human action and relationships without
themselves being philosophically justifiable. Thus, for him, they
contribute to what he sees as a major moral problem--moral
incommensurability.

Now this brief excursus into ways of looking at human
rights has been indulged in for a purpose. These three
approaches show that at the present, the concept of "human
rights" remains philosophically unjustified.[80] As such, economic
rights theories that seek to justify themselves by recourse to
arguments designed to qualify them as human rights, are bound
to be challenged because of current philosophical doubts with
regard to "human rights." Another way of stating this is that
economic rights are difficult to justify as valid moral concepts,
because their justification entails a reliance upon a foundational
premise that is itself unjustified: namely human rights. Thus,
much of the debate, in which, for varying reasons, parties are
challenging or affirming economic rights as human rights,
nevertheless misses the larger philosophical point: the debate
along these lines is largely academic until human rights

---

79 Ibid, 70. For an understanding of rights as useful fictions that also
explains some of the functions that rights play in society, see Jon P.
Gunnemann's enlightening essay, "Human Rights and Modernity: The
Truth of the Fiction of Individual Rights," *The Journal of Religious
Ethics* 16 (Spring 88), 160-189.

80 By philosophical justification I mean the formal demonstration
of the ultimate truth of human rights, in the form of a syllogism, from
first principles to a logically compelling conclusion. These approaches
do not even attempt to perform this task. I do not either.

themselves are philosophically justified. Though such rights may remain philosophically unjustified, such a conclusion does not preclude their consideration for inclusion into policy decisions. The reason for this conclusion is that economic rights are potentially in the same position as civil and political rights: useful for policy formation despite the uncertainty of their foundational premises.[81] Accordingly, this study will not attempt to prove philosophically the ultimate veracity of human rights: this is not what the dispute regarding economic rights is about in any event.   The dispute centers upon the appropriateness of including economic rights in policy formation because of their harmony or conflict with civil and political rights, and because their inclusion is demanded by the minimum requirements of social justice in a rights-claiming society.

Still to be considered is the interrelationship of human rights, moral rights, and economic rights. Human rights are considered, by most writers in the field, as being forms of moral rights.   Nevertheless, this association of human rights with moral rights does not define either term; to define moral rights or human rights is itself a difficult task.   It is troublesome, precisely in the same way as the task of defining the term rights was difficult: many definitions have been offered, but none has achieved a universal consensus.   In fact, widespread and prolonged debate on the meaning of human rights has generated increasing numbers of definitions. Alan Gewirth has a useful definition of moral rights and human rights that shows their interrelationship. Gewirth writes that:

> Human rights are a species of moral rights: they are moral rights which all persons equally have simply because they are human. To call them "moral" is to say that they are based upon or justifiable through a valid moral principle. To call a principle "moral," in turn, is to indicate that it sets forth as categorically obligatory certain requirements for action that are addressed at least in part to all actual or

---

[81] MacIntyre's criticism gives one pause when considering the foundations of human rights. But MacIntyre's dismissal of human rights, because of the absence of a philosophical justification, in no way dissuades one from considering them for the purposes of policy formation.

prospective agents and that are concerned with furthering
the interests, especially the most important interests, of
persons or recipients other than or in addition to the agent
or the speaker.[82]

Gewirth's careful definition uses moral language concisely
and rightfully emphasizes and integrates the concepts of agency,
interests, obligation, action and personhood. These concepts
are essential for any ethically perceptive theory of rights. Even
Maurice Cranston, an economic rights skeptic, defines human
rights as, ". . . a form of moral right, and they differ from other
moral rights in being the rights of all people at all times and in
all situations."[83] In classifying human rights in universal terms,
and characterizing them as being a species of moral rights,
Gewirth and Cranston are, to this extent, in agreement. Where
Gewirth and Cranston differ is found primarily in Cranston's
qualifications that human rights are human rights at "all times
and in all situations."[84] "At all times" implies that human rights
should have a universal and timeless application: it thereby
functions as a normative statement. With such a timeless
application, "classic" first generation rights such as the right to a
trial by jury, or the freedom of the press *do not* appear to qualify
as "human rights." To qualify them as human rights according
to his definition would require Cranston to demonstrate that the
recognition and implementation of such rights (or at least their
underlying values--as cultural or social norms) should be
mandatory for all societies. Such a task appears on its face to be
doubtful. It makes little sense to say that all societies should
have trials by jury, though it might make some sense to say that
all societies should have due process.[85] Thus, Cranston's
transhistorical and transcultural definition appears, as a

---

82 Gewirth, 1.

83 Cranston, 21.

84 Ibid., 49.

85 Even this more qualified statement might look very odd to the
modern eye. Such due process might turn out to be trial by contest
(jousting) or magical procedures (witch-dousing). These two methods
were once normative in our own legal systems.

normative claim, to be problematic.[86] Equally suspect is the
"situational" qualification, which implicitly assumes that every
historical situation is analogous to other historical situations.
Thus to qualify for the status of a "human right" in Cranston's
thought, every human right claim should be comprehensible in
every society in every situation.[87] Clearly, a "classic" first
generation right to freedom of the press makes little sense in a
non-literate society. It is for these reasons as well as others that
a definition of human rights, borrowed from Gewirth, will be,
provisionally, adopted for this work. Cranston's definition
problem is simply a good example of the types of problems that
are frequently found in the literature in this field.

In contrast, Gewirth's definition presents fewer
problems. Gewirth merely maintains that all persons possess
human rights (whatever they are) solely because they are
human. Thus Gewirth makes no claim to a timeless application,
relying instead on characterizing human rights as moral rights,
which are "based upon or justifiable through a valid moral
principle." By separating his definition of human rights from his
"valid" moral principle, Gewirth can write more precisely
regarding both the principle and the rights. Gewirth's full

---

86 Rights that can be considered as being transhistorically and
transculturally normative, must be of a very basic sort. Henry Shue, a
social philosopher, argues for rights to security, subsistence, and
freedom across cultures and generations. Shue's rights, as we will see in
chapter four are very basic and minimal; as such, it is not unreasonable
to call unjust any society that intentionally violated such rights. Thus,
slavery can now be seen as having always been immoral (a denial of
one's rights to freedom) and this moral assessment can be applied to all
societies. That such a moral judgment may prove to be chauvinistic, or
imperialistic is unavoidable. Yet to say that every society should take
care that none of its members are intentionally deprived of food,
clothing, shelter, security, and freedom does not appear to be too
demanding. The alternative view is that all moralities are, more or less,
equal and self-authenticating. This viewpoint is the essence of a moral
and cultural relativity that disables the ethicist from judging any moral
system, other than her own, and, finally, from assessing critically even
her own system.

87 Clearly Cranston's position is a normative statement, not an
empirical-descriptive one.   That no rights are transhistorically
normative is not herein suggested. I am simply calling into question
some of the ones that Cranston offers as being transhistorical.

explanation of his human rights theory cannot now be explored, but will be fully addressed in Chapter Four.

Turning, finally, to the term economic rights, we see that for our purposes, these rights are often considered a subset of human rights. This would also make them a subset of "moral rights."[88] The Covenant on Social, Economic, and Cultural Rights, which is the focus of much of the economic rights debate, has an extensive list of economic rights that are internationally though not universally recognized.[89] If Gewirth's definition of human rights is related to the subset known as economic rights, at least four problems immediately arise. First, economic rights must be shown to be possessed by all humans by virtue of their humanity (if those rights are to qualify as "human rights"). Secondly, their "valid moral principle" must be demonstrated (if they are to be "justified" regardless as to their status as "human rights"). Thirdly, if economic rights are to be demonstrated as inherently related to and interdependent with civil and political rights, their compatibility to such rights must be clearly and convincingly displayed. For example, the distinction between positive rights and negative rights must be shown as not disqualifying economic rights. Fourthly, since many theories for economic rights are based upon justifying them by some connection to dire need, as a necessary, though insufficient

---

[88] It is of course equally possible that economic rights could qualify as a subset of legal rights. The location of economic rights as moral rights or legal rights depends on whether such rights are positivized in a nation's or league of nations' legal system. Thus, in socialist countries, positive legislation creates and enforces economic rights. In contrast, in America welfare legislation is passed that provides for economic benefits and the provision of certain goods and services to certain people, *without* many recognized claims that the beneficiaries have a "right" to such goods, or that the legislation in question is positivizing "economic rights."

[89] Article 11 of the Covenant on Economic, Social and Cultural Rights reads in part as follows, "1. The States parties to the present Covenant recognize the right of everyone to an adequate standard of living for himself and his family, including adequate food, clothing and housing, and to the continuous improvement of living conditions. The States parties will take appropriate steps to ensure the realization of this right, recognizing to this effect the essential importance of international cooperation based on free consent."

element in a theory of rights, certain facts regarding basic need theses must be clarified.[90] Such economic rights theories based upon "needs" considerations need to show: (a) that all human beings deserve to have their basic needs met; (b) that an adequate method for identifying basic needs is possible; (c) that the demonstration that all people "deserve" to have their basic needs met must be connected to, or entailed in their "valid moral principle"; (d) that the correlativity of rights to duties problem is not fatal to justifying economic rights; and (e) that there is a clear basis for their theory of obligation--how the duty-bearer becomes obligated to perform the assigned burden. In short, our thesis can be sustained only if the major objections to economic rights are effectively rebutted and a clear and convincing moral theory for their recognition offered. These tasks will be addressed in Chapter Four.

A Brief History of the Economic Rights Debate

This study is most interested in the economic rights debate surrounding the Carter Administration's endorsement of economic rights. Our classification of rights into distinct types and our evolutionary generation of rights investigation demonstrate the varieties of rights conceptions and common debates that were current at the inception of the Carter Administration. This information demonstrates that there was an absence of consensus regarding economic rights and a school of thought that gravely doubted the possibility of economic rights. It is not surprising, therefore, given the state of the debate, that Carter was met with opposition. However, to understand fully the central problems addressed in this dissertation, it is necessary to reconsider the formal debates

---

90 Only by clarifying the concept of need can that concept be used in the justification of economic rights. Indeterminacy is one of the primary objections to the recognition of economic rights; it is a condition in which the class that constitutes the Objects of Rights is insufficiently defined so as to admit an unlimited number of objects. By doing so, the class itself breaks down into meaninglessness: this elemental breakdown triggers a breakdown of the notion of rights. Chapter Three shows how Cranston, Kirkpatrick, and others dismiss economic rights as "valid" rights because of the unaddressed problem of indeterminacy.

over economic rights that took place in the United Nations after World War Two and prior to Carter's election.

As most writers concede, the intense concern with what we now call human rights grew out of the massive destruction of human life and social and political arrangements, caused by World War Two.[91] This destruction dispelled whatever remaining notions of "unidirectional progress" that the First World War had not already exhausted, and placed a demand on governments to create an organ to promote international peace. The United Nations replaced the failed League of Nations, and began to establish moral and legal norms that would persuasively transcend the law of any one state. The hope was to find an international arrangement of interests in the system of nation-states that could avoid wholescale war and genocidal tragedies in the future. The conceptual result of this attempt was the reiteration of natural law claims, albeit recast in the language of human rights. Participants in the U.N. debates believed that the recognition of these rights would facilitate a check on the arbitrary and capricious power of any one state, and might expose the *ultra vires* actions of a state to international moral scrutiny, and, if necessary, censure. Their primary concern was for the establishment of civil and political rights designed to insure security for individuals (in a world in which fascism had "grossly violated" such rights) and international peace.

However, prior to World War Two, and the subsequent United Nations debates, certain changes that are important to our discussion had taken place on the American scene. One of the most influential voices raised on behalf of economic rights was that of President Franklin Delano Roosevelt, who endorsed a theory of economic rights during the war. Roosevelt, who was not a socialist, introduced a clear governmental commitment to addressing economic woes in his New Deal

---

[91] Robert A. Traer, "Human Rights: A Global Faith," 73. See also Louis Henkin, "Economic Social Rights as Rights: A United States Perspective," *Human Rights Law Journal* 2 nos. 3-4 (1981), 223-36. See also James Nickle, *Making Sense of Human Rights* (Berkeley: University of California Press, 1987).

approach and in his "Four Freedoms Doctrine."[92]   His
contribution to Western support in favor of economic rights
cannot be overestimated, although it cannot now be examined
at length and will be addressed in Chapter Two.   What is
important about Roosevelt's support for economic rights is that
it was a clear rejection of the prevailing view in the United
States that traditionally denied the conceptual coherency of the
term "economic" rights.   A representative example of the
traditional view of the United States is that of President Grover
Cleveland.   In 1887, Cleveland maintained that:

> [he did] not believe that the power and duty of the General
> Government ought to be extended to the relief of
> individual suffering which is in no matter properly related
> to the public service or benefit. A prevalent tendency to
> disregard the limited mission of this power and duty
> should, I think, be steadfastly resisted, to the end that the
> lesson should be constantly enforced that though the
> people support the Government, the Government should
> not support the people.[93]

Roosevelt's rejection of the traditional view (an American,
democratic, liberal rejection) upheld by Cleveland, initiated a
domestic economic rights debate that manifested itself after
Roosevelt's death in the United Nations debates. These debates
were carried on, primarily, by the winners of the Second World
War. One of the winners was the Soviet Union. As our brief
history of the evolution of rights has made clear, some

----

[92] It should be remembered from our generational study that
nonsocialists such as Thomas Paine and John Locke had certain theories
supporting what we now call economic rights. Since Roosevelt was not
a socialist, he may have formed his support for economic rights out of
the streams of support that flowed from Paine, Locke or others. In any
event, his theories did not draw on socialist traditions. Although
socialist thought has clearly endorsed economic rights, the authorship
of such rights cannot be assigned to its register, precisely because of the
previous influences of Paine, Locke, the French Declaration of the
Rights of Man and others.

[93] As quoted by Andrew R. Cecil, "Economic Freedom: The Rights
and Responsibilities of the Entrepreneur in Our Mixed Economy," *Our
Freedoms: Rights and Responsibilities*, ed. W. Lawson Taitte (Dallas:
University of Texas Press, 1985), 196.

European socialists did not reject rights talk out of hand, despite the criticism of Karl Marx. Instead, they championed rights that most easily fit their current society, economy and government. These rights influenced the creation of the rights now listed in the Covenant for Social and Economic Rights. Since Roosevelt's view of economic rights was still new, and contradicted a traditional American view, the socialist view (which was of course quite different from Roosevelt's view) found little American support, and much American opposition. A paradigmatic representative of the American economic rights skeptic position was that of Frank Holman, a past president of the American Bar Association, who opposed the inclusion of social and economic rights in the Universal Declaration of Human Rights. He maintained that such putative rights were spurious, because they were:

> ". . . predicated upon the unAmerican theory that basic rights can be created by legislative action and that, along with basic rights, the social and economic well-being of our citizens may be defined, fixed, and limited by international declaration."[94]

His rejection of economic rights was, of course, a variation on the positive/negative rights distinction that we have discussed in our typology of rights theories. He was opposed, nevertheless, by a new international economic rights partisan group, headed by Eleanor Roosevelt and Dr. Charles Malik, a Lebanese philosopher and Lebanese Ambassador to the United Nations. Malik maintained that understanding rights talk was an evolutionary task. He characterized the task as requiring stages:

> There were three logical steps to this transition. The first is to say, the civil, political and personal is primary, but the economic, social and cultural also has its place. The second is to move insensibly from this position to the view that

---

[94] Frank Holman, "International Proposals Affecting So-Called Human Rights," *Law and Contemporary Problems* 14 (Summer 1949), 481.

both types of rights are equally important. And the third obviously is to say, what is the use of the civil, political and personal if the economic and social is not first guaranteed? Ergo, the social and economic is primary and more important.[95]

Thus, two Western views claimed intellectual and moral ascendancy regarding the issue of economic rights and governmental economic duties. They opposed each other in an international forum on human rights in general and economic rights in particular. What became evident, even in the early nineteen fifties, within the American contingent alone, was the evidence of a struggle for power: the power to define the term "human rights" and to name the appropriate objects of those rights.[96] One group of American human rights advocates (the larger group) wanted to champion human rights as a simple reinterpretation of Western "natural rights." The other group (a smaller contingent) wanted to internationalize and formalize the "Roosevelt" tradition.

The socialists, on the other hand, wanted to challenge the American traditional view, in a neo-Marxist fashion, because of its "bourgeois" understanding of rights. Simultaneously, they emphasized their "socialist" understanding of economic rights. Though each group was disinclined to compromise, compromise they did. The compromise was necessary, because all of the groups in question wanted to advocate "human rights." The compromise was conceptually awkward, because none of the debaters gave up their ideological positions regarding the

---

[95] Charles Malik, "Human Rights and the United Nations," *United Nations Bulletin* 13 (1 September 1952), 253. Malik's use of the term "insensibly" must be understood as describing an unnoticed mental process in which his mind became changed from opposition to economic rights to support for the same.

[96] The recognized right to set the terms of a debate or the elements in a definition are often overlooked in the heat and smoke of a debate. An excellent article that focuses on the politics of interpretation is Nancy Fraser's "Talking About Needs: Interpretive Contests as Political Conflicts in Welfare-State Societies," *Ethics* 99, no. 2 (January, 1989), 291-313.

content and the implementation of "human rights." Accordingly, the compromises that took place were ones in which the concept of human rights had within it the inclusion of conflicting ideas. Thus, the 1948 Universal Declaration of Human Rights had passages that included **both** civil/political rights and economic rights. This compromise kept the differing positions in tension by implementing the Declaration as a manifesto of social ideals, rather than as an empowering constitution.[97] To make the provisions of the Declaration binding, the parties agreed to enabling legislation through a ratification process to create a distinct enabling Covenant.[98] This compromise was further qualified by a later determination to create two covenants, rather than one.[99] Both Covenants were approved by the General Assembly in 1966. The liberal democratic statement was encapsulated in the Covenant on Political and Civil Rights: it contained what we have previously described as first generation rights. This Covenant was designed to be immediately binding on all the parties that signed and ratified it. For its implementation, it was understood as requiring merely domestic legal systems that could recognize the ratification, and

---

[97] For two differing accounts of this history, see David Hollenbach's *Claims in Conflict* (New York: Paulist Press, 1979), Chapter One, and Maurice Cranston's *What Are Human Rights?*, 34.

[98] Eleanor Roosevelt, the chairperson of the committee, described the compromise process as follows: "Later it was decided that this Charter should be in two parts, first the Declaration and then the Covenant. The Declaration would set standards and voice aspirations, but not be legally binding on the nations whose representatives had accepted it in the General Assembly. The Covenant, however, would be drawn in the form of a treaty and would therefore have to be ratified by each nation in whatever way they ratified treaties and it would then be legally binding." Hollenbach, *Claims in Conflict*, 29. The original citation may be found in "Human Rights," *Peace on Earth*, ed. Robert E. Sherwood (New York: Heritage House, 1949), 65-66.

[99] James Nickel notes that, "To accommodate those who believed that economic and social rights were not genuine human rights or that they were not enforceable in the same way as civil and political rights, two treaties were prepared, the Covenant on Civil and Political Rights and the Covenant on Economic, Social, and Cultural Rights," *Making Sense of Human Rights* (Berkeley: University of California Press, 1987), 5.

use its provisions to limit the power and interventions of the state.[100]
    The Covenant for Social, Economic and Cultural Rights met a different fate, running into a series of further debates and lobbies. Since many of this Covenant's provisions had been covered in the Universal Declaration of Human Rights, which had been ratified since 1948, provisions for economic rights were clearly accepted as having some moral meaning, yet their implementation as effective rights was vigorously opposed.[101] This lack of closure on human rights has meant that the debate could (and did) continue unabated as various sides promoted their views while castigating their opponents' views. Henry Shue, a modern economic rights proponent, still complains about the historic imposition of the process of "gradualism" on the Covenant on Social, Economic and Cultural Rights.[102] Shue believes that the gradualism was implemented by the traditional American liberal democratic contingent because they wished to delay as long as possible the recognition and implementation of economic rights, while having their version of human rights internationally recognized and implemented. This gradualism was accomplished by putting a time table into the implementation of the Covenant that required only a "progressive attainment" in implementing the rights.[103] However, the effect of the change in the recognition and implementation of economic rights meant that their acceptance as "human rights" was also delayed. The delay also subjected

---

    100 Surprisingly, even this Covenant was not immediately signed by American liberal democrats, who were afraid of being subject to the intervention of an international, moral, supra-governmental organization, which could, conceivably, interfere in their national sovereignty. For a full history of this point see Maurice Cranston's *What Are Human Rights?*, 53-57.

    101 Maurice Cranston interpreted the mere inclusion of the so-called "economic rights" in the Universal Declaration as a "considerable diplomatic victory for the Communist members of the United Nations." *What Are Human Rights?*, 34. Cranston's view gives the impression that only Communists intelligently wanted "economic rights;" all others were simply "misled by good intentions."

    102 Henry Shue, *Basic Rights* (Princeton: Princeton University Press, 1980), 159.

    103 Ibid.

the Covenant to continued opposition to their inclusion within the "pantheon" of human rights.

In addition, the concept of economic rights was further confused by the onset of "third generation" rights that we discussed in our brief history of rights development. In short, though the Covenant for Social, Economic and Cultural Rights went into effect in January of 1966, the United States did not sign it until President Jimmy Carter signed it at the United Nations on October 5, 1977. To date, it remains unratified by the United States, though 92 other countries have seen fit to ratify it. Thus, the historical status of "economic rights" at the time of the Carter Administration was one of uncertainty: the American opinion on the matter was mired in an endless debate between two wings in the Western liberal tradition regarding the validity of economic rights and their relationship to human rights. Not only did Jimmy Carter sign the Covenant for Social, Economic and Cultural Rights, he forwarded it to Congress for ratification with his clear and unequivocal support for it. His support electrified the economic rights debate, and his position was understood to be charting a new course in foreign policy and a new expression of American mores and governmental responsibilities. His actions were berated as pious, misunderstood, or cravenly solicitous to Third World countries. Yet he believed (as did Roosevelt) that his support for economic rights was merely a reflection of current American moral sentiments in harmony with international foreign policy ethics. This confidence shows that Carter did not fully understand the radical quality of his position and the depth and strength of his opposition.

The Problem of Economic Rights

As previously stated, the purpose of this study is to explore the moral foundations of economic rights to determine their appropriateness for use in the process of formulating and implementing United States public policy, including foreign policy. Our examination reveals a serious problem that must be addressed if the moral foundations of economic rights are to be adequately understood. The problem is concerned with the approaches that have commonly been used for explaining the moral foundation of economic rights. There have been two primary approaches. The first approach claims that economic rights are morally important because they are valid human rights. This approach is predicated, of course, upon a prior understanding of human rights as a valid and necessary moral concept. The claim, therefore, that economic rights are important for public policy because they are forms of human rights, is dependent upon two prior considerations. The first consideration is that economic rights be shown to be a subset of human rights, and the second is that there be a showing that human rights are themselves viable, justifiable ethical concepts. Our previous discussion on the relationship of human rights, moral rights and economic rights, adequately demonstrates that indeed, economic rights constitute a subset of human rights.[104] However, our discussion has also shown that the second consideration, the demonstration of a philosophical justification for human rights is a very difficult endeavor.

It is for this reason, i.e., the difficulty of establishing a foundational justification of human rights upon which to ground economic rights that our thesis investigates the justification of economic rights indirectly. Our thesis justifies economic rights in moral foundations that are not in dispute: namely American civil and political rights, the first generation rights positivized in the Bill of Rights and the Constitution.[105] As was maintained previously, this study presupposes the existence of a deep and broad American consensus on the moral and legal validity of civil and political rights as human rights. These civil and political rights constitute the foundation out of which public policy is determined. Given this consensus, economic rights also should win widespread acceptance as human rights, if they can

---

[104] This demonstration is of course applicable only to economic rights supporters. For them economic rights, unless positivized by law, constitute a subset of human rights. Skeptics, of course, dispute this conclusion.

[105] By the phrase, "not in dispute," all I mean is that these rights are accepted as valid by most Americans, and by both sides of the economic rights debate. I also emphasize that civil and political rights have been made positive in our Constitution and upheld in our courts. These rights are of course disputed by various philosophers for various reasons.

be shown to be inherently interconnected and interdependent with civil and political rights. If such a showing can be made, then the actualization of civil and political rights would necessarily entail the recognition and implementation of economic rights in public policy.

However, a demonstration that economic rights are inherently interdependent and in harmony with civil and political rights is the crux of the economic rights debate. For economic rights partisans, such rights do not conflict with civil and political rights. Moreover, such rights function to protect people from standard recurrent threats much as civil and political rights do.[106]

In contrast, for economic rights skeptics, such as Jeane Kirkpatrick, Maurice Cranston, Joshua Muravchik, Michael Novak, and Charles Frankel, modern human rights are the conceptual successors to Enlightenment "natural" rights, what we have called first generation rights. As such, in their eyes, human rights are a species of moral rights that restrain the government from interfering in the pursuit of the maximization of liberty by the radically free modern individual. These "protective" rights are, for them, "negative" in their nature; they require acts of omission, not acts of provision. Thus, for them, economic rights are conflictual and confusing encrustations on "sacred" moral rights. Therefore they reject economic rights, because they understand that economic rights demand governmental provision, (which they do not favor) rather than rights that restrain a government (which they do favor). It is this undesired interventionism that conflicts with their vision of society and social responsibilities, and it is this factor that they wish to minimize.[107] Cranston, Novak, Kirkpatrick, and others

---

[106] The importance of acquiring immunity from standard threats, i.e., securing well-being, will be fully argued in Chapter Four. It can be seen, in part, even in this chapter, as inarticulately addressed in the economic rights listed in Vance's Law Day Address, and in certain section of the Covenant for Social, Economic, and Cultural Rights. The economic rights listed therein are designed to insure well-being.

[107] For example, one economic rights skeptic, H. L. A. Hart, a jurist (who wrote in regard to natural rights), held that economic rights would unacceptably conflict with the "preferred" (a lexical priority) political rights of the liberty of the individual. "Are There Any Natural Rights?,"

worry that if economic rights are characterized as human rights, a proliferation of "rights-claims" will be generated--that is, that economic rights will be mistakenly perceived as nothing more than thinly disguised wishes or desiderata--and a profusion of them may have the effect of undermining the "true" concept of human rights. Skeptics are disinclined to acknowledge any economic rights as human rights, or as compelling moral rights, lest such a recognition acts to compel the government to interfere in the affairs of people. In the skeptics' opinion, people should handle such matters themselves through the market, or through private organizations. Such rights could, in their opinion, even obligate the state to reorganize itself and implement a planned economy in a socialist state.[108]

The Structure of this Study

I intend to argue, then, that economic rights skeptics are wrong, that economic rights *are* interdependent with civil and political rights. This thesis will be demonstrated in the following order and ways.

Chapter Two examines at length former President James E. Carter's position on economic rights. This chapter shows how Carter was a carrier of Roosevelt's tradition that championed "second generation rights," while continuing to support "first generation rights." Also demonstrated are his use of moral language, the influence of his subordinates, his response to critics, and his support for the Covenant on Social, Economic, and Cultural Rights. Most importantly, this chapter will demonstrate how economic rights, supported by the Carter administration, actually affected the economic rights debate and the course of public policy, and how such rights presented a

---

Theories of Rights, ed. Jeremy Waldron, (Hong Kong: Oxford University Press, 1984), 77-90.

[108] As our brief history of rights has made clear, economic rights were most clearly and forcefully claimed by socialists; accordingly, the association of economic rights with socialism is not without considerable historical merit. However, it should also be noted that Franklin D. Roosevelt was an economic rights supporter who was influential in the U. N. debates (by his Four Freedoms Doctrine and by proxy, through his wife's leadership), but was not a socialist and did not draw on the socialist tradition.

unique moral stance. Lastly, Carter's approach to economic rights is evaluated as to its internal logic and effectiveness in rebutting standard objections to economic rights.

Chapter Three fully exposits economic rights skepticism. The arguments of Carter's detractors are analyzed along with the standard objections to economic rights. These criticisms are then evaluated as to their clarity, coherence and persuasiveness.

Chapter Four presents selected economic rights theories that demonstrate that economic rights are inherently interdependent with civil and political rights, and therefore crucial for public policy formation. These theories will also show why economic rights are morally compelling rights even without reference to civil and political rights. Two commentators will be discussed at length, Henry Shue and Alan Gewirth. Shue, a professor of social philosophy at the University of Maryland, is crucial to this study, because of his vigorous claim that "basic rights" are inherently interdependent.[109] If Shue is correct, and all basic rights are, in fact, interdependent, then given the deep commitment to civil and political rights, some economic rights must also be conceded as "necessary," if not "justified." Similarly, Alan Gewirth is important because of his rigorous analysis of rights language and his support for economic rights.[110] In summation, Chapter Four demonstrates the plausibility of our thesis.

Chapter Five demonstrates how religious bodies and commentators have impacted the economic rights debate. This material is important because it greatly affects the future recognition and implementation of economic rights. This chapter also shows how the work of Shue has been appropriated and clarified by Nicholas Wolterstorff, a Reformed theologian. Lastly, this chapter demonstrates how recent Catholic Social Teachings have addressed this question and how the work of Gewirth and Shue can contribute to these teachings. The views of David J. Hollenbach, S. J., a Catholic commentator, and proponent of economic rights, will be examined at length to see how well they address standard

---

[109] Henry Shue, *Basic Rights* (Princeton: Princeton University Press, 1980).

[110] Alan Gewirth, *Human Rights*.

objections to economic rights and how they enrich and correct certain weaknesses found in the supports for economic rights featured in Chapter Four.

Chapter Six reexamines the conclusions of this study and their implications for policy formation. Certain practical problems inherent in the implementation of economic rights are addressed, such as the continued evolution of rights concepts (in particular the problem of indeterminacy) and the difficulty of determining the appropriate time for international intervention on behalf of economic rights. Finally, suggestions are offered in support of economic rights and the direction that the debate is likely to move in the future is fully explained.

Limitations in the Research and Its Relation to the Literature

Every study must have its limits and this one is no exception. Significant questions regarding the relationship of group rights to individual rights will not be addressed. Group rights are third generation rights, and while many of them are concerned with economics, their structure and focus are too different from economic rights as individual rights to be easily encompassed within the time and space limitations of this study. However, it is not unreasonable to assume that if economic rights are not compelling moral concepts for the protection of individuals, they will not likely be considered compelling for whole groups of people. On the other hand, the establishment of a widespread consensus on individual economic rights may well serve as the beginning point for new discussions on group rights. But those discussions constitute different projects.

This study is unique because it is interested solely in the question of economic rights, but it is, nevertheless, related to current literature in the field. It differs from Shue's approach, however, in that other basic rights are not addressed, such as the right to security.[111] It is, nevertheless, dependent upon Shue's basic premises. I extend Shue's argument to the extent that I address all of the standard objections to economic rights, whereas Shue concentrates upon establishing his

---

[111] Shue is equally concerned with the issue of security, for example.

interdependency principle. In addition, in Chapter Five I explain in ways that Shue does not, who rights-claimants are and why they are sufficiently valuable to be accorded rights.

In some respects this work is a response to a prior case study (looking at the Carter Administration), which was also concerned with economic rights, conducted by Joshua Muravchik. However, in contrast to Joshua Muravchik's recent work on Carter's human rights policy, this work has an extended discussion of the problem of defining human rights and the process by which one should include or exclude economic rights.[112] This study is, of course, also an analysis and criticism of Alan Gewirth's work. Most of the popular criticism of Gewirth has focused on what his critics believe to be conceptual flaws in his moral system. This study does not address whether Gewirth's project succeeds as a foundational moral system. Instead, Gewirth is examined regarding how his work explains the necessity of economic rights. Importantly, this study shows how secular moral arguments for economic rights can and have been related to theological arguments for economic rights. For example, the work of David Hollenbach in demonstrating the progressive revelation aspects of Catholic Social Teachings is examined and criticized in light of the Shue and Gewirth projects. Hollenbach's work argues that economic rights are important for Catholics. This work maintains that such rights are important for all people.

The Significance of Economic Rights

This work is important, not just because of the uniqueness of its approach. It is important because it addresses vital moral concerns. As citizens of the United States of America, members of an economic and political world power, we need to examine the concept of economic rights to discover and understand our moral obligations to each other and to the international community. We live and work in relation to market conditions, often for multinational corporations, all within a welfare

---

112 Joshua Muravchik, *The Uncertain Crusade: Jimmy Carter and the Dilemma of Human Rights Policy* (Lanham, Maryland: Hamilton Press, 1986).

entitlement state. In theory, few Americans should perish from
starvation; few need die homeless of exposure, yet thousands
do. What duties do we owe each other in this world of
widespread scarcity (for many) and relative abundance (for a
fortunate few)? Should haves go about their pursuit of life,
liberty and happiness, oblivious to the fates of have nots? Can
economic rights be ethically justified, or must the needs of the
poor be addressed solely through charity?

The significance of this project is in direct proportion to
the mounting numbers of homeless and starving people, here in
America, and abroad. The nature of our inquiry is moral; it
demands that we look beyond our immediate interests and
critically examine our current understandings of the rights and
duties we may owe to each other as members of a moral
community. In a country founded in part upon the violation of
the economic rights of aboriginal peoples (the immoral
appropriation of their land) and captive Africans (the immoral
appropriation of their persons and labor), in a world of
continuing scarcity, this work is needed for the process of
identifying principles for determining economic responsibility
for a wealthy society that is neglecting many desperately poor
people.

Michael Walzer has maintained that, "No community can
allow its members to starve to death when there is food
available to feed them; no government can stand passively by at
such a time--not if it claims to be a government of or by or for
the community."[113] If Walzer is correct, modern governments do
have "positive" economic duties. It should be remembered that
the modern world is inescapably interconnected. Modern
international relations are facilitated by global communications,
travel and debate: this "global village" phenomenon has made
human relations problematic. The modern poor (and the
wealthier classes) are more aware of poverty than previous
socioeconomic classes. And, where opulence and squalor are so
easily seen in close proximity, human dignity and human life are
called into question. This study is in part an exploration into the
truth of Walzer's observation.

---

[113] Michael Walzer, *Spheres of Justice: A Defense of Pluralism and
Equality* (New York: Basic Books, 1983), 79.

This examination of the Carter administration is not accidental. Carter promoted economic rights without clearly explaining and justifying them. He did so at a time when the economic rights debate was reaching a boiling point and the direction that America should take regarding rights was in question. He attempted to win the debate and to positivize economic rights. As we shall see in Chapter Two, he also sought to bring America into conformity with the prevailing mood of Western Europe. By doing so, he sought to realign America with its cultural and political allies and peers. Yet his position was controversial. His successors have attempted to reverse his course. The moral justifiability of this reversal has not been fully demonstrated and will be explicated, by implication, by our study of his position. Carter's position demonstrates how a nation can have an economic rights policy without a broad based consensus on its validity; but it also shows how such a position can be reversed, by successors, if a widespread moral consensus is not evident.

In conclusion, this study is an investigation into the moral implications of the economic rights debate. The moral obligations entailed in the recognition of economic rights are scrutinized. In addition, the moral implications of failing to recognize and to implement economic rights are evaluated. The present state of confusion regarding economic rights creates doubts regarding many aspects of international morality. Human life and human dignity must never be trivialized in a post-Holocaust world in which most of its inhabitants are poor, and many are starving. These circumstances have been partially recognized in the literature, but a new and systematic examination and analysis is overdue. Chapter Two begins this examination by detailing our case study: the Carter Administration. Former President Carter believed that the United States was morally committed to recognizing economic rights. Was he correct in his supposition?

CHAPTER TWO

BRIDGING THE GENERATION GAP IN RIGHTS

This chapter is a case study of President Jimmy Carter's economic rights policy. The way in which he served as a bridge between first generation accounts of rights and second generation accounts of rights will be fully explained herein. Carter formed this bridge by incorporating economic rights with civil and political rights in his human rights policy. To accomplish this task he employed three rights accounts: first, a first generation of rights account; second, a moral appeal to the American compassion for the poor; and third, an adoption and adaptation of President Franklin Delano Roosevelt's *Freedom from Want Doctrine*. Thus Carter and Roosevelt are both bridge figures in American rights theories. These changes in economic rights understandings are then accounted for in Carter's progressive realization of rights theory. Special attention is paid to Carter's most revealing bridge right, the right to work, which was interpreted by him as a first rather than a second generation right.

Next, the actual implementation of Carter's economic rights theories as policies is examined. This examination reveals that they were interpreted as providing benefits in

Carter's explanation of the welfare state, rather than as implemented specifically as rights. Our attention then turns to criticisms of Carter's policies. Since this examination is only a preliminary one a full discussion of economic rights skepticism will be held in Chapter Three. Though Carter was criticized for his human rights approach, our discussion focuses upon economic rights skepticism, particularly regarding the question of whether or not his endorsement of economic rights made civil and political rights difficult to understand. In particular, the perceptiveness of Carter's critics in noting his tendency to understand economic rights as "goals" rather than "rights" is highlighted. Next, we formally evaluate his economic rights approach. The exhortative qualities of his policies are analyzed with a focus on how poorly he answered his critics and how unsatisfactorily he established a viable justification of economic rights as being interdependent with civil and political rights.

Finally, the lessons of the case study are considered. The ramifications of Carter's theoretical failures are addressed as well as the ongoing need for a proper justification of economic rights. What is demonstrated in this case study is that a permanent and radical change in human rights policy requires a clear explanation of the proposed change coupled with constant, unequivocal support for the change. Thus, this chapter concludes with the realization that Carter never adequately grounded economic rights, yet was, nevertheless, successful in proposing them.

When President James E. Carter came into office on January 20, 1977, the economic rights debate was in full flourish. The Covenant for Social, Economic and Cultural Rights had received (in 1976) the requisite number of ratifications to bring it into full force as to its ratifying parties. Lobbying for further ratifications by other states was continuing apace. In the United States, Carter succeeded Gerald Ford and Richard Nixon, both Republican presidents. His election was widely interpreted as a political housecleaning. The newly elected president had promised never to lie to citizens of the United States, and this promise appealed to the moral sensibilities of many.[1] The United States was recovering from the Viet Nam War and the shock of losing the war. Loss of confidence was also one of the consequences of the abuses of Watergate.[2] American morale was at a low ebb and this depression was in part a moral depression. President Carter appeared to sense this mood and to respond to it.[3] His response was one that was personal and social. Personally he represented himself as one to whom personal integrity was important. More importantly, however, for this work was the fact that Carter believed that he had discovered a way for the United States to regain its moral self esteem and tarnished reputation. This reclamation of political morality was to be addressed by a fresh approach to what appeared to be a popular policy that his predecessor had de-emphasized. The Ford Administration, by way of its Secretary of State, Henry Kissinger, had minimized the importance of human rights policy in the formation of foreign policy.[4] This

---

1   A New York Times editorial, published January 21, 1977 (the day after Carter's inauguration), entitled, "From Micah to the New Beginning" expressed the opinion that Mr. Carter was right in restoring lost moral confidence, stating, "His main task is to make us proud again of the purposes and competence of Government. Without that, there is no reaching for any other goals. The value of yesterday was that it showed a nation listening again to its leaders hoping to hear its mission defined."

2   Before his swearing in ceremony, Carter attended a prayer service at the Lincoln Memorial that was presided over by United Methodist Bishop William R. Cannon Jr., and the Reverend Martin Luther King, Sr. Bishop Cannon called for repentance from the sins of Watergate. Rev. King admonished the president to remember the least in the Kingdom. All of this met with Carter's approval. For a full description of this service, see "Plea by King's Father Adds Touch of Revivalism to the Day," *The New York Times*, (21 January 1977).

3   Reflecting on American morale prior to his election, Carter said, "I really felt when I came into office that something needed to be done just to raise a banner for the American people to admire and of which they could be proud again. From "Interview With the President," *Weekly Compilation of Presidential Documents*, (19 December, 1977): 1848.

4   Nicolai N. Petro writes of this era, "Congress' backlash against Henry Kissinger's Realpolitik found further expression in the Fraser Subcommittee hearing on human rights entitled, 'Human Rights in the

position was opposed in Congress by Congressman Tom Harkin, Donald Fraser, Senator Edward Kennedy and others, who were appalled at the application of Realpolitik to human rights issues.[5] This dissatisfaction manifested itself politically in the democratic platform that developed a new approach to human rights.[6] Carter sensed, in this new human rights approach, a fairly safe issue and one that was popular to sponsor, morally uplifting and personally appealing. Thus even prior to his election, he began to champion human rights. This early enthusiasm was buoyed by Carter's private polls that showed that human rights was a hot political issue.[7] Convinced that he had the means by which to place the United States on the high moral ground Carter wholeheartedly endorsed human rights. Yet his human rights policy was anything but clear and settled at the beginning of his presidency. It was also unclear what position economic rights had in that policy. Sandra Vogelgesang, a Carter Administration official, maintains that a thoughtful consideration of economic rights as human rights

---

World Community: A Call for U.S. Leadership'." The report concluded that "the human rights factor is not accorded the high priority it deserved in our country's foreign policy" and that "too often it becomes invisible on the vast foreign policy horizon . . . " The report found the administration's record to date "random," and "unpredictable," and came up with a list of recommendations. "A higher priority for human rights," the Fraser report concludes, "is both morally imperative and practically necessary." In *The Predicament of Human Rights: The Carter and Reagan Policies V* (Lanham, Maryland: University of America Press, 1983), 11-12.

5   Joshua Muravchik, a Carter critic, maintains that the human rights issue was one that Carter inherited from the democratic party. Muravchik writes, "The human rights issue emerged not in any Carter speech, but in the writing of the 1976 Democratic Platform. 'It was seen politically as a no-lose issue,' says Patrick Anderson, Carter's chief speech writer during the 1976 campaign. 'Liberals liked human rights because it involved political freedom and getting liberals out of jail in dictatorships, and conservatives liked it because it involved criticisms of Russia'." *The Uncertain Crusade: Jimmy Carter and the Dilemmas of Human Rights Policy* (Lanham, Maryland: The American Enterprise Institute, 1986), 2.

6   Ibid., 4, 5.that

7   Muravchik concedes that the "issue had resonance, in Carter's soul and in his polls." Ibid., 7.

was made belatedly, and was far from intentional. Vogelgesang recalls:

> That increased emphasis on economic and social rights, stated first and most comprehensively in a major policy speech by Secretary of State, Cyrus Vance in 1977, made few headlines. There was scant commentary at the time about why the Carter administration had included those rights in its overall policy or what difference they might make for most Americans. The administration itself did not call attention to this new focus of its foreign policy. Indeed, that emphasis on economic and social rights may have emerged more by accident than design. It was a belated addition to the draft text for Vance's initial human rights speech. The secretary's address, in turn, filled a vacuum in the early months of the Carter administration. The human rights issue had taken off faster than most administration officials had expected and before they had mapped out a comprehensive policy on human rights.[8]

Thus a critical examination of the early Carter administration policy reveals impressive support for an impressive issue. It is also clear, however, that Carter's human rights policy was publicly presented before he had time to formulate a systematic foundation for it, and a plausible explanation of its function in his overall domestic and foreign policy.

Joshua Muravchik, a Carter Administration critic, is correct in his assertion that the process which led to the decision to incorporate economic rights into the overall human rights policy is extremely unclear.[9] Carter's human rights policy was

---

8   Sandra Vogelgesang, *American Dream? Global Nightmare*, (New York: W. W. Norton and Co., 1980), 184.

9   Muravchik assumes, however, that the primary reason for the Carter Administration's adoption of economic rights was to simply curry favor with Third World regimes who were, in his opinion, economically destitute and politically repressive. Muravchik cites Carter speech writer, Hendrik Hertzberg as saying, ". . . I think the main motivation behind it was a desire to get the Third World to buy a package, [as if] this was the toy inside the Cracker Jack box. [It] was supposed to pull them into the idea of human rights . . . and then they would find that there was this package that involved freedom of speech and stuff like that." (In *The Uncertain Crusade*, 89.) Muravchik does

the product of several persons and was developed upon the foundation of other administrations.[10] Clearly Carter publicly endorsed human rights in general and economic rights in particular before he had constructed a formal understanding of these policies.[11] By endorsing a policy first and considering its ramifications afterwards, he found himself with a human rights policy which embraced both first generation rights and second generation rights. Furthermore, his harmonization of rights did not alert the United States public to the fact that these rights did not all come out of one uncontested tradition. Chapter One established that many commentators regard first generation rights and second generation rights as being incompatible. Carter's position is, therefore, like that of a grafted tree. His roots were in the soil of the Anglo-American natural rights tradition, a first generation rights tradition, yet Carter's branches were extended to economic rights, second generation rights. To see how Carter harmonized civil and political rights with economic rights we need to examine the contents of his policies.

---

recognize that there were other reasons for the emphasis on economic rights, saying, "There was probably more than a single reason behind the administration's decision to give this emphasis to a concept of rights that stands somewhat outside the American tradition." Ibid., 89.

10 Muravchik is aware that some Carter officials genuinely believed (for other than purely ideological purposes) in the valence of economic rights. He notes that, Patricia Derian said that "the dichotomy . . . between civil and political rights on the one hand, and economic and social rights on the other, is much overrated." UN Ambassador Andrew Young took the view that the two kinds of rights are "inseparable." And Jessica Tuchman, the human rights specialist of the National Security Council, was quoted as saying: "In much of the world the chief human right that people recognize is 800 calories a day. We're beginning to recognize that fact." Ibid., 89. What should be noted in this review of Carter functionaries, is the fact that each of these individuals worked in a separate political arena and or bureau. This implies that the approval of economic rights and their assumed relationship with civil and political rights was fairly widespread in the administration.

11 Carter developed his support for economic rights quite late in his campaign; a review of a speech he made before the B'Nai B'rith Conventon, in Washington, D.C., on September 8, 1976, entitled, "Human Rights" makes no reference to economic rights. From Jimmy Carter, *A Government As Good As Its People* (New York: Simon and Schuster, 1977), 166-72.

Carter's Economic Rights List

The Carter administration's fullest statement on the issue of human rights in general, and economic rights in particular, was set forth in Secretary Cyrus Vance's major address wherein he listed the following "rights":

1. The right to be free from governmental violation of the integrity of the person. Such violations include torture; cruel, inhuman, or degrading treatment or punishment; and arbitrary arrest or imprisonment. And they include denial of fair public trial and invasion of the home.

2. The right to the fulfillment of such vital needs as food, shelter, health care, and education. We recognize that the fulfillment of this right will depend, in part, upon the stage of a nation's economic development. But we also know that this right can be violated by a government's action or inaction--for example, through corrupt official processes which divert resources to an elite at the expense of the needy or through indifference to the plight of the poor.

3. The right to enjoy civil and political liberties: freedom of thought, of religion, of assembly; freedom of speech; freedom of the press; freedom of movement both within and outside one's own country; freedom to take part in government.[12]

Carter's policy had three categories of rights: first, the right to maintain the integrity of one's person; second, social/economic rights; and third, civil/political rights. It is the second category which is crucial to this work.

---

[12] Cyrus Vance, "Human Rights and Foreign Policy, "Law Day Address at the University of Georgia, *Department of State Bulletin* 76 , no. 1978, (30 April 1977): 505. This economic rights list looks like a selective listing of the economic rights found in Articles 22-27 of the Universal Declaration of Human Rights and Part II, Article 2(3), Article 3, and Part III, Articles 6 and 7, of the International Covenant of Social, Economic, and Cultural Rights. Sandy Vogelgesang also acknowledges the aforementioned rights as being the foundation for Carter's economic rights policy. (185).

His position was noteworthy for a United States administration, because he recognized an inherent economic factor embedded in the concept of human rights. In addition, he recognized the government's responsibility, where possible, to provide "economic assistance" for the realization of those rights. Notably absent from Vance's statements was a precise formulation as to how any of these rights came to be designated "human rights." Vance's failure to justify the content of the Administration's understanding of economic rights, or to identify the process wherein the content of economic rights was established, was paradigmatic for the Carter administration.[13]

Accordingly, Carter presented this position without explicitly acknowledging the ongoing debate over economic rights. By doing so he created the impression that he believed that there was no substantive dissonance between the generations of rights. As time passed, however, he was asked to account for his support for human rights. To justify his policy, he offered three substantive approaches designed to operate simultaneously. He also offered a process of progressive revelation which posited an evolution of rights. Let us now examine Carter's three substantive approaches: the first generation account; the moral appeal to compassion; and finally the adoption and expansion of Franklin D. Roosevelt's four freedoms doctrine.

Carter's Account of First Generation Rights

Carter justified economic rights in part by not calling attention to them, and by specifically addressing the larger concept of human rights. For example, Carter's Human Rights Day and Week proclamations seldom made a specific reference to economic rights. These latter rights he interpreted as simply representing a part of the historic American "inalienable" rights

---

13 In particular, Zbigniev Brzezinski, Carter's National Security Advisor, did not appear to care much regarding rights theory. His memoirs do not give much time and attention to the justification of economic human rights. His chapter that devotes the most attention to human rights considerations is revealingly entitled "Good Intentions at High Cost." See *Power and Principle: Memoirs of the National Security Advisor, 1977-1981* (New York: Farrar, Straus, and Giroux, 1983), 123.

tradition, a first generation of rights tradition, those rights listed in the Bill of Rights. He often cited the history and tradition of the Bill of Rights and the views of a "Founding Father"--usually Jefferson--in order to justify his view of rights.[14] Cyrus Vance, Carter's first Secretary of State, similarly interpreted modern human rights as being a modern restatement of inalienable rights. In Vance's eyes, the United States was the fortunate beneficiary of the expanded notion of "inalienable rights" that was part and parcel of the heritage of English justice and politics. This rights tradition was, in itself, the product of a long political and legal evolution. Similarly, for Carter's other theorists, the quintessential understanding of the United States was to be found in the Bill of Rights, and modern human rights were (at least in their own minds) nearly identical in content to the common understanding of the Bill of Rights.

Vance's proposed justification for the Carter Administration's version of human rights was of a first generation kind and appears to be as American as apple pie and as plausible as the Declaration of Independence. Indeed, this reading of United States natural rights tradition appears to be reasonably accurate.[15] However, what is problematic for Carter is that Vance's graft of social/economic rights onto the first generation natural rights stock (which was concerned chiefly

---

14 Jimmy Carter wrote, "The Bill of Rights culminated the Founders' efforts to create for their new country a national life grounded in liberty and respect for individual rights. The Declaration of Independence proclaimed the inalienable rights of lights of life, liberty, and the pursuit of happiness. The Constitution formed a "more perfect Union" in which those rights could be fulfilled. And the first ten amendments to the new Constitution placed the keystone on this new edifice of human rights. The immediate application of those rights extended only to one country, and only to some of the people in it. But because those rights were proclaimed as the natural birthright of all human beings, the documents that embodied them were rightly seen to have a profound and universal significance." From "Human Rights Day and Week," *Department of State Bulletin* 78, no. 2010, 38.

15 One of Carter's harshest critics, Jeane Kirkpatrick, has a similar reading of history. See her "Dictatorships and Double standards," *Commentary* 68 (November, 1979), 34-45, and "Establishing a Viable Human Rights Policy," in *Human Rights and U.S. Human Policy*, ed., Howard J. Wiarda, (Washington: American Enterprise Institute, 1982).

with "civil and political" human rights) was patently artificial. This mistake was belatedly recognized by Carter theorists, but not before much of their credibility as theorists was lost. As was demonstrated in Chapter One, Carter's social/economic rights cannot be located easily in the United States natural rights tradition which Vance sought to embrace.[16]

While Carter never abandoned his support for first generation rights, he offered alongside this account a second, simultaneous appeal for human rights in general and economic rights in particular: the moral appeal to the United States' traditional compassion for the poor.

Carter's Moral Appeal to the American Compassion for the Poor

Carter's second approach was to make a moral appeal, first to his fellow citizens of the United States, and secondly, to the world at large. A fundamental question which is posed by this study is, "Do the people of the United States understand and care about economic rights?" Carter believed that the citizens of the United States cared. He believed that the destiny and character of the United States was irrevocably tied to leading the world in its search for peace, freedom and prosperity within the present system of independent nations. At his inauguration, Carter said,

> Because we are free we can never be indifferent to the fate of freedom elsewhere. Our moral sense dictates a clear-cut preference for those societies which share with us an

---

16 Of the so-called "founding fathers" only Thomas Paine had a full theory of economic rights, and Paine was never followed by other "founders" on this point. For a discussion of Paine on economic rights see, *Political Theory and the Rights of Man*, ed. D. D. Raphael, (Bloomfield, Indiana: Indiana Univ. Press, 1967), 62. John Locke, a major influence on Thomas Jefferson, also had at least an implied right to subsistence, an economic right. Later on in Carter's presidency, in response to criticism, his Administration acknowledged their real source of justification of economic rights: the Roosevelt tradition and the new international declarations and covenants.

abiding respect of individual human rights . . . our commitment to human rights must be absolute.[17]

It should further be realized that Carter genuinely believed that his furtherance of human rights made a moral claim that was likely to accrue to the benefit of the United States. Carter was not, therefore, simply carrying out what he perceived to be a popular policy. As Secretary Vance, Carter's main spokesperson put it, "We seek these goals, because they are right and because we, too, will benefit."[18] Carter believed that his actions would run some risks, but would "benefit" the United States. What is most revealing regarding the motivations and attitude of the Carter administration can be seen in Vance's revealing remark regarding the relation of human rights to practicability, "Finally, does our sense of values and decency demand that we speak out or take action any way, even though in the short run there is only a remote chance of making our influence felt?"[19] Vance's surprising answer is, "yes!"[20] Vance also made a direct appeal to some unarticulated notion of shared beliefs and values. Yet despite the confidence the Carter Administration had in their position, their statement was not self-explanatory. As previously mentioned, Vance never revealed in his Georgia speech, or elsewhere, why he felt that near absolute support for human rights is (or should be) self-evident to citizens of the United States.[21] At his inauguration, Carter also said,

---

[17] Jimmy Carter's Inaugural Address, 122.

[18] Cyrus Vance, Department of State Bulletin 76, no. 1978, 508.

[19] Ibid., 506.

[20] Ibid., 506.

[21] The subject of economic rights is almost absent from Vance's best known book, *Hard Choices* (New York: Simon and Schuster, 1983). Recently, Vance has written a new statement on human rights, but he still fails, therein, to answer many foundational questions about human rights. See his "The Human Rights Imperative," *Foreign Policy* 63, Summer, 1986. The need to adequately explain and justify an economic rights policy was, apparently, a fact of life which only Sandy Vogelgesang (in the Carter Administration) seemed to have appreciated. Sandy Vogelgesang, *American Dream? Global Nightmare* (New York: W. W. Norton and Co., 1980), 184.

To be true to ourselves, we must be true to others. We will not behave in foreign places so as to violate our **rules** and **standards** here at home, for we know that the trust which our nation earns is essential to our strength.[22] (Emphasis added)

In a similar vein, Secretary of State Cyrus Vance, in his Law Day Address, noted that,

Our own well-being, and even our security, are enhanced in a world that shares common freedoms and in which prosperity and economic justice create the conditions for peace.[23]

An even clearer form of this moral appeal can be seen in the Carter Administration's extension of their views on supplying international aid. Carter's basic governmental objectives were outlined in an early statement by Vance, who maintained that some fundamental foreign policy objectives were to:

. . . demonstrate America's **compassion for the poor and dispossessed around the world**--those who, through no fault of their own, are exposed to daily suffering and humiliation and are struggling to survive; . . . to make our fair contribution to the enormous task of the social, economic, and technological development of poor countries, an investment which in this interdependent world can pay us handsome dividends; . . . to take the lead in encouraging the evolution of a world order based on an open economic system, a political structure reflecting a just balance of rights and obligations for all nations, and social progress and human rights for individuals wherever they might be.[24] (Emphasis added)

Since this work is not a study of foreign policy, scant attention will be paid to the ramifications of these objectives for foreign policy. What is of importance to this project is the clear moral commitment to economic rights made by the Carter

---

22 Jimmy Carter, *Inaugural Address*, 123.

23 Cyrus Vance, *Department of State Bulletin* 76, no. 1978, 508.

24 Cyrus Vance, "Secretary Testifies on Administration's Approach to Foreign Assistance," *Department of State Bulletin* 76, no. 1968, 236.

Administration on a national and international scale. This commitment makes it clear that his support for domestic and foreign economic rights was not simply a pragmatic response to domestic political pressures, but, instead, an expression of commitment to what were perceived to be the *basic moral values of the United States. And these commitments were designed to help usher in a new world order.* In other words, Carter genuinely believed that what he was doing was "right" because he felt that his moral sensitivities and values reflected the "shared" moral commitment of his constituency (United States citizens) and the sentiments of the international moral community.[25] Whether or not Carter was correct in his assessment of these sentiments is unimportant. When the Carter administration asserted that their support for economic rights was morally correct and morally necessary, they made thereby an explicit appeal for support. Yet their appeal also functioned as a justification for their policies. Helping the poor, they maintained was morally correct and was a fundamental American custom. They did not reveal in this appeal that this "traditional" custom was not and is not articulated in American traditional rights language. This moral appeal was used alongside Carter's first generation of rights argument. This second approach adopts a certain reading of United States history and mores: it presupposes that United States citizens believe that the poor should be helped. It is intuitive to the extent that Carter felt that the rightness of his approach was

---

[25] Cyrus Vance, also wrote, "In addition economic issues have assumed increasing political importance. Disadvantaged people everywhere are rejecting the proposition that poverty must be their fate, and governments everywhere are putting the goal of economic development at the top of their national agendas." "Secretary Testifies on Administration's Approach to Foreign Assistance," *Department of State Bulletin* 76, no. 1968, (14 March 1977): 237.

self-evident. Still the Carter administration was not satisfied with just these two approaches; their strongest approach (from an historical point of view) was their Roosevelt account.

Carter, Roosevelt, and Economic Rights

Carter developed one of Franklin Delano Roosevelt's four freedoms--freedom from want.[26] Warren Christopher, one of Carter's under secretaries of State, clearly invoked Roosevelt's four freedoms doctrine in one of the administration's official explanations of human rights.[27]

Andrew Young, Carter's Ambassador to the U.N., also referred to Franklin D. Roosevelt in justifying his economic rights position. In reference to Roosevelt's four freedoms, Young understood the freedom from want as applying to:

> all inhabitants of every nation of the world. The present Administration confirms our country's commitment to all four, a commitment manifested over the past 30 years by our cooperation in a series of economic development programs.[28]

To understand fully what the Carter Administration was attempting to do by relying on Roosevelt's understanding of the four freedoms requires a short excursus into Roosevelt's doctrines. Roosevelt wrote in relation to freedom from want:

> We have come to a clear realization of the fact that true individual freedom cannot exist without economic security and independence. Necessitous men are not freemen. People who are hungry and out of a job are the stuff of which dictatorships are made. In our day these economic truths have become accepted as self-evident. We have accepted, so to speak, a second Bill of Rights under which a

---

26 Roosevelt's four freedoms were: freedom of speech, religion, from want, from fear (i.e., security).

27 Warren Christopher, *Department of State Bulletin* 76, no. 1970, (28 March 1977): 290-91.

28 Andrew Young, "The Challenge to the Economic & Social Council: Advancing the Quality of Life in All Its Aspects," *Department of State Bulletin* 76, no. 1977, (16 May 1977): 496.

new basis of security and prosperity can be established for
all--regardless of station, race, or creed.[29]

Roosevelt named several different freedom-from-want
rights, most of which were obviously economic in nature.[30]
President Roosevelt, as the author of the four freedoms
doctrine, clearly described his four freedoms, but did so without
giving an ethical justification for his theories.[31] He assumed that
the correctness of his position was self-evident. What is
important to notice at this juncture, is that Roosevelt's term
"freedoms" is not synonymous with the term "rights." What is
more important, is the fact that Roosevelt saw his four
freedoms, freedom of speech, freedom of religion, freedom from
want, and lastly, freedom from fear, as being universal
freedoms necessary for the flourishing of human life. Just as
clearly, he did not see freedom from want as being a right in the
sense we adopted in the First Chapter (a claims-right).
Roosevelt observed in relation to freedom from want:

> The beginning has been made. The right to work. The
> right to fair pay. The right to adequate food, clothing,

---

[29] See Franklin D. Roosevelt, "Economic Rights," *The Human
Rights Reader*, ed. Walter Laqueur and Barry Rubin, (Philadelphia:
Temple University Press, 1979): 269.

[30] Among other rights, Roosevelt specified, "The right to a useful
and remunerative job in the industries, or shops or farms or mines of
the Nation; The right to earn enough to provide adequate food and
clothing and recreation; The right of every farmer to raise and sell his
products at a return which will give him and his family a decent living;
The right of every family to a decent home; The right to adequate
medical care and the opportunity to achieve and enjoy good health; The
right to adequate protection from the economic fears of old age, sickness,
accident, and unemployment; The right to a good education. All of
these rights spell security . . . America's own rightful place in the world
depends in large part upon how fully these and similar rights have been
carried into practice for our citizens. For unless there is security here at
home there cannot be lasting peace in the world." Ibid., 270. See also
Franklin D. Roosevelt, "Economic Rights." *The Human Rights Reader*,
ed. Walter Laqueur and Barry Rubin, (Philadelphia: Temple University
Press, 1979), 269.

[31] Franklin D. Roosevelt, *The Four Freedoms*, (Washington, D.C.:
U.S. Office of War Information, 1942), 3-15.

shelter, medical care. The right to security. The right to
live in an atmosphere of free enterprise. We state these
things as "rights"--not because man has any natural right to
be nourished and sheltered, not because the world owes
any man a living, but because unless man succeeds in
filling these primary needs his only development is
backward and downward, his only growth malignant, and
his last resource war.[32]

Clearly, Roosevelt thought of freedom from want as being
an ideal. He also believed it to be an obtainable ideal within the
near future relying upon the anticipated economic surplus he
expected from future scientific and industrial discoveries. But
Roosevelt's four freedoms are not a philosophical/ethical
theory. Quite to the contrary, it was his expression of his
understanding of the self-understanding of United States
citizens of his generation--people who were at war--people
who needed a word as to what they were fighting for.
Roosevelt's Bill of Rights Day Proclamation linked the concept
of inalienable rights to human rights and may have started a
tradition which Ford, Carter, and Reagan have continued.[33]
Clearly, Roosevelt felt that the obligation to obtain freedom
from want was a crucial and necessary one. He recognized the
global village aspect of modern life, writing:

The world is all one today. No military gesture anywhere
on earth, however trivial, has been without consequence
everywhere; and what is true of the military is true, also, of
the economic. A hungry man in Cambodia is a threat to
the well-fed of Duluth.[34]

The prudential quality of Roosevelt's view is easily seen in
this last quote, and its cautionary quality was also absorbed into
the Carter Administration's position. For Roosevelt the

---

32 *The Four Freedoms*, 11, 12.

33 Franklin Delano Roosevelt, *The Public Papers and Addresses of F.
D. R.*, (New York: Harper & Row, 1942): 498. Ford and Reagan did not
endorse economic rights, only the practice of celebrating Human Rights
Day and Week.

34 *The Four Freedoms*, 10.

problem of want was not primarily scarcity or production; it was distribution and consumption. Roosevelt observed that,

> In the short space of a few decades we have changed scarcity to abundance and are now engaged in the experiment of trying to live with our new and as yet unmanageable riches. The problem becomes one not of production but of distribution and of consumption; and since buying power must be earned, freedom from want becomes freedom from mass unemployment, plus freedom from penury for those individuals unable to work. In our United States the Federal Government, being the common meeting ground of all interests and the final agency of the people, assumes a certain responsibility for the solution of economic problems. *This is not a new role for the Government, which has been engaged since the earliest days of our history in devising laws and machinery and techniques for promoting the well-being of the citizen,* ... [35] (Emphasis added)

Roosevelt was careful to be vague; he committed the federal government to intervene in order to prevent catastrophic want, while stopping short of specifying exactly what steps should be taken by the government. Furthermore, he claimed that this intervention was not a recent invention, but an ongoing government policy. He understood his freedom from want as being a moral obligation which required the government of the United States to take undefined steps (a political as well as a moral obligation) to prevent the needy from suffering due to a failure in their securing of their "basic human needs." Roosevelt, however, never identified the source of the compelling obligation to aid the poor. His freedom from want would seem, therefore, to be grounded in some sort of tradition of distributive justice; a tradition apparently arising out of customary duties of haves to aid have nots. Such a tradition does not arise out of the natural rights history of England and the United States, but may be an expression arising out of a biblical social morality, a kind of civil religion, once removed from the Bible and embedded into the mores of the United States. Be that as it may, our focus here does not allow us to explore the roots of Roosevelt's assessments of American moral

---

[35] *The Four Freedoms*, 11.

obligations, or even to precisely identify his foundation for his sense of duty. Instead we are compelled to apply his vision to our consideration of economic rights.

Roosevelt's understanding of economic rights demands that we live in a society which does not allow (if it can help it) people to starve to death, or to perish from exposure to the elements. His understanding of governmental obligation and economic rights flow logically from the values demanded by his conception of society, and, what is important for this work, *Carter followed Roosevelt completely and uncritically in this area.*

It is not important for this discussion whether or not Roosevelt correctly read the character and mores of the United States (assuming there are such identifiable concepts). What is more important to note is that he was an enormously popular president, one who believed in these obligations for United States citizens, and who was followed in this vision by a Congress that passed legislation which ushered in social security and other welfare state programs. Equally important is the fact that Carter, over forty years after Roosevelt, came to the same conclusions as he did. Carter did so after the creation of *additional* social and economic benefits in what became clearly a welfare state.[36] By appropriating the Roosevelt legacy, the Carter Administration was able to promote economic rights without addressing many of the objections of economic rights skeptics. Apparently, Roosevelt, Christopher, Young and Carter all seemed to have understood economic rights in a "welfare entitlement" fashion.

Summing up, Carter's adoption of economic rights was coherent and justifiable, but not in the manner in which Vance and others initially tried to justify it. Carter's understanding of social/economic rights do not spring out of the historic natural rights theories, and cannot be defended by recourse to them.[37]

---

[36] Carter came along after the New Deal, the New Frontier, and the Great Society.

[37] Arthur Holcombe, *Human Rights in the Modern World*, New York: New York University Press, 1948), 5 notes that: "There were no provisions in any of the state bills of rights for securing a right to work and nothing about the conditions of employment or what is now called social security. The independent farmers and tradesmen who

Carter's economic rights policies were, as he later admitted, an American version of the economic rights expressed in the Roosevelt tradition and in the Universal Declaration of Human Rights and the International Covenant on Economic, Social and Cultural Rights. His reliance upon Roosevelt's "four freedoms doctrine" (an historical precedent) emphasized the need for his policy to have a justification that was more than just intuitionist in nature. Yet the Roosevelt justification is itself primarily prudential in quality, rather than moral. It was designed to eliminate the incentive for the desperate to start a war or revolution.

These three approaches were offered to justify Carter's economic rights policy. Since these approaches were obviously not directly traceable back to the foundation of the United States, Carter needed and employed a theory of progressive revelation which accounted for the belated American recognition of economic rights.

Carter's Progressive Realization of Rights

In the foreword to a publication entitled *The International Bill of Human Rights*, President Carter explains his commitment to economic rights.[38]   After reaffirming the Universal Declaration of Human Rights (and the two international covenants on human rights) and the Declaration of Independence, Carter equated all of those documents (in terms of their value and pertinence) by observing that, "Though separated by a century and a half in time, these visions are identical in spirit."[39]   Carter went on to say that, "The International Covenant on Civil and Political Rights concerns

constituted the bulk of the free population in 1776 were more interested in equality of opportunity to subjugate the wilderness and exploit the natural resources of the country than in what we now call social and industrial justice. Instead of a right to work there was a popular demand for the kind of liberty that consists of leveling natural barriers to profitable enterprise rather than organizing the market for labor and regulating the conditions of employment in the interests of a special class of wage earners."

[38] United Nations Publication, *The International Bill of Human Rights*, foreword by Jimmy Carter, (Glen Ellyn: Entwhistle Books, 1981).

[39] Ibid., x, in the foreword.

what governments must not do to their people, and the
International Covenant on Economic, Social and Cultural
Rights concerns what governments must do for their people."[40]
Carter maintained that,

> . . . a government commits itself to its best efforts to secure
> for its citizens the basic standards of material existence,
> social justice, and cultural opportunity. This covenant
> recognizes that governments are the instruments and the
> servants of their people.[41]

Since these last statements were made in 1981, it would
seem to be clear that Carter's commitment to economic rights
did not slacken over time, but became more developed and
nuanced. Carter recognized in these observations that all of the
rights outlined in the Declaration of Independence and the Bill
of Rights were not enjoyed by all of the people who inhabited
the United States in the eighteenth-century.[42] He also finally
acknowledges here the clear functional differences between
civil/political rights and economic rights. Nevertheless, in his
opinion, the "beliefs" contained in these "ideal" documents were
strong enough to bring about a realization of those rights for all.
Why? Carter believed that:

> . . . beliefs expressed in these documents were at the heart of
> what we Americans most valued about ourselves, they
> created a momentum toward the realization of the hopes
> that they offered . . . Some of these hopes were 200 years in
> being realized. But ultimately, because the basis was there
> in the documents signed at the origin of our country,
> people's discouragements and disappointments were
> overcome and these dreams prevailed.[43]

Carter had an enormous confidence in the power of ideas.
To Carter, a powerful idea would prevail in the end over less
forceful elements in the historical process, and he considered

---

40 Ibid.

41 Ibid.

42 One of the historical truths that champions of first generation
rights often fail to mention, is the extremely limited and parochial
application of those rights in the history of rights recognition.

43 Ibid., x.

human rights to be such an idea.[44] Carter concluded his foreword with the hope that the same process would take place for the International Bill of Human Rights.[45] Apparently Carter believed that the idea of radical equality embedded in the founding instruments was instrumental in causing an evolution in the status of certain "nonmembers" of colonial American society, even though those members were not a party to the instruments, nor even considered by the "Framers." This sense of a "progressive" realization of rights was a Carter Administration trademark.[46] Whether or not such a confidence in the power of ideas is defensible is not important. What is important is that Carter saw the Bill of Rights of the United States and the new International Bill of Rights as being of one whole moral cloth. By associating these two documents in this fashion Carter tried to borrow some of the moral capital that is commonly accorded the American Bill of Rights. The American Bill of Rights constitutes a "shared meaning" in American thought; it is a widely accepted, morally approved, legally

---

[44] I am less confident that most of the signers of the Declaration of Independence envisioned a day when all of the inhabitants of America, slaves, women, and indentured servants would have an equality of opportunity and equal legal standing. Carter's position is much more defensible if it is interpreted as representing a progressive realization and expansion of civic membership to classes of people whose ancestors were not considered to be fully human, or, if human, obviously not fully equal. Thus if Carter means that the founders were incorrect in their narrow extension of rights, and that the struggles in America have resulted in a correction of that error, then his argument is much more plausible.

[45] The International Bill of Rights contains second generation, economic rights.

[46] Warren Christopher echoes this view, writing, "We recognize that these first steps we have taken are just that. Change takes time--as demonstrated by the evolution of human rights within our own country; from religious freedom through the Bill of Rights, the abolition of slavery, universal suffrage, *the four freedoms, the civil rights movement, and the struggle against poverty to the Equal Rights Amendment*. It is a long, hard climb. But the course is firmly set." (Emphasis added). From "Human Rights: An Important Concern of U.S. Foreign Policy," and address made before the Subcommittee on Foreign Assistance of the Senate Committee on Foreign Relations on March 7, 1977. *Department of State Bulletin* 76, 290.

binding, "institution" in American society.[47] This Bill of Rights has, however, only civil and political rights, not economic ones. The new International Bill of Rights starkly contrasts the old Bill of Rights, and is, of course, still, vigorously disputed. By taking up for the new International Bill of Rights, Carter was implicitly interpreting the two generations of rights as being harmonizable, but this approach is precisely what is contested in the economic rights debate.

To show how these three accounts of human rights worked uneasily with each other, we should consider the most troublesome right for Carter's theory, the right to work.

Carter's Ties to the First Generation:
The Right to Work

Michael Allen's lengthy examination of Carter's human rights policy is a good illustration of the awkwardness of Carter' position on the right to work.[48] Although Allen expends considerable time and energy exploring Carter's human rights policy, he spends little time discussing the exact meaning of the umbrella term "human rights." As a consequence, he makes claims about Carter's economic rights policy that can be easily misunderstood. A prime example of this problem can be seen in how he understood Carter's "right to work" theories. Allen correctly maintains that Carter recognized a "right to work."[49]

Nevertheless, though Carter clearly did have a "right to work," and was also greatly influenced by the modern UN Covenant on Social, Economic, and Cultural Rights, he did not

---

[47] By the term "shared meaning," we are simply referring to a concept utilized most extensively by Michael Walzer. Waltzer's "shared meaning" is a common understanding of certain important values in a given society. *Spheres of Justice* (New York: Basic Books, 1984).

[48] Michael Leroy Allen, "The Human Rights Policy of Jimmy Carter: Foundations for Understanding." (Phd. diss., The Southern Baptist Seminary, 1987), hereinafter referred to as Allen.

[49] Ibid., 83.

have a "right to work" in the sense that that Covenant uses the term.[50]

Carter's view on one's right to work is made clear in his conversation with a Yazoo City housewife in which Carter said,

> And, of course, our religious beliefs emphasize compassion, love, concern about down trodden people, equality in the eyes of God, basic human freedoms, courage to stand up to one's convictions, and so forth . . . we admire . . . not only the right but the duty of people to stand on their own feet, to make their own decisions, to manage their own affairs, to support themselves if they are able, kind of an independence of spirit which also, of course, persists in a lot of other parts of our Nation. Here again the value of individual human beings is very important . . . we have been filled with the words of Thomas Paine and Thomas Jefferson, Benjamin Franklin and George Washington, and others--that all men are created equal, that we are endowed with certain inalienable rights, and that we have a government designed not to control us but to guarantee our rights.[51]

Nowhere in this extensive quote does Carter maintain that the government must create jobs so that those who are unable to find jobs in the open market will have a government created job as a guaranteed alternative. As we will discuss shortly, the absence of this type of declaration is important. Carter's unfortunate phrase, "We have a government designed not to control us but to guarantee our rights" unfortunately is not self-explanatory; nevertheless, he apparently felt that the government had an obligation to "promote programs that provided jobs." Yet he did not feel that the government of the United States had an obligation to guarantee every citizen a job. In this respect, Carter has a traditional, first generation understanding of rights in which a government is duty-bound to remove obstacles to equality of opportunity, but is not obligated

---

[50] That is a right to work that is constantly monitored by, and enhanced by, an active, interventionist state in conjunction with market forces. See the International Covenant of Social, Economic, and Cultural Rights, Part III., articles 6 and 7.

[51] Jimmy Carter, *Papers*, 1977, 1328.

to guarantee equality of outcomes with regard to employment.[52]
In reflecting back on his South, Carter acknowledged:

> In the South we were guilty for many years of the
> deprivation of human rights to a large portion of our
> citizens. Now, to look back 20 years, when black people
> didn't have a right to vote, didn't have a right to go to a
> decent school, quite often did not have equal opportunity
> to seek or acquire a job, or to get a decent home, is an
> indictment on us.[53]

Here he clearly regrets, *inter alia*, the violation of the
"economic right" to equal opportunity to work, rather than the
failure to provide Blacks or anyone else guaranteed jobs, or
even to properly promote job programs. This quote also reveals
Carter's commitment to the creation and maintenance of a
society in which there are no citizens who are systematically
excluded from economic opportunities. Carter wished to insure
that the recognition of equal opportunity for all which had been
achieved in the Civil Rights Movement of the nineteen fifties
and sixties would not atrophy during his administration. The
right to work that Carter most clearly supports in these quotes
is, in Hohfeldian terms, an immunity from being deprived of the
opportunity to obtain remunerative labor. Carter's theories of
rights proceed out of this social understanding. But this social
vision is not "socialist." Allen mistakenly reads Carter's
understanding of a "right to work" as if it were the equivalent to
the United Nation's Covenant on Social and Economic Rights.[54]

----

52 By having a more modest understanding of the right to work,
Carter is not subject to the standard objection that to ensure a right to
work one must create a planned economy and a totalitarian state. Ernest
Lefever was a staunch critic on this point, writing, "The third, are
so-called economic and social rights, such as the right to a job or health
care. These are really objectives and aspirations, not rights, because they
cannot be guaranteed by any government unless it is totalitarian. The
price of gaining these 'rights' is the sacrifice of freedom itself." "Human
Rights and U. S. Foreign Policy: Security or Pax Sovietica," *Vital
Speeches of the Day.* 48, (March 15, 1982): 343-346. At 343.

53 Jimmy Carter, *Papers*, 1977, 1328.

54 Carter's understanding of the right to work completely contrasts
to the socialist understanding of the right to work, as we have
demonstrated in Chapter One. The socialist right to work is a positive

However, a misreading of his understanding of economic rights is a fate that he shares with other economic rights promoters; this type of confusion is a frequent source of controversy in the economic rights debate. What Carter's understanding of the right to work demonstrates, however, more clearly than his position on other rights, is his basic commitment to assist the market in the creation of abundant employment opportunities in preference to gaining control of the market. This approach is a first-generation-of-rights approach. Presumably, if this approach failed to provide the indigent with "basic goods," welfare, subsidized housing, medicare and other "welfare entitlements" would catch the unemployed in a "second-generation-of-rights-safety-net." In this way, Carter supported first and second generation rights.

Economic Rights Policy Implementation:
The Carter Approach

Surprisingly the Carter Administration established no new, domestic, or foreign economic rights programs.[55] Though he resurrected Roosevelt's support for economic rights, he did

right. Carter's right to work may (depending on the state of the economy) occasionally require positive government action, but usually requires on a permanent basis a duty to restrain discriminatory economic forces.

[55] Jimmy Carter's explanation attendant to this welfare reform proposal never associates welfare benefits with "welfare rights" or any other type of economic rights. The term economic rights is not even used in connection with the proposal. In fact, his support sounds many of the themes that are most often associated with his critics (especially Michael Novak). Carter writes, regarding the welfare system, "It is a crazy-quilt patchwork system stitched together over decades without direction or design. It should offer opportunity, but often breeds dependency. . . .The guiding principles of my proposals are simple: those who can work should; and there should be adequate support for those who cannot. . . . America's people, particularly her poor, have waited long enough for important progress in this area. A society like ours must be judged by what we do for the most needy in our midst. America must meet this challenge. " In, "Message from the President of the United States, Transmitting His Recommendations for Welfare Reform: A Message referred to the Committees on Ways and Means, Education and Labor, and Agriculture, "*House Document No. 96-131*, Washington, D.C.: GPO, 1979.

so without the creation of new New Deal programs.[56] What Carter did do administratively is name the first director of a new human rights bureau, Patricia Derian, who became the first Assistant Secretary of State for Human Rights and Humanitarian Affairs.[57] Much of Derian's responsibilities were to monitor the actions of foreign governments in regards to how well they recognized human rights related to security rights, i.e. rights to emigration, and other civil and political rights.[58] Derian's job specifically did not consist of creating new domestic or foreign welfare programs. The Carter Administration took the position that the United States already had in place economic rights programs which were already being administered. Andrew Young is also representative of this philosophy of improving the already existent economic rights of United States citizens. Young concluded that civil/political

---

[56] Warren Christopher makes this point clearly when he talks about the ongoing task of implementing human rights: "Much of President Carter's domestic program is directed toward the enhancement of the human rights of Americans. Proposals for welfare reform, efforts to cut the cost of health care, and the commitment to full employment are obvious examples." From these remarks, it is obvious that Christopher and Carter felt that the requisite human rights programs were already in place and merely needed continued supervision and improvement in performance. Warren Christopher's remarks are from a speech he made before the American Bar Association, entitled, "The Diplomacy of Human Rights: The First Year," Bureau of Public Affairs, Office of Public Communication, Washington, D. C., (13 February 1978): 4.

[57] Carter did not even create the new bureau, Congress did. Carter did propose to create a new independent agency within the executive branch, The International Development Cooperation Administration (IDCA). "International Development: A Message from The President of the United States, Transmitting: A Report on Steps He has Taken and Proposes to Take To Strengthen The Coordination Of U.S. Economic Policies Affecting Developing Countries, Pursuant to Section 303 of Public Law 95-424," *House Document No. 96-70*, Washington, D.C.: GPO, (8 March 1979).

[58] These duties grew out of the Congressionally legislated Harkin Amendment and the Jackson-Vanik Amendment. For a good discussion of this legislation see David Forsythe, *Human Rights and U.S. Foreign Policy: Congress Reconsidered* (Gainesville, Fla.: University of Florida Press, 1987), 10-13.

rights were not enough: Blacks also needed "economic rights."
Young observed that:

> One of the things we learned was that civil rights weren't
> enough. We had to struggle to get our people some
> economic power, too. If they just had the right to vote but
> were still poor, they were still at the mercy of powerful and
> sometimes hidden economic elites. This is true, I believe,
> in every society, no matter what kind of political or
> economic system it has.[59]

Furthermore, Young felt that a concern with economic
considerations was essential to policy formation. His
justification of economic rights was not grounded in a system of
philosophy, ethics, politics, or religion, but was based upon his
own experiences as an "change agent" in an oppressed and poor
community.[60] Nevertheless, it must be concluded, that Young
and Carter both believed that the duty to meet basic needs was
no longer debatable in the United States and was in the process
of being met.[61]

Nevertheless, while Young's understanding of Carter's
human rights policy expressly cites Roosevelt's four freedoms,
his convictions seem to be most deeply grounded in his own
moral experience as an oppressed person. Yet the full meaning
of this moral experience is never fully explored by him. Still,
what is most important, is the fact that the economic programs
Young associated with economic rights were, primarily,
domestic "welfare" programs. They were financed, at least in
part, through income taxes. Thus the government's strict
commitment to providing for the "poor" was from his

---

[59] Andrew Young, "Anew Unity and a New Hope in the Western
Hemisphere:Economic Growth with Social Justice." Department of State
Bulletin 76 no. 1979, (30 May 1977): 576.

[60] Ibid., 570. Young also wrote: "For we have learned not only by
observing the sometimes bitter lessons of world history of recent decades
but repeatedly in our own domestic experience that separating the
economic considerations form the social, political, and cultural goals is
not only an illusion, but it produces unintended and harmful effects for
both the social and economic process."

[61] Ibid., 571. Here Young shows that he, at least, believed that all of
these rights were interdependent.

perspective already in place. In addition, this commitment excluded the possibility of tolerating the complete lack of governmental control on market forces required in a laissez faire, capitalist economy. As a consequence, the Carter position was antithetical to the basics of a minimalist state.

We can see from these quotes that, for Carter and Young, previous legislation positivizing the poor's claim--i.e. the right to basic necessities, acted to change (at least in their minds) the poor's moral rights into legal rights--from hopes into welfare entitlements.[62] This positivization of moral rights into legal rights may have convinced Young and Carter, who were not philosophers, to focus on problem solving rather than ideological arguments.[63] Carter and Young were apparently willing, within the means and consent of the United States populace, to extend largess to needy nations in the form of foreign aid.[64] Carter and Young considered all of humanity to be

---

[62] One example could be the 1946 Full Employment Act: a piece of legislation growing out of the Roosevelt era.

[63] The confidence of Carter and Young on this point is crucial. It gives evidence that they believed that they were carriers of a certain American social justice mission. They seem oblivious, however, to the fact that no American court has ever upheld a governmental duty to provide welfare or subsistence benefits to citizens. For a full discussion of the case law in this area see Martha H. Good, "Freedom from Want: The Failure of United States Courts to Protect Subsistence Rights," *Human Rights Quarterly* 6, (August 1984): 335-65.

[64] Carter's clearest impact on American foreign aid was manifested by his occasional ban on the provision of aid to poor countries that were also human rights violators. It is this linking of aid with human rights compliance which is most distinctive about the Carter administration,rather than any significant increase of aid during his term of office. In no way should Carter's arguments for economic rights necessitate the use of goods for the implementation of other human rights, or other national interests, though this is what Carter sometimes did. According to Nicolai Petro, in 1973, Congress passed The Foreign Assistance Act which "directed bilateral assistance, away from large capital transfers to food production, nutrition, rural development, population planning, health, education, and resource development." This act also required a president to deny any economic or military assistance to the government of any foreign country which practiced the internment or imprisonment of that country's citizens for political purposes. *The Predicament of Human Rights,* 12.

members of their moral community and, therefore, entitled to appropriate and interventionist responses from government.[65] But neither Carter or Young clearly identified the source of the special obligation to service the needy.[66] Carter, Young, Vance, and others made propositions, rather than supplying clear definitions. Instead of defining their moral terms, such as "right" or "just," they simply stated them as given propositions. Similarly, instead of stating exactly why and how the government was obliged to care for the needy, they simply maintained that the government *was* so obliged. They spoke as if their concept of society was obvious to all "moral" people.

---

[65] Young wrote, "Man is born to be free, and all that we do must be devoted to the well-being of human beings--every type of human being, of whatever race or religion, of whatever sex, and in all societies, new and old, rich and poor . . . It is the duty of public officials, and especially the governing elite, of every nation, to do their utmost to realize these common goals of humankind." Ibid., 495. Andrew Young, "The Challenge to the Economic & Social Council: Advancing the Quality of Life in All Its Aspects," *Department of State Bulletin* 76, (16 May 1977): 495.

[66] One theory which the Carter Administration advanced was the need to create a new economic order in relation to the foreign aid assistance. Cyrus Vance's testimony before the Foreign Relations Committee's subcommittee on Foreign Assistance explained this view stating: "Any fair and just international order must apply not only to political considerations but also to economic ones. Poorer countries must not be excluded from the benefits of the world economic system. A fair and just economic order must be evenhanded and allow each country a reasonable opportunity to fulfill its aspirations. The role of development assistance in such an order should be to strengthen the economies of poorer countries which by whatever historical circumstances cannot at present participate in the full range of international economic activities enjoyed by more affluent nations. By giving these countries, and poorer people of those countries, a stake in the international economic system, we reinforce the system itself and help its constructive evolution." Clearly Vance saw foreign aid as being more than altruism, as being a form of long term self-interest. He also was willing to consider some form of group rights or rights to peoples. His testimony can be found in, "Foreign Assistance Authorization, Hearings before the Committee On Foreign Relations and the Subcommittee On Foreign Assistance, Ninety-Fifth Congress," *Washington, D. C.: GPO*, (23, 24, and 25 March 1977).

Thus, with few exceptions, the Carter Administration's ethical justifications were settled in a noncritical fashion by fiat.

Carter thus pronounced, administered, modified and maintained his human rights theories without the benefit of a clear ethical justification, and did so with much success. Carter, like Roosevelt, acted pragmatically, and simply interpreted modern entitlement programs as being the necessary steps to preventing want. He believed such actions were demanded by American mores. He justified his economic rights by maintaining that he had the consent of United States citizens, who, in his political judgment, had previously approved of the entitlement benefits, and, by implication, some form of entitlement rights. Carter saw himself as merely fulfilling his duties, much as his predecessors had done (Roosevelt among others), for the people of the United States, in conjunction with a supportive Congress. But was Carter correct? Did everyone in the United States see economic rights as a moral necessity?

Carter's Critics

Clearly everyone did not. Shortly after his inaugural address, critics began to challenge Carter's policies. In an article published in the New York Times, entitled, "The Rights Standard," Ernest Lefever set forth what he believed to be the correct standard for human rights.[67] He maintained:

1. Giving human rights a central place subordinates, blurs or distorts all other relevant considerations. After all, the central objectives of our foreign policy are security and peace . . . Fundamentally, the quality of life in a political community should be determined by its own people, but outsiders should urge governments that adhere to international rights covenants to honor their obligations. . . The advocacy of human rights in other states, supported by policies of denial or punishment, leads to a kind of reform intervention that we rightly detest when others do it. We have no moral mandate to remake the world in our own image. It is arrogant to attempt to reform the domestic behavior of our allies or our adversaries. But we have a

---

67 Ernest W. Lefever, "The Rights Standard,"*New York Times*, (24 January 1977): 24.

right and obligation to attempt to alter their external policies that threaten the peace.[68]

Lefever declared that the tail should not wag the dog, but the dog, the tail. Human rights for him must fit into the larger policy considerations of foreign policy, which was to be interpreted along the lines of Realpolitik, i.e. designed to secure the "national interest." Arthur Schlesinger, Jr., reiterated this theme declaring that, "A nation's fundamental interest must be self-preservation; and, when national security and the promotion of human rights came into genuine conflict, national security had to prevail . . ."[69] Essentially a pragmatist, Schlesinger asked a telling question: "Is the point of foreign policy to discharge moral indignation or to produce real changes in a real world?"[70] Carter was doomed to inconsistency in his emphasis on human rights in relation to foreign policy because the two policies do not have the same priorities. Foreign policy must be concerned with the health and security of a nation; human rights are designed to protect individuals, often from the power of the state.

His position was seen, therefore, to be one of good intentions but confused idealism. Lefever believed that Carter overestimated the ability of the United States to further human rights internationally, and confused domestic policy with foreign policy.[71] Yet these criticisms of Carter do not address the central issue at hand, namely, whether economic rights are inherently interdependent with civil and political rights. Thus most of the criticisms against Carter's human rights policies, no

---

68 Ibid., 24.

69 Arthur Schlesinger, Jr., "Human Rights and the American Tradition," *Foreign Affairs* 57, Extra Edition no. 3., 519.

70 Ibid., 509.

71 Ernest W. Lefever, "The Trivialization of Human Rights," in *Policy Review* 3, (Winter 1978): 13-34. Reiterating his Times article, Lefever wrote, "The mode and quality of life, the character and structure of institutions within a state should be determined by its own people, not by outsiders, however well-intentioned. The same is true for the pace and direction or social, political or economic change. " At 18.

matter how incisive, do not address the concerns of this study.[72] However, criticism of his policy on economic rights does concern this study, and such was not long in coming.

The chief criticism of Carter's position, which reliance on the Roosevelt tradition exacerbated rather than answered, was the claim that economic rights constituted ideals and goals rather than rights. This is, of course, precisely how Roosevelt characterized his rights to freedom from want. The very phrase, "freedom from want" is something of a circumlocution; it fits in well with Roosevelt's other three freedoms while being a very awkward way of expressing a right to subsistence. Carter needed, therefore, a way to claim the Roosevelt tradition while at the same time using a new rights vocabulary and distinguishing its understanding of responses to need as being rights which individuals could claim (rights-claims), rather than charities which it would be good to attend to, or possible goals superior governments could aspire to obtain. Carter claimed the Roosevelt tradition, without employing a sharply defined vocabulary distinct from it. Ernest W. Lefever, who was nominated subsequently by the Reagan administration to take Derian's place as the new Assistant Secretary of State of the Human Rights and Humanitarian Affairs Department, focused precisely on the rights/goals distinction.[73] Earlier, Walter

---

72 For example, whether or not Carter should have used the threat or withdrawal of economic aid to a human rights abusing nation is an issue of policy implementation, and cannot determine the viability and status of economic rights. It should be noted however, that Carter unsuccessfully opposed the Harkin Amendment, and was criticized from the left and the right. Wes Michael's article explains the basis for the left's criticism, see "Jimmy Carter, Jacques Ellul, and human rights," in *Sojourners* 6, no. 6, (June 1977). The right criticized Carter for not playing more Realpolitik, even after his opposition to the Harkin Amendment.

73 Ernest W. Lefever, "Human Rights and U.S. Foreign Policy," in *Vital Speeches of the Day* 48, (15 March 1982): 343-48. Lefever maintained that, ". . . so-called economic and social rights, such as the right to a job or health care. . . . are really objectives and aspirations, not rights, because they cannot be guaranteed by any government unless it is totalitarian. The price of gaining these "rights" is the sacrifice of freedom itself," 343.

Laqueur had raised this point.[74] Several other critics followed this lead, such as Jeane Kirkpatrick (who became the Reagan Administration's ambassador to the United Nations), and Michael Novak, who also became affiliated with the Reagan administration.[75] Kirkpatrick and Novak also emphasized the place and function of supporting institutions for the implementation of rights.[76]

Thus, many of the criticisms fired at Carter's policies were merely polemical. Some of them were not directed so much at his ideas as at his inability to stick by them. Arthur Schlesinger, Jr., who initially had some sympathy for Carter's human rights policies, became convinced that he was hopelessly incompetent, in large part because of Carter's interpretation of human rights.[77] Schlesinger rightfully points out the prototypical response Carter had for critics: silence. As an alternative to silence, Carter would simply retreat from some of his policies. Regarding Carter's economic policies, Schlesinger writes:

> The reason for Carter's horrible failure in economic policy is plain enough. On such matters he is not a Democrat--at least in anything more recent than the Grover Cleveland

---

74 Walter Laqueur, "The Issue of Human Rights," in *Commentary* 63, no. 5, (May 1977). See also Walter Laqueur, "Third World Fantasies," *Commentary*, (February 1977): 550-56.

75 Kirkpatrick cites Carter's use of goals language in place of rights language in her most influential essay, "Dictatorships and Democracy," *Commentary* 68 (November 1979): 34-45, and in "Establishing a Viable Human Rights Policy," *World Affairs* 143, no. 4 (Spring 1981). Michael Novak's criticism can be found in "Human Rights and Whited Sepulchres," a keynote address, given at a conference on Human Rights at Kalamazoo College, Kalamazoo, Michigan, 26 April 1978, published in Human Rights and U.S. Human Rights Policy, ed. Howard J. Wiarda (Washington: American Institute for Public Policy, 1982): 79-82, and in "The Rights and Wrongs of 'Economic Rights': A Debate Continued," *This World* 17, no. 17 (Spring 1987).

76 Kirkpatrick, "Dictatorships and Double standards," and "Establishing a Viable Human Rights Policy," Novak, "Human Rights and Whited Sepulchres." See also his editorial entitled, "The Reagan Approach to Human Rights Policy," in the *Wall Street Journal*, (28 April 1981).

77 Arthur Schlesinger, Jr., "The Great Carter Mystery," *The New Republic* 182, cover page, (12 April 1980).

sense of the world.   Let him speak for himself:
"Government cannot solve our problems. It can't set the
goals. It cannot define our vision. Government cannot
eliminate poverty, or provide a bountiful economy, or
reduce inflation, or save our cities, or cure illiteracy, or
provide energy" No, children, this is not from a first draft
of Ronald Reagan's inaugural address. It is from Jimmy
Carter's second annual message to Congress. Can anyone
imagine Franklin D, Roosevelt talking this way? If he had
taken Carter's view of government, we still would be in the
Great Depression.[78]

Carter's second annual message, which Schlesinger is
referring to in this quote, was a typical response. Instead of
saying what limited things government could do Carter
sometimes focused on its limitations. Accordingly, Carter's
critics were not effectively answered during his administration,
though Carter was aware of their criticisms.   Sandy
Vogelgesang, a Carter administrator, was quite familiar with
the critiques of Cranston, Vernon Van Dyke, Richard Claude,
and others. Whether or not Vogelgesang ever discussed these
problems with Carter and the rest of his staff is unclear; it is
clear, however, that an ethical defense of his economic rights
policy was not timely mounted.[79]   Many of Carter's
critics--Alexander Haig, Jeane Kirkpatrick, and Michael
Novak--became important officials in the succeeding Reagan
Administration, which promptly attempted to reverse much of
Carter's policies on human rights and all of Carter's policies on
economic rights.[80]   However, President Reagan and his
economic rights skeptics found that public and Congressional
support for human rights was too strong to allow it to be buried
as a policy of the United States.[81]   Nevertheless, Reagan was

---

[78] Ibid., 21.

[79] Sandy Vogelgesang, *American Dream? Global Nightmare*, (New
York: W. W. Norton and Co., 1980),184.

[80] Ernest Lefever's hostility to human rights was so well-known
that his appointment to be Patricia Derian's successor was blocked.

[81] See Tamar Jacoby for a full discussion of the attempt and failure
of the Reagan Administration to bury human rights in relationship to
foreign policy. "The Reagan Turnaround on Human Rights," *Foreign
Affairs* 64, nos. 4, 5, (Summer 1986).

able to redirect human rights to exclude economic rights and to address, exclusively, the human rights abuses of communist countries.[82] The process by which Reagan was able to bury economic rights is quite important, and must now be addressed as it helps to explain certain weaknesses in Carter's policies.[83]

An Evaluation of the Carter Economic Rights Legacy

Former President Carter's economic rights policy should be evaluated on several levels so that its strengths and weaknesses can be identified and discussed. First to be evaluated will be his first generation rights account, then his moral appeal, and finally his Roosevelt adaptation. Also analyzed will be his use of moral language and his comprehension of the main problems associated with the economic rights debate.

Carter's first generation of rights account is well within the American tradition. This account is primarily a continuance of the policies of previous administrations and politics in the United States in general. What is striking, however, is his implicit importation of economic rights into this account. For example, consider his remarks upon signing the International Covenant on Economic, Social and Cultural Rights and the International Covenant on Civil and Political Rights at the Economic and Social Chamber of U. N. Headquarters on October 5, 1977.[84] Carter writes in reference to the economic rights covenant:

[82] Reagan attended to this task as quickly as possible. His Deputy Secretary of State William Clark, prepared a human rights memo, which excluded economic rights out of hand. An account of this matter is reported in an article published in the *New York Times* (5 November 1981).

[83] For those interested in Ronald Reagan's Cold War focus , see Jacoby's article, "The Reagan Turnaround on Human Rights," previously cited.

[84] From "President Carter Signs Covenants on Human Rights," in *Department of State Bulletin 77*, no. 2001, (31 October 1977): 586-87.

> By ratifying the other covenant on economic, social and
> cultural rights our government commits itself to its best
> efforts to secure for its citizens the basic standards of
> material existence, social justice, and cultural opportunity.
> This covenant recognized that governments are the
> instruments and servants of their people. Both of these
> covenants express values in which the people of my
> country have believed for a long time.[85]

Here Carter gives the misleading impression that there is
no economic rights debate. For him, the economic rights in the
covenant he is signing have been shared beliefs, "for a long
time." In this quote, Carter interprets economic rights as if they
were interdependent with civil and political rights, and *always
understood to be so*. In this approach, none of the principals in
the Carter Administration (Carter, Vance, Christopher, Young,
Brzezinski, or Derian) even attempted to justify their version of
human rights, in general, and economic rights in particular.[86]
Carter attempted thereby to leap over a theoretical chasm by
proceeding as if it were not even there. As we will discuss more
fully in Chapter Three, his critics savaged him on this point.

Carter's second approach, his moral appeal to
compassion, has one major weakness: it is in no way historically
or conceptually tied to rights language or rights orientations.
United States citizens do indeed have a deep and abiding
commitment to help the needy. However, the moral appeals for
compassion for the needy are usually couched in the language of
charity, rather than rights, and usually responded to along the
same lines.[87] Thus no matter how well such appeals may be

---

85   Ibid., 587.

86   In fact, Vance's best known work, *Hard Choices*, (New York:
Simon & Schuster: New York, 1983), does not discuss economic rights at
all. The concept simply drops out of consideration. More recently Vance
has written briefly on this issue, see note 105.

87   Among others, Alan Keith-Lucas' work is conclusive on this
point, see his *The Poor You Have With You Always: Concepts of Aid to
the Poor in the Western World from Biblical Times to the Present* (St.
Davids, Pa.: North American Association of Christians in Social Work,
1989).   David Forsythe makes this same point in reference to the
legislative action in Congress: "For example, a congressional report
about human rights lists a number of acts having to do with global
hunger and food policy. A close reading of this list, however, coupled

constructed they do not actually justify Carter's human rights policies except that they are given as reasons for having economic rights. But the connection between the appeals for charity and the designation of economic rights as rights is not addressed. To be kind may be good, but governments are usually required first to avoid being cruel, rather than required to be kind. Charity is an imperfect moral duty and can generate only an imperfect moral obligation or duty. These elements are distinct from what we have called rights-claims.

Turning to the Roosevelt tradition, Carter finds more solid ground. Roosevelt represents a nexus between first generation rights and second generation rights. Roosevelt's economic rights were in response to the Great Depression and the Second World War. His work stimulated the incorporation of economic rights into the Universal Declaration of Human Rights. Thus, Carter's reliance upon the Roosevelt tradition allowed Carter to claim that economic rights were not incompatible with civil and political rights, as such a claim is implicit in Roosevelt's stance. Yet Roosevelt's rhetoric clearly distinguished between rights language and ideals and goals language, and his understanding of civil and political rights was couched in the former language and his economic rights in the latter. Thus, though Roosevelt's freedom from want was useful in integrating differing types of rights, it did so by subordinating economic "rights" to civil and political rights. It also confused the issue by referring to such "rights" as "ideals." Actually it proved counterproductive for meeting some of the criticisms of Carter's economic rights skeptics on this very point, i.e., confusing "rights" with "goals." Carter's economic rights

with a broader understanding of American approaches to these socioeconomic subjects, leads to the conclusion that Congress has dealt with food policy out of moral concern or for the sake of U.S. political expediency. It has not approached the subject of hunger from the perspective that people have a right to be free from hunger just as they have a right to be free from torture. Congress has endorsed the latter right but never, specifically the former." In, *Human Rights and U.S. Foreign Policy: Congress Reconsidered* (Gainesville, Fla.: University of Florida Press, 1987), 3. Forsythe correctly notes that not even the International Security and Development Cooperation Act of 1981, which was devoted to the elimination of hunger and its causes, actually acknowledged that, ". . . freedom from hunger or malnutrition is an internationally recognized human right." Ibid., 4.

theories were, therefore, unsubstantially explained while being vigorously promoted. The effect of this support must now be examined.

David Forsythe has an insightful understanding of Congressional action that by analogy helps to explain some of the problems with Carter's support of economic rights.[88] Forsythe has a category of Congressional action which he designates as "hortatory." By hortatory, what Forsythe means is simply that the policy in question is brought into being only on a formal basis. It is not, however, attached to any active legislation designed to change any one condition. Its function is purely explanatory and inspirational; it is designed to express a certain attitude about American political life. Carter's economic rights policy functions in much this way. Though Carter signed the Covenant for Social, Economic, and Cultural Rights, it could not be an active piece of legislation without further ratification, by Congress. In the absence of this action, Carter's speeches, human rights day proclamations, and campaigns were essentially exhortative. This does not mean that they were not important, nor that they did not express the official attitude of the government. However, it is clear that unratified, economic rights could simply be buried by a different administration which ceased to sound the economic rights trumpet and took no efforts to have international covenants ratified. This exhortative quality of Carter's rhetoric, coupled with the fact that he did not introduce any legislation for economic rights allowed Reagan to recast human rights talk in different terms.[89] But this criticism is primarily a practical one; other problems are more foundational.

Carter had three substantive accounts for his economic rights foundation, yet he never addressed whether or not these foundations were adequate, and if adequate, complimentary. We have seen from Chapter One and our earlier discussion in this chapter, that the first generation of rights tradition of the

---

[88] Once ratified, it would act as treaty and be superior to most legislation. A claimant serving in a United States court could, at this point force the government to provide help.

[89] The Humphrey-Hawkins Full Employment Act was grossly watered down prior to its passage during Carter's term, and was not specifically his bill anyway, though he was in favor of it .

United States, with a few notable exceptions, did not encompass economic rights. Thus Carter's reliance upon it to justify his version of economic rights was doomed from the start. Carter's second approach--his moral appeal to the United States' compassion for the poor--was well-grounded in American shared meanings, but those meanings were ones grounded in charity and not in rights. These sentiments were expressed and enacted by the vitality of voluntary charities in the United States. Such meanings, so deeply cast in the mold of charity, needed a recasting in the language of rights if they were to be characterized as rights. Carter never provided for such a change, except by means of his third approach via the Roosevelt tradition. However, Roosevelt's freedom from want predates many of the economic rights debates, and was, in any case, an intuitional and prudential policy. It was intuitional in that Roosevelt never offered any moral reasoning or justification for it: to him it was self-evident. He believed it to be such for all citizens of the United States. It was prudential in that it was designed to insure national security and peace through a form of kindhearted appeasement. As such, it was not a morally compelling theory. Moreover, it did not have a firm moral justification.

No one in the Carter Administration perceived that Roosevelt had not really used rights language in the precise, rights-claims sense detailed in Chapter One. Accordingly, no one realized that Roosevelt had never justified his understanding of "freedom from want." Since no one realized that Roosevelt's view was not justified, no one realized how slender a reed such a doctrine was to lean upon in terms of moral justification. Thus this vision of society that enthralled Roosevelt and compelled Carter, was championed on a peculiar reading of American mores, and was believed to be intuitively self-evident. Such a foundation is adequate *only* when championed by a Congress and the White House. So, when Carter left office, this aspect of human rights left with him; at least to date.

In summation, none of the three substantive accounts of economic rights actually addresses their construction and status as rights and moral norms. Accordingly, Carter exhorted economic rights in a country which already provided economic benefits, but did so without systematically connecting the rights language with the economic provisions.

In addition, Carter's theory of progressive revelation of a generations of rights was not well communicated or integrated with his economic rights theories. It may be recalled from the first part of this chapter, that he maintained that the realization of human rights comes about in a slow generational process. Yet Carter's account of these changes does not actually explain how economic rights came into being. For example, consider Carter's observation regarding the Bill of Rights of the United States and the new International Bill of Rights, "Though separated by a century and a half in time, these visions are identical in spirit."[90] Yet it is not at all clear to partisan or skeptic, that the visions held by those two documents are identical in spirit. The case **can** be made that these documents are not in conflict, but such an argument needs to be made, and Carter did not attend to this task. Consider again Warren Christopher's position on economic rights:

> We recognize that these first steps we have taken are just that. Change takes time--as demonstrated by the evolution of human rights within our own country; from religious freedom through the Bill of Rights, the abolition of slavery, universal suffrage, *the four freedoms, the civil rights movement, and the struggle against poverty to the Equal Rights Amendment.* It is a long, hard climb. But the course is firmly set.[91](Emphasis added)

This perspective is troublesome in that the process of struggle and change is not well described. What, for instance is the relationship (if any) between abolitionism with the widespread slaughter in the Civil War? How do rights come into being? Where is the claiming done and by whom? If a right is denied, can the putative right holder simply start a war?

---

90 Jimmy Carter, United Nations Publication, *The International Bill of Human Rights*, x.

91 Warren Christopher, "Human Rights: An Important Concern of U.S. Foreign Policy," an address made before the Subcommittee on Foreign Assistance of the Senate Committee on Foreign Relations on March 7, 1977. *Department of State Bulletin* 76, 290, (28 March 1977).

These rhetorical questions point out the gaps in the Carter Administration's theories.

Recently, Cyrus Vance, Carter's Secretary of State, attempted to address one central criticism of his economic rights policy, its assignment of importance in relationship with civil and political rights.[92] One of the common criticisms of Carter's economic rights policy was the fact that he did not make it clear whether or not economic rights were on a par with civil and political rights, or superior to them.[93] Vance, several years later, finally states what are, at least for him, the most important rights, namely, security rights.[94] Since some of the security rights that Vance refers to are group rights, such as immunity from genocide, a third generation of rights concern is also present within this policy. And since Vance believes that these rights are more important than economic rights or what he calls civil and political liberties, both first generation rights and second generation rights are relegated to an inferior position to at least some third generation rights: this relegation presents a whole new set of theoretical problems. Nevertheless, since the political defeat of the Carter Administration, the Covenant for the Prevention of Genocide has been ratified by the United States, so that Vance's ideas may not be very radical at all.[95]

---

[92] Cyrus Vance, "The Human Rights Imperative," *Foreign Policy* 63, (Summer 1986).

[93] For the clearest example of this criticism, see Joshua Muravchik's, *The Uncertain Crusade*, 89-111.

[94] Vance writes, " The most important human rights are those that protect the security of the person. Violations of such rights include genocide; slavery; torture; cruel, inhuman, and degrading treatment or punishment; arbitrary arrest or imprisonment; denial of fair trial; and invasion of the home. In the United States, many of these protections are enshrined in the Bill of Rights." "The Human Rights Imperative," 4.

[95] David Forsythe assumes that the reluctance of Americans to ratify international conventions is on the wane. He writes: "As noted, there is still an American imprint to congressional human rights activity. Congress, after making reference to 'internationally recognized human rights,' frequently defines them largely in terms of the civil and political rights found in the U. S. Constitution. There still is not much congressional interest in economic, social, and cultural human rights recognized in international law. Nevertheless, some international

Last to be considered is the language that Carter employed. The Carter Administration used moral language in a vague and uncritical fashion. In actuality, the justification of economic rights required the use of precise language. For example, Carter's references to rules and standards, common deontological terms, are never clearly defined, or even illustrated by examples. Similarly, Carter's use of abstract terms such as honesty, fairness, and justice are simply left to the free interpretation of his listeners. Patricia Derian, former Assistant Secretary of State for Human Rights and Humanitarian Affairs, understood the term "right" to mean, "that which is logically compelling and necessary for the maintenance of human life."[96] But Derian's understanding of the concept "right"is too ambiguous to be very useful.[97]

---

human rights policy made indirectly through congressional action. The United States is not as impervious to international developments action on human rights as a legalist might believe. The Senate's consent to ratification of the Genocide Convention in 1986, after almost forty years of debate, may indicate less formal resistance to international developments as well." In, *Human Rights and U.S. Foreign Policy: Congress Reconsidered*, 168.

[96] Patricia Derian's comment was a reply to an inquiry as to her meaning of right, asked by this author on April 22, 1987, in Atlanta, Ga., in reference to her use of the term during the Carter presidency. Derian was, during her service as Assistant Secretary of State, apt to follow Vance's lead in explaining theory. One minor theme of note was the notion that America sometimes inadvertently assisted foreign elites with their depredation of their locals. Derian associated this theme with her recitation of economic rights: "Second, all people desire and have a right to such basic and vital needs as food, shelter, health care, and education. Recognizing the varying stages of development around the world, hunger and privation cannot be condoned when a nation's government diverts limited resources from its citizens." From her address before the National Association of Human Rights Workers in Nashville given on October 15, 1978, entitled, "Human Rights: A World Perspective." published in *Current Policy Statement*, 42, Washington, D. C., (2 November 1978).

[97] In fairness to Derian, though she was not always clear on just what constituted human rights she was a consistent advocate of human rights and held up well under criticism. She made several effective rebuttals to Kirkpatrick's criticisms in a debate in print entitled, "Overhaul U.S. Policy on Human Rights?," in *U.S. News and World Report*, (2 March 1981): 49.

Still, her concept of rights was tied to a "needs based" theory which she did not fully explain in her published explanations of human rights.[98] Undersecretary of State Warren Christopher's discussion of the "right to work" is similarly flawed, because he indulges in "goals" language in reference to rights and lays no foundation for his views.[99]

Since Carter has been considered one of America's brightest presidents, his failure to attend to the examination of his language is difficult to explain. The easiest explanation is that Carter felt that economic rights were self-evident. This explanation assumes that Carter employed an intuitionist approach similar to Roosevelt's. Although intuitionism has fallen into philosophical disfavor, this is also how Jefferson understood inalienable rights.[100]

The Lessons of the Carter Administration

What the Carter Administration's handling of economic rights makes clear to us, for future policy considerations, is the fact that effective, and permanent policy must be both clearly explained and championed. If economic rights are to be

---

[98] The importance of this observation must await its full discussion in Chapter Three.

[99] In a major policy statement Christopher called the "right to work a "goal." Christopher went on to say, regarding the Covenant on Economic, Social, and Cultural Rights, that, "It commits states to take steps toward the future realization of certain economic, social, and cultural goals for the individual. These goals are ones to which the United States has long been committed, including the . . . right to work . . . freedom from hunger." In "Four Treaties on Human Rights," Washington, D.C.: GPO Policy no. 112, (14 November 1979): 2. What is problematic about these comments is that Christopher calls the right to work a goal rather than a right, thus giving credence to the criticisms of Lefever, Novak, Laqueur, and Kirkpatrick. His statements do have the advantage of making it clear that there was no proposal from the administration to create a planned economy. This position makes it clear that Carter was no socialist.

[100] For the intuitionist basis for rights, its defectiveness as a justification and its use by Thomas Jefferson, see Alan Gewirth, *Human Rights: Essays on Justification and Applications* (Chicago: University of Chicago Press, 1982).

understood as being on par with civil and political rights they cannot be assigned such a designation by fiat. In the United States the current status of economic rights is of an hortatory quality. This hortatory language, established by the Carter Administration, needs to be concretized by specific legislation. One unambiguous way would be by means of the ratification of the International Covenant for Social, Economic, and Cultural Rights by the United States. But the ratification of this covenant is unlikely without a clear refutation of the many criticisms of economic rights.[101]

It must be recognized that the passage of such an international instrument opens up the United States to domestic and international criticisms of both its domestic and foreign economic policies. Such exposure to international scrutiny will not be tolerated lightly, particularly if the rights in question appear to threaten previously established legal and moral norms, such as the Bill of Rights of the United States. Accordingly, what is needed is not an approach that attempts to obfuscate the possible conflicts among rights, but one that explains how the conflict is either not a serious conflict, or is a conflict inherent in all rights accounts. Carter's approach to these problems, which attempted to adopt and adapt modern economic rights without attending to the conceptual conflicts in this area, which were well known at that time, provides us with important lessons. One lesson is that moral idealism coupled with power and zeal are not enough to establish a specific new policy on a permanent basis. For a permanent policy change, a whole new articulated theory must also be presented.

Furthermore, this theory must demonstrate itself as being obviously superior to the established policy. Carter's championing of the broader concept of human rights was successful in this regard.[102] Though his own handling of human

---

[101] The ratification of this covenant has been languishing before the Senate Foreign Relations Committee of Congress, since February 23, 1978.

[102] Carter's position on human rights (not economic rights) has proven to be sounder than Kissinger's. It is also conceptually superior to Reagan's approach that initially attempted to jettison human rights. This claim is for Carter's theoretical approach; no claims are made herein with regard to his diplomatic prowess.

rights disputes was not completely successful, his emphasis on the importance of human rights in policy formation was. Its importance is now seen to be permanent. This is just one example of the triumph of human rights that Louis Henkin identified for us in Chapter One.[103]

Yet the enduring triumph of human rights provides merely a foundation for an additional and necessary demonstration that economic rights should also be similarly revered. As was maintained in Chapter One, if economic rights are to be "positivized" in the mores and law of the United States, then the criticisms of economic rights must be shown to be faulty, and the logic, coherency, and plausibility of economic rights in interrelation with civil and political rights must also be demonstrated (the task of Chapter Four).[104] The Carter Administration proved that speaking exhortatively economic rights could be successfully championed, even amid controversy. But such views, posited without dispelling the doubts of skeptics, were successful largely within that administration. When the Carter Administration ceased, the exhortations ceased. Thus, the economic rights debate during Carter's term and shortly thereafter seemed to favor economic rights skeptics, at least in the United States.

There is, however, a second lesson to consider. Assuming that Carter is right in understanding rights as evolving out of a progressive and revolutionary process, then the Carter position itself may be seen as not just an inarticulate failure at establishing economic rights as human rights. On the contrary, his administration can be seen as merely one stage in an ongoing process of change in the conceptualization and implementation of economic rights. According to this scenario, Roosevelt could be understood as a first stage, or bridge, in which a president exhortatively establishes economic rights and, without a full explanation, attempts to put them in the same moral category as civil and political rights as they function as human rights. Carter could be seen, therefore, as a second bridge figure, one

---

[103] Foreign policy assessments are now never considered to be complete without a consideration of human rights concerns.

[104] It is in these chapters that the inherent interdependence of economic rights with civil and political rights will be demonstrated.

who capitalizes on the start made by Roosevelt (which was primarily prudential in nature), and attempts to give a more cogent and morally compelling explanation of economic rights, particularly as he relates such rights to prior legislative action and post-Roosevelt international law and international consensus.

In this interpretation Carter constitutes a second stage in the establishment of economic rights in the United States. It could even be argued that Carter better advanced the establishment of economic rights precisely through his failure to explain their origins and foundation. Thus his exhortation of such rights, and his emphasis on a new bureau were more effective in furthering economic rights while that concept was still in hot debate. If this scenario is at all accurate, then the debate is far from finished and is simply moving from one stage to another with the election of Ronald Reagan and the presidential abandonment of economic rights as human rights.

That this progressive revelation and evolution is what is actually happening is not completely demonstrable at this point in time. The Carter Administration could have been merely an odd exception to the rule that a democratic society with a limited state cannot effectively champion economic rights. Thus, Carter's progressive evolution of rights could merely be a case of wishful thinking, rather than a evolutionary stage in a unidirectional process. Perhaps Carter's endorsement of economic rights should be considered a policy aberration until a subsequent endorsement of economic rights surfaces. Yet, despite an apparent plausibility to this explanation, it is on closer examination unsatisfactory. It is unsatisfactory because if this criterion was applied to Franklin D. Roosevelt, from the time of his death until the Carter administration, economic rights could have been considered by concerned theorists as being at best controversial, and at worst nonsensical. Yet, of course, during that period most of the legislation that confers economic benefits to the citizens of the United States was passed. And when Carter did appear upon the scene strongly endorsing economic rights, he was not met with complete puzzlement or derision, which he would have been had his position been considered nonsense. Neither was his actual policy quickly and permanently discredited. The Reagan

Administration preferred to call economic rights "goals," not rights, but it did not actually campaign for this reconceptualization. Furthermore, they did not say that those goals were not worthy; they simply preferred to say that those responses were goals, rather than rights.[105] Since that time, the issue has continued to be widely discussed.

We conclude, however, that this debate is in the process of being lost by economic rights skeptics. Chapter Three presents Carter's critics, as well as the formal objections to economic rights in the pertinent literature. Chapters Four and Five show why economic rights do not conflict with civil and political rights, why the latter are in fact dependent, on the former, why the debate is not finished, and why the recognition of such rights will probably, eventually, prevail.

Perhaps the Carter Administration's greatest lesson is a simple one: that economic rights partisans need to be as vigilant and constant in stating, explaining and campaigning for economic rights as Jeffersonian democrats have been for the protection of civil and political liberties.

----

[105] A typical Reagan administration position is given by W. Scott Burke, a Deputy Assistant Secretary of State for Human Rights and Humanitarian Affairs, who maintains: "Also, as long as it is insisted that economic and social rights are of equal dignity or importance to other rights, there will be no consensus in our country on the proper role of human rights. I—and I think most conservatives, such as myself—view so-called economic and social rights not as rights at all. Rather, they are desirable goals. Whether they are made an objective of a government's policy and have a place among the other goals of a government's policy is something that is best determined according to the legal and constitutional procedures that exist in a democratic society. In an undemocratic society, so-called economic and social rights frequently serve only as a pretext to deprive citizens of other, I would say, more basic human rights, such as the right not to be tortured or murdered or the right to freedom of speech, to freedom of religion, and the other rights enshrined in our Constitution and national documents." In this quote we see the Reagan Administration's attempt to use human rights as a club against communism coupled with their denial of economic rights.   At the same time, W. Scott Burke acknowledges that the objects of what we have called economic rights are probably good to obtain, but only as a loose governmental obligation. W. Scott Burke, "In the American Tradition Rights," *The Center Magazine*, (July/August, 1984), 40.

CHAPTER THREE

ECONOMIC RIGHTS: NONSENSE ON STILTS?

Chapters One and Two foreshadowed and outlined certain objections to the consideration of economic rights as being interdependent with civil and political rights. Chapter Two focused on objections to economic rights that were specific criticisms of the Carter Administration. This chapter examines deeper and more comprehensive criticisms of economic rights.

There are three primary categories of objections to economic rights. The first category of objections maintains that economic rights make no sense, and further asserts that their confused association with civil and political rights threatens the continued acceptance of those rights. These objections we will call incomprehensibility objections. The second class of objections assert that economic rights are comprehensible, but that they are fundamentally incompatible with civil and political rights, and constitute a clear and present danger to them. These objections we will categorize as incompatibility objections. The third major group of objections we will call pejoristic objections.[1] Some pejoristic objections assert that economic rights are unable to overcome poverty, or, in the alternative, are counterproductive, and actually increase the level, intensity and threat of poverty. Some of the pejoristic objections pose no categorical rejections of economic rights, but instead challenge and limit the applications of those rights.

This chapter details these three categories of objections that have made the economic rights debate so interesting, and so prolonged. Some of the critics and criticisms of the Carter Administration's position, previously referred to in Chapter Two, are reiterated here in a more formal and comprehensive fashion. There are two primary goals for this chapter. The first goal is to show why so many first generation rights defenders, primarily proponents of civil and political rights, oppose economic rights. The second goal is to test the persuasiveness of their arguments. Since economic rights skeptics, like most Westerners, presuppose that civil and political rights are sacred moral foundations for modern liberal society they believe that economic rights have to be opposed systematically in order to insure the continuity and power of civil and political rights.

It should be noted that these objections constitute a rejection of our main thesis that maintains that economic rights **are** interdependent with and compatible with civil and political rights. We maintain that they should be accorded the respect and recognition ascribed to the latter rights. Thus this chapter is one in which our main hypothesis is rigorously challenged. Chapter Four will respond to the views of this chapter, and present arguments in support of our main thesis. Since Carter's

---

1   Garret Hardin explains pejoristic objections as follows: "The adjective "melioristic" is applied to systems that produce continual improvement; the English word is derived form the Latin meliorare, to become or make better. Parallel with this it would be useful to bring in the word pejoristic (from the Latin pejorare, to become or make worse). This word can be applied to those systems that, by their very nature, can be relied upon to make matters worse. A world food bank coupled with sovereign state irresponsibility in reproduction is an example of a pejoristic system." Pejoristic objections are objections that maintain that the recognition of economic rights will only exacerbate the problem of poverty. Garret Hardin, "Living on a Lifeboat," *BioScience* 24 no. 10 (October 1974): 564.

critics focused initially upon the first category of criticisms, the incomprehensibility objections, our discussion will begin there. Our exposition will start with Maurice Cranston, the foremost proponent of these objections.[2]

Economic Rights: Nonsense on Stilts?

Maurice Cranston has been the quintessential economic rights skeptic. His books and essays constitute the primary theoretical opposition to the recognition of economic rights. While Cranston has opposed economic rights he has also been a champion of what has been called, in Chapter One, first generation rights, i.e., civil and political rights. In fact, as this chapter will demonstrate, it is his unswerving devotion to these rights that causes him to reject economic rights. Cranston insists that the economic rights partisan's drive to include economic rights in the same category with civil and political rights is completely mistaken. He charges:

> that a philosophically respectable concept of human rights has been muddied, obscured, and debilitated in recent years by an attempt to incorporate into it specific rights of a different logical category. The traditional human rights are political and civil rights such as the right to life, liberty, and a fair trial.[3]

Regarding economic rights as human rights, he insists that:

> What are now being put forward as universal human rights are social and economic rights, such as the right to unemployment insurance, old-age pensions, medical services, and holidays with pay.[4]

Cranston has two objections to economic rights:

---

2 Among Cranston's many publications, the following are concerned with human rights: Maurice Cranston, "Are There Any Human Rights?," *Daedalus: Journal of the American Academy of Arts and Sciences* 112, no. 4 (Fall 1983): 1-18; *What Are Human Rights?* (New York: Basic Books, 1962); "Human Rights, Real and Supposed," *Political Theory and the Rights of Man*, ed. D. D. Raphael (Bloomington: Indiana Univ. Press, 1967), 43-54.

3 Maurice Cranston, "Human Rights, Real and Supposed," 43.

4 Ibid., 43.

> The philosophical objection is that the new theory of human rights does not make sense. The political objection is that the circulation of a confused notion of human rights hinders the effective protection of what are correctly seen as human rights.[5]

Cranston is correct in being concerned that economic rights may confuse the traditional understanding of "human rights." He is additionally correct in his assessment of the problems of implementing a confused notion of rights. "Human rights," as we have seen in the first chapter, are not easy to define or to implement. Of his two objections the more fundamental one is his philosophical objection: if human rights theories make no sense, if they are incomprehensible, then they are indeed likely to be abandoned by policy makers. This first objection must be examined and evaluated carefully.

In addressing Cranston's philosophical objection we must turn to his threefold test of human rights. The first test is the practicability test. For Cranston rights must be correlated to duties.[6] Thus, if there is no duty to perform a task, there can be no right to have the task performed. Since duty turns upon the feasibility of an action, where feasibility is not possible no duty arises. The right is not, thereby, "practicable."[7] Thus, as Cranston observes:

> You cannot reasonably say it was my duty to have jumped in the Thames at Richmond to rescue a drowning child if I was nowhere near Richmond at the

---

5   Ibid., 43.

6   Cranston is a subscriber to the correlation thesis fully discussed in Chapter One.

7   I have used the term feasibility in relation to Cranston's practicability test to highlight the difference between the two terms. For something to be feasible, it must be possible for an actor to perform. For example, as a male human being, it is not feasible for me to give birth to a child. Practicability is a less stringent term: something practicable is an act that is not only possible, but also not arduous to perform. It is impracticable for me to run for President, but it is not impossible or infeasible. This distinction is an important one that Cranston does not observe.

time the child was drowning. What is true of duties is equally true of rights.[8]

He then claims that:

> If it is impossible for a thing to be done, it is absurd to claim it as a right. At present it is utterly impossible, and will be for a long time yet, to provide "holidays with pay" for everybody in the world.[9]

Cranston concludes that the economic incompetence of some countries precludes the guaranteed provision of certain economic goods. Since these goods cannot be assured, rights to them are impracticable. As part of the practicability test Cranston compares economic rights with civil and political rights. He understands these latter rights to be secured by simple legislation. Accordingly, in his opinion, civil and political rights qualify as "human rights." In contrast, economic rights fail these tests.[10]

---

8   Ibid., 50.

9   Ibid., 50. Cranston's use of the term impossible here shows that he is really referring to feasibility rather than practicability.

10   For Cranston simple legislation is all that is necessary to implement these rights. He writes: "The natural rights to life, liberty, and so forth have always been understood as categorical rights, rights nobody could find any excuse for not respecting. Such 'political rights' can be readily secured by legislation. The economic and social rights can rarely, if ever, be secured by legislation alone. Moreover, the legislation by which political rights are secured is generally very simple. Since those rights are for the most part rights against government interference with a man's activities, a large part of the legislation needed has to do no more than restrain the government's own executive arm." Ibid., 37. Similarly Paul Streeten maintains that negative rights (non-economic rights) do not require "resources though opportunity costs may be involved." "Basic Needs and Human Rights," *World Development* 8, (February 1980) 109.   See also Charles Fried, *Right and Wrong* (Cambridge, Mass: Harvard University Press, 1978), 120-22.   The supposed expensiveness of economic rights was discussed in Chapter One. Though it would not seem to be theoretically demanded, ease in implementation is, apparently, a necessary element in practicability. Other commentators also emphasize the "inexpensiveness" of civil and political rights. Feinberg, joined by Jan Narveson, another social philosopher, also is impressed with the seemingly cost-free quality of "negative" rights: neither the individual nor the government need

Cranston's second test is the universalizability test.   He describes it in relation to economic rights in this way:

> Another test of a human right is that it shall be a genuinely universal moral right.   This the so-called human right to holidays with pay plainly cannot pass. For it is a right that is necessarily limited to those persons who are paid in any case, that is to say, to the *employé* class. Since not everyone belongs to this class, the right cannot be a universal right, a right which, in the terminology of the Universal Declaration, 'everyone' has.[11]

For Cranston, universalizability requires that putative rights have universal application if they are to be considered "true" human rights. Thus, the right to be free from interference is a right that purports to protect everyone all over the world at any point in time. It is, accordingly, a universal right. The universalizability test is closely associated with his practicability test, the two appear to be opposite sides of the same coin. This closeness in concept makes the tests repetitive in application.

Cranston's third and final test is the "paramount importance" test. For Cranston, a genuine human right must protect something that is of an "ultimate" interest. With regard to this test, Cranston maintains that:

> A further test of a human right, or moral right, is the test of paramount importance. Here the distinction is less definite, but no less crucial. And here again there is a parallel between rights and duties. It is a paramount duty to relieve great distress, as it is not a paramount duty to give pleasure. It would have been my duty to rescue the drowning child at Richmond if I had been there at the time; but it is not, in the same sense, my duty

---

dispense "goods" in order to "guarantee" negative rights: this sentiment also echoes Cranston's belief in the simple, cheap, and automatic implementation of civil rights through legislation. It is this "cost free" quality of "negative rights," which, for skeptics, always seems to make them "practicable."

11   Ibid., 51.

to give Christmas presents to the children of my
neighbours. . . . Liberality and kindness are reckoned
moral virtues; but they are not moral duties in the sense
that the obligation to rescue a drowning child is a moral
duty.[12]

Thus Cranston is unconcerned about his "failure" to give
Christmas presents to the children of his neighbors. Since
giving Christmas presents to one's neighbor's children is a
gratuitous pleasure, it cannot be a paramount duty. Because he
focuses on, what is, in his mind, the dubious right to a "paid
vacation," he does not seriously entertain the possibility that
other economic rights may be, as he puts it, "sacred things."[13]
Thus he characterizes the recognition of economic rights as
being as morally compelling as playing Santa Claus with his
neighbor's children. If Cranston is correct and no economic
rights protect interests of paramount importance, i.e., interests
that may relieve great distress, or that protect "sacred things,"
then any arguments for economic rights as moral rights would
be extremely doubtful.[14]

Cranston's concerns have shaped the economic rights
debate in many ways. Some writers accept his tests as being
valid tests, although they come to different conclusions.[15]

---

[12] Ibid., 51.

[13] See Note 15.

[14] Cranston associates paramount importance interests with the
objects of first generation rights. These latter rights are sacred things,
such as freedom of movement. Cranston's classic example is the
unjustness of denying a South African student the freedom of
movement (to England) so as to accept a scholarship to Oxford. Cranston
observes that: "In considering cases of this kind, we are confronted by
matters which belong to a totally different moral dimension from
questions of social security and holidays with pay. A human right is
something of which no one may be deprived without a grave affront to
justice. There are certain deeds which should never be done, certain
freedoms which should never be invaded, some things which are
supremely sacred." Ibid., 51-52.

[15] D. D. Raphael, a dialogical opponent of Cranston, nevertheless
accepts his tests as being diagnostically sound. See Raphael's comments
in "Human Rights Old and New," Political Theory and the Rights of
Man (Bloomington: Indiana Univ. Press, 1967): 63 and 109. Susan
Moller Okin also accepts the validity of Cranston's tests. See "Liberty &
Welfare: Some Issues In Human Rights Theory," Human Rights,

However, most commentators have refined Cranston's theories into what we have previously called the three primary categories of objections to economic rights: incomprehensibility, incompatibility, and pejoristic concerns. These objections are derived from or harmonize with his threefold tests, and are fully consistent with his views.

Incomprehensibility objections constitute three distinct types: the first type is a confusion of rights with goals; the second is the wrongful connection of needs to rights; and the third is the failure to distinguish between positive rights and negative rights. In addition to the incomprehensibility objections we will examine three distinct incompatibility objections. The first incompatibility objection is that economic rights misrepresent the proper relationship of duty to rights. The second objection is that economic rights limit individual freedom. The third objection is that economic rights unduly burden and compromise the state. Pejoristic objections maintain, in a variety of ways, that "the poor cannot or should not be helped." In order to demonstrate the persuasiveness of these refinements upon Cranston's objections they must be examined at length, beginning with incomprehensibility concerns.

Incomprehensibility Objections:
Rights and Goals Distinguished

Chapter Two introduced this objection, which was a favorite of former President Carter's critics. This objection evokes, in an odd kind of way, Cranston's incomprehensibility objection; specifically his characterization of economic rights as

---

Nomos XXIII (New York: N. Y. Press, 1981). See also Warren Lee Holleman, The Human Rights Movement: Western Values and Theological Perspectives (New York: Prager, 1987), 90-91. Joshua Muravchik utilizes Cranston's ideas and comes to the same conclusions as Cranston. See Muravchik's published dissertation-based book The Uncertain Crusade: Jimmy Carter and the Dilemmas of Human Rights Policy (Lanham: Hamilton Press, 1986), 95. The best known ethicist to follow Cranston on this point is Reinhold Niebuhr, who enthusiastically wrote the preface to Cranston's What Are Human Rights?, viii.

being "ideals" or "goals."[16] We may recall that Cranston rejects
economic rights because they are, in his opinion, not practicable,
i.e., not subject to immediate implementation. Because of this
defect they should, in his opinion, be considered to be merely
"aspirations." Cranston is followed in this conclusion by several
theorists. For example, former Ambassador to the United
Nations, Jeane Kirkpatrick, criticized President Jimmy Carter's
support for economic rights by pointing out Carter's tendency to
confuse "rights" and "goals."[17] She also criticized the "shopping
list" or Santa Claus mentality inherent in some international
human rights documents, such as the Universal Declaration of
Human Rights that Carter signed and endorsed.[18] Kirkpatrick
also joins Cranston and Ernest Lefever in maintaining that the
careless and indiscriminate characterization of every
conceivable right as a human right does nothing for the "human
rights movement," except to trivialize it.[19] Kirkpatrick and
Cranston both deny that the economic right to a state-paid
employee's holiday is a "human" right. Rights to a paid
vacation fail to explain, to Kirkpatrick's satisfaction, how such
rights could be universal, and how and why the state should
bear the obligation for paying for such entitlements. These
universalizability concerns harmonize nicely, of course, with
practicability concerns. This incomprehensibility objection is, of
course, a restatement of Maurice Cranston's "practicability"
test. Thus the putative right to a paid vacation is unequalled in

---

16 Cranston writes: "An ideal is something one can aim at, but
cannot by definition immediately realize. A right, on the contrary, is
something that can, and from the moral point of view *must,* be
respected here and now. If this were not so, we should have to agree
with Bentham; if the Rights of Man were ideals, to talk of them as rights
at all would indeed be rhetorical nonsense." In "Human Rights, Real
and Supposed," 53.

17 See Kirkpatrick's "Dictatorships and Democracy," Commentary
68, (November, 1979): 34-45. See also "Establishing a Viable Human
Rights Policy," World Affairs 143, no. 4 (Spring 81) 323-34.

18 For a similar view, see Midge Decter's "Understanding Human
Rights: An International Social Welfare System," *Vital Speeches of the
Day,* presented at a World Leadership Conference of the United Nations
at Wabash College, Crawfordsville, Ind., on October 10, 1987, 139-42.

19 See Ernest Lefever, "The Trivialization of Human Rights," *Policy
Review* (Winter, 1978): 11-26.

drawing the ire of skeptics.[20] Charles Frankel, a Columbia University professor of philosophy, former assistant secretary of State, and former UNESCO delegate, writes in regards to economic rights:

> What, then, are they? They are statements of aspiration, proclamations that governments should set themselves certain goals. Individually and jointly, they should seek to establish full employment, to improve the production of food and see to its more equitable distribution, to provide education and health care. But this is not to say that people in need have here and now, or even in the short- or middle-term, a right to the actual fulfillment of their needs. It is to say, at most, that *they have a right to their government's and the international community's best efforts to repair their situation.* (Emphasis added.)[21]

It is clear from a review of the literature that no modern human rights theorists insist that governments are obligated to treat aspirations as rights. Frankel is no exception to this rule. However, Frankel, unlike most other commentators, clearly distinguishes between the obligation to "guarantee" the immediate recognition and implementation of "rights," and the obligation to immediately "endeavor" with one's best efforts to

---

20 Michael Novak writes in one essay: "In short, the true conceptual force of the argument in favor of economic rights (to income, food, shelter, a job, etc.) is not that the latter are truly 'rights' inhering in the nature of human persons, but rather that they are 'goods' indispensable to a full human life." Michael Novak, "The Rights and Wrongs of Economic Rights," *This World* 17, no. 17 (Spring 1987): 45. Novak goes on to say: "Not only are 'welfare rights' not 'rights' in the full sense, and not only are they conditional (being first responsibilities, and claims upon others only under certain conditions): they are better to be described in terms of objectives, ends, goals--that is, as highly important social goals, part of the 'general welfare.'" Ibid., 49. Similarly, regarding the "right" to a state paid holiday, Harvard history professor, Walter Laqueur, insists, that: "This right cannot be universally enforced at the present time since, among other reasons, many countries do not have the resources. Moral considerations aside, it is quite clear that a law that cannot be enforced is not a law but an aspiration." Walter Laqueur, "The Issue of Human Rights," Commentary 63, no. 5 (May 1977) 30.

21 Charles Frankel, *Human Rights and Foreign Policy*, Headline Series 241 (New York: The Foreign Policy Association, 1978), 39.

"repair their situation." Frankel briefly entertains the possibility that governments do not need to discharge their duties absolutely and perfectly in order to discharge them successfully. In other words Frankel's thought haltingly considers that economic rights might only require good faith efforts on the part of government to count as a successful discharge of their duties. What distinguishes Frankel's view from other skeptics is that he entertains the idea that governments have a duty to put forth immediately their best efforts to "realize" certain economic rights.[22] He implies thereby that a "right" vests citizens with the authority to demand that their government immediately put forth its best efforts to recognize and implement economic rights. Such actions may be mandatory even though, due to economic factors, they might not be successful for some indefinable length of time. Thus the right contemplated by Frankel is one of dutiful governmental action rather than successful governmental results.[23] Frankel is, thereby, not as consistent in his distinction between rights and goals as other skeptics and is therefore more sympathetic to economic rights. Despite all of his protestations to the contrary, Frankel seems to recognize that economic rights are not incomprehensible. This recognition implies that there is a growing end to the economic rights argument in which some economic rights will have to be recognized.

Frankel's views of 1978 anticipate, or at least complement, an interpretation of economic rights that has been adopted by international jurists regarding the Covenant on Social and Economic Rights; namely the Limburg Principles.[24]

---

[22] The theoretical problem that Frankel's position implies for skeptics is that if a government simply has to immediately put forth its best efforts in order to implement economic rights, then by doing so their actions could indeed be considered as recognizing rights, rather than entertaining ideals or aspirations. To this extent, Frankel is a friend to economic rights supporters and a theoretical problem to economic rights skeptics.

[23] Rights are, as we saw in Chapter One, ethical responses that are deontological. They are rules oriented, rather than consequentialist.

[24] See "The Limburg Principles on the Implementation of the International Covenant on Economic, Social and Cultural Rights," *Human Rights Quarterly* 9, no. 2 (May 1987), 122-35. Since the Limburg Principles are principles in support of economic rights their full

This understanding of governmental duties is the direction in which the international economic rights debate is moving. Frankel, however, is not unaware of the import of his observation, and is careful to draw back from it. He maintains, therefore, that though looser talk may be useful in pushing "helpful" programs, in the final analysis such talk is "dangerously utopian." For Frankel "wisdom lies on the side of restraint in the use of the phrase 'human rights.'"[25] Thus he desires to keep a clear distinction between rights and goals, but has trouble doing so. His difficulty is not necessarily a weakness. Frankel's insight shows that though rights and goals are distinctly different terms there is always a relationship between the concepts. Rights give rise to duties that people commonly understand as being strictly obligatory. Ideals, on the other hand, create looser duties that are much less strictly obligatory. In the West, however, we consider people without ideals cynics. If they have no goals we categorize them as being imprudent, lazy, or hopelessly confused. Moral individuals are assumed, by most, to have some goals they wish to reach, and some ideals that they attempt to achieve.[26] This judgment is not limited to individuals but is also applied to societies and governments. Thus, though rights and goals are distinctly different, they are clearly not unrelated in terms of moral reasoning.

Be that as it may, the economic rights partisan's misconstruing of goals as rights is, for Cranston, Frankel, and others, a sound reason for rejecting economic rights claims. Cranston, Lefever, Kirkpatrick and Frankel, are all realists. True rights for them are concrete and invaluable claims in and on the modern world, subject to immediate implementation. Within their conception of that world, the clear recognition,

discussion will be held in Chapters Four and Six where arguments for economic rights are given full coverage. The length and demands of this chapter necessitate a postponement of their discussion herein.

25 Frankel, *Human Rights and Foreign Policy*, 41. Frankel is nearly an economic rights enthusiast, but does not, in the final analysis, step over the line of skepticism. Though he must be considered an economic rights skeptic, his position implies an acceptance of economic rights.

26 Most of the debates in recent ethical discourse ha not been over whether one should have ideals, but over the difficulty in discerning "shared meanings," or common ideals.

conceptualization, and implementation of these rights is an imperative. Anything short of such results constitutes, for skeptics, a utopian fantasy.

Our second incomprehensibility objection may now be addressed by turning to Donald Van De Veer's well-known essay entitled, "A Right To Be Saved From Starvation?"[27] Van De Veer believes that economic rights are incomprehensible because one of the common justifying causes for recognizing them, their supposed quality of being mandatory due to the existence of unrequited basic human needs, cannot, in his opinion, be adequately explained. Van De Veer poses this question in as dire a form as possible. If this purported economic right should fail all other such efforts should, logically speaking, also fail.[28] Van De Veer answers his title question in the negative.[29] He does concede, however, that "that serious human need is of moral relevance is rarely disputed."[30] What he chiefly objects to is the contention that "the needy, due to serious human needs, thereby have rights."[31] His essay is a rejection of William Aiken's claim for economic rights.[32] Van De Veer constructs Aiken's argument as follows:

> 1.   Any person involuntarily undergoing extreme deprivation which would lead to his or her death has a moral right to the goods and services required to prevent that death. So,
> 2.   Any such person has a right to be saved from starvation.
> 3.   Such a right is claimable against any persons in a position to provide the necessary goods and services.

---

[27] Donald Van De Veer, "A Right To Be Saved From Starvation?" *The Personalist* 60, no. 2 (April 1979) 216-20.

[28] To his credit Van De Veer picks a putative right that clearly has a "paramount interest, "a "right to be saved from starvation," rather than challenging its weakest economic rights sister, the "right to a paid vacation." Donald Van De Veer, "A Right To Be Saved From Starvation?"

[29] Ibid., 216.

[30] Ibid., 216.

[31] Ibid., 216.

[32] See William Aiken, "The Right to be Saved from Starvation," *World Hunger and Moral Obligation*, ed. William Aiken and Hugh LaFollette (Englewood Cliffs, N. J. : Prentice-Hall, Inc. , 1977), 85-120.

4.   Persons in such a position (see (3)) have a duty to provide such goods and/or services.[33]

Van De Veer rejects Aiken's conclusion by rejecting Aiken's first premise. He does so by way of an analogy that supposedly demonstrates the invalidity of Aiken's position:

A.   Portnoy is involuntarily undergoing extreme sexual deprivation which would lead to his being chronically depressed.
B.   Portnoy has a moral right to the goods and services required to prevent chronic depression (from those "in a position" to provide them).[34]

Van De Veer believes that he has painted Aiken into a corner, but his criticism is not completely persuasive. Aiken is not cornered for the simple reason that Van De Veer's analogy is bad. Aiken's marginalized person is facing a deprivation that inevitably leads to death--i.e., starvation. In comparison, Van De Veer's Portnoy is undergoing a deprivation that presumably makes him unhappy. Van De Veer makes much of the fact that malnourished people are also often dreadfully unhappy, but perhaps no more than people who are extremely sexually deprived. However, Van De Veer has made the classic mistake that is usually associated with proponents for economic rights, that is, of mistaking wants for needs. In a sexually ideal world, every Portnoy would have a mate (or mates, if necessary) to fully satisfy their desires. But no serious economic rights advocate is demanding a utopian sexual cosmos; at least Aiken is not. Thus Van De Veer is successful only in knocking down his own hastily constructed straw man. He demands correctly, however, that Aiken justify a "right" to be saved from starvation. Clearly, an undeniable need can not immediately be equated with a "justified" right.[35] Van De Veer shows us that

---

33 Van De Veer, "A Right to be Saved from Starvation?", 217.

34 Ibid.

35 C.B. MacPherson explains the problems posed by the consideration of the concept of need in liberal thought. He writes: "Classical political economy and neo-classical economics are built on the same postulate: the infinity of wants provides the incentive that propels the market economy. And twentieth century pluralist political science has strong traces of the same postulate, insofar as it treats the democratic

what a dire need demonstrates is that the sufferer should, logically speaking, make a claim.[36] The claim itself, however, cannot ripen into a rights-claim (in the sense that we use the term) without an accompanying justifying principle.[37]

Aiken's proffered justifying principle is in fact defective.[38]

political system as a market in political goods. This classical liberal individualism holds that this endless increase of wants is good-just the opposite of Rousseau. And this theory is unlike Rousseau's in another way : it is totally unhistorical. Individuals are by nature, at all times, creatures of unlimited wants   This unhistorical quality of the Hume-to-Bentham concept of wants cripples it morally: it would confine mankind forever in a predatory market society. And perhaps because it is so unhistorical, this liberal theory, and liberal-democratic theory insofar as it accepts the capitalist market society, makes no distinction between wants: every want is as good as every other. So there is no place in the liberal theory for a distinction between 'needs' as more essential and 'wants' as less essential. Nor does it admit a distinction between natural and artificial wants, that is, between wants supposedly inherent in man's nature and those created by the capitalist relations of production and the operation of the market. No such distinction can be made if one postulates universal innate emulation, for on that postulate whatever new thing one man gets, another will therefore want, and this want will flow from his innate nature just as much as his apparently more basic or natural wants." In "Needs and Wants: an Ontological or Historical Problem," *Human Needs and Politics*, ed. Ross Fitzgerald (Rushcutters Bay, Australia: Pergamon Press, 1977), 30. MacPherson endorses Marx's understanding of needs and wants, in preference to Abraham Maslow's typology, or the liberal tradition's views. One need not share MacPherson's enthusiasm for the Marxist approach in order to see that wants and needs present a complex problem of differentiation for interpreters of liberal political thought.

[36] As Cranston has rightly maintained, a need must justify a "paramount" interest. The alternative view would be to consider seriously every claim and every need, at which point the notion of a rights-claim would break down.

[37] As was maintained in Chapter One, according to Gewirth, every right has five elements, one of which must be a "justifying principle." The demonstration of a paramount importance value in the object of a right, is not, in itself, sufficient to justify a right.

[38] Van De Veer's further argument with Aiken is irrelevant to our discussion. This discussion is irrelevant because Aiken's rights position is a utility-oriented maximizing theory that is rife with problems. This study is a study in rights, rather than a study in utilitarianism. Van De Veer finds that Aiken's theories lack a clear formulation. On this last point Van De Veer appears to be correct. Donald Van De Veer, "A Right

But Van De Veer has only shown that Aiken's argument is not a good one. So although Van De Veer's first rebuttal is weak, specifically his Portnoy analogy, his demand for a justifying principle is undeniable; and it is a demand that Aiken cannot satisfy. More important for this study, however, is that Van De Veer demonstrates why such a justifying principle is necessary: because of the danger that spurious claims may hopelessly obfuscate human rights discussions. For example, without a morally compelling justifying principle, Portnoy's claims for sex may seem as compelling as claims for sufficient food to sustain life. However, since Van De Veer only claims that Aiken does not make a persuasive demonstration, the possibility that such a demonstration can be made by others remains open.

Van De Veer's view demonstrates the difficulty of connecting needs to rights. With regard to the issue of "paramount importance" difficulties abound. The foremost difficulty is in providing a self-evident paramount importance. What is paramount to some people is not *paramount* to others. What is needed, if "basic needs-based" economic rights theories are to be persuasive, is a theory for clearly discerning "paramount" interests. In addition, the connection between the manifestation of basic needs of a paramount importance and the recognition of rights must be made clearly and without confusion. If not, economic rights could indeed be incomprehensible. Economic rights skeptics doubt that such a connection can be made, but their correctness on this point is not completely clear.

Clearly, needs cannot automatically generate appropriate corresponding rights and correlating duties. If such were the case one would have as many rights as there are "important needs." Such a proliferation of rights would endlessly confuse rights theory. Connecting needs to rights is a difficult proposition as Van De Veer has shown. Cranston's paramount importance test can be used to pinpoint the difficulty. In Van De Veer's hypothetical example, Portnoy's need for sex can be seen to be paramount in one sense; sex is a basic human drive and fundamental to human reproduction. Although Portnoy's need may seem to pass Cranston's "paramount importance" test, it falters in its comparison with

To Be Saved From Starvation?," 219-20.

starvation issues. Meeting Portnoy's "right" for sex would require a sexual partner; that is, a personal relationship and a provision of service that is more akin to a right to an organ transplant than a right to a sack of flour.[39] Unless a society is willing to create and sustain a system of public prostitutes, Portnoy's "rights" could never be systematically met. While the freedom to engage in sexual intercourse may well be accepted as a basic moral or "human right," it is clearly to be understood as a freedom right, implying mutual consent, rather than a "positive" right to the provision of any goods, or Good.[40] In short, Portnoy really is asking for a "freedom right," rather than the provision of any good. Portnoy's argument is, therefore, a far cry from a justified demand. Instead it is a dubious demand that society provide citizens with sex as a basic social guarantee.[41] By contrast, in most societies sex is not a commodity such as a sack of grain, and sexual relations are reasonably accessible without the intervention of the society in general and the state in particular.[42] More precisely, Van De Veer's comparison of sex with food fails to take into consideration that some persons abstain from sex for a lifetime, whereas no one can do so regarding food.[43] Still while Van De Veer's challenge to "needs-based" economic rights is unsuccessful, his failure does not settle the issue. It is quite conceivable that other commentators may successfully challenge such rights. Thus

---

[39] Organ transplants always require a specific duty-bearer, although the identity of the duty-bearer may be withheld because of the norms of the health industry. A liver or a kidney is much more personal item than a sack of flour, in that it is a provision of human matter rather than a commodity. Consent to engage in sexual intercourse is similarly a very personal affair.

[40] By a positive right, I mean a right that requires some party to provide some good, rather than to require a person to refrain from acting.

[41] That some societies have in the past, or could have in the future, such a systemic provision of sex misses the point. Such a provision is not a "paramount" need in the way that Cranston uses the term.

[42] See George Orwell's groundbreaking novel, *1984* (New York: Harcourt, Brace & Jovanovich, 1982), as an example of what a truly sexually constrained society would look like.

[43] I owe this further criticism of Van De Veer to my director, Dr. Theodore Weber.

economic rights partisans must continue to clarify the connection between needs and rights.

L. Duane Willard offers another criticism of attempts-to-connect-needs-to-rights projects. Willard is concerned about:

> . . .[the] considerable energy expended by some in an attempt to ground the notion of moral rights on a certain kind of fact about human nature, namely, human needs.[44]

Willard correctly senses that exponents of economic rights theories are trying to ground moral rights in certain kinds of facts about human nature. He also assumes economic rights proponents want to connect moral rights to human nature by way of human needs.[45] He concludes that justifying this connection is difficult, and that the failure to connect them could make the resulting economic rights theory incomprehensible. He therefore rejects certain attempts to state human needs as constituting facts that logically compel their satisfaction and recognition as basic rights. Willard may be correct in refusing to connect human needs to human rights, but his rationale for this refusal is contestable if not incomprehensible. Willard writes that:

> needs are not psychological, physiological, or chemical states, events, processes, or properties at all; they are neither empirically observable nor logically inferable facts of any kind. In familiar terms, I am suggesting that to think of needs as facts is to make a category mistake, for needs are simply not among the "furniture" of human nature.[46]

To Willard, understanding needs as facts confuses values with facts, and he maintains, ". . . needs are not facts about individual human beings or human nature, but are values."[47]

---

[44] L. Duane Willard, "Needs and Rights," *Dialogue* XXVI (Spring 1987): 43.

[45] Chapter Four will demonstrate that both Henry Shue and Alan Gewirth assume that basic needs have a vital connection to basic rights.

[46] Willard, 46.

[47] Willard, 47.

His observation is a very good point: values are values, and facts are facts. However, he never considers the possibility that while needs express values, and values clearly are not facts, needs may nevertheless also express facts. For example, if the need for food for living organisms is not a fact, it is doubtful that any observable phenomena will qualify as facts. While it is true that the physiological and psychological state that is called "hunger" is technically not exactly the same thing as the "need" for food, the two phenomena are so closely associated as to be considered, in the normal course of living, as equivalents. So, even if an organism, such as a monkey in a behavioral study, rejects food in favor of another "need," as for instance cocaine, scientists do not say that the monkey does not "need" food. Nor do scientists say that the monkey never gets hungry; scientists merely maintain that the monkey prefers the cocaine. The subsequent deaths of the experimental monkeys only emphasize the point that basic needs cannot permanently be denied without death ensuing.[48] The assertion that the lack of food results in death is simple common sense, and while appeals to common sense are always a form of question-begging, Willard's position demanding the complete separation of value and facts is so completely counter-intuitive as to justify recourse to common sense justifications. Furthermore, in terms of the other social forms of behavioral control, namely legal duties and responsibilities, the need for food is a given in assessing legal and moral accountability.. Thus a failure to feed one's child is considered negligence and abuse. Attempts to argue that such needs are not facts or are not self-evident are not defenses against a charge of child abuse. Nevertheless, even if we assume arguendo that some needs are facts, Willard is correct in arguing that their factual status does not automatically qualify them for recognition as rights.[49] However, Willard contradicts himself on this point when he attempts to distinguish between

---

[48] For a description of the actual experiments that this hypothetical example is based upon see a monograph by Chris Johanson, entitled, "Assessment of the Dependence Potential of Cocaine in Animals," *National Institute on Drug Abuse Research Monograph Series* (Chicago: University of Chicago, 1984), Mono 50, 54-71.

[49] The fact that people in Ethiopia need food does not in itself create for them a right to food, or a duty on my part, to provide it.

luxuries and "genuine" needs. Willard correctly asserts that:

> On the one hand, luxuries (by definition?) are not things that people ought not to be without. On the other hand, a "genuine" need is thought of as something people ought not to be without, that is, ought to have satisfied.[50]

In saying this Willard himself has shown a possible nexus between needs and rights. **Rights are, if they are nothing else, claims for the meeting of needs that "ought" to be satisfied.**

The philosophical problem in connecting rights to needs is not, as Willard would have us believe, a problem of confusing values with facts, but of finding a satisfactory principle for discerning between claims based on "desires," and claims based on "genuine" needs (Kirkpatrick's desiderata problem revisited).[51] The real problem, therefore, is the difficulty in recognizing "genuine" needs, and explaining the process for distinguishing between trivial needs and basic needs. This problem must be confronted and resolved because the alternative is to consider all needs as covalent. Once one assumes that all needs are covalent, rights based upon the category of needs become incomprehensible because the class of possible needs is too vast and indeterminate and breaks down. With a conceptual breakdown in the class of need-based objects, the rights based on that class also break down and become incomprehensible. If the class of needs is determinate, it must still be limited in size. If is too large then the extent of the duties necessary to address the class of objects becomes so onerous as to discourage the performance of the duties. The unwillingness to shoulder questionable duties is one of the principal reasons for economic rights skepticism. Thus, as we saw in Chapter One, there is a clear distinction between positive rights and negative rights, and between positive duties and negative duties. This distinction needs a few additional remarks.

A reconsideration of the nature of rights, positive and negative, calls to our attention the connection between incomprehensibility objections and incompatibility objections.

---

50 Willard, 48.
51 See also Sheldon Wein's reply to Willard in "Rights and Needs," *Dialogue* XXVI (Spring 1987): 55-57. Wein observes that the need for oxygen is not a value, but a fact that can be rapidly tested.

No clear line lies between the two categories. However, the distinction between positive rights and negative rights helps to explain why the two kinds of objections must be associated and how they might be distinguished. For some economic rights skeptics their concept of rights is so determined by their understanding of correlative duties that differing understandings of correlative duties and rights are "incomprehensible" to them. For others their concept or definition of rights is established in such a way that differing understandings of correlative duties and rights are not incomprehensible, but incompatible with their own definitions. These latter commentators favor their own definitions and norms over others by declaring that competing notions of rights and duties are not incomprehensible, but incompatible with their own conceptions, which they assume to be conceptually superior. In short, the positive/negative rights distinction, that was touched upon in Chapter One must be further discussed.

Richard Pierre Claude, states the distinction clearly:

> In political theory economic and social are distinguished from political and civil rights as "positive" rather than "negative" rights. The state enforces the latter by refraining from certain practices that infringe upon individual freedoms and assuring standards of judicial procedure. The positive rights must be promoted by legislative, administrative and executive planning to ensure basic human needs such as jobs, education, shelter, health care that the individual alone cannot provide. To guarantee positive economic rights a government must direct the state apparatus to action on behalf of segments of the population who otherwise would not benefit from these rights. By implication the state also acts against those elements whose power and disproportionate share of national resources inhibit state action in this direction.Theoretically, economic and social human rights can be promoted by assuring minimum standards in a society characterized by substantial economic inequality. Economic and social rights cannot be promoted, however, under conditions of laissez-faire capitalism, and the scarcer the resources, the more planning and careful priority setting is likely to be required. [52]

---

[52] Richard Pierre Claude, "The Western Tradition of Human Rights in Comparative Perspective," *Comparative Juridical Review* 14, (1977): 3-66.

It should be noted that Claude's use of the term positive rights is quite distinct from Cranston's use of that term. Cranston used the term positive rights to refer to rights that were secured by "positive" law (i.e., secured by legislation).[53] In Cranston's opinion true human rights were rights that, "nobody could find any excuse for not respecting."[54] These latter rights he called "categorical rights." In contrast, Claude and others distinguish between rights of provision (which Cranston would call "ideals" for provision) and rights to governmental restraint, i.e., negative rights (categorical rights in Cranston's nomenclature). Cranston objected to what Claude calls positive rights under his "practicability" test because many states simply did not have the mechanism to "provide" much of anything.[55] Thus, for Cranston, such claims were not rights at all, but ideals, or goals. This practicability concern has been extended from Cranston's initial observations. Not only are more recent economic rights skeptics concerned with the feasibility of "positive rights," they are also hostile to the idea of correlative "positive duties." As we discussed in Chapter One, rights-claims, as we have used the term, demand that someone recognize them. And if such recognition requires a positive action, the one who recognizes the rights is thereby saddled with a "positive duty." This positive duty requires people to utilize their time and/or energy in fulfilling the duty. It is this performatory burden that skeptics find objectionable, either incomprehensible or incompatible, to their projects.

Michael Novak, a Catholic lay scholar, and Joel Feinberg, a social philosopher, recognize the difference between positive and negative rights and relate this distinction to the notion of duty.[56] As Novak puts it, "If there is no one to fulfill such obligations, then the alleged human right has no substance; it is merely a form of words."[57] For Novak, every human right

---

53 Cranston, *What Are Human Rights?*, 8.

54 Ibid., 37.

55 Ibid., 37.

56 Joel Feinberg, "The Nature and Value of Rights," *Rights*, ed. David Lyons (Belmont, Calif.: Wadsworth,1979): 91.

57 Michael Novak, "Human Rights and Whited Sepulchres," *Human Rights and U. S. Human Rights Policy*, ed. Howard J. Wiarda (Washington: American Inst. for Public Policy Research, 1982): 79. Here

has a corresponding human obligation; a provider must be available if subsistence rights are to be provided. Joel Feinberg, whose views differ in many respects from Novak's, nevertheless shares Novak's insistence on the correlativity of duties and rights.[58] Accordingly, for Feinberg, for there to be a "genuine" duty to provide for the poor such a duty must be feasible. However, Feinberg argues that, due to scarcity, such a duty is impossible to fulfill. Accordingly, its purported correlative right must be a mirage. This argument is, of course, simply a variation on Cranston's "practicability test." Feinberg thus insists upon the possibility of the actual fulfillment of a correlative duty and the actual enjoyment of rights prior to assigning them status as "justified" rights. For Feinberg, negative duties create "perfect" obligations, i.e., duties whose performance can be guaranteed. As we may recall from Chapter One, Feinberg believes that he can discharge his negative duties, his mirror concept to negative rights, to millions, simply by minding his own business. To do so he must only refrain from interfering with a person's right to speak, worship, contract, travel, or to live secure from assault. On a personal level, Feinberg is undeniably correct; by simply minding his own business, he does not interfere in the liberty and security of others. By contrast, a positive right, demanding a corresponding duty would, by definition, interfere with the freedom of others.

Further discussion of positive rights in contradistinction to negative rights is needed, but it should be conducted under the associated rubric of duty. It is at this point that we pass from incomprehensibility objections to incompatibility objections.

Novak emphasizes the incomprehensibility of "positive rights." Novak holds the George Frederick Jewett Chair in Public Policy at the American Enterprise Institute.

[58] Joel Feinberg, "The Nature and Value of Rights," *Rights, Justice, and the Bounds of Liberty* (Princeton N.J.: Princeton University Press, 1980): 143-58.

These latter objections posit that economic rights are comprehensible but impermissible because they conflict with lexically prioritized civil and political rights.[59]

The Conceptual Incompatibility Objections: The Relationship of Duties to Rights and The Limitation of Freedom Objection

The relationship of duties to rights, and the limitations on freedom that duties entail constitute a two part, interrelated objection to economic rights.   Prior to looking at these objections, we should first examine the deeply rooted liberal inclination to prefer rights to freedom over rights to well-being.[60] It is this long standing inclination that is the source of the rejection of economic rights.   By rights to freedom I mean at least two understandings of those rights.   The first understanding of a right to freedom is the right of the individual to be immune from the coercion of any other party.   This understanding of liberty is given its clearest expression by a celebrated political philosopher and social economist, F. A. Hayek.[61] Hayek's understanding of liberty is defined negatively. One is free, from his perspective, as long as he is free from interference or coercion.[62] The meaning of one's freedom is, however, left to the individual's imagination.   In this understanding of freedom, how people use their freedom is basically irrelevant provided that they do not interfere with the freedom of others. Thus the individual is to be left alone to contract and covenant freely with other free, atomized

---

59 These last commentators concede that economic rights theories are not conceptual nonsense, while maintaining that the demands of economic rights systematically conflict with preferred civil and political rights.   The process of having a lexical priority for civil and political rights simply means that these rights are weighted or preferred rights. As such if they conflict with other rights, they cannot be overridden by the other classification of rights.   Thus in the case of a conflict with economic rights civil and political rights would always be preferred.

60 For a definition of a right to well-being see Chapter One.

61 See F. A. Hayek, "Liberty and Liberties," *The Constitution of Liberty* (Chicago: University of Chicago Press, 1960), 11-21.

62 Ibid., 133.

individuals. Hayek's freedom is a freedom from interference, rather than a freedom for any particular purpose. Since Hayek's idea of freedom is totally disassociated from any elements of well-being, aside from freedom from coercion, it is no surprise to find that he opposes social redistribution schemes such as governmental taxation designed to take from the rich to assist the poor.[63] Similarly, other free-market enthusiasts, Milton Friedman and Isaiah Berlin all oppose economic rights, especially in relation to rights to liberty.[64] However, liberalism, as we have seen in the first chapter, has produced more than one position on the relationship between liberty and other values. In addition to Thomas Paine's *Agrarian Justice* and

---

[63] Hayek's position on the government's intervention on behalf of the indigent is complex. He seems to have some genuine sympathy for the poor. He writes: "There is no reason why in a free society government should not assure to all protection against severe deprivation in the form of an assured minimum income, or a floor below which nobody need to descend. To enter into such an insurance against extreme misfortune may well be in the interest of all; or it may be felt to be a clear moral duty of all to assist, within the organized community, those who cannot help themselves. So long as such a uniform minimum income is provided outside the market to all those who, for any reason, are unable to earn in the market an adequate maintenance, this need not lead to a restriction of freedom, or a conflict with the Rule of Law. The problems with which we are here concerned arise only when the remuneration for services rendered is determined by authority, and the impersonal mechanism of the market which guides the direction of individual efforts is thus suspended." *Law, Legislation and Liberty: The Mirage of Social Justice* (Chicago: University of Chicago Press, 1976), 87. On the other hand, however, Hayek adamantly opposes economic rights, as being both incompatible and incomprehensible. Ibid. See his "Appendix to Chapter Nine: Justice and Individual Rights." There he exercises every objection that Cranston makes to economic rights. Hayek must see, therefore, the government's duty to intervene as being a loose moral duty or goal that should be accomplished without interfering with the free play of the market. See also *The Constitution of Liberty*, 231-33.

[64] As Berlin observes, "I am normally said to be free to the degree which no man or body of men interferes with my activity. Political liberty in this sense is simply the area within which a man can act unobstructed by others. If I am prevented by others from doing what I could otherwise do, I am to that degree unfree . . ." From Isaiah Berlin, *Four Essays on Liberty* (London: Oxford University Press, 1969), 122.

John Locke's concern with basic subsistence, and the duty to refrain from exhausting the "commons," other liberals have given different definitions of liberty.[65] In particular, Thomas Hill Green, a noted British social philosopher, understood freedom as having a positive component as well as negative considerations. Green believed that freedom had to be more than an immunity from the constraint of others. Green wrote of freedom, that:

> When we speak of freedom as something to be so highly prized, we mean a positive power or capacity of doing or enjoying something worth doing or enjoying, and that, too, something that we do or enjoy in common with others.[66]

Green's understanding of freedom is a freedom for, rather than merely a freedom from. It is therefore, a liberal understanding of freedom that differs significantly from Hayek's. It is concerned with well-being from a positive perspective. In this understanding of freedom one has a responsibility to develop oneself, and to realize one's fullest potential in relation to others. Green's moral agent is located and embedded *in* a society, wherein one is supposed to find meaning and self-realization. This understanding of freedom and responsibility has to be concerned with well-being. In addition, this type of liberalism could not legitimate a purely negative freedom. Most liberal thinkers have positioned themselves between these two poles on the political spectrum, with Hayek on the right and Green on the left.

This brief characterization of liberal political thought is by no means exhaustive, yet it allows us to address the question of duties in relation to rights, which is where the balance between liberty and well-being is most often struck. Prior to doing so, however, one other historical observation should be

---

65 See Chapter One for a brief discussion of Paine and Locke. For an interesting discussion of Locke's right to subsistence, see Jeremy Shearmur, "The Right to Subsistence in a 'Lockean' State of Nature," *The Southern Journal of Philosophy* XXVII, no. 4, (1989): 561-68.

66 T. H. Green, "Liberal Legislation and Freedom of Contract," *The Political Theory of T. H. Green*, ed. John R. Rodman (New York: Appleton-Century-Crofts, 1964): 51-52.

made. Anthony Arblaster, a historian of liberal political theory, recounts the Irish potato famine and the resulting social chaos and wide-scale death caused by, at least in part, the British government's refusal to intervene in the famine to minimize loss of life, and to mitigate suffering.[67] Arblaster maintains that the refusal of the British to intervene in the Irish famine was not based upon scarcity, since they continued to promote the export of food from Ireland. Rather, their refusal was based upon an absolute commitment to being a non-interventionist state that allowed people to fend for themselves in complete freedom. This austere state was, as Arblaster observes, the England of the New Poor Law and the new workhouses, and this new spirit of non-intervention, aside from preserving law and order and property, prevailed in Ireland as it had in England.[68] This was a new relationship of economics and politics, one that had been influenced by Thomas Malthus and the rising industrial world market. In such a world the individual was to be guaranteed freedom from interference even if it resulted in insuring freedom to starve to death, as many Irish did. Thus in this wing of liberal thought it was theoretically incorrect to weigh well-being against the needs of liberty. Well-being was the primary responsibility of the risk-aversive atomized individual who was the basic political, social, and moral unit in the new social contract society.

It should be recognized that liberal thought has never abandoned the tension between the demands of freedom and well-being. For example, H. L. A. Hart is a classic champion of individual liberty to the exclusion of well-being concerns. Hart in a celebrated essay entitled, "Are There Any Natural Rights?," concludes that if there are any rights, they are only rights to liberty.[69] It is for this reason that Hart contemplate the

---

[67] Anthony Arblaster, *The Rise and Decline of Western Liberalism* (Oxford: Basil Blackwell Publishers, 1984), 257-60.

[68] As Arblaster relates, intervention was always seen as interference. He also writes, "Liberal political economy did not allow the recognition that poverty and unemployment had structural causes; they were seen as misfortunes whose remedy lay within the power of the individual." Ibid., 255.

[69] H. L. A. Hart "Are There Any Natural Rights?," *Philosophical Review* 64 (1955): 175-91.

disturbing dilemma of a "free, but starving poor." Hart's lack of concern for the perishing poor is not attributable to hardheartedness on his part, but primarily to Hart's lexical priority preference of liberty over any other value.[70] In summation, even for modern economic rights skeptics, it is difficult to show how the needs, even the basic needs of human beings, can be used to justify a curtailment on the liberty of others, since liberty is for them a higher value. And, in today's busy world, with a multiplicity of duties, and obligations, these writers want to limit any further demands on individuals and governments.[71]

Jan Narveson, a noted economic rights skeptic, also contrasts negative rights to positive rights. In doing so, he shows that he does not find economic rights to be incomprehensible. Instead he understands them to be incompatible with rights to freedom. Narveson, like Hart and Hayek, maintains the lexical priority of liberty over other rights. For Narveson, the right to lounge on the beach would be limited

---

[70] This position is also precisely that of Charles Trevelyan, Assistant Secretary of the Treasury, in England, who was in charge of the "relief" of Ireland during the potato famine (1845-48). Arblaster writes of this policy, "Once again, it was not a question of personal hardheartedness. It was that the ministers and officials most responsible for policy in Ireland--above all Trevelyan, Wood and Russell--were committed to an ideology that frowned on intervention and even resigned itself to famine as, in some circumstances, an unavoidable evil." Arblaster also notes that at least one and one half million Irish died during the famine, not counting the possible deaths of some of the one million that emigrated during this period. *The Rise and Decline of Western Liberalism*, 259.

[71] In contrast to Hart and Friedman, is Noel Farley, an economist. Farley recognizes the differences between economic rights (as the provision of a minimum economic security) and the traditional human rights (which we have termed first generation rights) as creating trade offs in policy decisions, rather than creating conceptual incoherence. For Farley, though the choices may be somewhat incompatible, the important discussion lies in choosing between the trade offs and justifying one's choice. See, Noel J. J. Farley, "Human Rights in the Contemporary World: Some Notes from an Economist," *Human Rights in Religious Traditions* ed. Arlene Swidler (Pilgrim Press: New York, 1982): 93.

if one had a duty to rescue a drowning person.[72] Thus for
Narveson, the duty to rescue, which cannot be discharged
simply by minding one's own business, cannot be allowed to
interfere with his "right to lounge."[73] Narveson is not averse to
rescuing potential drowning victims; he simply does not want to
be compelled to do so by society. But society specifically employs
coercion, if necessary, to implement rights.   Narveson
recognizes this coercive element, and, preferring liberty, rejects
certain positive rights and positive duties.   In another essay
Narveson restates this argument in a clearer fashion. In his
youth, Narveson argues, he had to weed potatoes. He accepted
this duty because it related to his own personal household. But
he objects to any extension of such duties:

> If the people across the street had a right that I supply
> them with potatoes, then they had a right that I do (or
> that I get someone else to do) things like that. Whereas
> when I was peacefully napping away the afternoon,
> gazing at the distant meadows and idly savoring the
> country air, I was respecting not only their rights to
> noninjury, but in fact, the similar right to noninjury of
> everyone in the entire world![74]

Narveson correctly shows that the purported duty to
provide "basic necessities" to others does entail some sacrifices,
and those sacrifices must be justified if they are to be compelled
by the state. Narveson, Milton Friedman, and others, do not
want to become the slaves of the lazy, profligate, or imprudent.
Narveson raises the question as to how one person's
responsibilities, for instance to feed herself or her family, can

---

[72] Jan Narveson, "Negative and Positive Rights in Gewirth's
Reason and Morality," *Gewirth's Ethical Rationalism* ed. Edward Regis,
Jr. (Chicago: U. of Chicago Press 1984), 96. Paul Streeten also makes this
distinction between negative "rights" and positive "rights" and what the
distinction implies for the creation of new and possibly onerous duties.
Streeten interprets the Universal Declaration as demanding: ". . . for
everyone, . . . a right to benefit from the services of a full-fledged welfare
state, however poor the society." Paul Streeten, "Basic Needs and
Human Rights," 109.
[73] Narveson, 97.
[74] Jan Narveson, "Positive/Negative: Why Bother?," *Positive and
Negative Duties*, ed. Eric Mack (New Orleans, La.: Tulane Univ.), 56.

become another person's responsibilities. How does the second person become obligated? He brings to our full attention, in ways that are more concrete than Hart's, the general preference of economic rights skeptics: the lexical priority of negative rights to liberty over any positive rights to well-being.[75]

---

[75] Nearly all economic rights skeptics prefer rights to liberty, over rights to well-being. Besides Narveson, see, H. L. A. Hart, "Are There Any Natural Rights?," *Philosophical Review* LXIV (1955): 175-91. For Hart (who wrote in regard to "natural rights") economic rights would unacceptably conflict with the "preferred" political rights of the liberty of the individual. Similarly, Milton Friedman, an economist, shares Hart's lexical priority for liberty rights, to the limited extent that he discusses rights. Writing in regards to the right to work, Friedman unconditionally favors the government's guaranteeing freedom of opportunity to work while adamantly opposing all movement towards governmental provision of jobs. Friedman (like Narveson) refuses to be compelled by government to provide for anyone. He insists upon the freedom to provide charity, voluntarily. See Milton Friedman, *The Essence of Friedman* (Stanford: The Hoover Institution Press, 1987), 137-38. See also, Tibor Machan, "Are There Any Human Rights?," *The Personalist* 59, no.2, (April 1978): 169. Douglas J. Den Uyl and Tibor Machan, "Gewirth and the Supportive State," *Positive and Negative Duties*, ed. Eric Mack (New Orleans: Tulane Univ. Press, 1985), 167. Clifford Orwin and Thomas L. Pangle, "Restoring the Human Rights Tradition," *This World* 3 (Fall,1982): 22. Joshua Muravchik, *The Uncertain Crusade: Jimmy Carter and the Dilemmas of Human Rights Policy* (Lanham: Hamilton Press, 1986), 96-97. John Rawls, despite his commitment to his maximin principle, has, nevertheless, a lexical priority of values, with its highest value being a right to liberty. *A Theory of Justice* (Cambridge: Harvard Univ. Press, 1971): 43. Christian Bay writes with regard to Rawls' lexical priority for liberty, "It turns out that Rawls, too, operates with a peculiarly narrow conception of liberty, one that bears more closely on the likely preoccupations of comfortably-off academics than on the most basic needs of human beings in general, in the vast, unsheltered expanses of the real world around us. If a person is too poor or too ignorant to make use of supposedly available liberty, this, to Rawls, does not make him or her less free. Instead, it affects negatively the *worth* of liberty, although Rawls makes it clear that, with the two basic principles taken together, the end of social justice requires that 'the basic structure is to be arranged to maximize the worth to the least advantaged of the complete system of liberty shared by all." From *Strategies of Political Emancipation* (Notre Dame: University of Notre Dame Press, 1981), 21.

Many economic rights skeptics, in this modern debate, are also libertarians. For such skeptics the limitation of an individual's freedom is suspect; it can be overridden, but only by a showing that the limitation actually works to **secure** the individual's liberty. It can also be overridden by a showing that the limitation is a check on outlandish actions that are likely to harm other individuals, particularly in the expression of their liberty. Thus one is not free to falsely shout "fire" in a crowded theater, or to take whatever catches one's eye without compensating the owner of the property. Such curtailments on liberty are defended as actions taken to secure the liberty and security of all individuals in society, as well as their rights to property. Narveson's previously referred to preference for individual liberty is a characteristic preference of economic rights skeptics.[76]

In direct contrast with these views, proponents for economic rights tend to favor an equal emphasis on "well-being."[77] Are these human values mutually exclusive, independent, or mutually interdependent? Skeptics maintain that well-being is, at best, independent from liberty; at worst it is incompatible.

The Undue Burden on the State Objection

This objection is another incompatibility objection that directs our attention away from the rights and duties of the individual, and focuses on the obligations of states in a rights-based society. Tibor Machan, a libertarian, insists upon the need to show the legitimacy of governmental force in the process of protecting rights.[78] Machan's response is well-grounded in traditional liberal understandings of the State. According to liberal theory, the State has the strict

---

[76] For a good discussion of this inclination as well as its problems, see Christian Bay, *Strategies of Political Emancipation* (Notre Dame: Notre Dame Press, 1981), Chapter One.

[77] A full determination of this economic rights partisan preference will be demonstrated in Chapter Four.

[78] Tibor Machan, "Moral Myths and Basic Positive Rights," *Positive and Negative Duties*, ed. Eric Mack (New Orleans: Tulane University Press, 1985): 37.

obligation to maintain law and order, and to do so without violating the liberty rights of individuals.[79] By keeping its part in the social contract, the State is entitled to have the monopoly on the use of force to settle disputes as well as the right to collect taxes to maintain the society. For Hayek, Machan, and others, all interventions beyond these minimum actions are suspect. Such interventions have to be justified by special pleading, and they have to be carefully examined to see what effect they might have on the autonomy and agency of the individual, as well as the legitimate limited powers of the government. For all of these reasons Machan cannot countenance economic rights. His objection echoes Cranston; namely, that the State should not be unduly burdened in providing goods to its citizens.[80] Such actions give the State too much power and involve it in affairs that are none of its business. Machan writes:

> Shue, along with Ronald Dworkin and James Nickel, fails to understand that the existence of the government or state is morally problematic. For example, where did the state derive its authority to restrain those who would violate our rights, that we might enjoy without this violation? Not just anyone is justified in breaking up a fight, halting a trespasser, apprehending and incarcerating embezzlers, etc. And how does its rights to the resources needed to provide protection arise? Not just anyone is justified in securing fees and property from potential victims of murder, assault, and theft for

---

[79] For a classic statement of limited duties, see Hayek, *The Constitution of Liberty*, Chapter 12.

[80] The basic responsibility of the liberal State is to protect rights. This duty can be complicated by an illegitimate proliferation of rights. Further, the State is to be entrusted with as little power as necessary for the protection of rights. To insist that the State attend to tangential duties, and to empower it to do so is bad for several reasons. First it is bad because it may distract the State from attending to its main duties. Secondly it is bad in that it may give the State more power than it needs and tempt it to be intrusive. Thirdly it is bad because new false rights may require the State to do more than is possible. Thus the duty of the State to protect the rights of individuals is closely related to, but not identical with, its duty to refrain from using too much power or to perform tasks that are intrusive or impossible.

the sake of rendering the services which fend off such actions.[81]

Machan justifies government on neo-Hobbesian grounds; individuals must submit to the State, the one power under the rule of law that is capable of preventing the war of all against all. It is for this reason that he insists on the lexical priority of negative rights and duties over positive rights and duties, as did Feinberg, Hayek, and Narveson. For Machan, the state is justified, if it is justified at all, precisely because it serves to protect negative rights, without taking on other "questionable" duties. Similarly, the ability of the State to tax is also derived from its primary duty to protect negative rights.[82] Even the notion of duty is, in his thought, tied to the State. He writes:

> Citizens, upon having established and/or consented to live under a government which exists so as to protect their basic rights, owe their government certain (agree upon) duties--payments for services, participation in administration, cooperation in crime detection and prevention, offering testimony in the pursuit of justice, etc.[83]

Still, he is aware of an obvious concern, namely, the contested assertion that government should not limit itself to protecting only negative rights. Machan's response is that:

> Government ought to be established to do something unique, namely fend off and contain human aggression through very precise and well specified means - due process of law. It ought to do this because human aggression is morally culpable. It is not just any obstacle or danger. Inviting it to handle categorically different tasks-e.g., combat the dangers we face from nature, our own folly, etc.-would threaten its integrity. Government's unique task, securing our (negative) rights to life, liberty, property, etc., ought not be mixed

81 Tibor Machan, "Moral Myths and Basic Positive Rights," 37. For a similar libertarian view, see Sheldon Wein's essay, "Libertarianism and Welfare Rights," *Philosophical Essays on the Ideas of a Good Society*, ed. Yeager Hudson and Creighton Peden (Lewiston: Edwin Mellen Press 1988), 157-67.
82 See Machan, "Moral Myths and Basic Positive Rights," 39.
83 Ibid., 39.

with the tasks that human beings ought to strive to carry out in peaceful cooperation.[84]

Machan's explanation for a limited government is, however, problematic. He is correct in assuming that human aggression is a real danger in the world. Yet he offers us no compelling reason to distinguish between human aggression expressed by tyrannical forces in a market economy from the human aggression expressed by a tyrannical government. If social aggression and tyranny are bad for people, does it make a real difference that private super-forces, giant corporations for example, are terrorizing people, on a wide-spread basis, rather than the State?[85]

Machan writes as if only civil and political rights (the rights to be free from assault, false imprisonment, censorship, religious freedom, and freedom of speech) were of value, and were the only rights susceptible to threats from societal forces. It is in this way that he is a proponent of a certain wing in the liberal tradition. Unfortunately Machan seems to be unduly influenced by the history of just one stream of first generation rights discourse in which the State was characterized as both the securer of many natural rights as well as the chief threat to many natural rights. So influenced, Machan's view of security is too limited. Hobbes' war of all against all may have been, initially, a root metaphor based upon physical security from violence, but in the further developed world economy of modernity the war of all against all may also be a good root metaphor for laissez-faire capitalism. As we will soon see in

---

84 Ibid., 40.

85 This question demonstrates additional rhetorical force if one considers, for example, the Colombian drug cartel. In this instance a giant corporation is able to threaten and destabilize a government as well as violating the security, freedom,and economic rights of citizens. No one questions the rights of the Columbian government to oppose and destroy this cartel (with due process of law of course). Is this acceptance given only because the drug cartel is breaking the law and killing people? Would the government be morally entitled to oppose a cartel if the cartel's offense consisted of the diversion of land from the production of local food staples into the production of a cash crop whose profits were not distributed to the growers and led to an equal number of deaths? This is a question that will be addressed in Chapter Four.

Chapter Four of this study, Henry Shue, an economic rights partisan, makes this claim. The persuasiveness of Machan's position cannot be fully assessed without Shue's response and a critical assessment of his arguments. As it stands, Machan's position flags certain issues that will have to be addressed by economic rights partisans. Partisans will have to show how and why a limited government should use coercion on behalf of economic rights. If they cannot do this, their endorsement of economic rights *will* conflict with civil and political rights. Since this kind of conflict is unacceptable to the West, the case for economic rights should fail at that point. We must now address the pejoristic objections.

Pejoristic Objections: The Case Against the Irresponsible Poor

Pejoristic objections are our third and final family of economic rights objections. These objections are not directly derived from Cranston's work, yet they can be considered a practical extension of Cranston's practicability test. These objections are powerful because they make the other objections moot if they are accepted. If aid to the poor cannot effectively help them satisfy their basic needs to subsistence because it encourages the poor to act irresponsibly, then their rights claims are pointless. In such a world, all of the state's or societies' actions will be, like the King's horses and the King's men in the old nursery rhyme, unable to "put Humpty Dumpty back together again." These objections that we have called pejoristic objections have two relatively simple theses. The first thesis is that the poor should not be helped because they simply reproduce more poor people and exhaust the "commons" in the process of maintaining and developing life. The primary theorist for this objection is a noted bio-ethicist, Garrett Hardin. For Hardin, the poor cannot be helped because scarcity will not allow poverty to be eliminated, and the poor insist upon reproducing themselves. By doing so they insure on a permanent and inter-generational basis that the "poor will be with us always."

In two influential essays Hardin makes it clear that Malthusian logic is not dead, albeit recast in modern ecological engineering terms.[86] Hardin, a professor of human ecology, concludes that, "The population problem has no technical solution; it requires a fundamental extension in morality."[87] For him, the population problem must be controlled by the poor themselves, and they should not be prevented from solving their population problems by misguided assistance from the wealthy. In short, Hardin offers a modern version of Malthus' warning regarding population.[88] Hardin favors coercion--a mutual coercion in which society compels its members to refrain from breeding at a rate above the carrying rate of the commons.[89] For

---

[86] Garrett Hardin, "The Tragedy of the Commons," *Science* 162, no. 3859 (13 December 1968):1243-1251. See also, Garrett Hardin, "Living on a Lifeboat," *BioScience* 24, no. 10 (October 1974): 561-569.

[87] Hardin,"The Tragedy of the Commons," 1243.

[88] Thomas Malthus wrote the well-known essay entitled, *An Essay on the Principle of Population* (Homewood, Illinois: Richard D. Irwin, Pub., 1963). Malthus' argument was deceptively simple and stated in a mathematical formula: population, if unchecked, increases geometrically while food supplies are increased only arithmetically. If people do not control their rate of reproduction, it will swiftly outstrip their productive capacities. Nature will then have to intervene to restore the balance by means of famine and diseases. With such an understanding of the world, Malthus objected to the provision of basic goods to the poor as interfering in the natural course of events, as in fact, promoting poverty and suffering, and as threatening the well-being of "haves." Arblaster, liberal theory commentator, understands Malthus as maintaining that: "any thing that improves the condition of the poor will encourage them to have children, thus creating more poor, but not creating more wealth. Therefore the poor will get poorer as they get more numerous." See Anthony Arblaster, *The Rise and Decline of Western Liberalism*, 245. Not surprisingly then, Malthus was constrained to oppose the socially ameliorating legislation of his time: the Poor laws. Malthus may rightfully be called the father of "lifeboat ethics." In a lifeboat conceptualization of life, people are caught in a zero-sum game. If the poor are to do better in society, it can only be at the expense of the wealthy. For Malthus, duties to provide for others were first and foremost familial: a poor man and his wife simply should not have many children if they could not adequately provide for them. The State on the other hand, clearly did not incur certain obligations just because, within its territorial limits, new needs in the form of new mouths were created.

[89] Hardin, "The Tragedy of the Commons," 1246.

him, the possibility of an optimum population can be arrived at, if at all, when a given population growth rate is zero. He demands therefore that births and deaths hit an equilibrium. Like Malthus, Hardin cannot logically agree to meeting the needs of the "irresponsible poor."[90] The responsible poor, in his opinion, curtail their breeding until they become self-sufficient. Accordingly, for him, economic rights are simply counter-productive, or pejoristic. Hardin makes this position clear in his use of the root metaphor of the "lifeboat":

> Metaphorically, each rich nation amounts to a lifeboat full of comparatively rich people. The poor of the world are in other, much more crowded lifeboats. Continuously, so to speak, the poor fall out of their lifeboats and swim for a while in the water outside, hoping to be admitted to a rich lifeboat, or in some other way to benefit from the "goodies" on board. What should the passengers on a rich lifeboat do? This is the central problem of "the ethics of a lifeboat."[91]

His solution to this dilemma is to:

> Admit no more to the boat and preserve the small safety factor [a margin of error in carrying capacity]. Survival of the people in the lifeboat is then possible (though we shall have to be on our guard against boarding parties).[92]

Just as Malthus opposed the Poor Laws of England, Hardin rails against the possibility of a World Food Bank.[93] And he is diametrically opposed to unlimited immigration. Rights, for him, are never "sacred things" (to borrow Cranston's term). The rights to reproduction, food, immigration and other benefits are all contextually and prudentially derived. In his thought, the concern of "haves" is not with their rights, but with their duties:

---

[90] It should be noted that Malthus was influential. As Arblaster recounts, the reasons that British officials gave for not intervening in the Irish potato famine were primarily Malthusian. So also were the reasons for the implementation of the New Poor Law and the creation of workhouses. See Arblaster, *The Rise and Decline of Western Liberalism*, 244.

[91] Hardin, "Living on a Lifeboat," 562.

[92] See Arblaster, *The Rise and Decline of Western Liberalism*, 245.

[93] Hardin, "Living on a Lifeboat," 567.

specifically their duties to their posterity. Lest Hardin be thought to be absolutely egoistic and cynical we must consider the driving motive behind his work: our duties to our posterity. As Hardin puts it:

> To be generous with one's own possessions is one thing; to be generous with posterity's is quite another. This, I think, is the point that must be gotten across to those who would, from a commendable love of distributive justice, institute a ruinous system of the commons, either in the form of a world food bank or that of unrestricted immigration.[94]

So, for Hardin, a form of Social Darwinism is the logical order of the day. In his opinion, economic rights are not just a trivialization of "true" human rights, but life-threatening concepts for creating disastrous policies. Pleas for aid are, in his opinion, the abject grasping of drowning people for life-preservers in a tempestuous sea that has a permanent shortage of life-preservers. By enabling the poor to live and breed, economic rights only insure, in his opinion, the inevitability of a larger "emergency" in a later generation. By way of Malthusian premises, Hardin is thus able to come to his conclusion: the poor cannot be effectively helped, so they should not be assisted. His argument is, nonetheless, distinctive in economic rights skepticism since he departs from traditional American "natural," or first generation rights discourse, as his primary focus is not on liberty, but sustainability and security. For Hardin no individuals are to maximize their interests without reference to the others in the "lifeboat." Thus he is one economic rights skeptic who does not categorically prefer liberty over welfare. Hardin's position is, however, a full-blown extension of Cranston's "practicability" test. He obviously does not believe, however, that even civil and political rights are immune to the necessary application of coercion. This position contrasts with that of most economic rights skeptics. Economic rights are, from his perspective, incompatible with civil and political rights. They are also objectionable due to their "impracticability" in terms of successful performance.

---

94 Paul Streeten, "Basic Needs and Human Rights," *World Development* 8, (February 1980), 107.

Turning to another pejoristic objector we find Paul Streeten of the World Bank. Streeten asks bold and important questions:

> Is the satisfaction of basic needs a human right? Are minimum levels of nutrition, health and education among the most fundamental human rights? Is there a human right not to be hungry? Or are human rights themselves basic needs? Are there basic needs other than material needs which embrace human rights? Do the respect for rights and the satisfaction of needs go together or can there be conflict?[95]

Streeten's argument is that the poor cannot be effectively helped by the recognition of their economic rights. This thesis is based upon his historical reading of economic rights implementations. With regard to the economic right to education, Streeten writes, "In Africa and Asia, the experience has been that a very high proportion, sometimes as many as four-fifths, of those educated in primary schools drop out or forget what they learn soon after, so that educational efforts on them are wasted."[96]

----

[95] Streeten also raises the familiar problem of calling aspirations--needs. Streeten is careful to break the concept of human rights down into four categories, placing economic rights in the fourth category that he calls "most controversial" Streeten, "Basic Needs and Human Rights. 108. Part of what makes such rights controversial for some skeptics is their cost. However, Streeten never compares the economic costs of recognizing and implementing civil and political rights to the costs of providing economic rights. By fiat Streeten dismisses the costs for the former rights, while exaggerating the costs of the latter rights.

[96] Streeten's reasoning is similar to Lord P. T. Bauer, who maintains that aid to the foreign poor is poor policy, because the foreign poor are inherently incapable of using outside help. Such aid is given (mistakenly, in Bauer's opinion) to ease the bad consciences of the West. See Bauer's *Equality, the Third World, and Economic Delusion* (Cambridge: Harvard University Press, 1981), 23-5 and 120-21. Bauer maintains that colonialism and slavery were good for the Third World, because of the elimination of certain diseases and the introduction of modern economic practices. Ibid., 73. Bauer also writes, "As late as the second half of the nineteenth century, Black Africa was without even the simplest, most basic ingredients of modern social and economic life." Ibid., 72. Such views are ridiculous, especially in regards to

Streeten's pejoristic objection constitutes a second thesis, and a weaker pejoristic objection. This thesis maintains that the poor are incapable of using the benefits of their economic rights due to defects in their nature, and/or defects in their economic system.[97] Streeten points out that even those who become educated, that is who prove themselves to be normal rather than defective, have gravitated to cities. There they became unemployed and "frustrated" due to the scarcity of jobs suited to their training. In this scenario, the prevailing economies cannot properly utilize their newly acquired skills. The weakness of this argument lies in how Streeten employs it. He uses his historical examples as if they expressed some sort of immutable, political law. For Streeten, most Asians and Africans don't learn, and if they do, their economies are too underdeveloped to absorb "the learned" and to effectively use their education. Streeten offers no data for these conclusions, but even assuming that his assertions are empirically true, they do not provide us with a principled argument against economic rights. Streeten's observations instruct us, if they instruct at all, that policy makers should take great care to construct and implement economic rights theories that are well coordinated with the overall economy. Furthermore, his argument never questions the appropriateness of the education that has been "given"

African social life. In Bauer's mind, Africans must have simply fumbled around for millennia, waiting for the West to give them a social life. Bauer's views do not constitute a direct formal argument against economic rights. Yet if they are given credence, the result would be to incline people to reject the distribution of foreign aid. If such aid is an economic right designed to assist "foreigners," then the effect is the denial of their economic rights. Since what is at issue in this argument is not the "foreignness" of the international poor, but their inability to benefit from aid, Bauer's arguments are easily transferable to our domestic poor and our domestic understandings of economic rights.

[97] Whether or not educational rights are in fact economic rights, cannot now be discussed. Chapter Six discusses the problems that the designation of educational rights as economic rights poses for economic rights theory. Our examination of the issue here is due solely to the construction of Streeten's argument. Here he is challenging the notion of economic rights by challenging educational rights. Streeten is not wrong to conclude that many consider educational rights to be economic rights, since they are listed as such in the International Covenant for Social, Economic and Cultural Rights.

historically to Africans and Asians, or the possible intrinsic value of education for other then purely economic uses.[98]

Streeten's arguments show that some historical implementations of economic rights have been mismanaged; but his arguments do not constitute logical, persuasive objections to the concept of economic rights.[99] And his arguments do not show that the poor cannot be effectively helped by aid. At best, Streeten's arguments may demonstrate that the economic rights that he refers to were, historically, ineffectively implemented.

Pejoristic objections, however, more than any of the other objections, discourage people who are concerned about poverty from considering economic rights, or investigating the causes of poverty. They discourage investigations because they often interpret economic rights claims as attempts by "losers" to blame the successful for their "failures."[100]   For example consider Charles Frankel's observation regarding economic rights:

---

[98] Even assuming for the sake of the argument that Streeten is correct, and only one fifth of the Africans and Asians who receive "education" actually learn from "Western" education, at least those students have benefitted from their education, and, presumably, are now better prepared to handle social, economic, and political responsibilities. If they are not, then the education was obviously ill-suited to their needs.

[99] The management of rights is a continuous public discussion. Civil rights regarding affirmative action are criticized as being mismanaged. Constitutional protection for criminals is currently being criticized as being mismanaged, or misinterpreted. The important point is not which side is correct on the issue of mismanagement; rather, what should be recognized is that rights are never absolutely fixed in their interpretations. Rights are constantly being reinterpreted, as they are subject to changes in human relations.

[100] Myron Magnet recently wrote an influential essay along these lines, entitled, "The Rich and the Poor: Are the Haves Responsible for the Disquieting Plight of the Have-Nots?," *Fortune* 117, (6 June 1988): 206-20.   Magnet dismisses William J. Wilson's book, *The Truly Disadvantaged*, in favor of the culture of dependency thesis of Thomas Sowell, *Civil Rights: Rhetoric or Reality?* (New York: William Morrow, 1984).   The debates between Wilson and Sowell are likely to rage for years.   Economic rights are unlikely to be effective if their implementation must await a consensus with regards to the causes of poverty.

> But the language of rights gives them [sources of poverty, such as corruption, callousness, a desire to maintain positions of privilege] excessive attention. It simplifies and obscures the underlying issues. It suggests that peoples' deprivations are due in the main neither to the scarcities of nature nor to their own habits and preferences but to the misdeeds of others. It encourages a search for villains, and an impatience with the slow ways of freedom.[101]

Frankel's remarks imply that poverty is caused primarily by forces primarily attributable to the poor. Accordingly, attention to outside forces "simplifies and obscures the underlying issues." If in fact the poor are a significant cause for their own poverty, as is implied in Frankel's comments, then aid to them may well be fruitless, and or counter-productive. But his assertion that the claim for economic rights "encourages a search for villains" fails to offer any proof regarding the causes of poverty. It is therefore problematic. Frankel's comments imply that people spend too much time looking for scapegoats rather than finding the "real" cause of poverty. He also implies that there is a correlation between sustainability and the "slow ways of freedom." That there may be a correlation between the establishment of freedom and the establishment of economic sufficiency is not, however, the issue. Frankel is inclined to deny economic rights because the claims for such may encourage a search for villains, that is, the wealthy as villains. His position presupposes that there are no "wealthy villains" to be found, i.e., he presupposes that the wealthy do not contribute significantly to poverty. This presupposition would be much more convincing if it were accompanied by a demonstration, theoretical or otherwise, that the wealthy seldom victimize the poor. Frankel implies, however, that people are poor not because of the possible misdeeds of "haves," but because of the scarcities of nature and/or their own bad habits and foolish

---

101 William J. Wilson's review of Charles Murray's *In Pursuit of Happiness and Good Government,* appears to be devastating, Wilson criticizes Murray for ignoring wholesale, vast sources of literature that "flatly contradicts the premises of his argument." From Wilson's "The Charge of the Little Platoons," published in the *New York Times Review of Books,* (23 October 1988): 12.

preferences. Claims that poverty might have some external causes are, in his opinion, a dangerous overstatement. Economic rights claims are, in this scenario, self-seeking, delusional, and projectionist. However, Frankel never seriously considers the possibility that poverty might be caused, at least in part, by forces external to the poor. He never seems to seriously consider that the external causes for poverty might be attributable to organizations and causes that the government ought to be able to regulate, or at the least, to try and regulate.

Frankel's failure to consider this possibility constitutes a form of question-begging. If poverty is presumed to be caused primarily by the poor themselves, then there can be few other forces for the government to regulate, and therefore only a slight chance that the government has failed to perform its duties. From this perspective, the poor can have no rights/claims against the government because there is little "positive" that the government can do. The performance of a duty always implies the ability to perform the duty. In summation, the "poor cannot be effectively helped" objection is only as persuasive as its explanations of the causes of poverty and its evaluation of the use that the poor make of aid to them. Yet Frankel's assumption that the wealthy are innocent of any contributions to the creation and continuation of poverty conflicts with classic liberal economic theory that has continued to influence these discussions.

Classic liberal theory assumed that poverty was a necessary by-product of laissez-faire capitalism and ineradicable from a free-market society. This thesis posited that without a free market there could be no great wealth; however, with a free market, there was no way to eliminate poverty.[102]

---

[102] Barry Bluestone, A modern critic of capitalism, concludes that capitalism is the primary cause of poverty. As a consequence, governmental interventions into economic relations are mandatory in his opinion. He writes: "Within the context of a capitalist economy, expanding public welfare programs are the only significant alternative to explosive political discontent. And they will remain the only alternative, for to remove the *cause* of uneven development would require the replacement of the fundamental principle of capitalism--private investment decision. Within a capitalist economy, then, poverty is the natural outcome. Whether it is 'functional' or not is an incidental question. The ultimate contradiction of capitalism is

Finally, this thesis maintained that government was not designed to be distributive, but to protect the economic hegemony of the wealthy. Adam Smith, the father of modern liberal economics, bluntly acknowledged this position when he wrote, "Law and government, too, seems to propose no other object but this; they secure the individual who has enlarged his property, that he may peaceably enjoy the fruits of it . . ."[103] Smith also wrote:

> Law and government may be considered in this, and indeed in every case, as a combination of the rich to oppress the poor, and preserve to themselves the inequality of goods which would otherwise be destroyed by the attacks of the poor.[104]

Smith assumed that laissez-faire capitalism would generate substantial inequality: "Wherever there is great property there is great inequality. For one very rich man there must be at least five hundred poor, and the affluence of the few supposes the indigence of the many."[105] Yet as Arblaster rightfully argues, Smith was troubled by poverty.[106] Smith also

---

that it tends inevitably to lead to a secular deterioration between classes in society. In the long run this secular deterioration or uneven development leads to political instability. the only recourse to this process imposes an ever greater economic cost on the bourgeois state." "Capitalism and Poverty in America: a discussion," *Monthly Review* 24, no. 2, (June, 1972): 65-77, 71.

103 Adam Smith, as quoted in Donald Winch's work, *Adam Smith's Politics* (Cambridge: Cambridge University Press, 1978), 68.

104 Ibid., 58. The original quotation is from Smith's *Lectures on Jurisprudence*, ed. R. L. Meek, D. D. Raphael, and P. G. Stein, (Oxford: Oxford Univ., 1977): 15.

105 Adam Smith, as quoted by Anthony Arblaster in *The Rise and Decline of Western Liberalism*, 241. The original quotation is from Smith's *The Wealth of Nations* II (London: Dent/Everyman, 1910): 199.

106 Arblaster notes that, although Smith understood poverty to be a byproduct of capitalism, he did not believe that it was a permanent feature of society. Arblaster comes to this conclusion by maintaining that Smith was ambiguous in this area, and confident that the prosperity of capitalism would eventually drive out poverty. Amartya Sen understands Smith to be more compassionate than many of his followers. He notes that in regards to the Poor Laws: "He was opposed to suppressing or restricting trade. But this did not imply that he was against public support for the poor. Indeed unlike Malthus, Smith was

maintained that: "No society can surely be flourishing and happy, of which the greater part of the members are poor and miserable."[107] Yet despite his uneasiness, Smith believed that the market system, with checks on monopolies, was the engine to create more wealth and a better life for people. Poverty, in this scenario, can only be minimized by the poor themselves. The State, in particular, must be careful not to intervene, since it is usually considered to be the chief threat to individual rights.[108] Yet the State is also often the guardian of rights. From this point of view economic rights should not be extended to the poor because to do so would be to abrogate the freedom rights and responsibilities of the poor. Constant intervention would also encourage dependency in the poor: this response would be pejoristic, i.e., only likely to exacerbate the problem.

It should be noted that some pejoristic objectors maintain that poverty is not caused by the structure of the market system, but by character defects in the poor themselves. Streeten, among others, is not making categorical objections to economic rights. Instead he is making categorical qualifications on economic rights. His understanding of economic rights is to recognize and to extend them, but to do so only under certain conditions and only to certain poor people. These theories of economic rights maintain that some people in the world are defective, but since the defect is in the character of the indigent, attempts from the wealthy cannot help because there are some

---

not opposed to Poor Laws, though he did criticize it for the harshness and counterproductive nature of some of the restrictive rules affecting the beneficiaries." *On Ethics and Economics* (Oxford: Basil Blackwell, Pub., 1987), 25-26.

[107] Arblaster, *The Rise and Decline of Western Liberalism* , 242.

[108] For a good article on classical economic thought on the ineradicability of poverty (which ascribes such views to Malthus and David Ricardo) see Vernon E. Sweeney's article, "A Note on Classical Economics," *Social Science* 52, no. 2 (Spring 1977): 90-93. Sweeney notes: "Following the Industrial Revolution, classical economics of the 18th century becomes in the 19th century a theory of economic development, a doctrine of capital. If the increase of the wealth of nations depends on the accumulation of capital, then poverty is justified as involuntary saving and the poor suffer currently for the future good of all. This is a proposition well known to citizens of developing countries. The doctrine of capital is more optimistic than the doctrine of sin; but for both, evil exists." Ibid., 91.

things that money can't buy, such as character and a work ethic.[109]

According to this pejoristic thesis the foreign poor are the unfortunate occupants of poor, economically primitive countries. These foreign poor may be subjects in authoritarian societies in which a ruling elite is unable, or unwilling, to use basic goods at hand (domestic surplus, or donated foreign aid) for meeting the needs of the people.[110] The economy in these countries is characterized as needing development, usually along the lines of Western democracies. At some point in the

---

[109] Hans Morgenthau expresses succinctly this argument, on an international scale in his discussion of the appropriateness of foreign aid: "Yet a nation may suffer from deficiencies, some natural and insuperable, others social and remediable, which no amount of capital and technological know-how supplied from the outside can cure. The poverty of natural resources may be such as to make economic development impossible. Nations such as Jordan and Somalia are in all likelihood permanently incapable of economic development for that reason. Many of the nations which are the perennial recipients of subsistence aid are likely to fall in the same category. A nation may also suffer from **human deficiencies** which preclude economic development. As there are individuals whose qualities of character and level of intelligence make it impossible for them to take advantage of economic opportunities, so are there nations similarly handicapped. To put it bluntly: as there are bums and beggars, so are there bum and beggar nations. They may be the recipients of charity, but short of a miraculous transformation of their collective intelligence and character, what they receive from the outside is not likely to be used for economic development." (Emphasis added) Hans Morgenthau, "Political Theory of Foreign Aid," *American Foreign Policy in International Perspective* (Englewood Cliffs: Prentice-Hall, 1971), 246.

[110] Ibid., 247. Morgenthau's criticism is not a racist understanding of differences among differing humans. It is instead a pragmatic understanding of the power relations, especially the land control issues, that often persist between Third World elites and have nots. For Morgenthau, donor nations have the extremely difficult task of trying to help the poor while trying to also uphold a basic tenet of foreign policy ethics: namely, that nations should be very careful to avoid intervening in the internal affairs of foreign nations. Aid that may assist the poor in overthrowing oppressive elites must be understood as a form of interventionism. If so, it must, from an ethical point of view, be justified as a morally acceptable form of intervention. This second justification is a difficult one and is also beyond the scope of this study.

future, provided civil and political liberties are honored, impoverished countries should be able to duplicate enough of the success of the West so as to meet the basic needs of their people.[111] Since they will be able to take care of themselves in the future without outside aid they will not need it then, and cannot effectively use it now. Many, but not all, of the domestic poor, are characterized as persons who have never learned or acquired employment skills, or have never developed good work habits, or have never striven to stay in the job market (that is why they are bums).[112] Instead, these domestic poor have been content to live off of a public dole of varying sorts, and to make irritating demands for more aid from the economically successful and responsible. In this objection, aid for the "depraved" foreign and domestic poor is simply a dependency inducing palliative that acts to curb initiative, good work habits, innovation, and risk taking. According to this view, the easiest, surest, and most demeaning option for the poor to exercise is to accept the dole. Good government should not, however, give

---

[111] Ibid., 246. Michael Novak echoes this sentiment, writing: "Many in the world are indeed hungry. But there is a prior issue. Less than half the world--barely a third is free. More than two-thirds is slave. . . Hunger, or at least poverty, is the long-trend line of the human race. Such poverty did not begin with the present generation or with present-day economic systems. . . If [President Carter] wishes to end hunger and poverty, let him first break the shackles of whole empires of the unfree." *The March of Defeat: Morality and Foreign Policy* (Washington, D. C.: Georgetown University Press, 1978), 38, 41-42.

[112] Charles Murray, author of *Losing Ground: American Social Policy, 1950-1980* (New York: Basic Books, 1984), is a major theorist regarding the moral inadequacies of the domestic poor. Murray's work is not extensively reviewed herein because he is not a rights theorist. Murray's work, however, is worthy of notice because of its attribution of poverty to the failures of the poor, which implies that economic rights recognitions are pejoristic in their results. Michael Novak also notes along these lines, that: "Yet optimism about workfare must be tempered by the facts of behavioral dependency. Too many citizens are not employable, less because they lack skills--since many new jobs require only minimal skills--than because their life patterns and habits ill-prepare them for the independence of free citizens." From Novak's editorial, "Attacking Problems Money Can't Solve," *New York Times,* (22 March 1987), sec. F, p. 2.

them this opportunity. As a consequence of economic dependency, and passivity, the "depraved" poor never effectively interact with economic institutions, or create new wealth. They are, instead, "drains" on the economy. The specifics of this objection in relation to economic rights take differing forms.

The only commentator of note on this point is Michael Novak, who has been previously characterized as an economic rights skeptic.[113] Novak's association with economic rights skepticism is based upon a 1982 essay.[114] Novak's most recent writings have recanted his previous position, opting instead for a qualified support for economic rights.[115] His support is, however, for the "deserving poor" and an indictment of the "depraved" poor. In a recent essay entitled, "The Rights and Wrongs of 'Economic Rights': A Debate Continued," Novak attempts to state more precisely his views on economic rights and why some of the poor should not be helped. Novak explains that, "Able-bodied persons do **not** have a right to be dependent upon others, **unless** through no fault of their own they cannot meet their own responsibilities."[116] For him, people who can work should work. Within his qualified support for an "economic right," he blames at least some of the poor for their poverty. What he is trying to get at is the notion of "fault" with regard to poverty, or at least in terms of aid. Novak desires to aid the "innocent needy" with a conditional right to economic help. Simultaneously, he wishes to spur malingerers and the

---

113 Novak is resident scholar at the American Enterprise Institute. He was also the former chairperson of the U. S., delegation to the United Nations Human Rights Commission during part of the Reagan Administration.

114 See in particular, Novak's provocative essay, "Human Rights and Whited Sepulchres," *Human Rights and U. S. Human Rights Policy*, ed. Howard J. Wiarda, (Washington: American Institute for Public Policy Research, 1982), 79-82.

115 This shift in Novak's position will be fully addressed in Chapter Five.

116 Michael Novak, "The Rights and Wrongs of "Economic Rights": A Debate Continued," *This World* 17, no. 17 (Spring 1987): 43.

unprepared into maximizing their earning capacities.[117] To do any less would, in his opinion:

> . . . suggest that human persons are universally and necessarily dependent on others, society, or the state for their material necessities, . . . (and to) . . . ignore their inherent and primary responsibilities, which are the very ground of their liberty and dignity.[118]

In Novak's opinion "depraved" poor people are simply lazy: they could, but will not work. They could but will not marry and stay married. They could, but do not use their money wisely. Thus, Novak's partial economic rights objection, which either assigns the causes of poverty to at least some of the poor, and maintains that they cannot or should not be assisted except under very limited circumstances, acts to make claims for economic rights difficult. Yet these pejoristic objections *do assign and concede economic rights to the "deserving" poor, for whom economic rights are not pejoristic.* These arguments acknowledge therefore, albeit grudgingly, the rights to economic assistance to the "working poor." Novak's objection to helping certain poor people has a certain internal logic. If aid does not help people to become self-sufficient, then the aid must be permanent. But a further argument needs to be made to make this objection compelling. Novak should argue that to

---

[117] Novak correctly notes in his most recent writings, the Census Bureau figures that show that three conditions are commonly found in the hard-core poor: eighty-three percent did not work full time year round (in 1988); ninety-three percent did not graduate from high-school; and more than half of the households were families headed solely by women. Thus Novak's prescription for avoiding poverty is to at least graduate from high school, get married, and stay on a job, even if it is minimum wage. Novak concludes from his reading of the census that, "By contrast, the Census Bureau figures show clearly that most poverty in America results from behavior: regarding work, education, and marriage." See "The Truth About Poverty," *Forbes* (11 December 1989), 82. His advice is fine if one wants to marry, and there is a readily available pool of marriageable people, and if one has a sufficiently stable family to allow one to stay in school till graduation, and if one lives in an area with jobs for high school graduates. Assuming that a person may lack one of these conditions, he/she could be in for a tough life.

[118] Ibid., 44.

enable people to be irresponsible, lazy, and dependent is more morally objectionable than allowing them to perish. In contrast to the classic liberal position of Adam Smith, Novak, to his credit, does attempt to explain why aid should be given to the "down-on-their-luck-yet-willing-to-work-poor." In short, this last pejoristic objection is not a complete rejection. It is a qualification that concedes a conditional right to an economic entitlement. This concession is only for those individuals who have basic needs to be met, which remain unmet, due to no fault of their own.

*A Critical Analysis of Economic
Rights Objections*

All of these objections and qualifications are serious and require careful analysis. One of the central questions of this dissertation is whether there is a single, demonstrably "correct" understanding of "human rights" in general, and economic rights in particular. The difficulty of this question was made apparent in Chapter One and has not been resolved.

Cranston, for example, assumes two things in his work. First, he assumes that there is only one way of understanding "human rights," essentially a first generation way. Secondly, he assumes that this traditional way of "interpreting" human rights is, in fact, the "correct" way of interpreting human rights. So predisposed, the three-fold test that Cranston devises, practicability, universalizability, and the paramount importance test "prove" his case. However, Chapter Four will maintain that only one of these tests, the paramount importance test, is applicable to every understanding of economic and other rights. Be that as it may, what is clear at this time is that Cranston, while not a legal positivist, as was Bentham, nevertheless believes that economic rights theories make "no sense." This conclusion is strikingly similar to that which Bentham arrived at in regards to natural rights, that such rights were "nonsense, nonsense upon stilts."[119]

---

[119] Jeremy Bentham believed that even first generation "natural" rights were fictions, due primarily to their lack of positive enactment in English law. It should be noted that Jeremy Bentham was a political liberal as well as a legal positivist. Bentham desired to quell dubious

Turning to the specific categories of objections made against economic rights, we find that these objections center on dialectical relationships between three fundamental values and the power to determine the priority of these values in regard to the State. The first and most important dialectic is concerned with the balance between liberty and well-being, and the social arrangements that are necessary for achieving this balance. The second dialectic to be considered is between the identification of the holders of rights and the bearers of duties. The third dialectic addresses the problem of determining which economic rights express a "paramount importance," i.e., constitute claims for "sacred things." This last dialectic includes the problem of distinguishing between morally compelling objects worthy of rights protection and "desiderata." We conclude our discussion of these dialectical concerns with a consideration of the role of the state in implementing rights. Our critical evaluation will begin with the first dialectic; welfare v. liberty values.

Well-being in Tension with Liberty

The rejection of economic rights is, primarily, a rejection of well-being as an equal value to liberty in the construction and operation of modern society. For many of these theorists liberty is the primary interest, and the State is designed to insure the security of that liberty (a Lockean value orientation). Rights theories that suggest anything other than the lexical priority of liberty over equality, or well-being, are, for these theorists, simply incomprehensible, or incompatible. Such theories introduce values into our society that are, in their opinion, secondary, if not trivial. For most economic rights skeptics, real rights are sacred; they constitute the true moral and political values, not just for America, but for the whole Western world. H. L. A. Hart, for example, may not have felt that liberty was of the highest value, but he did believe that the free ability to

---

claims for "natural" rights because he believed that such claims allowed the powerful in his society to give lip-service to the task of helping the powerless. For Bentham, positive law was the only efficacious protection for the rich and poor, and he wanted help for the poor by recourse to it. Thus he felt constrained to regard natural rights as being, "nonsense, nonsense on stilts." "Anarchical Fallacies," *Human Rights*, ed. A. I. Melden (Belmont, Calif.: Wadsworth, 1970), 30-31.

choose one's actions was. Thus while not having an identifiable "telos" for his theory, he nevertheless realized the difficulty of assigning a universal and absolute value to any rights talk. It was for this reason that he did not insist upon the self-evident quality of rights. Instead, he insisted upon the lexical priority of liberty as the axiological starting point for any rights discussion. The greatest human need for most of these skeptics is freedom. And their understanding of freedom is quite limited. It is not a **freedom to** do anything, or for anything. Rather it is a **freedom from** being coerced into doing things. As we have seen, this view of freedom contrasts greatly with others in the West.[120] The more restrictive notion of freedom, the freedom from, has the benefit of not being morally or culturally imperialistic. Possessors of this type of liberty need answer to no one with regard to what they do with their action and agency. On the other hand, this type of freedom is philosophically and spiritually barren. Freedom here has no content and little sense of social cohesion. It projects a view of society that has no shared goals in sight, or in discussion.

In contrast to "negative freedom," we should consider Green's positive freedom. This understanding of freedom highlights the demands of responsibility to others in ways negative freedom does not. Narveson's right to savor the afternoon sunshine rather than to dig potatoes seems to be self-evident. However, his right to lounge on the beach while another person drowns, where he could have easily effectuated rescue, is not self-evident. It is fairly obvious, therefore, that one's liberty is extremely important, while one's leisure is much less so. As was made clear by L. Duane Willard, rights to liberty are rights that "ought" to be protected, whereas rights to leisure

---

[120] As Rosenbaum observes regarding this issue: "In support of socio-economic rights as human rights, Melvin Rader criticizes certain liberals for their failure to interpret freedom in both its negative and positive senses. Rader insists that negative freedom (translated as civil or First Amendment liberties) is often too narrowly construed as the absence of **governmental restraint** on the unduly powerful can actually facilitate negative freedom. Rader cautions that although civil liberties are necessary, they are not sufficient for a free society." Alan S. Rosenbaum, *The Philosophy of Human Rights: International Perspectives* (Westport: Greenwood Press, 1980), 30.

evoke a lesser moral concern. Accordingly, Narveson's rights theory in which liberty, threats, and assets are described individualistically is psychologically striking, but is also systemically naive. Narveson's analogies fail to consider that modern societies address problems of rights and threats with institutions and systems.[121] More perceptive skeptics, such as Jeane Kirkpatrick and Michael Novak, accept the importance of institutions for the effective implementation of rights. Accordingly, for most theorists the meeting of most paramount importances should be handled, by institutions, systemically. Thus, in a "just" society a system of lifeguards could be instituted to safeguard unfortunate or careless swimmers. In a similar fashion other institutions can also put in place practices that attend to the duty of "digging" potatoes, so to speak, for the societies' indigents, particularly if poverty is seen as a necessary systemic by-product. Such tasks can be financed through taxes and regulated through political representation. Thus Narveson never really needs to fear the dilemma of choosing between savoring summer air and digging potatoes, as long as he is willing to pay his taxes.

What is also problematic for skeptics is their confidence that liberty guarantees happiness or success. For many of them, it is a confession of faith that any and all other goods are obtainable by dint of hard work and luck once liberty has been secured. Thus it cannot be said that they are heedless regarding well-being. It is, however, a secondary concern for them. This confidence in the success of hard work hails back to Adam Smith, who wrote,

> In all the middling and inferior professions, real and solid professional abilities, joined to prudent, just, firm, and temperate conduct, can very seldom fail of success. Abilities will even sometimes prevail where the conduct is by no means correct.[122]

For these writers liberty cannot be secured unless the State's powers have been checked. Rights are therefore trumps

---

[121] The relationship of rights to implementing institutions was addressed in Chapter One. It will be readdressed in Chapter Four.

[122] Adam Smith, *Theory of Moral Sentiments* (Indianapolis: Liberty Classics, 1982) § iii.3.5 (Of Propriety), 63.

by which the State may be kept from interfering in the individual's pursuit of life, liberty and happiness. Social arrangements, such as they are, must be organized along these lines.

Rights Claimants in Tension with Duty-Bearers

From the skeptic's perspective the second value dialectic, the identification of rights-holders and duty-bearers, flows directly from the first. All of these theorists correctly insist upon the correlation of duties to rights embedded within a system of social arrangements. Since they see the implementation of human rights as a struggle between the individual citizen and the State, their identification of the duty bearer of civil and political rights is never at issue. For example, citizens have the responsibility of cooperating with the courts if society is to have a system of law. In this scenario, both rights-claimants and duty-bearers are clearly designated. The State, in this context, must constrain itself to the bounds of the Constitution, Bill of Rights and appropriate case law if these precious rights are to be upheld. Accordingly, the State takes on the self-limiting mantle of restraint as a major governmental duty. The consequences of these social arrangements (for maximized liberty) are such that citizens should, logically speaking, not expect anything but restraint from the government. For such an arrangement it is confusing and distasteful to say that citizens should make, and the government should entertain, demands for anything more then self-restraint. In such a conception of the world, economic rights are unacceptably contradictory whenever their recognition requires a limitation on one's liberty, and the assignment of extra duties and powers to the government. This conclusion is especially appropriate when such rights could also coercively assign "new," and noxious duties to individuals and to governments. What is not acknowledged by the skeptics is the fact that the choice of liberty and a minimalist State (the usual concomitant social arrangement) is not self-evident; it is not a given. Their rights theory, therefore, coordinated with certain appropriate social arrangements, is made in strict accord with an a priori value determination for the lexical priority of liberty. Thus their rights theory is no more justifiable than their a priori value assessment in favor of negative liberty. If in fact the a priori value assessment is incorrect or arbitrary, or limited rather than absolute, then the subsequent rights theories are equally deficient. In any event, such rights can be no more persuasive than their foundational values. Nevertheless, if economic rights skeptics are able to win the value debate, that is, that a good society must first be concerned with liberty over well-being, then ultimate victory in the economic rights debate may fall like a ripe plum in their laps. Turning now to our third dialectic, the problematic contents of and application of economic rights to basic needs, certain concerns come to the fore.

Indeterminacy Problems Reconsidered

Economic rights are, for skeptics, intolerably vague and contradictory when they are not vague. Such rights are vague, for Van De Veer, Willard, Lefever, Cranston, Kirkpatrick, and others, because there is, currently speaking, no universal standard of economic well-being. This is a serious criticism because the content of economic rights appear to be indeterminate. This conclusion is a logical one, since the Object element in the rights definition, is, all too often, difficult to identify. For example, consider the much maligned economic right to a paid vacation. How can the government determine the cost of a "standard" vacation, or even what activities qualify as a vacation? Is a government-paid vacation needed for the "wealthy?" Can such vacations be tied to government jobs, pay levels, or civil service? Should they be? Why? The failure to set forth a limited number of rights-claims objects constitutes a fatal defect to economic rights theory. If economic rights advocates cannot clearly explain how the objects of rights can be identified and limited, then they are bound to lose the economic rights debate. This last problem is also related to the problem of connecting needs to rights, which is usually understood to be a "justifying cause" problem. Economic rights partisans must account for the nexus between needs and rights. If economic rights are to make sense, the skeptics' charge that the connection of needs to rights cannot be made must be dispelled. Van De Veer and Willard were unable to demonstrate that such a connection cannot be made. Yet they clearly showed that economic rights partisans have the burden of putting forth clear explanations of how needs can be connected to rights. How the work of Shue and Gewirth address this challenge will be examined in Chapter Four.

This problem of indeterminacy demands further discussion. If as Hayek suggests the poor could be identified and legally entitled to a negative income tax, some putative economic rights still would not be adequately addressed. For example, a negative income tax will not sustain a critically ill indigent for an extended hospital stay. Illnesses are occurrent, unpredictable and expensive; they are best addressed therefore with a national health service rather than through the poor's attempts to meet their medical needs through market mechanisms. On the other hand, a negative income tax does have the benefit of addressing the problem of indeterminacy on a practical rather than theoretical level.[123] A clear definition of a paramount interest, or a basic good, would not seem to be necessary, theoretically, if the poor were guaranteed through their work and supplemental income sufficient income to meet their basic needs. Yet further reflection reveals that the level of negative income tax needed to address the basic subsistence problems of the poor highlights rather than eliminates the ongoing problem of indeterminacy. How much of a negative income tax is necessary to sustain even the deserving poor? What exactly do the deserving poor need? These rhetorical questions demonstrate the likelihood of a continued debate on the amount of negative income tax needed to adequately assist the poor. Thus, the debate as to what constitutes basic goods and "paramount importance" interests need not stop, or even slow down, with the implementation of a negative income tax.

The Role of Government in the
Implementation of Rights

With regard to the "minimalist State," a few additional critical remarks are in order. Feinberg, Narveson, Streeten and

---

123 Hayek and Friedman suggest the implementation of a negative income tax in lieu of economic rights.

Machan all fail to appreciate certain facts about their preferred minimalist state. First, as even Novak admits, all rights cost![124] Thus simply "minding their own business" by these theorists does respect negative rights, but such "self-restraint" will not, by itself, effectively "implement" even negative rights. All rights, as Kirkpatrick understands the term, are implemented by institutions; some by society, some created by the State. The right to security within a system of procedural justice requires a fairly expensive and active system of police, courts, and prisons.[125] Most importantly, as Machan surely realizes, the system of justice that implements and preserves his beloved negative rights requires the compulsory acquisition of property through taxes along with a host of other civic duties. For example, the duty to go to war in defense of one's country is a fairly heavy duty: one can get killed! Nevertheless, this burden is borne willingly to keep and secure liberty. And, in times of conscription, it is borne even by those who do not value liberty. Assumedly, this form of compulsion is a duty willingly born by economic rights skeptics who champion the maximization of the individual's liberty. It is, of course, a limitation on their liberty.[126] Yet these same theorists resist spending some of their

---

[124] Novak, unlike Feinberg, Narveson, and others, understands that the recognition and implementation of rights are expensive: "Rights do not come free. Each right has a corresponding cost." See "Human Rights and Whited Sepulchres," 79.

[125] As previously mentioned, these costs are not figured into the calculus that Feinberg, and others use. Thus the claim that no real costs are needed to secure rights to liberty is erroneous. The costs of securing liberty rights should be determined and should be compared to the costs of securing economic rights; neither set of rights are free.

[126] Hayek comments extensively on taxation and conscription: "Of course, in some respects the state uses coercion to make us perform particular actions. The most important of these are taxation and the various compulsory services, especially in the armed forces. Though these are not supposed to be avoidable, they are at least predictable and are enforced irrespective of how the individual would otherwise employ his energies; this deprives them largely of the evil nature of coercion. If the known necessity of paying a certain amount in taxes becomes the basis of all my plans, if a period of military service is a foreseeable part of my career, then I can follow a general plan of life of my own making and am as independent of the will of another person as men have learned to be in society. Though compulsory   military

taxes on welfare assistance.[127] They are willing to risk their lives
for the well-being of fellow citizens in a military war, but they
remain unwilling to risk their purses for the well-being of their

---

service, while it lasts, undoubtedly involves severe coercion, and
though a lifelong conscript could not be said ever to be free, a predictable
limited period of military service certainly restricts the possibility of
shaping one's own life less than would for instance, a constant threat of
arrest resorted to by an arbitrary power to ensure what it regards as good
behavior. The interference of the coercive power of government with
our lives is most disturbing when it is neither avoidable nor predictable.
Where such coercion is necessary even in a free society, as when we are
called to serve on a jury or to act as special constables, we mitigate the
effects by not allowing any person to possess arbitrary power of coercion.
Instead, the decision as to who must serve is made to rest on fortuitous
processes, such as the drawing of lots. These unpredictable acts of
coercion, which follow from unpredictable events but conform to
known rules, affect our lives as do other 'acts of God,' but do not subject
us to the arbitrary will of another person." *The Constitution of Liberty*,
143. Hayek's reasoning on taxes and conscription is very interesting. It
should be noticed that his points can easily be applied to economic
rights. A lottery could be devised to conscript young people into serving
a domestic "Peace Corps" that could be assigned any number of tasks that
aid the poor. In the alternative, we could simply pay a certain amount
of taxes to support a negative income tax program. In any case, what can
be done for civil and political rights and benefits can also be done for
economic rights and benefits.

127 Not all libertarians are disturbed over the economic costs of
economic rights. Sheldon Wein, a self-professed libertarian, recognizes
the welfare proviso made by the poor on the rich. However, Wein
comes to a totally different conclusion regarding that proviso. Wein
takes the position that the proviso runs with the title to all property and
therefore he would insist that even under libertarian theory, the rich
should be divested of their property by the state if dire economic needs
demand such an act. This position is similar in effect to that of Thomas
Aquinas, concerning common property although Wein and Aquinas
have totally different views of the world and social justice. This view is
also quite surprising for a libertarian. See "Libertarianism and Welfare
Rights," *Philosophical Essays on the Ideas of a Good Society*, ed. Yeager
Hudson and Creighton Peden (Lewiston: Edwin Mellen Press,1988):
157-67.

fellow citizens in an "economic" war. Of course, fighting a war to keep a country free secures the rights of all of its citizens, rich and poor alike.

Streeten, for example, maintains that the resources that are needed to ensure economic rights must always come from the "rich" and must, therefore, always deprive them of some of their private resources.[128] Streeten never acknowledges explicitly that in the modern world civil and political freedoms are financed basically through taxes. Accordingly, he never explains why it is proper to sacrifice some resources (which presumably come from "rich" individuals and corporations--by way of taxes) to finance police forces and courts, but improper to sacrifice some of those same resources for the systematic protection (including provision of basic needs) of economic rights.[129] Yet the crux of the criticism concerning the role of the State centers upon its supposed functions and its integrity. For Tibor Machan, the integrity of the government is compromised by attempting to compensate for scarcities. Yet Machan, like Frankel, and Streeten, makes this claim by fiat: he offers no explanation or examples to show how helping the poor compromises the government. Hayek asserts the same point by offering a "slippery slope" argument; namely, that once coercion is exercised by government to guarantee anything more than liberty, order, and property rights, it will head unidirectionally and imperceptibly into a totalitarian, chauvinistic State, which absorbs all the power and opportunities that are available.[130]

---

[128] Streeten, "Basic Needs and Human Rights," 109.

[129] Ibid., 109. Streeten never discusses such costs because he is too concerned with addressing what he calls opportunity costs. Opportunity costs, for him, are the costs for compensating the owner of compensated property due to the eminent domain actions of the state. Apparently, Streeten can only assign costs to the compensation of property, rather than the cost of operating a free and democratic society that does not allow the homeless to perish from exposure.

[130] Hayek makes a clear distinction between society and government. Government is to be limited, and is self-limited by means of its recognition of negative rights. Society on the other hand is the proper organization to address positive economic rights. Yet such a society would, in Hayek's opinion, always operate on totalitarian premises. Hayek writes in regards to "employment rights": "It is evident that all these 'rights' are based on the interpretation of society as a deliberately

Since, for example, the United States of America has, at least since Roosevelt's New Deal policies, coerced funds through taxes to secure social security,   Hayek's claims must be thoroughly flawed.   As we will see in Chapter Five, Michael Novak, in contrast to Hayek at least offers the subsidiarity argument to explain why governments should not do some things that smaller organizations could do. [131]

Conclusion

The essential ethical weakness in these positions is now evident. Economic rights skeptics are willing to give up some of their freedoms, such as the right to own and dispose of their property. They are also willing to endure taxation, and even the confiscation of their property in the interests of eminent domain. But these limitations on freedom are tolerated because they are designed to secure their freedom and well-being through specific, acceptable institutions (police, courts, and prisons). Yet, at the same time, they refuse to pay for other institutions and provisions that provide for meeting needs that they can individually acquire: food, shelter, and adequate health care. They believe that civil and political rights benefit both the rich and poor, and therefore should be supported. In contrast, they also believe that entitlements, for which the self-sufficient do not qualify, benefit only the poor. This view is essentially an investment concept of society. In this conception risk aversive calculators of interest reason that since they do not presently need certain goods and services, and do not envision needing them in the future, those goods and services must be secondary values. These secondary values are, in essence, gratuities that

---

made organization by which everybody is employed. They could not be made universal within a system of rules of just conduct based on the conception of individual responsibility, and so require that the whole of society be converted into a single organization, that is, made totalitarian in the fullest sense of the word." In *Law, Legislation and Liberty: The Mirage of Social Justice*, 104. It is for this reason, that Hayek favors only a negative income tax.

[131] Chapter Five discusses subsidiarity fully in relation to the duties of the state; it is primarily a concept most commonly associated with Roman Catholic theorists.

generous people may provide for the unfortunate, voluntarily.[132] Yet if society is simply an investment scheme, the tax paying poor are perhaps being preyed upon rather than the wealthy. The tax paying poor help, of course, to finance the freedom and security of all, including the rich. Yet if their economic status is such as to prevent them from enjoying some of their civil and political rights, then at least some of their money is actually financing the freedom of the wealthy.[133] One right that illustrates this point is the right to foreign travel. Though the poor possess this right legally and morally, it is highly unlikely that they can exercise it.

We must now address certain weaknesses in Novak's arguments. They can be seen by considering the nature of modern poverty, in particular the distinction between the "deserving poor" and the "depraved" poor. Though the causes of poverty are disputed, the occupants of those classes are not. Most studies show that the poor are, to a disproportionately large extent, children.[134] Though many children are, assumedly, able-bodied, they are not usually considered to be the front-line employment force. Accordingly, children, the most vulnerable members of society, created in the imago Dei, might not be assisted under Novak's reading if their parents are shirkers. But

---

[132] See for example the views of one of Reagan's representatives, Jeane Kirkpatrick. She wrote, in "Doctrine of Moral Equivalence," regarding 15.9 billion in economic and military assistance in fiscal year 1985 that such funds served four U.S. interests, one of which was, "Our humanitarian interest in alleviating suffering and easing the immediate consequences of catastrophe on the very poor." "Doctrine of Moral Equivalence," Current Policy No. 580, U. S. Department of State, Bureau of Public Affairs (Washington, D.C.: GPO, 9 April 1984).

[133] This is the point of Christian Bay's criticism of Rawls' lexical priority of liberty. Rawls makes a distinction between equality of liberty and equality of the worth of liberty. Bay feels that the distinction has little merit. From his point of view, not only are the poor unable to equally value some rights, due to their poverty, they also are unable to exercise some rights. See note 76 herein for Bay's criticism.

[134] See Henry Shue, for one such source, *Basic Rights* (Princeton: Princeton University Press, 1980): 97-102. See also William J. Wilson, *The Truly Disadvantaged*, 174-77. Michael Novak is somewhat aware that many of the poor are children. See his provocative article, "The Truth about Poverty," 82.

if children cannot be held morally responsible to feed and clothe themselves, and if their true worth and dignity lies in their recognition as being created in the imago Dei (as is asserted in the Catholic social doctrine that Novak seems to employ), what difference should it make that these permanently deprived children have parents who are shirkers?[135] In contrast, children of poor but willing-to-work parents would be helped and fed in Novak's policy recommendation. Clearly, Novak's distinction could result in an absurd application of policy. Thus, his "real" qualifications for help are not located in the human dignity resulting from one's creation in the imago Dei, but rather lie in presenting evidence of "rugged individualism" and a strong work ethic for the would-be self-reliant poor. Novak never explains, however, how independence and self-sufficiency are encouraged by abandoning people in dire straits, even if their suffering is of their own doing.[136]

What is also doubtful about these qualifications is the complete lack of empirical data that would seem to be needed to present a persuasive argument that poverty is caused by laziness and an unwillingness to work.[137] An unsupported claim that the recognition of economic rights causes people to become subservient also requires some empirical data.[138] These

---

[135] This criticism of Novak anticipates his position that is fully explicated in Chapter Five. Though the fullest statement of his position is located elsewhere, sufficient exposition of his views has been given in this chapter to enable us to discuss some of its strengths and weaknesses.

[136] Novak's point that a government should not encourage dependency is a reasonable one. At the same time, there does not seem to be much sense in refusing to make a bad situation better after a person has exercised bad judgment.

[137] Most observant people have noticed "lazy" people. I have often noted that many of them are not poor. On the other hand, I have known many hard-working, but poor people. I am not offering a theory as to the causes of poverty so much as personal observations that hard work and wealth are not always directly connected. Idleness and leisure are often considered one of the advantages of being wealthy.

[138] Novak's essays clearly make this claim."The Rights and Wrongs of Economic Rights," 44. In another essay, "Free Persons and the Common Good," *Crisis* October 1986, at 19, Novak insists: "Yet it is natural enough that families, provident for their future, desire under modern conditions the sort of security that rural living once afforded. It

arguments, unlike the others, make empirical claims that demand accordingly, empirical proofs. Empirical proof both for and against economic rights is, however, difficult. It is difficult because the reasons for poverty are usually in dispute.[139] Yet Novak's qualified acceptance of economic rights must not be overlooked. From Novak's "Human Rights and Whited Sepulchres" to his latest essays there has been a gradual, evolutionary change in his understanding of rights. Whereas he initially understood economic rights to be categorically incomprehensible, now he sees some of them as being objectionable, and others as necessary. Novak stands, therefore, as a forerunner in the evolutionary movement from economic rights skepticism to a qualified economic rights acceptance. He is, therefore, an example of where the economic rights debate is headed.

As we have seen, however, it is unusual for economic rights skeptics to examine closely the causes of poverty. Instead, they usually assign the causes of poverty to the poor's moral ledger, or attribute the existence of poverty, in a vague fashion, to bad luck, or nature.[140] Still if Garret Hardin is correct, that the State cannot sucessfully intervene to provide basic

---

is not mean of them to do so. But the provision of universal security does choke liberty, innovation, and advance. As parents who overprotect their children reap unintended consequences, so some forms of compassion reduce citizens to a dependence upon the state not altogether different from serfdom. The liberal party cannot only speak of liberty. It must distinguish rigorously among the legitimate and the illegitimate desires for security. The liberal state is certain to be to some extent a welfare state." Novak writes as if people in welfare states are not also dependent on the State for many of the amenities of modern life, such as police protection and fire protection. In any case, it is not self-evident that abandoning lazy people is morally preferable to assisting them.

[139] The causes of poverty are frequently distorted because of class interests and philosophical loyalties. The debates in this area tend to fall into various camps. Charles Murray vs. William J. Wilson, or Michael Harrington (See Harrington's "The Future of Poverty: Faith and Economics-A New Numbers Game," *Commonweal* 111, (November 1984): 625.

[140] Novak's work can be seen as primarily attending to the task of explaining the creation of wealth not poverty.

necessities to the poor, since intervention is per se pejoristic, then logically speaking the State also does not have the duty to put forth its best efforts to intervene sucessfully. According to this logic, the State should only attempt to advise the poor as to how to find employment, or how to run a business, or how to save money, or how to refrain from reproducing. If this logic is pushed to its conclusion one might conclude that the State has, as a reasonable obligation, the duty to hand out free condoms or other contraceptive devices to its poor citizens, but not the duty to distribute even surplus food to starving citizens during a time of excess private production.[141] Hardin's practicability challenge is difficult to meet, but some of the practical conclusions of his policy suggestions appear to be morally absurd. Nevertheless, his pejoristic objections must be dispelled if economic rights are to make any sense.

Finally, we must ask whether economic rights skeptics can give an adequate theoretical explanation for the presence of "welfare" States. Our world is one in which, on an everyday basis, governments enforce antitrust laws, recognize Medicare and welfare, subsidized lunches, and employ the language of rights to do so. Our government, through the FDA, carefully screens what drug manufacturers put on the market. They curtail the freedom of the public to use laetrile, or other unregulated drugs. They regulate the freedom of drug manufacturers to develop markets. In short, modern, industrialized governments already act in a paternalistic fashion, and already provide economic benefits. They do so in democratic societies with majorities that publicly applaud and willingly pay for such paternalism. Such approval cannot itself justify the actions of the government. These actions may be popular, unethical, and unwise. The point is, however, that in addition to making and financing these policies the public apparently feels that what it is doing is not just necessary, or popular, but "right" in the moral sense of that word. This is the importance of the understanding of moral obligations that was demonstrated in Chapter Two in the sentiments and policies of

---

141 The use of condoms or other contraceptives would, presumably, help to limit population, whereas the provision of food could encourage overpopulation.

Presidents Roosevelt and Carter, namely, that the provision of economic benefits is considered to be a duty of the government. Skeptics pay too little attention to the need to account for the current state of social arrangements. This criticism takes on added force if we consider other societies similar to our own.

One of our closest neighbors, geographically, culturally and philosophically is Canada. Canada has an explicitly interventionist system of socialized medicine that has not, apparently, reduced its citizens to child-like dependency.[142] Hayek and Cranston often ask their readers to consider countries that have a full panoply of economic rights, such as communist countries.[143] This comparison to American democracy and wealth always makes our understanding of life, and rights, more attractive than the communist examples. Yet Hayek and Cranston cannot account for the overall success of democratic socialist countries that have had success in implementing economic rights. These countries are not totalitarian, and do not appear to be moving in that direction. Such phenomena cast doubts on Hayek's slippery slope argument that maintains that any coercion on behalf of economic rights guarantees, in the future, the creation of a totalitarian state.[144]

What is most problematic in the economic rights skeptic's theories is their willingness to accept absurd outcomes. From their perspective it is better that the poor die of starvation in freedom than for anyone to have their rights to liberty limited. Hart's lexical priority for liberty is, therefore, constructed so that a person could never demand economic assistance as a matter of right. This conclusion is inescapable no matter the level of over-abundance available in the hands of the wealthy, or the absolute squalor or deprivation of the poor. The rich in such a scenario are doomed to act always as philanthropists and never as siblings or peers. Both parties are doomed here to relate to each other (until the empirical fact of scarcity passes away, or is overcome) through a hazy curtain of deference. In

---

[142] A brief argument for health rights as valid economic rights will be raised in Chapter Six.

[143] Hayek, *Law, Legislation, and Liberty*, 103-4. Cranston, *What Are Human Rights?*, 34.

[144] Ibid.

this caste system haves may help have nots, but never as social equals. Such a system makes servility a permanent feature of modern life; and if haves should not feel generous have nots can simply starve. Not only is equality irrelevant under economic rights skepticism, the evidence of gross inequality is equally immune from philosophical attacks, at least from attacks on the basis of justice considerations. If Malthusian logic is correct, then Walzer's observation is incorrect.[145] If Malthus, Hart, and Hardin are correct, then all that can be said about societies that tolerate gross inequalities in wealth, and allow deaths due to deprivations is that such societies lack charity and compassion, not justice. Chapter Six will demonstrate that not even Adam Smith, no radical egalitarian, accepted this modest an understanding of justice.

It must be acknowledged, however, that equality is not itself a self-evident human value. Accordingly, arguments for economic rights, and the necessary social arrangements such rights demand, must be raised. While it should be recognized that well-being may be a self-evident norm, in that it is self-evident that it is better to be healthy than sick, adequately fed and housed than homeless and starving, these norms do not in themselves impose any duties on anyone other than each individual seeking his/her own well-being. To impose such duties on others requires a persuasive justification. Thus, it must be conceded that economic rights must be clearly justified, economic rights advocates cannot merely explode some economic myths. They must also show how economic rights make sense and why they are morally compelling. The way some have taken up this task is fully detailed in Chapter Four.

---

145 In Chapter One Walzer's criticism of the British abandonment of the Irish during the monumental potato famine maintained that such a government was unquestionably unjust. See Chapter One, page 63, note 117.

CHAPTER FOUR

ECONOMIC RIGHTS--
INDISPENSABLE RIGHTS?

Chapter Three presented us with many objections to economic rights; individually and severally, these objections raise a rebuttable presumption that economic rights trivialize and contradict civil and political rights. Our central hypothesis maintains that these objections to economic rights are incorrect. We suggest that economic rights are inherently interdependent with civil and political rights, and must be recognized and implemented if civil and political rights are to be adequately recognized and implemented. This interdependency thesis is grounded upon the American consensus that clearly interprets civil and political rights as human rights. We posit that the designation of human rights status that has been extended to civil and political rights should also be extended to economic rights. This extension would make economic rights a constant concern and element in public policy formation, including foreign policy. Thus, if our thesis is sustained, economic rights should acquire the deep respect and wide-spread recognition that civil and political rights have acquired. From the viewpoint of economic rights skeptics, however, economic rights are conceptual errors, suspect human rights, novelties, or incomprehensible ideological attempts by the poor to coerce the provisions of basic goods from the wealthy through the distortion of traditional human rights discourse.

The purpose of this chapter is to demonstrate the correctness of our thesis. Accordingly, cogent and coherent

169

moral justifications of economic rights will be presented in order to rebut the economic rights skeptics' negative presumptions. In addition, to be fully persuasive, the proffered theories will specifically answer the previously voiced objections against economic rights. These objections are of three types: incomprehensibility objections, incompatibility objections, and pejoristic objections. The contrasting explanations also will be related in a harmonious fashion to our empirical case study, the human rights theories of the Carter Administration. Most importantly, economic rights will be shown to be inherently interdependent with civil and political rights in a society with a government of limited powers in a democratically constituted welfare entitlement state, such as the modern day United States of America. This chapter presents several explanations of economic rights that meet these criteria. Gewirth, Nickel, Plant, Okin, Peffer, Bay, Kleinig, Sadurski, Shue, Couto, Waldron, Fletcher, and others present us with theories that purport to justify economic rights.[1] The views of these writers vary from each other in many ways, and the issue of their joint

---

1   Alan Gewirth, *Human Rights: Essays on the Justification and Applications* (Chicago: University of Chicago Press, 1982). James Nickel, Making Sense of Human Rights (Berkeley: University of California Press, 1987). Raymond Plant, "Needs, Agency and Rights," *Law, Rights and the Welfare State*, ed. C. J. G. Sampford and D. J. Galligan, (London: Croom Helm, 1986), 23-48. Susan Moller Okin, "Liberty and Welfare: Some Issues in Human Rights Theory," *Nomos* 23, ed. Pennock and Chapman, (New York: New York University Press, 1981). Rodney Peffer, "A Defense of Rights to Well-Being," Philosophy and Public Affairs 8, no. 1 (1982), 65-87. Christian Bay, "Self-Respect as a Human Right: Thought on the Dialectics of Wants and Needs in the Struggle for Human Community," Human Rights Quarterly 9 (1982), 53-75. John Kleinig, "Human rights, Legal rights, and Social Change," Human Rights, ed. E. Kamenka and A. Ehr-Soon Ray, (New York: St. Martin's Press, 1978), 36-47. Wojchech Sadurski, "Economic Rights and Basic Needs," Law, Rights, and the Welfare State, ed. C. J. G. Sampford and D. J. Galligan, (London: Croom Helm, 1986), 49-66. Henry Shue, *Basic Rights: Subsistence, Affluence, and U. S. Foreign Policy* (Princeton: Princeton University Press, 1980). Richard Couto, "Property, Pinmakers and Physicians: Liberal Myths and America Health Care," Soundings 42, no. 3 (Fall 1979), 275-92. Jeremy Waldron, *Nonsense Upon Stilts* (New York: Methuen, 1987). David B. Fletcher, "Must Wolterstorff Sell His House?" *Faith and Philosophy* 4, no. 2 (April 1987), 187-97.

compatibility is seldom absent from consideration. The accounts of human rights reviewed here are conceptually compatible with Carter's formulation of human rights and could have served to ground and justify his thought, provided the principals had taken the time to learn and employ them. Of these various arguments Henry Shue's interdependency theory most clearly demonstrates the defensibility of our hypothesis. Alan Gewirth's theory most clearly addresses the objections of economic rights skeptics. A formal response to economic rights objections will follow the presentation of the economic rights partisans. Explanations of economic rights should begin with Henry Shue, who best expresses the clearest argument for the interdependency of rights.

Henry Shue and the
Interdependency of Basic Rights

Henry Shue claims that the ability of a human agent to claim anything is predicated, at least in part, upon the ability of that agent to claim. Shue directly challenges Hart's notion that the starving poor should be considered as being truly free. True freedom, for Shue, is not just the ability for one to go or come as one pleases, but also the ability to resist being wrongfully coerced into giving up one's freedom of choice. He therefore challenges a widely known defect in Hobbes' theory of social contract: the validity of coerced concessions.[2] Shue maintains that basic freedom consists of unforced choices. Such choices are dependent, however, upon the ability of people to resist standard threats to their freedom, security, and well-being.[3]

---

2 Thomas Hobbes, *Leviathan*, ed. C. B. MacPherson, (Baltimore: Penguin Books, 1968) Part I, Chapter 14, 198. Hobbes believed that coerced concessions or promises should be honored, even though the concession was obtained without honor. The importance of this point cannot be gainsaid because Shue's theory is deeply grounded in the notion that basic rights function to protect people from being forced into making coerced concessions.
3 While Shue's understanding of freedom concentrates on a freedom from coercion, it does not stop there. Shue's freedom from coercion necessitates a concern with well-being that goes beyond the limited notions of Hayek and Machan that were discussed in Chapter Three.

Shue explains his rights theory without discussing the
evolutionary process of the formulation and interpretation of
rights that was fully discussed in Chapter One. Instead he gives
a simple definition of a right, "A right provides the rational basis
for a justified demand."[4] Rights to him are a special sort of
claim. Shue closely associates the claiming of a right with the
claiming of one's dignity or humanity, following Joel Feinberg
on this point.[5] He then proceeds briskly into his specific theory of
basic rights. His approach is a direct challenge to the
first-generational bias of Western economic rights skeptics.
Clearly he is less interested in the foundational principles by
which rights may be justified, and more interested in how rights
function in modern societies. For him rights are characterized
by interrelatedness. This interrelatedness is fully accounted for

---

4   Henry Shue, *Basic Rights*, 13. It should be remembered from
Chapter One, that definitions of rights are always provisional.

5   Shue quotes Feinberg on this point as follows: "Legal claim-rights
are indispensably valuable possessions. A world without claim-rights,
no matter how full of benevolence and devotion to duty, would suffer
an immense moral impoverishment. Persons would no longer hope
for decent treatment from others on the ground of desert or rightful
claim. Indeed, they would come to think of themselves as having no
special claim to kindness or consideration from others, so that
whenever even minimally decent treatment is forthcoming they would
think themselves lucky rather than inherently deserving, and their
benefactors extraordinarily virtuous and worthy of great gratitude. The
harm to individual self-esteem and character development would be
incalculable. A claim-right, on the other hand, can be urged, pressed, or
rightly demanded against other persons. In appropriate circumstances
the right-holder can "urgently, peremptorily, or insistently" call for his
rights, or assert them authoritatively, confidently, unabashedly. Rights
are not mere gifts or favors, motivated by love or pity, for which
gratitude is the sole fitting response. A right is something that can be
demanded or insisted upon without embarrassment or shame. When
that to which one has a rights is not forthcoming, the appropriate
reaction is indignation; when it is duly given there is no reason for
gratitude, since it is simply one's own or one's due that one received. A
world with claim-rights is one in which all persons, as actual or
potential claimants, are dignified objects of respect, both in their own
eyes and in the view of others. No amount of love and compassion, or
obedience to higher authority, or noblesse oblige, can substitute for those
values." At 14-15. The original citation is from Joel Feinberg's *Social
Philosophy* (Englewood Cliffs: Prentice-Hall, Inc., 1973), 58-59.

in his theory of basic rights. For Shue basic rights must include economic rights because human agents have permanent, basic, economic needs. Shue's three covalent values are freedom, security, and subsistence. Subsistence consists of sufficient food, clothing, shelter to survive, and freedom. He believes that these human needs must be guaranteed by any society.[6] Accordingly, in a rights claiming society, every member must have a right to these goods. Further, each member cannot tolerate a continued absence of these items, or a deprivation of them. Though the threat to economic needs is a minor feature in Gewirth's writing, which we shall review later in this chapter, this reality of desperation is emphasized by Shue. He reveals, at least to his satisfaction, the interdependency of rights by demonstrating the interdependency of needs. Deprivations of what he calls subsistence rights, which we have called economic rights, must be guarded against constantly.

Shue's classic illustration in support for this position focuses on the effect that a change in production can make on all social relationships. Shue writes:

> Suppose the largest tract of land in the village was the property of the descendant of a family that had held title to the land for as many generations back as anyone could remember. By absolute standards this peasant was by no means rich, but his land was the richest in the small area that constituted the universe for the inhabitants of this village. He grew, as his father and grandfather had, mainly the black beans that are the staple (and chief--and adequate--source of protein) in the regional diet. His crop usually constituted about a quarter of the black beans marketed in the village. Practically every family grew part of what they needed, and the six men he hired during the seasons requiring extra labor held the only paid jobs in the village--everyone else just worked his own little plot. One day a man from the capital offered this peasant a contract that not only guaranteed him annual payments for a 10-year lease on his land but also guaranteed him a salary (regardless of how the weather, and therefore the crops, turned out--a great increase in his financial security) to be the foreman for a new kind of production on his land. The contract required him to grow flowers for export and also offered him the opportunity, which was highly recommended, to purchase through the company, with

---

6 Though these needs must be guaranteed by society, they do not need to be guaranteed by a system of rights.

> payments installments, equipment that would enable him
> to need to hire only two men. The same contract was
> offered to, and accepted by, most of the other larger
> landowners in the general region to which the village
> belonged.[7]

Shue's illustration describes a sudden change in customs,
agriculture, and economics that spells disaster for many of the
villagers. Landowners, in his hypothetical, are able to grow rich
rapidly; however, there is a price for this individual
maximization of interests. Because of the subsequent collapse of
the black bean economy, the vast majority of villagers are soon
suffering from malnutrition. Shue is careful to point out that
the actions of the major landowners and the foreign flower
buyer need not be malicious in intent in order to be morally
objectionable. He maintains, however, that both parties are
callous, particularly if they continue the flower growing once
the harms to society are evident. But he does not demand a
state-run economy to supervise all economic relations. He
argues, instead, that the government has the obligation to
intervene, perhaps by taxing the new agriculture and
redistributing it (perhaps even as black beans) to the people who
have a right to it (the villagers in question, who are suffering
from malnutrition). Starving villagers are not lazy or foolish,
though they still wind up being "deprived." Shue characterizes
the major landowner, the foreign buyer, and the government as
all having duties to insure that people not be deprived of their
basic right to sustenance. These duties correlate to the rights of
villagers to be able to work to provide for themselves, and to be
assisted when sudden economic changes make their customary
ways of working and living impossible. Shue maintains that this
illustration is really a prototype of modern "economic
development".[8] He sees basic rights to be both first generational
in nature and negative. For the implementation of these rights

---

7   Shue, 41.

8   Shue, 45. Regarding this hypothetical, Shue states that he has,
"simply presented a stylized sketch of a common pattern. Most
anecdotes are in the form of 'horror stories': about transnational
corporations switching land out of the production of the food consumed
by the local poor." He cites many sources, the most important being:
Robert J. Ledogar, *Hungry for Profits: U. S. Food and Drug
Multinationals in Latin America* (New York: IDOC, 1976), 92-98.

the government must be limited and people must have civil and political liberties. He also understands basic rights to be second generational. These latter rights demand that the government must intervene when others can't or won't, to prevent suffering due to standard threats, such as starvation in a serious regional depression. Shue cannot tolerate a minimalist state because, from his point of view, such a state would fail to properly carry out all of its duties.

He further maintains that the historical development of rights confers no lexical preference in value upon what we have termed first generation rights. That the recognition of "first generation rights" may have preceded the recognition of other generated rights does not in itself make such rights more necessary and valuable to the protection of the individual or society. More important to him is the obligatory power of rights based upon the meeting of certain basic needs. As such the rights that respond to these needs are basic rights and are equal in value without any respect to their chronological recognition. Writing regarding basic rights, Shue also insists upon the recognition of security rights, i.e., freedom from arbitrary imprisonment, and house arrests, as well as what he calls subsistence rights, which we have called basic economic rights. In addition, he insists upon the liberal tradition's favorite, the right to liberty. Since security rights are considered normative in this study, our attention can be exclusively focused upon rights to liberty and the limited economic rights that Shue classifies as subsistence rights.[9] With regard to these rights Shue maintains:

> Basic rights are a restraint upon economic and political forces that would otherwise be too strong to be resisted. They are social guarantees against actual and threatened deprivations of at least some basic needs. Basic rights are an attempt to give to the powerless a veto over some of the forces that would otherwise harm them most. Basic rights are the morality of the depths. They specify the line beneath which no one is to be allowed to sink.[10]

---

[9] All parties to the economic rights debate agree that security rights must be recognized and protected.

[10] Shue, 18.

One can see from Shue's recitation that unlike Machan he has no confidence in the minimalist state to protect the powerless from the deprivations of the powerful. In contrast to Machan, he assumes that market forces are unable to regulate themselves by means of Adam Smith's "invisible hand."[11] Shue therefore wishes to extend the power of the State to intervene in economic affairs on behalf of the powerless. He hopes to obtain by this intervention a form of commutative justice, and an elimination of the possibility that the poor will be coerced into giving up their liberty or security in order to guarantee their subsistence. He also rejects the classic liberal notion that what the individual needs most is the Garboesque right "to be left alone." He considers the failure to intervene, on behalf of the powerless to be a form of "poison."[12] Intervention is necessary because he rejects the assumption, which he attributes to classical liberal thought, that the world is in a state of mild scarcity. The world, for him, is a place of radical scarcity (1 billion people threatened by a lack of basic goods).[13] The scarcity is not of production, because, in his opinion, there are sufficient existent good to meet the demands of scarcity. The problem is that a minority of people retain a lion's share of basic

---

11 Couto and Walzer share Shue's pessimism regarding the self-regulating abilities of the free market. Couto's analysis of foundational political myths and the need to demythologize social relationships makes Shue's point, in a clear and convincing manner; namely, that the market cannot be left unregulated in crucial areas. Couto shows how our health care system is based upon Lockean and Smithian political myths: myths that turn health care into a form of private property. The correct analogy for Couto is not health care as a sack of flour, but as a service similar to police or fire protection. Couto insists that if our political myths can be recast, so as to limit the economic forces in our country that demand that health care be deemed a commodity, then health care may begin to be widely understood as a basic human right. With this understanding of health care its provision will be extended to all, with no regard of their ability to pay. The cost for this protection could be provided for out of a communal chest. In this way health care would be understood as a right in the same way that fire and police protection are understood, and would be justifiable therefore, by theories that justify those rights.

12 Shue, 19.

13 Ibid., 101.

goods. He believes this situation constitutes an uneven distribution of goods, and is grossly unjust. Shue should not be misunderstood, however, as demanding a radically egalitarian redistribution of goods. Like Gewirth, the logic of his arguments wanes in direct proportion to the supplying of goods. Shue does not make any claims for any kind of equalization of wealth. His position implicitly tolerates wide disparities in wealth *provided* everyone's basic needs are being adequately addressed. Thus he does *not* defend a system of rights in which an equality of outcomes is assured. He also does not discuss the distinction between the "deprived poor" and the "depraved poor." He relies instead upon the statistics that show that most of the poor are children, and thus are helpless victims of poverty rather than lazy beggars looking for a dole. Shue constructs a safety net with which to catch those who cannot sustain themselves with basic necessities, despite their good faith efforts. Furthermore, he is careful not to make the mistake of being overly specific in defining basic rights. For example, he writes:

> A right to subsistence would not mean, at one extreme, that every baby born with a need for open-heart surgery has a right to have it, but it also would not count as adequate food a diet that produces a life expectancy of 35 years of fever-laden, parasite ridden listlessness.[14]

Thus his understanding of a basic right is a right to a range of "enabling conditions." He observes, ". . . people may have rights to subsistence even if they do not have any strict rights to economic well-being extending beyond subsistence. Subsistence

---

14 Ibid., 23. Shue's range of "subsistence" is not designed to cover every possible need. Thus, open heart surgery is illustrative. It represents a real need that is very costly and unusual. Its illustrative value lies in the fact that it demonstrates that Shue wants to guarantee only subsistence for all, not every contingency for all. In the same way, Shue avoids any specific, culturally bound formula for a "subsistence" diet. Whatever people are entitled to is not precise, but it must, at a minimum, provide a maintenance of basic health and avoid chronic nutritional deficiencies. Shue's standard appears to be universal. No culture desires a fever-laden, parasite ridden existence for its members.

rights and broader economic rights are separate questions."[15]

It is for this reason that, as previously stated in Chapter Three, Cranston's dismissal of the dubious "right to paid vacations" is, in Shue's opinion, an insufficient investigation of the propriety of other economic rights.[16] Addressing the crucial question of the interdependency of rights, he explains what basic rights really are:

> When a right is genuinely basic, any attempt to enjoy any other right by sacrificing the basic right would be quite literally self-defeating, cutting the ground from beneath itself. Therefore if a right is basic, other, non-basic rights may be sacrificed, if necessary, in order to secure the basic right. But the protection of a basic right may not be sacrificed in order to secure the enjoyment of a non-basic right. It may not be sacrificed because it cannot be sacrificed successfully. If the right sacrificed is indeed basic, then no right for which it might be sacrificed can actually be enjoyed in the absence of the basic right. The sacrifice would have proven self-defeating.[17]

Shue contends that the right to assemble is really a right to assemble peacefully without interference, and that a right to freedom is directly tied to a right to security.[18] He likewise ties subsistence rights to other basic rights. Thus, starving people cannot really be free since they may quickly alienate their liberty to the one who can provide them with bread. Images of Dostoevski's Grand Inquisitor, from *The Brothers Karamazov*, come to mind: unfortunate, sheep-like people debased by the manipulation of a basic need. At the heart of his interdependency theory is a pessimistic pragmatism. Shue recognizes that various social forces do not always work for the "common good," but prey, instead, upon the weak and defenseless in society: it is for this reason that we have rights. For him, the fact that the need for rights may have been first recognized for civil and political interests to protect individuals from civil and political threats, is no reason in itself to assume

---

15 Ibid., 34. Whether or not Shue's lack of specificity with regards to the Objects of rights is fatally indeterminate will be discussed later on in this chapter.

16 Ibid., 98.

17 Ibid., 19.

18 Ibid., 27.

that other vital interests have not, cannot, and will not be threatened. As a consequence, there is no reason why other rights should not be recognized and employed to protect these interests.[19]

He is also careful to answer one of the standard incomprehensibility objections to the recognition of economic rights: namely, the positive rights/negative rights distinction. Chapters One and Three maintained that economic skeptics prefer the recognition of civil and political rights over economic rights because the former rights are said to be cost free, while the latter are alleged to be expensive to implement. Shue argues, however, that civil and political rights also present costs for the social arrangements that guarantee people these "rights." Whereas Feinberg, Machan and others insist that the rights to liberty and security are free, but "welfare rights" are costly, Shue shows how all such rights have both social obligations and real costs.[20] This cost/benefit analysis is always an important aspect of the positive/negative rights distinction.

The effect of Shue's argument is striking. He makes it extremely difficult to hold to what I call the "have your cake and eat it too" position. This position, held by Frankel, Machan, Cranston and others, allows them to freely reject economic rights, while they still support other "human rights." They employ the fiction that civil and political rights are costless to implement, while economic rights are supposedly costly to implement. Shue's argument explodes this fiction. His insight is, therefore, a valuable contribution to this field.

Shue does not specifically address each and every one of the major objections to economic rights. He does present, however, a rights theory that accounts for most of the concerns of the skeptics. This approach may be seen more clearly by

---

[19] This point is, of course, a rejection of Tibor Machan's argument about the duty of the state to only protect individuals from social harms caused by governmental interference in the exercise of their "negative" rights.

[20] Shue shows that to recognize the "right to a trial," a society has to have an extensive police, court, prison and parole system, and must tax its citizens in order to create and maintain these systems. Thus the right to a trial is no more "free" than food stamps or welfare. See also Sadurski on this point, 55.

reconsidering Cranston's threefold test. Shue maintains that
his basic rights are universal.[21] He insists that all human beings
need sufficient goods to at least subsist. He also insists that
everyone has to have a minimum level of security to enjoy any
other rights, whether basic or not and of any kind or quality.
Since his overall theory insists that all people are entitled to
certain basic rights, he clearly believes that his rights theory
addresses universality concerns. Since Shue also strongly
follows Feinberg with regard to rights being primarily
claims-rights (in the Hohfeldian sense of the term) and also
adopts the correlativity thesis, he is constrained to connect the
question of universality to the issue of correlative duties. For
Shue individuals have, universally, a strict duty to refrain from
depriving others (without cause) from exercising their own
respective rights. Thus it can be said that Shue has consciously
addressed Cranston's universality test. Further, he addresses
Cranston's practicability test by calling into question Cranston's
use of the term practical. He correctly shows that Cranston's
practicability test is not one of pure reason, but a pure
pragmatism. Economic rights to subsistence may be impossible
in an economically inept country, but that impossibility is usually
local: other countries could step in and provide the aid. For
example, an economic right to even subsistence may be doubtful
in Ethiopia, as an immediate claim of the Ethiopian government
during a famine, but not at all doubtful for other generous,
economically competent nations or organizations. In a global
village world practicability cannot be limited only to the assets
or institutions of a local government. Shue charges Cranston
with the mistake of short-circuiting the process of moral

---

21 At 120. It is also true, however, that Shue does not use the term
universality in the same way that Cranston does. Shue does not assert
that "basic rights" is a concept that must be used universally, especially
by societies whose social arrangements and philosophy do not use the
concept of rights. Nor would he say that even basic rights have been
applicable over all time periods (as Cranston does with human rights).
Instead, Shue insists that the security from standard threats to basic
goods and resources is universal, though the social arrangements and
institutions that establish that security are culturally and historically
relative, and often explained in different moral languages, such as
custom, virtue, or duty.

reasoning by refusing to consider all of the possible avenues of aid from a variety of human agencies.[22]

Shue addresses Cranston's paramount interests test, by means of his whole theory of basic rights. For him a basic right is, if it is nothing else, absolutely concerned with interests and goods of paramount value. Thus basic rights are basic rights *only* if the objects of those rights, and their interests, are of a basic or paramount value. This is the reason why Shue's basic rights argument limits itself to only three values: security, well-being, and freedom.[23] Rights based solely upon these three values are the foundation for any other rights discussion. Thus any other rights that come up for discussion must be compared to and weighed against these three rights. If a right to privacy, for instance, came into conflict with the three covalences, it would have to give way to the preferred values, and the rights that those values bring into being.

In summation, Shue shows that there can be no true liberty or political justice without some minimum of economic viability. Shue makes this argument in a way that should be pleasing to most of his libertarian critics: He insists that political participation is necessary to safeguard and maintain the social arrangements that are necessary for the recognition and implementation of basic rights. By insisting on participation he makes it clear that he is not unconcerned with the concerns of

---

22 Shue writes regarding Cranston, that, "Cranston obscures, or does not see, the terrible severity of his view's implications. The fact, if it be a fact, that resulting starvation within India would be only intentionally allowed to occur, and not intentionally initiated, is of little consequence. If preventable starvation occurs as an effect of a decision not to prevent it, the starvation is caused by, among other things, the decision not to prevent it. Passive infanticide is still infanticide. Part of the underlying logic of Cranston's position seems to be that one ought not to acknowledge any rights that fail the 'test of practicability,' where practicability is interpreted to be incompatible with transfers of 'capital wealth.'" At 98-99.

23 Shue's insistence on only three ultimate values enables him to dodge the bullet of indeterminacy. People are to receive, as rights, only goods and services that are absolutely necessary for their basic survival. Desiderata are left unaddressed in this scenario, but this rejection of them is precisely what saves Shue's theory from the fatal defect of indeterminacy.

liberals and libertarians for individual liberty, participatory democracy, and limited government. Shue also clarifies the great difficulty of making persuasive transgenerational social justice decisions.[24] Shue later disputes Hardin and Cranston's disinclination to help the starving as a matter of right rather than as a generous gesture. Thus Hardin's appeal to let some starve now so that our progeny will have more later is revealed to be more than just heartless; it is also shown to be empirically doubtful.[25] Shue is thus able to explode the underlying fiction of most pejoristic objections. He insists that the poor must be helped so that they *can* have sustainable lives that will enable them to control their own population.[26] Shue therefore rejects Hardin's approach, which he characterizes as population control by means of mass starvation.[27]

The weakness of Shue's endeavor is that it does not answer the communitarian criticisms of Alisdair MacIntyre, for whom all rights-claims are simply evidence of moral disarray

---

24 Ibid., 96-97.

25 Shue insists that there have been few theories of social justice that adequately address the additional factors of what he calls "temporal allocation and spatial allocation. " But Shue is insistent that Hardin's, Narveson's, or Cranston's refusal to intervene demands a strong moral justification that addresses the question of justice over time and between widely divergent groups of people. For Shue it is not at all clear that the resources due to people of our generation should always outweigh the demands of a future generation, or always be outweighed by posterity (the latter being Hardin's position). He is careful to concede however, that the steps that we take to address a small famine in the present can increase the chances of having to deal with a huge famine in the future. Nevertheless, Shue insists that most sustainability problems can be addressed in the present because poverty is not caused, primarily by the actions of the poor. From his perspective, scarcity is remediable. at present. For Shue full argument on this point, see Basic Rights ,99-102.

26 Ibid., 10l, n.22. Shue argues that marginalized people have more children, because their marginalization, with its high infant mortality rate, encourages this response: when the poor become sustainable, their inclination is to limit their family size as a rational attempt to further improve their lots. Recently this thesis was rejected by Garrett Hardin, who offered no statistical evidence for his rejection. "There is No Global Population Problem," *The Humanist* 49, no 4, (July/August 1989), 5-13, 32.

27 Ibid, 97-104.

and linguistic anarchy.[28] Shue's central point, that one must have all of one's basic rights, or none at all cannot dissuade MacIntyre, who simply believes that there are no human rights any more than there are unicorns.[29] MacIntyre's criticism,

---

[28] Alisdair MacIntyre, *After Virtue* (South Bend, IN: University of Notre Dame Press, 1981).

[29] MacIntyre's theories speak clearly on the meaning of human life and the value of the community and the individual. Alas, MacIntyre's approach is one that denies the ontological validity of human rights in general and economic rights in particular. MacIntyre's criticism is a specific criticism of the work of Alan Gewirth whose work we briefly examined in Chapter One. MacIntyre argues that human rights claims are akin to declarations of belief in witches and unicorns. (At 69). What MacIntyre means by this view is not that human rights are pure nonsense, but rather that claims for human rights are not rationally demonstrable. They are, therefore, mythical and magical. Human rights, for MacIntyre, may evoke images of ideal human relationships, or at least the rules by which ideal human communities might come into being and subsist. But for MacIntyre the content of human rights doctrine cannot be agreed upon because of the lack of a justifying principle. The lack of a justifying principle is due, at least in part, to the lack of a telos. There can be no justifying principle, in MacIntyre's opinion, because human rights claims are simply useful fictions that were created "as a social invention"' of the autonomous moral agent." Ibid. If correct, MacIntyre's point would be decisive; human rights, all human rights, not just "economic" human rights, would have to be understood as being simple fictions that are social constructs designed to help regulate human life. The logic of this position demands that as long as they help to do this, then they have a certain "utility." However, if they lose their effectiveness, then they may be abandoned easily because they do not express some sort of ultimate truth about human relationships. To bolster his argument, MacIntyre turns to the historically accurate point, that, "there is no expression in any ancient or medieval language correctly translated by our expression 'a right' until near the close of the middle ages: the concept lacks any means of expression in Hebrew, Greek, Latin or Arabic, classical or medieval, before about 1400, let alone in Old English, or in Japanese even as late as the mid-nineteenth century." At 69. MacIntyre interprets the relatively recent expression of human rights to be proof that they are merely a recent social invention. If MacIntyre is right and all human rights theorists are wrong, then human rights are like the "natural rights" that Bentham called "nonsense, nonsense upon stilts." But is MacIntyre right? MacIntyre, maintains that rights claims are always located in, "a highly specific and socially local character, and that the existence of

however, even if correct, does not dismiss Shue's interdependency thesis, at least not for people who are already committed to using rights language. MacIntyre's position constitutes a fundamental criticism of *all* rights discourse. Shue's theory is simply one of many that is built upon a rights foundation that MacIntyre calls into question. Be that as it may, <u>we must now turn to</u> some of the other weaknesses in Shue's

particular types of social institution or practice is a necessary condition for the notion of a claim to the possession of a right being an intelligible type of human performance. (As a matter of historical fact such types of social institution or practice have not existed universally in human societies.) Lacking any such social form, the making of a claim to a right would be like presenting a check for payment in a social order that lacked the institution of money." At 67. Of course, here MacIntyre is both right and wrong. MacIntyre is right, that rights are claimed in particular societies; and that if they are to be implemented, they must use rather specific language, and be implemented by some recognizing social institution. Yet, in spite of these verities, in some important ways, MacIntyre is wrong. On the modern scene, countries that have not had histories of democracy and freedom are recognizing the human rights that guarantee such. Conversely speaking, however, to say that rights claims are made, or have been made in locally specific language, is only to note the obvious. What other language is a putative rights holder apt to use? In most circumstances, communication is most effective by using the most customary terms. Nevertheless, in the modern world, human rights talk has taken on an international patina, one in which internationally recognized terms and norms are employed. It is in the implementation of these rights that parochialism too often predominates. Take, for example, the right to freedom of religion. Many Islamic countries formally recognize this freedom, having signed covenants to that effect. See Robert F. Drinan, *Cry of the Oppressed: The History and Hope of the Human Rights Revolution* (San Francisco: Harper & Row, 1987). Yet many of these countries, with their fusion and interrelation of religion and state, do not really tolerate the proselytization of other religions in their state. What they mean then by freedom of religion is that the faithful Moslem will be totally unrestricted in his religious beliefs and practices by the State. Thus these countries believe, in some real sense, in freedom of religion, though they do not share the West's understanding of that concept. What MacIntyre shows, however, is how modern and western Gewirth's PGC is; and how dependent it is on the modern conception of the individual. This is not the same as showing that rights language is simply a recent fiction. Alan Gewirth has a rejoinder on these points in the following essay: . "Human Rights and Conceptions of the Self," *Philosophia* 18 (July 1988), 129-49.

account.

Shue is subject to criticism by most liberals because he argues for the priority of rights to security and subsistence over freedom rights. This approach is a mistake that Gewirth's theory, which we will discuss shortly, avoids. Further, he is simply unable to show that reasonable people will always prefer security and subsistence to freedom. In such a world no martyrdoms would be comprehensible, and no revolutions for freedom would be reasonable.[30] It is not, of course, logically necessary for him to show that every human being equally prefers freedom, security and well-being; he is only logically obligated to show that most people would or logically *should* want these values equally. Shue is not obligated to account for the moral values of exceptional people; martyrs, patriots and saints. Rights are designed, however, to regulate human relationships in a world that is populated by people who are less than saints. Despite these faults, *Shue demonstrates, with unerring logic, that if there are any rights at all, they are inherently interrelated and interdependent, thus proving our thesis.*[31] Our thesis is proven because Shue demonstrates that civil and political rights are themselves real options only when people have sufficient well-being to effectively exercise these rights. In the final analysis, a starving peasant is only technically free. In most cases he is apt to become a slave to anyone who can provide him with food, clothing, or other basic necessities. Starving peasants who experience real freedom do so only existentially, heroically and briefly. Patriots and saints often become martyrs, their freedom being short-lived. Shue's basic rights argument shows how rights are universal while also showing the necessity of mediating institutions that can act to recognize and enforce those rights. By doing so, Shue is able to refute the particularism of Burke while demonstrating why

---

[30] One empirical study demonstrating that, on occasion, people prefer freedom to security and subsistence is found in an article by Marshall Carter and Otwin Marenin, "Human Rights in the Nigerian Context: A Case Study and Discussion of the Nigerian Police," *Universal Human Rights* 1, no. 2 (April-June 1979).

[31] Shue's argument has been in discussion for several years; to date, no argument has been put forth to show that Shue's interdependency argument is incorrect.

Burke, Novak, Lefever, and Kirkpatrick are correct for insisting on the action of social institutions in the enforcement of those rights.   Since Shue has demonstrated the inherent interdependency of economic rights with civil and political rights but has not answered every objection that has been raised against economic rights our study must turn to other theorists. This presentation of additional economic rights theories will be followed with our evaluation of the adequacy of these theories in meeting standard economic rights objections.   Our presentations should start with a consideration of Alan Gewirth.

Alan Gewirth's Principle of Generic Consistency

As applied to human rights, Alan Gewirth's theories are important because he has written extensively and frequently in an attempt to answer the objections of human and economic rights skeptics.   In doing so, he draws clear lines of disagreement with his many detractors, and has greatly influenced other writers in the field.   With regard to Cranston's tests for universality and practicability Gewirth maintains:

> One view is that these rights, including the right to be given food and the other goods needed for alleviating severe economic handicaps and insecurities, cannot be "human" rights because they do not meet two tests: universality and practicability.   According to the test of universality, for a moral right to be a human one it must be a right of all persons against all persons: all persons must have the strict duty of acting in accord with the right, and all persons must have the strict right to be treated in the appropriate way.   Thus, all persons must be both the agents and the recipients of the modes of action required by the right.   This test is passed by the rights to life and to freedom of movement: everyone has the duty to refrain from killing other persons and from interfering with their movements, and everyone has the right to have his life and his freedom of movement respected by other persons. But in the case of the right to be relieved from starvation or severe economic deprivation, it is objected that only some persons have the right: those who are threatened by starvation or deprivation; and only some persons have the

duty: those who are able to prevent or relieve this starvation by giving aid.[32]

To these objections Gewirth replies:

> The answer to this objection need not concede that this right like other economic and social rights, is universal only in a "weaker" sense in that whereas all persons have the right to be rescued from starvation or deprivation, only some persons have the correlative duty. Within the limits of practicability, all persons have the right and all have the duty. For all persons come under the protection and the requirements of the PGC insofar as they are perspective purposive agents. Hence, all the generic rights upheld by the PGC have the universality required for being human rights. It is, indeed, logically impossible that each person be at the same time both the rescuer and the rescued, both the affluent provider and the deprived pauper. Nevertheless, the fact that some prospective purposive agent may not at some time need to be rescued from deprivation or be able to rescue others from deprivation does not remove the facts that he has the right to be rescued when he has the need and that he has the duty to rescue when he has the ability and when other relevant conditions are met.[33]

Now regarding the "practicability test," Gewirth observes:

> . . . to the contention that the social and economic rights are not human rights because they do not pass the test of practicability, in that many nations lack the economic means to fulfill these rights. Now, it is indeed the case that whereas the political and civil rights may require nonaction or noninterference rather than positive action of the part of governments, the economic rights require the positive use of economic resources for their effective implementation. This does not, however, militate against governments' taking steps to provide support, to the extent of the available resources, to persons who cannot attain basic economic goods by their own efforts. There is a considerable distance between the position that the same high levels of economic well-being are not attainable in all countries and the position that a more equitable distribution of goods and of means of producing goods is not feasible for countries at the lower end of the scale.[34]

---

[32] Alan Gewirth, *Human Rights: Essays on Justification and Application* (Chicago: Univ. of Chicago Press, 1982), 64, hereinafter referred to as Gewirth's Human Rights.

[33] Ibid.

[34] Ibid., 65.

Gewirth's reply to Cranston's paramount importance test is more formal than his reply to the first and second tests.[35] His rights theory is grounded in what he calls the PGC.[36] Within his PGC Gewirth accounts for his own understanding of paramount importance.

These long quotes from Gewirth are indulged in because they disclose clearly his approach to Cranston's tests as well as his response to some of the major economic rights objections. These quotes also explain how economic rights are connected to needs. His response also shows how economic rights can be positive and necessary, thereby addressing the alleged defect attributed to economic rights that they fail to distinguish between positive rights and negative rights. Moreover, Gewirth shows how duties are to be related to rights and what impact economic rights have on freedom (thus addressing that standard objection). Finally, his replies explain how economic rights may be recognized and implemented without unduly burdening the State.

The pejoristic objection that opposes aiding the lazy elicits a clear response from Gewirth. He maintains that economic rights do not come into effect unless the would-be recipient has actually unsuccessfully attempted to secure the objects of the rights through his own efforts. This requirement addresses Novak's concern, that the lazy not be rewarded for their laziness.[37] Gewirth is also sensitive to the problem of indeterminacy. He posits that his economic rights would only justify those rights to goods or non-interference that allow for conditions that ensure basic human action and agency. Such goods would not provide for an equality of results, but only an

---

[35] As a quick provisional answer, we should note that Gewirth believes that, "The test of paramount importance is obviously met by the right to food for averting starvation." See Gewirth, *Human Rights*, 208.

[36] PGC stands for Principle of Generic Consistency; it will be described in full shortly.

[37] This objection is not a formal and categorical rejection of economic rights, rather it is a limitation of economic rights to the "deprived" rather than the "depraved" poor.

equal opportunity for successful human agency. The goods proposed create only an "even playing field," rather than significant unfair advantages for the unfortunate. In summation Gewirth rejects economic rights skepticism. He is convinced, as is Shue, that if the poor are helped they will be more likely to control their population so that the commons will not be overtaxed.[38] Finally, Gewirth subscribes to a theory regarding the causes of poverty that if true would obligate haves to reparatively assist have nots as a strict duty correlative to the poor's justified right to assistance in achieving well-being.[39] These brief responses are indications as to how Gewirth has responded to the primary economic rights objections. But these responses do not explain how his theory of economic rights work, and they do not demonstrate that his responses are themselves justifiable. A closer look at Gewirth is therefore required.

Gewirth's human rights theory, within which his economic rights theory is located, emphasizes the concepts of moral agency, human action, and basic goods. Gewirth's Principle of Generic Consistency, with which he addresses human rights has four main precepts:

> First, every agent holds that the purposes for which he acts are good on whatever criterion (not necessarily a moral one) enters into his purposes. Second, every actual or prospective agent logically must therefore hold or accept that freedom and well-being are necessary goods for him because they are the necessary conditions of his acting for any of his purposes; hence, he holds that he must have them. Third, he logically must therefore hold or accept that he has rights to freedom and well-being; for, if he were to deny this, he would have to accept that other persons may remove or interfere with his freedom and well-being, so that he may not have them; but this would contradict his belief that he must have them. Fourth, the sufficient reason on the basis of which each agent must claim these rights is that he is a prospective purposive agent, so that he logically must accept the conclusion that all prospective purposive agents, equally and as such, have rights to

---

38 Gewirth, *Human Rights* , 211-17.

39 Gewirth maintains that haves help to cause poverty. Gewirth does not point to the active exploitation of the poor by the rich. He does point to their failure to intervene on behalf of the poor. He also notes that haves coerce assumptions of risks on the poor. Ibid., 192.

freedom and well-being. This conclusion is equivalent to the PGC.[40]

Gewirth's theory of human rights seeks to bridge the gap between the empirical and the normative. Since it can be empirically shown that people must have food, shelter, and clothing in order to act with some hope of success, Gewirth concludes that people indeed have a right to such basic goods. Another way of saying this is that Gewirth attempts to move from an is to an ought. But again, as in Chapter Three, Van De Veer's question arises, "How can needs, even basic needs constitute a right?" As part of his answer, Gewirth ties needs to rights through his emphasis on action that he directly relates to the concept of agency. Gewirth takes the Kantian view that what makes people most valuable is not their mere survival, but their moral choices and actions made in freedom. For him these choices are freely made only when the agent has some level of both freedom and "well-being." Thus, for him, a person is not truly recognized by others as being "human" unless the person is allowed and is not prevented, to act in his/her own best interests. The agent must also, however, be "able" to make choices, that is the person cannot be comatose, or suffer from other restricting conditions. Gewirth settles the issue of the universality of human rights by locating them in the necessities of human action. He writes, "human rights are thus equivalent to "natural" rights in that they pertain to all humans by virtue of their nature as actual or prospective agents."[41] So for him any prospective or actual agent avoids being self-contradictory, and secures the possibility of successful action, by seeking basic human rights. Every agent must, therefore, also concede to all other prospective human agents, basic human rights. Only by doing so can the agent act rationally, in freedom, and can reasonably hope for the well-being of herself and others.

---

40 Gewirth, 20.

41 Ibid., 7. It is in this way that Gewirth also understands human rights to be "universal."

Accordingly, Gewirth's Principle of Generic Consistency can be succinctly stated as follows, "Act in accord with the generic rights of your recipients as well as of yourself."[42] Gewirth illustrates his principle in relation to the basic human need of nutrition as follows:

> Suppose Ames, a bachelor, has a very large amount of food while Bates, another bachelor who lives nearby, is starving to death. None of the voluntary factors mentioned above applies to Bates. Ames knows of Bates's plight but doesn't want to give away any of his food, despite Bates's appeals for help. Bates dies of starvation.[43]

The voluntary factors that Gewirth eliminates are the possibilities that Bates had irrationally decided to starve himself to death, or that he was wantonly careless and failed to work, or to properly buy and store food. Gewirth argues that Ames' failure to intervene on behalf of Bates is a violation of Ames' and Bates' PGC. Gewirth reasons that Ames has more than a *negative* duty to refrain from preventing Bates from acquiring food; he has a *positive* duty to supply it. This duty arises for Ames because the difficulty of providing food to Bates is negligible, his proximity to Bates is close, the threat to the loss of one of Bates' basic rights (in this case Bates' life) is imminent, and his failure to act constitutes a directly contributing cause to Bates' death. For Ames to stand by idly while Bates loses his life is not merely intuitively wrong; it is, according to Gewirth, irrational and equivalent to a "bad thing." Gewirth further argues that Ames' humanity and moral agency, his familiarity with the natural processes of hunger, and, in a cause and effect sense of the term starvation, positively obligates him to value Bates' generic rights (one of which is to have a basic good such as life-sustaining nutrition). For Gewirth the fact that other moral agents failed to act, such as the state, mediating institutions, or other individuals (besides Ames) did not excuse Ames from his moral responsibilities.

Gewirth then extrapolates this exercise in individual and personal morality to universal and international levels.[44] The

---

42 Ibid., 200.
43 Ibid., 203.
44 Ibid., 205-17.

duty to intervene under these circumstances is universal, barring some sort of special duty to refrain from intervention. Intervention is necessary because all humans need certain basic goods to guarantee their freedom, well-being, security and, concomitantly, their moral agency. Gewirth internationalizes this principle by arguing that nations in a system of states can be seen as acting like persons.[45] However, even if one accepts the steps that Gewirth makes in moving from a hypothetical individual, like Ames, to a country, such as America, certain other factors must be considered. For instance, with regard to a situation where a single state, such as Ethiopia, is in dire straits, and several states have an over-abundance of food, medical supplies and other basic goods, it is not always clear what any one state should do. Should a state stand by idly until others act? Should the most prosperous states act first, with other moderately wealthy nations standing by waiting to see whether or not the first provision of aid is effective? Should "have" countries act in concert, or not act at all? These questions are practical concerns that take into consideration the realities of the ongoing complexity and competition that is prevalent in the modern world of nation-states. Gewirth's reasoning would seem to indicate that any economically competent state should respond as soon as practicable to dire need, up until the point where the aid is "unduly" costly to them. As a practical matter Gewirth is aware of the responsibility of foreign states to avoid intervening into the affairs of other states.[46] Thus it could be said that the ideal practical response would be for several "have" states to work in concert to prevent, or alleviate, "famine." The reasons for this conclusion are simple: a league of states is more likely to have the necessary goods, the ability to transport them, and the international moral profile to allow a recipient nation to cooperate with the transmission of the aid.

Thus, in Gewirth's mind, if a prosperous United States with grain rotting in over-burdened silos, stands by idly, while Ethiopia starves, the U. S., has violated Ethiopia's generic rights. This conclusion follows barring the existence of logistical issues such as the possibility that the cost and feasibility of

---

45 Ibid.
46 Ibid, 214-17.

shipping food or aid is impossible or prohibitive. Gewirth assumes that nations are made up of persons (including their sovereign representatives) that are actual or prospective moral agents.[47] Thus they can be held morally accountable for their action on inaction in much the same way as individuals are brought to account.

Nutrition rights are used by Gewirth primarily for illustration. They are simply the most obvious examples of rights that are dialectically necessary to enable human beings to act purposefully in the world with some reasonable hope of success. Housing, clothing, medical care, and other objects of rights may also be necessary to ensure human agency and action. It is clear, however, that once one economic right is recognized, such as the right to subsistence, other basic rights can also qualify as valid rights. What is not clear, at this point, is the extent to which intervention into a foreign country on behalf of a right should go. In a recent essay, Gewirth observed that:

> As a political project, the positive rights of the persons threatened by starvation require certain political changes, including more control by local farmers over their producing and marketing activities. These changes are a matter, first, for indigenous forces within each nation and second, for the enlightened support of other nations and international organizations.[48]

On this same point Gewirth has also observed, that:

> It may be objected that if individuals' rights to freedom and property may be invaded whenever this is needed to prevent harm to other persons, then there will be no limit to such invasion and hence if effect no rights. This slippery-slope contention fails, however, because in the present argument the harms in question are limited to interferences with basic goods. These are serious enough in their destructive effects on agency to require, as a matter of strict justice, such legally sanctioned intervention.[49]

---

[47] Ibid., 207.

[48] Alan Gewirth, "Private Philanthropy and Positive Rights," 5. Gewirth's confidence in "enlightened" nations is both heart-warming and bone-chilling. "Enlightened" nations in one generation are often recognized as "imperialistic" in another. .

[49] Alan Gewirth, *Human Rights* , 213.

By being committed to the coequal values of freedom and well-being, Gewirth is committed to exercising caution in implementing rights to well-being that might curtail freedom rights. Thus, with regard to the use of coercive power to protect someone's rights to well-being, Gewirth replies:

> As against these extremes, the PGC requires that the freedom of one's recipients be maintained as long as possible, and that every possible effort be made to combine freedom with well-being. The use of coercive methods... would, indeed, be serious violations of the rights to freedom and to basic well-being in Nation B. In addition, it would open the door for other developed nations to impose enslavement and even genocide while proclaiming the same lofty motives. [Of providing aid of varying types to impoverished countries][50]

Gewirth acknowledges the limits of economic reconstruction and intervention in a foreign country. Because despotic elites may rule a famine-stricken country, and may enjoy increasing wealth and power by intentionally maldistributing goods and services, Gewirth is cautious about intervening in the "oppressed" country. Intervention in such instances would probably have to pass just war theory criteria.[51] Though Gewirth does not make such an argument, Joseph Allen does, and Allen's understanding of economic rights, though clearly distinct from Gewirth's is, nevertheless, harmonizable with Gewirth's on this point.[52]

---

50 Alan Gewirth, *Human Rights*, 214.

51 Gewirth takes the safe approach of saying that a country that would allow its citizens to starve when it could easily effectively act to prevent that starvation was not a just government. This position is similar to Michael Walzer's comments discussed in Chapter One. Ibid, 214. It is of course a rejection of the views of Malthus and Garrett Hardin.

52 Joseph L. Allen, *Love and Conflict* (Nashville: Abingdon Press, 1984), 203-17. I am not saying that Allen utilizes Gewirth's PGC. Rather what I am saying is that Gewirth could justify the exportation of food to a country with a hostile government, if such an exportation (which might constitute a political intervention) met Allen's just war theory criteria. If for instance one hundred government troops might be killed because one hundred thousand peasants violently took off of a dock, the necessary grain to preserve their lives (which presumably had been donated by a foreign government) then, provided other just war criteria

Looking again at Gewirth's approach to "practicability" we find that his concept of duty creates an obligation to provide assistance *only when a capable agent is available to assume the duty.* This precondition would seem, obviously, to be applicable to all duties. In other words, where the provision of a duty is patently impractical (if for instance Ames were only marginally better off than Bates), for Gewirth no duty would arise, although the recipient's needs would unrequitably persist. This perspective extrapolated to the system of nation states would indicate that an economically bankrupt Ethiopia has no strict duty to help an economically bankrupt Sudan. However, in contrast, rich Western states would have obligations to both countries. They would be obliged, at least in part, *because* they are economically competent. But to be perfectly clear, the obligation to help arises only when there has been a recognition of the lack of a basic need, as well as the availability of a capable duty bearer (someone who has the needed abundance of goods).[53] The duty of individuals and countries to sacrifice their goods, services, or freedom, is therefore, for Gewirth, a limited duty. In short, duties and rights are correlative, but rights arise out of basic needs that create duties and not the converse.

The strength of Gewirth's position is evident; needs are clearly, though abstractly defined; obligations are clearly limited, and human agency and action are adequately addressed. The issue of responsibility is also addressed, and the duty to provide aid is tied to the ability to help of the would-be-rescuer, as well as to the previous actions of the recipient. Presumably if a recipient has been wantonly derelict in the exercise of his agency he or she would not automatically be bailed out by the diligent and prudent. For Gewirth, the responsibility to act prudently never leaves a recipient. This fact highlights Gewirth's supreme value--human agency. In this theory, *dependency is not encouraged.* The reasonably prudent person would attempt to be self-sufficient, knowing that aid might be provided in a worst case scenario, but also knowing

were also met, both the taking of the grain and the exportation of the grain by the donor country might be morally justifiable.

[53] If, for instance, a government has concealed the existence of a famine, in an obscure part of the globe, other countries could not be held responsible for failing to act on a situation of which they had no knowledge.

that aid might be very minimal and might not come in time, if at all. From Gewirth's point of view, Novak's fears that the recognition of economic rights might encourage servility seems unpersuasive.

Gewirth's PGC only requires the provision of a safety net: haves are morally and rationally compelled to assist people in obtaining necessities for agency and action that is calculated to increase their minimum chances of success with the exercise of their agency. Most importantly, Gewirth's PGC does not call for an equality of outcomes, but the provision of the goods that guarantee the possibility of equality of opportunity.[54] Gewirth's establishment of an equality of opportunity without also an establishment of an equality of outcomes implies a certain view of human nature. Human beings are equal, in Gewirth's thought, in the sense that all are able and compelled by the logic of his PGC to claim the entitlements to the conditions that provide a reasonable chance to pursue happiness. Beyond this probability Gewirth does not speculate.[55]

The strength of Gewirth's scheme is that it is both universal in scope while still being subject to a case by case application: one may have only to rescue a drowning child out of a shallow pond, incurring a minor cleaning bill. Or, depending upon the precariousness of the child's position, one may also have to act like the Good Samaritan, and provide other basic needs to the child. The government, in Gewirth's view, need only do what it can, not what it cannot. If the state silos are empty the government may still have met its duty to feed starving people because its duty is to do the possible, not to do the impossible. Thus, the "practicability" objection with regard

---

54 Alan Gewirth, "Economic Rights," *Poverty, Justice, and Law: New Essays on Needs, Rights, and Obligations* (Lanham, MD: University Press of America, 1986), 26. He writes, "From these considerations, it is apparent that the equality of generic rights prescribed by the PGC is an equality of opportunity rather than of outcomes."

55 This recognition of an equal status for human beings with regard to how we must be treated, would confirm Gewirth's neo-Kantian approach; namely, that human beings must be treated as ends in themselves and never merely as means. Still, this is a thin theory of human nature, and it will lead shortly to a substantive criticism of his approach.

to the State is groundless. From Gewirth's perspective, it was always based on a misunderstanding of the concept of rights as exceptionless guarantees. At the same time, however, *they are morally* compelled to intervene. Thus Cranston's universality or practicability tests do not disqualify Gewirth's enterprise. In his explanation, the government is obligated to do its best in a prudent and responsible fashion in a world of scarcity. Some of the other objections to Gewirth's work are similarly specious.

Machan, for example, feels that Gewirth's understanding of obligation is unlimited. This objection is a variation on one of the standard incomprehensibility objections, the indeterminacy of economic rights claims. Machan would have us believe that Gewirth would commit the government to endeavor to prevent natural catastrophes such as earthquakes and floods because these disasters are tragic and rob people of their lives, agency and goods. However, a careful reading of Gewirth discloses that the government and other individuals who wish to act upon his PGC are not obligated to maximize utilities tirelessly: they are not obliged to prevent every conceivable loss. Economic rights adherents are obligated to act responsibly only when the need is obvious, the ability to successfully intervene is clear, and the interest is what Cranston would call of a paramount nature. Thus a modern government would certainly be obligated, provided they have the information, to warn coastal inhabitants about the approach of a hurricane, though they need not build, for coastal inhabitants, hurricane-proof homes. The government might be obligated, provided the national treasury is not depleted, to rebuild infrastructures in national disaster areas, particularly if, for national interests, people have been encouraged by the government to live in areas prone to natural disasters.

Turning to the problematic of work the government might not be obligated, by the PGC, to nationalize industries. It may, however, be obligated to: regulate labor relations; limit the exportation of certain national resources; supervise the enforcement of antitrust laws; encourage the creation of jobs.[56]

---

56 Ibid., 28. Gewirth maintains five responsibilities for government: first, to provide necessities such as food, clothing, shelter, and medical care (or their monetary equivalents) to persons who, despite their own good faith efforts, have not been able to obtain them; secondly, to

These proposed actions should be considered in light of Ernest Lefever's objection regarding economic and social rights; namely, that they are, "really objectives and aspirations, not rights, because they cannot be guaranteed by any government unless it is totalitarian. The price of gaining these 'rights' is the sacrifice of freedom itself."[57] Closely scrutinized, what Gewirth proposes is hardly the creation of a totalitarian state. Lefever's and Hayek's similar claim appear, therefore, to be unwarranted.

If we reconsider Cranston's test of paramount importance, Gewirth's position is particularly appropriate. Since Gewirth's obligation is a call to provide only that which is necessary to guarantee freedom and the probability of successful agency in action, *only* paramount needs should be contemplated. Gewirth calls the goods needed to meet paramount needs basic goods. Higher-order needs, such as paid vacations, or stylish clothing simply are not demanded by Gewirth. These latter goods do not obligate the state or anyone else to provide them to those who are without such goods. Non-substractive goods are another important concept for Gewirth. They are, ". . . the general abilities and conditions needed for maintaining undiminished one's level of purpose-fulfillment and one's capabilities for particular actions. . . Examples of non-subtractive goods are not being lied to, stolen from, insulted, or threatened with violence."[58] Also, to be considered are what Gewirth calls additive goods, which are, ". . . the general abilities and conditions needed for increasing one's level of purpose-fulfillment and one's capabilities for successful actions. Examples of additive goods are self-esteem, wealth, and education."[59] These last goods do not obligate the state or others to supply them, with the possible exception of the

---

encourage private industry to invest and retool wisely and timely; thirdly, buffering, temporarily, the shock of unemployment in benefits and in retraining; fourthly, educating youth in ways that enable them to find and keep work; fifthly, to provide protection of workers' rights to healthy working conditions and sustainable salaries.

57 Ernest W. Lefever, "Human Rights and U.S. Foreign Policy: Security or Pax Sovietica, " *Vital Speeches of the Day*, (15 March 1982), 343-46.

58 Gewirth, "Economic Rights."

59 Ibid.

provision of sufficient education, which may be needed to enable people to obtain and keep meaningful employment. Education generates a right because it is what Shue would call a necessary good, i.e., a good needed to ensure the reasonable prospect of getting and maintaining other basic goods. In contrast, a good such as self-esteem would not be the kind of good that any government could necessarily provide to any individual or group (though that government may, nevertheless, have a strict duty to protect some persecuted minority from assaults upon their dignity--for example, the prompt prosecution of violent Klansmen).[60] Paid vacations or stylish clothes, in contrast, would not be sought by Gewirth, as basic goods, for the simple reason that every need designated as a *basic* need obligates every adherent to the PGC to provide that need for another. This mandatoriness applies without regard to the providers' unfamiliarity with the recipient, or the recipient's lifestyle. Unwilling benefactors are logically obligated to provide benefits without regard to other plans they wish to pursue, or other ends they wish to realize. This threat of self-enslavement to others logically forces PGC adherents to temper their claims as they may be called upon to provide the satisfaction of those claims in others.

In Gewirth's vision participants find themselves in a situation akin to Rawls' Original position.[61] In Rawls' Original Position one postulates the rules of distribution and the ordering of institutions so as to maximize one's chances of success, with an additional desire to maximize procedural fairness. In this position there is no regard to one's actual position in society. Certain principles of distributive justice, which entail the concept of rights, are then freely constituted. Seen in this way, adherents to the PGC weigh two logical possibilities. The first possibility that they must consider is that they might be one of William Julius Wilson's "truly disadvantaged": a person at the

---

60 The recognition of such a right to a good would, therefore, be essentially negative. A just government might indeed be constrained not to disparage the identity of an individual or group nor to allow the arbitrary disparagement of an individual or group (within the confines of upholding the general preferred right to freedom of speech).

61 John Rawls, *A Theory of Justice* (Cambridge: Belknap Press, 1971).

bottom of the social barrel.[62] Conversely, as a second possibility, they may find themselves positioned somewhat higher on the social scale and therefore susceptible to the demands of those beneath them. Logic would demand that adherents of Gewirth's PGC should try to discern what it is that any human agent truly needs. They would thereby avoid the extension of a largess that might enslave all but the most wealthy, or the most destitute. Such a careful weighing of "needs" is also quite apt to eliminate the "Santa Claus" or "shopping cart" mentality that Jeane Kirkpatrick, Maurice Cranston, and others so rightfully scorn. This approach is one in which indeterminacy in the scope and application of economic rights is avoided. This type of prudent reasoning is also most likely to avoid the absurd situation of H. L. A. Hart's starving-yet-free humanity whose agency is severely hampered by want. It would also avoid, at the polar opposite of the spectrum, an enslaved, utilitarian provider--chained to an endless demand, from strangers, for "more."

Another way of looking at this situation is to realize that Gewirth recognizes an obvious fact that Van De Veer and others overlook: basic human needs are permanent, whereas the ability to provide for them is provisional. Gewirth argues that the adherent to the principle of generic consistency recognizes that her status as a self-sufficient member of society and as an agent in society is not guaranteed, whereas her basic needs, which provide her with freedom and well-being, and that enable her to exercise her human agency, *are* guaranteed--to persist. Every adherent to the PGC understands the frailty of human status, and human life. In seeing those personal threats one is able to appreciate those dangers in the plans, schemes and lives of others. It is this possibility of frustrated agency that creates Gewirth's "ought" out of the "isness" of human life. To reiterate, for Gewirth, in contrast to H. L. A. Hart, *freedom and well-being are equal values.*

But, Gewirth is, like Novak, aware that there is a basic conflict of rights problem in rights discourse. A conflict of rights

---

62 William Julius Wilson, *The Truly Disadvantaged: The Inner City, the Underclass, and Public Policy* (Chicago: University of Chicago Press, 1987).

problem is a situation in which two or more recognized rights are claimed by different parties for the same object of a right. A classic example is the conflict over prayer in schools. One party claims to have a right to exercise their religious beliefs while attending a public school. The other party feels that their First Amendment rights, which they interpret as restraining the government from establishing any religion, especially in school, mandates that school prayers be discontinued. The most common conflict of rights problem related to economic rights occurs between claims for liberty and claims for well-being. Gewirth does not resolve this conflict by relying upon a lexical priority of a right to liberty, as Hart does, but by employing a principle he calls his *criterion of degree of necessity of action*.[63] Simply put, this principle maintains that when two rights conflict with one another, the right whose object is more necessary for action must take precedence.

For example, Gewirth's non-subtractive right to not be lied to should, in his opinion, be overridden if it conflicts with the more paramount right to not be murdered. Gewirth's rights to well-being, fall, therefore, into a hierarchy of progressively less necessary conditions for action--basic, non-subtractive, and finally additive goods and rights. Freedom, Gewirth's other basic value, also gives rise to a hierarchy of goods and rights. When a conflict arises, freedom rights must also be weighed against well-being rights (the converse is also true). Thus, for example, Gewirth writes:

> if the affluent are taxed so that a relatively small part of their wealth is removed in order to prevent the destitute from starving, this is a far less significant interference with their freedom than would be the case if they were forced to surrender most of their wealth or were prohibited from supporting political parties, religions, or universities of their choice.[64]

Why Gewirth reasons in this fashion can again be seen by employing Rawls' Original Position as a heuristic device. If, as in the Original Position, one does not know what one's actual status in a society is going to be the reasonably prudent agent

---

63 Alan Gewirth, *Human Rights*, 58-60.
64 Gewirth, "Economic Rights," 24.

should be willing to give up the absolute right to dispense with her wealth (along with a small portion of that wealth) in order to establish a system of justice in which the destitute (whose ranks she may fill) are provided with basic goods. It is by this reasoning that her immediate demise is prevented. This reasoning is logical, but of course, since people are not perfectly logical, this action is not the only action that a person might take. Yet it is the only *logical* action that can be justified. Gewirth does not believe that his principle undervalues freedom, while he explicitly believes that the libertarian view, absolutizing freedom, overvalues liberty. Thus he does not believe that his approach is just a mirror image of Hart's absurdity, the starving, yet free peasant. Gewirth is not logically constrained to favor a well-fed prisoner because his theories are based more on human action and agency than they are on mere human existence. He realizes that well-fed prisoners can no more effectively exercise agency than starving peasants: true human agency and action requires both freedom and well-being. In short, for him, neither well-being nor freedom can be considered in and of themselves absolute or paramount values. His two basic values, freedom and well-being are values that create interdependent rights. Accordingly, Gewirth supports Shue's position that all basic rights are inherently interdependent. This finding, of course supports our thesis that economic rights are inherently interdependent with civil and political rights.

Another important theorist, Rodney Peffer, has a position similar to Gewirth's and Shue's. Peffer, in a compelling article entitled, "A Defense of Rights To Well-Being," is able to clarify some of the confusion that centers around discussions of economic rights. Peffer is most persuasive with his three categories of rights: freedom rights, rights to well-being and social contract rights. For him, ". . . rights to freedoms are traditionally said to arise from our respect for a person's autonomy (and hence may be referred to as autonomy rights), . . ."[65] Rights to well-being are, for him, rights that are concerned with human welfare. The first two categories are vague, but sound universal in definition and application. In contrast, his

---

65 Peffer, "A Defense of Rights to Well-being," 65.

definition of social contract rights is strictly particularistic. Peffer writes:

> Furthermore, I should like to distinguish a third kind of right which includes whatever rights to freedom and rights to well-being we may legitimately be said to have, but is not limited to them. These rights, which I shall call social contract rights accrue to individuals by virtue of their being members of a particular society at a particular time. They are defined as the rights which we, as members of that society, can justly claim, the rights that a just society, given its concrete conditions of production and so on, deems us to have. . . We do not possess these rights merely by virtue of being persons; given the principles of distributive justice and other such basic principles, they are rights that must be guaranteed by the particular society in which we live. Examples are the right to a free education, to adequate health care, to a fair trial and, I think it can be argued, the right to own property.[66]

His theory of rights accounts for many phenomena. Peffer is able to show, along lines similar to Gewirth's, how certain rights are absolutely necessary for action and agency in the world. At the same time, however, he is also able to explain how and why rights beyond the mere guarantees of freedom and subsistence may be defended. Peffer's theory of rights is a derivation of that of Gregory Vlastos.[67] Both theorists have as their ultimate value and beginning point the notion of human worth. Following Vlastos, Peffer writes:

> human worth, the intrinsic value we attribute to human beings regardless of their merit, is perhaps our most basic moral concept and the equal intrinsic value of all human beings perhaps our most basic moral principle. This concept underlies not only the concepts of justice and equality but also that of human rights.[68]

From these basic doctrines, whose correctness we will not presently address, Vlastos and Peffer conclude that:

> one man's well-being is as valuable as another's," that "one man's freedom is as valuable as another's," consequently

---

66 Ibid., 65, 66.
67 Ibid., 78, 79.
68 Ibid., 78.

that "one man's (prima facie) right to well-being is equal to that of any other," and that "one man's (prima facie) right to freedom is equal to that of any other.[69]

If Peffer and Vlastos are correct, their conclusion that the two major human values are freedom and well-being also appears to be sound. Equally correct therefore would be their understanding that these basic values are also the correct bases for freedom rights and rights to well-being. Rights to well-being are, for Peffer, "the rights to those things which we require if we are to survive and to have any sort of a life worth living."[70] These are rights similar to, but not as precise as, those given by Gewirth. Peffer gives examples to clarify the meaning of these rights. For him, rights to sustenance are valid well-being rights. Just as clearly, however, rights to a paid holiday are not. Peffer lists the latter rights in the social contract category. His rights theory attempts to account for social cooperation, or the lack thereof, in the actual recognition and implementation of rights. Thus freedom rights and rights to well-being are timeless and not bound by culture or economics. In contrast, clearly rights to paid holidays are merely the social contract rights of a planned economy in a socialist state.[71] Peffer shows how life requires both freedom and well-being without being tied into the "practicability" objections that Cranston and others have raised. In third world subsistence economies, rights to freedom and well-being may be all that may be recognized and implemented. As economies improve, social contract rights begin to be implemented by society as the culture, mores, and politics of the society allow and dictate, and as the social contract itself evolves in recognizing and responding to new social "needs."

Peffer's scheme, like Shue's and Gewirth's, does not call for radical egalitarianism, or for an equality of outcomes. Peffer, deeply influenced by John Rawls, emphasizes, as does Rawls, the role of institutions in recognizing and implementing

---

69 Ibid.

70 Ibid., 80.

71 This conclusion concedes the correctness of economic rights skeptics on paid vacation rights, without conceding the issue of other '"justified" economic rights.

rights. Like Gewirth and Shue, Peffer's theory calls for a new economic order. If membership in a society is extended universally, then the notion of the social contract, in Peffer's thought, must also expand, over a period of time, into some sort of international social contract applicable to a world community. Peffer's theories explain how rights can be both universal and particularistic, and how one can be distinguished from the other. Peffer, like Kleinig, is aware of the implicit coercion that is inherent in a concept like "rights."[72] Rights entitle one to call upon the community to act coercively to ensure that an individual has certain freedoms, or, for Peffer, certain provisions. Peffer is essentially a liberal theorist who does not want to invoke the power of the state to enforce any but the most basic rights. He also wants to enforce only those less basic rights that a given society has *already* acknowledged as valuable by means of an actual expression of a social contract (by means of a Civil Rights Act for example).

What are social contract rights? Peffer maintains that social contract rights are connected to theories of social justice maintaining that:

> we have a right to those benefits (goods, services and opportunities) which the principles of distributive justice dictate we should have, given the ability of our society to provide us with them--given its productive capacity and its population.[73]

In short, Peffer gives one a basis upon which to distinguish between basic rights and non-basic rights and a way for accounting for the differences between the two in international human rights schemes. If Peffer is correct, many of the rights that Americans think of as human rights are, in fact, simply social contract rights; those rights that are simply "understood" to be due to members of American society. These particularistic rights sound remarkably like Burke's "rights of Englishmen," as well they might. The essential difference between Peffer and Burke is that, unlike Burke, Peffer recognizes that there are universal moral rights that go beyond the rights dictated by

---

72 Kleinig, 45.
73 Peffer, 86.

custom or social contract.

Another scholar who has been deeply influenced by Alan
Gewirth is Raymond Plant, who helpfully fleshes out Gewirth's
structure. He ties it (like Shue) directly to social institutions but
in a clearer manner than does Gewirth. Plant also ushers in the
useful notion of human dignity. Plant relies on Gewirth's
Principle for Generic Consistency, but develops it in very
interesting ways. For Plant there are four elements in every
fully developed theory of rights:

> (1)   The agent to whom the rights are ascribed.
> (2)   The features of the agent which justify the ascription
> of such rights.
> (3)   The nature of the objects, resources, states of affairs,
> processes, or forbearances which the rights are rights to.
> (4)   The range of individuals or institutions who have
> the duties or obligations which correspond to the rights of
> other agents: that is, who or what has the duty to respect,
> implement, or satisfy the rights which individuals have.[74]

Though Plant is reliant on Gewirth, his argument works
more like Henry Shue's argument. His strategy is, as he puts it;

> to consider ways in which arguments in relation to the four
> features mentioned in Gewirth's formula are deployed in
> relation to rights such as life or liberty and then try to show
> that there are corresponding and equally cogent arguments
> in the case of the rights to welfare.[75]

Plant applies to Gewirth's formula his own two
fundamental criteria, universality and moral relevance.[76] Plant
maintains that raising claims assumes that agents possess moral
sensibilities: one cannot have duties or rights without the ability
to recognize them. Further, he grounds all rights discussion in a
matrix of social relationships that he presupposes are
essentially moral in nature. Recognizing the diversity of values
in the modern world he links universality and moral relevancy
together. He asks, "Are there any universal features of human
life which appear to be necessary presuppositions or conditions

---

[74]   Plant, 22.
[75]   Ibid., 23.
[76]   Ibid., 24.

for morality, whatever such moralities may turn out to be?"[77]

Such features, Plant insists, would be both universal and morally relevant. Not surprisingly, Plant adopts a Kantian approach: the preconditional human features are rational, autonomous agency, and the ability to formulate universal rules. If autonomy and rationality are to be the essential features of a theory of morality, then the rights that could arise out of these elements should be, at least initially, rights that are expressed by autonomy and rationality. These rights would be those understood traditionally as protecting the values of life and liberty. Thus for Plant basic human rights begin with the right to life and liberty: both understood as "first generation" negative rights. They are "negative" rights because they do not demand from society, ostensibly, acts of commission, simply acts of omission. The duties created, therefore, are merely duties to refrain from interfering with others. For Plant, a human being must get what she needs to live if she is to act as a rational agent. She must also be immune to a sudden or unnatural death, and free from the interference of others (coercion, assault, threats, etc.) in the expression of that agency. Plant recognizes that such a foundation is a difficult one upon which to construct welfare rights that are usually considered to be "positive" rights. That their recognition demands more than forbearance from interference but also the provision of "basic goods" presents problems. This line of reasoning shows how a liberal jurist like Hart can believe that if there are any "natural" rights at all, those rights must first begin with a right to individual liberty. It is with this liberty, agency, and rationality, that Kant and Plant believe that humans have the possibility of acting as moral agents. But Plant escapes Hart's dilemma, the starving-yet-free indigent, by turning to Rawls, who correctly raises the question as to the value of liberty. As Plant puts it, "Why do we want to be free from coercion? The answer must surely be that if we are free from coercion we shall be able to do more of what we want to do.[78] Plant thereby rejects the notion that the real value of liberty is simply to be able (in terms of our intelligence and rationality) to make independent choices.

---

[77] Ibid., 25.
[78] Ibid., 28.

Another way of illustrating this point is consider a menu in a restaurant. The ability to choose, and the freedom to choose, and even the resources to choose (i.e. having meal money) are all meaningless if one can choose any food or drink, but not get to eat or drink any of one's choices: one then suffers the tortures of Tantalus. Plant successfully argues, on the contrary, that part of the value of liberty is *the ability to successfully act upon one's choices*. Thus Plant is able to show that true liberty cannot simply mean freedom from the interference of others, but must also demand some measure of successful action.[79] If successful action demands certain resources, true liberty must be constrained to acquire or attempt to acquire those resources. This argument is, of course, quite similar to Gewirth's, and like Gewirth's requires a showing as to *why and how* the necessary resources of one independent agent become the responsibility (to supply) of another independent agent.

Plant begins this latter argument by distinguishing between freedom and ability. He acknowledges that he may have the freedom to do various things: to become a great mathematician, marathon runner, or child-bearer, without having the ability to do those things. In these cases no individual or institution in society can supply him with the resources for acting in those ways. Thus he is constrained to consider the class of basic goods that are the *necessary* conditions of agency, and not simply the possible objects of agency. Such goods would demand protection in terms of rights, and should be distinguished from all the other goods that a particular agent might desire. This task requires Plant to ask:

> . . . are there any needs which are basic to agency which can be defined independently of the specific needs which an individual may have in a particular culture or morality? If there are such needs they would then define the set of basic rights which would reflect such needs.[80]

Plant correctly posits that the needs that agency demands begin with the needs of physical survival. But he doesn't stop

---

[79] The methods and criteria for measuring the "successful" action are the concepts that generate controversy and discussion: not the notion of the necessity of "successful" action.

[80] Ibid.

there, also demading more more than just survival. He appears to have a genuine truth. What is the point, for a conscious being, of simply surviving when death is inevitable? Plant thus insists that some notion of well-being is logically necessary to account for agency. The alternative view merely reduces one's choices to actions that prolong life, or shorten it. Finally, Plant reveals his basic goods list that is, not surprisingly, rather short. Agency for Plant requires food, shelter, and some sort of health care. Thus he is really restating many of the elements found in Gewirth's formula. He does not, however, unreservedly maintain that Gewirth's principles are self-evident, or justified. Employing principles similar to those of Gewirth, but utilizing a method of argumentation that is closer to Shue's, Plant reminds us that if there are any rights at all, those rights *must* be both negative and positive rights. If he is correct, Jan Narveson's objections to positive rights, and other similar objections, must be erroneous.

His conclusion identifies providers for welfare goods. He recognizes the familiar objection that no single person can be seen as being perfectly responsible to supply the indigent with goods. But this axiom does not, in his opinion, disqualify economic rights from consideration as human rights. Instead like many skeptics he maintains that all rights in a modern society are embedded in the social arrangements and institutions of that society. Thus, just as a person might turn to the police for security, and to the courts for freedom from arbitrary arrests, so also might the indigent turn to the government, or some other social institution, for protection from want. Every competent individual would have, therefore, as a perfect, constant, but limited duty, not the obligation to act individually to protect the economic rights of the poor, but the duty to create, support and maintain institutional structures that can address particular and general cases of want; thus rationality and autonomy require both economic rights and rights to life and liberty.

Evaluations of Economic Rights Proposals

The economic rights theories offered have attempted to address the objections of the economic rights skeptics. What must now be determined is the extent of their success in rebutting the presumptions that economic rights are incompatible with civil and political rights. This question is a complex one. Clearly the economic rights that have been offered are not trivial; no one is seriously demanding, for all, a right to a paid vacation. These economic rights theories have had, as their objects, the minimum necessities for human survival. It is clear from our review of these theories that they all pass Cranston's paramount issue test: there is simply no demand for fluff. Turning again to the issue of universality, these approaches also pass muster. Shue, Plant, Gewirth and Peffer, each support economic rights for "universal enabling conditions." By universal enabling conditions I mean that the rights that they justify permit and maintain what is universally necessary for human life. This is not to say, however, that there are no societies in which the enabling conditions that these rights are designed to protect are absent, at least for some members. Such societies, however, have by definition grossly unjust distributions of goods and services, benefits and burdens.[81] What must be confessed therefore in regard to the use of the term universal is not that each enabling condition must have an actual empirical manifestation everywhere in the world. Instead what is meant by universal is that the rights that are offered are those that rights oriented people offer to the world as "candidates for truth"; as what we would offer as categorical imperatives.[82] In short, they are what we would propose as an international standard for human relations. This is obviously a different understanding of universal than what Cranston offers. The economic rights proposals considered herein, are, in contrast, less self-delusional.[83] Peffer recognizes

[81] Such societies are often genocidal and unstable; witness the state of Ireland, "run" by the British during the great potato famine. Ireland hemorrhaged precisely because of its lack of positive as well as negative rights.

[82] This phrase and the idea behind it I have borrowed from Jeffery Stout's *Ethics after Babel: The Language of Morals and Their Discontents*, (Boston: Beacon Press, 1990).

[83] They are less delusional in rights oriented societies. At the same time they concede that not all societies are or should be rights oriented. Human needs can be met in ways that do not use rights language.

that societies and their capacities differ. Thus these proposals are particularistic proposals for universal standards that are, admittedly, particularistic; that is, the standards are subject to the ethical, cultural, and historical influences of their authors, and their authors' contexts.

These responses explicitly challenge Cranston's practicability test. Essentially each of these authors maintains that there is a scarcity of the distribution of essential goods in the world, as well as a lack of industry. Each also maintains that there are more than enough goods in the world to address these scarcities. Thus each author maintains that the positive/negative rights distinction, while having technical merit, cannot invalidate economic rights concepts. As Shue emphasizes, the West could make it possible for everyone in the world to have their basic rights actually implemented and enjoyed. What that intervention would require, however, is a transfer of wealth, among other actions. This action is not logically impossible, but, for Cranston, morally impractical. In short, people like Cranston never seriously consider the transfer of wealth to a foreign country. By casting rights as the concern solely of each nation to its own nationals and others actually located within its territorial control, Cranston makes a moral problem look like a physical impossibility. Shue and others show why this reading of reality is incorrect.

Turning to the refinements on Cranston's tests, we find that the responses are effective rebuttals. First, none of the economic rights theories expressed is incomprehensible. Readers may disagree with their premises and or their conclusions, but each is a clear and coherent statement of economic rights. Thus these theories make sense, though they clearly will not appeal to everyone. Shue's thesis in particular, demonstrates the inherent interrelationship between civil and political rights and basic (including economic) rights. The incomprehensiblility objections are, therefore, in reality disguised claims that economic rights supporters fail to value the supreme values of the economic rights skeptics, i.e., liberty. On this point the skeptics are right; the co-equal values of freedom, well-being and security, are a different emphasis from the skeptic's supreme values of freedom and absolute property rights. But to say that the value choices differ is not the same as demonstrating persuasively that the rights based on differing value choices are incomprehensible. As has been argued throughout this study value choices are not automatically self-justifying and rights based on such choices are justified only to the extent that their underlying values are justified. Gewirth, Shue, and Plant are careful to show how basic needs may be used to create a short and simple list of basic rights, including economic ones. By doing so they adequately answer objections that decry that there is any connection between basic human needs and basic human rights.[84] These responses also show why the objects of economic rights are not endless. All economic objects cannot be claimed because even under these theories only a few basic objects can be morally justified. This closure as to the possible class of objects for economic rights also addresses both the limitation of freedom objections and interdeterminacy problems. If the number of objects and the scale of provision are limited, and if they are of a paramount value, than such objects and rights can and should be provided by institutional social arrangements and considered to be vital social provisions, like police, or fire protection.

Thus total negative individual freedom for some is given up as a trade off to secure basic positive freedom for all. The correlativity thesis is addressed along these same lines of thought. Duty-bearers are found among all those who propose to enjoy and uphold civil and political rights in a society that is concerned with a safety net for all. Those who have taxable assets, available to create and maintain such a society, make up the class of possible duty bearers. From Shue's perspective those who do not wish to pay for basic rights are shirkers; they want a society that has basic civil liberties and political rights without being willing to pay for the enabling conditions that permit that kind of society to function. There is no doubt that these arguments temper and limit certain understandings of liberty. If Shue is correct, the state has the responsibility to intervene to ensure that people do not succumb to standard threats. Indeed, this is one of Shue's major rationales for the

---

[84] The viability of Gewirth and Shue is further demonstrated in Chapter Five by theological adaptations of their approaches.

liberal state, notwithstanding Machan's arguments to the contrary. Machan's argument founders on his failure to justify his distinction between standard threats arising out of government, and standard threats arising out of economic institutions and relationships. In short Machan's criticism is itself defective. In contrast Shue's position, once one concedes the point that the individual in society is susceptible to standard threats, is self-evident.

Finally to be considered are the pejoristic objections. With regard to Hardin's objections, these neo-Malthusian complaints are, as we have seen, empirically doubtful. As moral arguments they are woefully defective. Gewirth and Shue show why Hardin is incorrect; he takes no notice of opposing empirical data. In addition, his argument is morally questionable because he favors a certain inhumane omission, or failure to act in the present, as a preferable response to a possible future problem of possible greater magnitude.[85] Hardin prefers the certain death

---

[85] The issue is not that the people of this generation have no moral obligations to the people of future generations. Rather, the issue is that one cannot say easily that certain actions that in this generation must be refrained from because they might make life more difficult in the future for future generations. Future generations may well have rights, but how they compare to a generation in being cannot be totalistic. Their rights, logically, cannot always outweigh our rights. The reasons why future generations cannot always matter more than the current generation are simple. First there can be no future generations without a current generation. Secondly, and perhaps equally important, to hold that the rights of future generations are always more important than the current generation is to engage in an infinite absurd progression. If future generations are always more important than current ones, solely because of their futurity, then they are also always less important than their successive generations. If this were true, then every generation would be less important than the following one and have consequently an absolute obligation to produce succeeding generations with no regard to present sacrifices, plans, etc. Moral agency in such a conception collapses into the pure reproductive instinct. People become merely a different sort of salmon, driven heedlessly into reproduction for the sake of reproduction. They would also be constrained by this logic to marshall all resources for the sake of a future generation. On the other hand, Hardin is not completely incorrect. This generation has (assuming it has some duty to continue the species) an obligation to reproduce and to steward the world in ways that do not penalize

of many in the present over the possible death of a greater number of people in the future.

In summation, the economic rights supporters answer every criticism of the skeptics. They show thereby that the skeptics represent a particular historical/political/economic position. Economic rights skeptics represent a position that wishes to have the sole power to define rights so as to lay down the ground rules for international relations, including economic relations in the present and the future. This struggle to have defining control over the concepts of human needs and human rights will be discussed extensively in Chapter Six. We must now turn to some of the weaknesses in the economic rights accounts.

A Criticism of Gewirth's Approach to Economic Rights

Alan Gewirth' s approach will be the primary focus of this evaluation. The reason for this emphasis on Gewirth is that he attempts to address more economic rights objections than any other theorist. In addition, Gewirth proposes that his PGC demonstrates, from first principles, the basis for moral obligation. Thus, his approach to economic rights, which is based upon his PGC is, from his perspective, self-evident. Though Gewirth may be correct in this claim, this study does not join him in making it. Further, I am unwilling to use his theories in the way in which he uses them. Gewirth's arguments demonstrate that economic rights are logically necessary for all rights oriented societies. Gewirth does not demonstrate, however, that all societies must be rights oriented. Thus, the PGC may well be compelling for Americans, while quite unnecessary and foreign for the Chinese. As Chapter One asserted rights are not the only way of construing moral obligations for all societies. Alisdair MacIntyre's criticism on this point has merit.

---

succeeding generations. The issues raised here are best addressed by environmental ethicists whose inquiries go beyond the limits of this work. What is clear, however, is that if the present generation has any rights they cannot be any less than the rights of future generations.

The chief weakness in Gewirth's work may be found in his inadequate explanation of human nature. One can deduce from reading him that he believes that people are *rational*, and that all individuals propose to be independent agents pursuing their own ends in the world. This rather empty conclusion highlights his vacuous characterization of human nature and human destiny. Gewirth does not have a fully articulated idea as to what is the meaning and value of human life, society, and destiny, offering no explanation of the Common Good.[86] He presents us with a moral construct that allows *individuals* the opportunity to pursue whatever ends they might fancy. Our only attendant obligation is the duty to eschew benign neglect. While pursuing life, liberty and happiness we are constrained to pause, when the occasion arises, to intervene on behalf of those who cannot act independently on their own behalf with any hope of success.

Susan Moller Okin criticizes Gewirth's position insightfully. Okin does not repudiate Gewirth as much as she attempts to correct him. Okin insists that all human rights theories are implicitly egalitarian. Accordingly, she accuses Gewirth of attempting to deny the inherent egalitarianism of his work. Gewirth, as Okin perceptively realizes, rejects the common anti-egalitarian ascription argument that since different people have differing abilities they should be accorded correspondingly different rights. Gewirth claims, to the contrary, that regarding agency, "actually being a prospective agent who has purposes to fulfill is an absolute quality, not varying in degree."[87] Accordingly, Okin points out Gewirth's consistency in denying full rights to those with restricted capacities, i.e., infants, the insane, and the mentally deficient.[88] She claims, however, that Gewirth's egalitarianism lies in the fact that he maintains that, with regard to the minimally competent, ". . . all human beings, as purposive agents, are equal."[89] Gewirth's refusal to differentiate between qualities or

---

[86] A focus on the Common Good is a primary concern of many philosophical and theological ethical inquiries. A brief discussion of this concern is addressed in Chapter Five.

[87] Okin, 233.

[88] Ibid.

[89] Ibid.

degrees of agency (beyond threshold competency) produces an egalitarian effect. Another way of putting this would be to say that because Gewirth will not second guess anyone's exercise of agency his position compels a nonvarying response that results in the appearance of egalitarianism. His theory thereby demands an equality of response without establishing an ontological human equality. Gewirth's theory of human nature is weak precisely *because* he cannot explain how, from a rights orientation, those who have no actual capacity for rationality, such as the comatose, idiots, the dead, or infants, are (or were) in fact human. Clearly, he does not deny their humanity, and yet he is confronted with the logical requirement to explain why those who are human must nevertheless be denied some of their "human" rights.[90] Okin attempts to correct Gewirth's theory by predicating human rights on human capacities, i.e., rationality,

---

[90] Gewirth tries to address the question of limited rights with a theory of limited capacity. Thus the comatose have rights to life while they have the capacity for life, even while they are unconscious. Why they should be accorded these rights Gerwith explains rather unpersuasively, writing: "What, however, of biological humans who are incapable of any kind of action, such as the famous case of Karen Ann Quinlan as well as infants who suffer from various disabling diseases? If human rights are rights to the generic features of agency, then how can any of these humans have such rights, let alone have them equally with normal human agents? The main answer to this question involves what I have elsewhere called the Principle of Proportionality: where humans lack the minimal rationality and other abilities that enter into normal agency, there have the generic rights to the degree to which they approach having these abilities. Hence insofar as there is any biological possibility that the humans in question will attain the normal abilities of agency, they have rights to the fostering of these abilities. Even where such attainment seems hopeless, they still have rights to be helped to attain as close an approximation of these abilities as possible." "Human Rights and Conceptions of the Self," *Philosophia* 18 (July 1988), 129-49, at 140.

What is troublesome in this approach is the fact that Gewirth never explains why someone who will never approach agency or action should be accorded rights. He never explains what the value is of people who are biologically fully human, "alive," yet permanently incapable of ever acting on their own behalf.

willing, choosing *and* human need.[91]   Thus, for Okin, permanently comatose persons may have certain rights to nutrition and health care even though they are permanently unable to exercise agency, or to experience well-being. Their rights are valid simply on the basis of their having human needs. But Okin's correction exacerbates rather than cures Gewirth's defect. Gewirth's enterprise is compelling, *only* because it is logically demanded of a *thinking and rational* human being who intends to act in the world with some probability of success. In such a scheme, infants may be considered as having "inherent" human worth because they are *potential* rational human agents in a maturation process necessary for their actual exercise of agency. The comatose, or autistic hold no such promise, and if they are not somehow intrinsically precious to society it is difficult to see why they should be accorded any rights including economic ones.

If human beings are not sacred, intrinsically valuable, in themselves, and not because of what they can do, what difference does it make that they have needs? How can bare needs command the provision of goods? Okin introduces the concept of human respect and dignity, but this does not solve this problem. Conscious human beings can sense respect, enjoy dignity, and can command respect. They can expect to be respected. It is difficult, however, relying purely on logic, to see how an idiot, or a comatose "body" merits the same consideration. This dilemma raises three serious questions that Gewirth avoids. The first question is whether there can be an adequate theory of human rights without an adequate explanation of the value of human life. The second question is similar: can we have a human rights theory without any teleology? The third question inquires into the importance of "individual" goals and their relationship to rights. Why should any rights be respected if human life has no purpose other than the pursuit of individual goals? What is so important about protecting the freedom and capacity for achieving individual

---

[91] Alan Gewirth, "The Epistemology of Human Rights," *Human Rights*, ed. Ellen F. Paul, Fred D. Miller and Jeffrey Paul, (Oxford: Basil Blackwell, 1986), 7. Gewirth specifically contests Okin's understanding of human rights, because of her dependency on definitions and what he perceives to be circularity in her arguments.

goals? Perhaps unintentionally, Plant raises these last questions when he employs Rawls' thought to question the value of liberty. Such evaluative questions cannot be limited, however, solely to the concept of liberty: they must be extended to question the value of all social meanings.[92] Plant argues that we have human rights so that we can be free to pursue life, liberty and happiness. But can the contents of human rights ever be determined without some consensus on human nature? Can we truly have a reasonable theory of human rights without some shared notion of happiness? If we have freedom and well-being we are able to pursue happiness, but to what end? How can the necessary social arrangements to enforce all types of rights be put into place and into practice if there is no consensus on the content and nature of happiness? More importantly, if human life is not somehow intrinsically valuable, how can the pursuit of happiness be important except to the pursuer, and only so long as the pursuit is pleasurable, or continues to present a real prospect of providing pleasure or happiness?

A recent essay by Gewirth attempts to take up these questions, and we shall turn to it shortly, but we must first note that he seeks to avoid the challenge of proposing and justifying a telos or goals in a modern, culturally pluralistic world. By doing so he avoids the problems of historical, cultural, and ethical relativism. He avoids the problems of relativism by choosing no specific goals or any specific ends that humanity should be obligated to fulfill or move towards.[93] But in doing so he presents us with an empty view of human destiny and a meaningless view of society and social cooperation. Okin is correct, therefore, in her decision to base her human rights theories on more than one basis, such as the rationality of the autonomous agent. Yet she too fails to propose a general theory

---

92 Plant, 22. Evaluations of primary values cannot be limited to a simple value, but must be extended to all of the primary values of a value system. Thus liberty is always understood in regards to equality and well-being. Much of the debate in this area is over how the values should be weighed and how such meta-ethical justifications can themselves be justified.

93 This refusal to suggest any goals to attempt to fulfill is similar to Hayek's negative liberty in that it gives no indication as to what constitutes the ultimate value of **positive freedom, "freedom for."**

of human value and human destiny. Indeed, Gewirth's problem in this area comes from his understanding of human nature and human worth, which he directly and irrevocably ties to his PGC. At the end of his epistemology of human rights, Gewirth finally attempts to comment on human dignity as the basis of human rights. For Gewirth, human dignity is personal and subjective. A human agent is a valuing agent, i.e., his/her goals have worth or value. Worth is, for him, an inherent, "ineluctable" quality of purposive human action. On the other hand, action that has no purpose has, assumedly, also no worth. He writes:

> Now, there is a direct route from the worth of the agent's ends to the worth or dignity of the agent himself. For he is both the general locus of all the particular ends he wants to attain and also the source of his attribution of worth to them. Because he is this locus and source, the worth he attributes to his ends pertains a fortiori to himself. They are his ends, and they are worth attaining because he is worth sustaining and fulfilling, so that he has a justified sense of self-esteem, of his own worth. He pursues his ends, moreover, not as an uncontrolled reflex response to stimuli, but rather because he has chosen them after reflection on alternatives.[94]

Gewirth argues that human worth can be asserted dialectically, and assertorically, but his arguments are not rigourous. There is good reason for this laxness, Gewirth's valuation theory, is, from an ethical point of view, no more persuasive than that of Nietzsche's. Nietzsche's will to power philosophy, tied to his theory of the Übermensch, centers on the notion that there is no objective reality regarding ultimate value.[95] Thus the Übermensch is required to impose value upon the observable world, including the slave races beneath him. What the Übermensch thinks is good, must be good; his ends are the only ends that matter. Gewirth's valuing individual is in the same position; that Gewirth's agent values (values here is used as a verb and not as a noun) is incontestable, however, the objectivity, relevance and universalizability of the end products of that valuing process (values as a noun, rather than a verb)

94 Gewirth, "The Epistemology," 23.
95 Friedrich Nietzsche, *The Gay Science*, Kauffman, trans. with commentary (1974), section 335.

are completely contestable. Thus, Nietzsche's Übermensch and Gewirth's agent are both left with the sheer fact of their willing value and worth. But though their act of valuing creates in them an undeniable psychological state of worth, it is a state that is present without also being inherently persuasive to others. Even the psychological state of Gewirth's willing is open to question. For example, a pedophile may feel that he must have the freedom and well-being that molesting children gives him. At the same time he is probably aware of the social taboos and prescriptions on his practice. Though he may not be able to control his irresistible impulses to crime, he may feel that his goals are valuable, hedonistically speaking, as well as reprehensible, conventionally speaking. He may in fact feel worthless, rather than worthy, precisely because of his effective exercise of his criminal agency. Presumably, Gewirth would say that pedophilia is not a basic good, and therefore should not be seen as necessary to any agent's freedom or well-being. This is a completely logical and rational response, but it misses the point. The pedophile is prudently aware of the dangers that his practices present to his freedom and well-being, yet he takes the risks, for what is, for him, a higher value. He is, simply put, not a purely rational being. One wonders if anyone is. This last point is is troubling. Gewirth's PGC binds rational people, yet we all know that no one is always rational, unswayed by emotion, and a sizable number of people are often irrational. The important point to note here, is however, *that Gewirth cannot derive human dignity from the individual act of a valuing agent.* At best, he can present for inspection a certain psychological state of consciousness. He can rightfully say that rational, autonomous agents should feel that their actions are worthwhile. Accordingly, they themselves have worth. But why, we must ask, should anyone else agree with them? Why should anyone else feel that anyone else's actions have dignity, or that anyone else is worthy of dignity? Logically speaking, it cannot be on the sheer basis of the other person's psychological state. If a madman insists that he is Napoleon he may get a salute while failing to convince anyone that he is Napoleon. Such a position brings to mind Hans Christian Anderson's tale of the "Emperor's New Clothes." The emperor's dignity was acknowledged as long as he and his subjects kept their decorum.

This dignity vanished, of course, as soon as one small child refused to play the decorum game.

Turning back to our three seminal questions for Gewirth we must conclude that he at least believes that his theory is fully justified. Thus he believes that we can have a theory of human rights with no theory of human value other than the one that is internal to his PGC. His argument for this is not explicitly made, but would have to be something along the following lines. Since every human agent has purposes or goals that he/she believes to be valuable, he/she must believe that, as the author of valuable goals, he/she is valuable. Thus every autonomous, rational, agent believes that human life is valuable, at least as that life is manifested by the agents themselves. Since every such agent believes that they are valuable they must also believe that the process of valuing is itself valuable and worthy of respect. If what makes each agent valuable is nothing inherent in the individual, other than the evaluation capacity and process of evaluing, every agent with this capacity who employs this process should be considered to be valuable, and equal in value to every other agent. Finally, since every agent is equal to every other agent, at least in this very limited sense, each agent should therefore be considered to be worthy of the respect that is due to valuing beings. This argument escapes circularity, however, only if the process of valuing can be given the high level of respect that this argument demands.

To make this second argument we inquire into the worth of valuing. Gewirth would probably reply, in a neo-Kantian fashion, to the effect that if nothing else in the world is valuable, at least the process or capacity to value must be. If in fact the process of valuing is valueless, or worthless, then no value assessments are possible for the simple reason that if the process of valuing has no value, how can the product(s) of this process be valuable? This argument is akin to Kant's absolutizing the good will as the ultimate source of the "good." Gewirth's valuation of valuing--functions like an ontological statement--like Kant's assignation of value to the good will. But what such statements are really saying is not that human beings are intrinsically valuable. Rather what such statements really maintain is that if there is any value, good or meaning in the world at all, it will be discovered only in the exercise of inquiry, evaluations and/or willing. For Kant, this meant that morality was completely autonomous, absolute rules or values existed, if they existed at all, only because they were brought into being by a Good Will.[96] Turning back to Gewirth, a comparison to Kant is unavoidable. Human dignity must be, for Gewirth, derived from the valuing process of rational, autonomous human agents. Humans are, therefore, valuable ontologically speaking, primarily because of their exercise of rationality and agency in conjunction with their actions in the world. The logical extension of this argument is, however, problematic, and has been touched upon previously. Non-rational, dependent beings, the retarded, autistic, or the comatose, are either not fully human, or somehow not (fully) entitled to human rights. Since they cannot value their actions, their actions have no worth to them. Accordingly, they themselves cannot have intrinsic self-worth. If such beings cannot value themselves, why should, and how can society value and respect them? Gewirth's logic cannot adequately address these rhetorical questions. Thus, as a practical matter, in any calculation where a conflict arises between these "second class citizens" and the rest of humanity, the resolution must be resolved in favor of the "valuing beings." Valuing beings become automatically valued beings. With this line of reasoning, in a world of scarcity, plugs should be pulled on the comatose. The retarded, or autistic, should be public policy afterthoughts, or, if they are competent to handle simple chores, employed in drudgery to the benefit of the "valuing" society. If the retarded can be employed as "drones," then at least they can be said to have some social value, even if they have no "intrinsic" value. These are grim, fascist thoughts. But where in all of this is the foundational notion that human rights, economic or otherwise, are rights to which all human beings are entitled, sheerly on the basis of their humanity? Such a notion may in fact be held by Gewirth, but it cannot clearly be derived from his theory apart from his high value on rationality and

---

[96] Immanuel Kant, *Foundations of the Metaphysics of Morals*, Lewis White Beck, trans. (Indianapolis: Bobbs-Merrill, 1981).

autonomous faculties of choice.[97] Vlastos' and Peffer's high esteem for "humanity in general" is missing from Gewirth's account.

Much time has been spent on highlighting this defect in Gewirth's theories for very important reasons. It is now apparent that human rights are not easily justified by resorting solely to moral principles and theories. Why this is so is demonstrated by the aforementioned problem as well as by attempts to answer the second critical question that Gewirth avoids. This second question is whether there can be a human rights theory without any telos. Gewirth's autonomous agents reveal no express understanding of the meaning of human life. Are we created, and if so, to what end or purpose? If we are not created, but are the simple products of necessity and chance, the thoughtless progeny of a mindless, purposeless process of evolution, what ultimate purposes can we have and how can they move from prudence and instrumental orientations to morality? It would seem, in such a world, that our human telos is simply to live with each other in as cooperative a fashion as possible, for as long as possible, deriving meaning catch as catch can, and moving unilaterally toward unknowable fates. Human rights in such a world, would be rules. These rules would be designed to minimize friction, and maximize "happiness," whatever that proved to be. Our human telos would be to live as harmoniously as possible until our Sun dies out and extinguishes all life. This bleak picture may be the only real one, but if it is, it is unlikely to inspire anyone to live "morally," or to recognize human rights. As austere as this vision is, it is still morally preferable to an antinomian muddle.

Our third seminal question also helps to show the problems of Gewirth's scheme. This question centered upon the value of individuals seeking and obtaining their own goals. Gewirth's autonomous agents each have their own purposes, but Gewirth makes no attempt to harmonize or cohere their purposes. Gewirth's human beings resemble, in an odd way, Hobbes' "man" in a state of nature. Individuals are not situated

---

[97] Since this study is not an examination as to the metaphysics of rights, but an evaluation of policy formation, Gewirth's failure on this point is not a fatal defect.

in families or in other institutions in society, and they seem to pursue singularly individualistic goals. There is no real explanation, from Gewirth, as to how his central principle would actually express itself in a society that is differentiated, pluralistic, and in great need of social cohesion. For Gewirth, every agent is psychologically prepared to be totally self-reliant. Individuals are not encouraged thereby to alienate themselves from others, but they are psychologically ready to fend for themselves if they need to. As a consequence, Gewirth's human agent seems to act in a vacuum, and it is unclear how such an individual could easily arrive upon shared strategies for creating and maintaining the institutions that are necessary to implement rights. Gewirth's agent seems, therefore, to work without a specific social vision. He or she merely wants to exercise his/her freedom in an experienced condition of well-being. Beyond these features Gewirth does not speak. It is fairly easy to show that this high value on the realization of individual goals is a product of the modern, liberal, social contract tradition. However as critics of this tradition we are constrained to ask why the realization of individual goals should be accorded so much value. For Gewirth, it is not of paramount importance that individual goals are of the highest value. Instead, it is a realization, on his part, that his PGC, cannot, as constituted, differentiate between *any* goals, nor properly evaluate shared social concerns. It cannot assess shared social goals because he has no explicit general theory of society. Gewirth's PGC is structured to consider first person attempts at reasoning, evaluating, and goal setting, rather than exploring shared moral propositions, exchanges and compromises. But shared social goals in a modern, pluralistic society are freely arrived upon, if at all, only after debate and compromise. Gewirth's theories cannot take this process into account. Thus his implied theory of society is that it is made up of a collectivity of risk aversive calculators of interest who merely want to exercise their agency and help others (when necessary) to exercise their own respective understandings of agency and action.[98] Such an atomized society lacks the social

---

98 The essential difference between Gewirth's moral individual and Hayek's consists in the fact that Gewirth's agent recognizes certain moral claims that Hayek's does not. Neither agent is, however, firmly fixed in

cohesion necessary for establishing and supporting the mediating institutions that are necessary for the continued recognition and protection of human rights, however they might be defined. Or, speaking more positively, if there is sufficient social cohesion present, such cohesion cannot be accounted for in his theory and remains, therefore, a conceptual mystery.

Gewirth's theory helps us to understand, however, that the recognition of economic rights is, or should be, compelling to rational, non-delusional beings: this is an important point. But, in the final analysis we are left with the further necessary determination as to whether or not human beings are as rational, logical, honest and consistent as Gewirth's theory implies. Gewirth simply does not give his theory of human nature and/or sin. What this criticism requires, therefore, is a continued search for more adequate explanations of economic rights that are grounded in a fuller and more satisfactory understanding of human society. Such theories may be able to successfully address Gewirth's shortcomings. More satisfactory understandings of society in relation to rights theories will be addressed in Chapter Five. We must now turn our attention to the question of how to interpret economic rights in interdependency *and* conflict with civil and political rights.

The Balancing of Rights

Economic rights skeptics insist correctly that economic rights sometimes conflict with civil and political rights: yet they miss the full import of this truism. On occasion, all rights conflict, even civil and political rights. Thus the economic rights skeptic's lexical priority for liberty is an inadequate way of dealing with the problem of the conflict of rights since civil and political rights also occasionally conflict.[99] Gewirth's approach with his criterion for degrees of necessity is, therefore, a superior response to this problem. It is a preferable response because he is able to address the conflict of rights problems of all types of rights, not just the conflict between civil and political rights with economic rights. What Gewirth's approach forces us to do is to understand, with regard to rights, that there must be

---

a cooperative social matrix.

[99] Even various rights to liberty conflict with other rights to liberty.

a balancing of rights. This requirement encourages us to consider the notion of prima facie rights.[100] For example, my right to own property, undisturbed by the State, is always only a provisional, prima facie right since the state can take my property by means of eminent domain. Of course I must be compensated for the taking, but a compensation is the constitutionally mandated response to the fact that my right to own my own real estate has been overridden by the state. My property right has not been violated, but overridden. It is, therefore, only a prima facie right. Similarly, my freedom to go about life, liberty, and the pursuit of happiness is limited by conscription. In America, even my liberty rights are not immune to being overridden by other needs of the State. That the conscription may be fairly and justly applied does not obviate the fact that my liberty rights are not absolute and have been overridden. How this relates to our discussion of economic rights can be seen by reconsidering the relationship between rights and duties. Economic rights are most concerned with those qualifications and exceptions that separate correlative prima facie duty presumptions from actual duty conclusions. If rights are correlative to duties, that is, that duties also create rights then in fact any genuine duty positively creates prima facie "rights" subject only to being ignored or overridden by important qualifications and exceptions. Such prima facie "rights" are not always realized as actual rights, but this circumstance is due solely to the fact that their realization is circumvented by the actual presence of appropriate overriding qualifications and exceptions. We should pause briefly now to consider such qualifications and exceptions.

Let us consider two hypotheticals. It is a common rescue procedure for lifeguards to resolve difficult rescue situations in a clear and quick fashion. If, for instance, a lifeguard is faced with the problem of saving two drowning victims he will commonly save first one drowning victim, and then, if it is not too late, the other. If his non-selected drowning victim (in a state of panic) impedes him from saving his selected drowning

---

[100] Peffer's essay, previously cited herein, has a good discussion of prima facie rights.

victim (his selection is arbitrary), the lifeguard customarily assaults the impeding victim so as to free himself to aid the first selected individual. There is no malice in either the selection or the assault, only the intent that at least one life be saved rather than two lives surely lost. Both potential victims have equal prima facie "rights" to be saved from drowning, but only one necessarily gets saved. However, no one questions the integrity of the lifeguard, or the wisdom or fairness of this practice, as the practice is self-evident. Now in terms of ethical analysis, prior to the actual rescue, though both victims have prima facie rights to being saved the lifeguard knows that he has only an actual duty to save both if circumstances permit. The lifeguard has, however, if circumstances do not permit, an actual duty to save only one. If one of the rescuees drowns they will not have had their rights ignored, or violated; they will simply not have had the implementation of their rights. Thus, for the unfortunate one, a prima facie right does not ripen into an actual right--still no one would say that the deceased did not have a right to be saved. The deceased simply did not have his right implemented. Now this right to be rescued can be applied in a similar fashion to the notion of economic rights. We have seen similar arguments by Shue, Gewirth, Plant, and Peffer. But even Michael Novak, an extremely tepid supporter of economic rights, can show us how this works. Novak, as we saw in Chapter Three, maintains that economic rights are conditional rights. His conditions for such rights are standard. The first concerns the capacity of the government or some other body to intervene if and when an emergency economic situation arises. The second condition is that the emergency economic condition expresses a paramount importance. The third condition is the one concerning Novak's pejoristic qualification. This condition demands that the would-be holder of the economic right must try, unsuccessfully, prior to his making a claim for help, to meet the economic emergency. Thus Novak's "conditional" economic right is best understood as a prima facie right, with prima facie duties. If the claimant passes all of the qualifications, and the claim passes all of the qualifications, and the duty-bearer passes all of the qualifications, then and only then can there be said to vest an actual economic right with an actual economic duty. However, when all of the conditions have been met, then the intervention by the government, organization, or individual is not a loose, gratuitous, charitable duty, *but a strict moral obligation that justice mandates.* Those who can help the innocent "needy" have a strict duty to do so. Conversely, the threatened innocent has a correlative actual right to help.

Consider another hypothetical, a "bad thing" is about to happen. A small child is in the process of drowning in a shallow pool. If there are no positive duties, or positive rights, than that child may call out repeatedly to no avail to nearby inactive "loungers" (Narveson's hypothetical).[101] Without a positive right to rescue such an occurrence might be a tragedy, but the failure to rescue, the carefree lounging by the pool would be perfectly acceptable moral behavior on the loungers' part. Their failure to intervene should not trouble the loungers, nor should others, having heard of this incident afterwards, be upset with the loungers. Yet, this scenario is patently absurd. Most cultures would frown on if not condemn such behavior. In the Judaeo-Christian heritage, even Pharaoh's daughter pulled Moses out of the bullrushes. Yet our analysis saves us from having to rely on intuition to account for the wrongness of the refusal to intervene. The paramount importance in preserving the child's life has not been preserved by the inaction of the loungers. Their rights to freedom in this instance are provisional and prima facie. Since they had no good reason not to intervene and the criterion of necessity was clearly in favor of preserving the child's right to life, they should have seen that the child's right was superior to theirs. Thus the child's rights automatically overrode their rights and therefore strictly obligated them, morally speaking, to intervene. If they fail to do so their failure cannot be justified by a reference to their rights to freedom. Such a conclusion is not reliant upon intuition, but rights analysis, strictly construed. Their prima facie right was to lounge. Their actual duty, however, was to intervene. In this case the child's prima facie right was to be rescued *and* her

---

101 This hypothetical presumes that the "loungers" are expert swimmers who can effectuate an easy rescue with a minimum effort

actual right would be to be rescued.[102] What is really at issue is not whether or not economic rights are "valid" human rights, but rather what should constitute the qualifications and exceptions and limitations pertinent to prima facie economic rights that might excuse or override their prima facie rights presumption and prevent them from being recognized and implemented as actual rights: rights that are important and potent, to be implemented by individuals and institutions.[103]

We come, finally, to a clear statement showing how economic rights (among other rights) should be conceded by all rational individuals (Gewirth's views-- shared by others), which cannot, however, clearly explain human nature, a viable telos, the value of humanity and the value of individual goals.

That theological explanations of economic rights theories better address the weaknesses that we have pointed out in our criticism of Gewirth's account is an hypothesis that must be explored. Hopefully these theories value human beings convincingly and can relieve the empty logic of Gewirth and Shue of their responsibility to explain and justify human worth. Gewirth and Shue's accounts are, nontheless, very important for handling the problems of conflicts among rights and the indeterminacy of rights objection.

Conclusion

This chapter has shown that economic rights are interdependent with first generation civil and political rights. Shue, Plant, Okin, Peffer and Gewirth, all explain why one cannot have "civil liberties" without also having economic rights. Gewirth has shown us that there is nothing that is inherently self-contradictory in the concept of economic rights. Further, he has shown us that human rights are logically necessary for rational beings who hope to have success in the

---

102 If, on the other hand, loungers cannot swim or get help in time, or otherwise intervene, the child could be characterized as simply an unfortunate drowning victim. Duty always implies an ability to act: where there is no ability to act, there is no duty to act.

103 This conclusion can also be reached with regard to civil and political rights. The classic qualification on free speech restrains the false exclamation of "fire" in a crowded, darkened theater.

exercise of their free agency when they are located in rights claiming societies.

More satisfactory accounts of economic rights are needed, which we can find in theological commentators. Better accounts are needed because the moral rights theories that we have examined are logically correct without being morally compelling. They lack compelling moral suasion because they cannot account for the nature and value of human beings adequately. Further, they do not show how human rights relate to human life beyond the assurance of human subsistence, and life has to be more than sheer subsistence. In addition, human dignity, that form of experience that the West has craved since at least the time of Hobbes is better addressed by theological economic rights theories.

Chapter Five profiles theological explanations of economic rights that incorporate or harmonize with the commentators in this chapter. Chapter Six shows how ethical and theological explanations of economic rights are not in contradiction to the Carter presidency's understanding of economic rights and how they might be incorporated into future economic rights policy statements. Chapter Six will also show how and why these explanations are still important to public policy formation. Our attention must now turn to Chapter Five and the theological debates.

CHAPTER FIVE

DIVINE DEVELOPMENTS

Chapter Four demonstrated the central thesis of this dissertation, namely that economic rights and civil and political rights are inherently related and interdependent. Accordingly, civil and political rights should not be recognized without also recognizing and implementing economic rights. With this conclusion, it might seem that the status of the economic rights debate is moving towards the "growing end of an argument"; that is, towards closure. This closure is a recognition of the validity of economic rights for implementation and policy formation. This growing closure is a logical one given the settled disposition of United States citizens to uphold and implement civil and political rights, and it is demanded despite the apparent reluctance of Americans to accord "second generation" rights the same policy status as "first generation" rights.

The present chapter reviews theological theories of economic rights. There are two major reasons for reviewing these materials and writing this chapter. The first reason is that although my central thesis has been demonstrated in Chapter Four, the moral justifications for economic rights were themselves less than satisfying for several reasons: first, they were unable to account for economic rights for human beings with defective capacities, i.e., those without rationality--the comatose, retarded, and the like; thus, their theory of human nature is too thin. Second, they failed to integrate rights within a clear conception of society. Third, Gewirth and Shue do not present a clear and common destiny for humanity, a telos that transcends their immediate era and place.

The failure of the moral accounts to satisfy these questions collapses economic rights into mere trumps in an endless card game of life with no meaningful resolution. Part of the task of this chapter is to show that these theological explanations ground economic rights theories in meaningful communities and contexts, in a social, rather than in an atomistic fashion. In addition, these theological economic rights theories must account for a common life together in a society that recognizes rights. Furthermore the theological theories present a value of human nature that is not dependent on human capacities, such as reason, and are able to explain more clearly who rights-claimants are and why they should be accorded rights.

The second major reason for looking at this material is more practical. The economic rights debate has not been argued without the input of religious debaters or the expression of theological concerns. Thus, a discussion of economic rights without a review and discussion of theological contributors and doctrine is simply an incomplete and inadequate approach to the subject. Economic rights have been discussed widely by religious thinkers and religious bodies and in ecumenical conferences. However, the influence of religious discussions of economic rights has not been limited to religious circles, but directly affects formalized economic rights debates. Theological economic rights theories and religious organizations have played and continue to play a significant role in contributing to the discussion in the economic rights debate. Robert F. Drinan's study of this phenomenon describes the extensive lobbying conducted by religious groups for the passage of economic rights legislation.[1]

---

1   Drinan writes in regards to the lobbying effort of religious groups on behalf of the Covenant for Social, Economic, and Cultural Rights, that, "The National Council of Churches (NCC), the United States Catholic Conference, and representatives of the Jewish community, were lavish in their praise of these treaties. Msgr. Frank Lally, testifying on behalf of the nation's 350 Catholic bishops, noted that in 1976 thirteen hundred representatives of diocese and Catholic organizations, in a unique assembly to commemorate the bicentennial of the nation,

It should be recognized further that some of the principals in the debate have worn two hats; they have represented secular organizations such as the State as well as religious bodies. For example, Michael Novak, a Catholic, and resident scholar at the American Enterprise Institute, was also the Chair of the United States delegation to the United Nations' Human Rights Conference in Geneva. And as Robert Bellah's classic essay on American civil religion suggests, every United States president has had to wear, even if unwillingly, some mantle of religiosity.[2] Further, as Chapter Two demonstrated, former President Carter's support for economic rights was founded, at least in part, upon his own understanding of religion and the ethical demands that the civil religion of the United States makes upon its citizens. This active involvement in the debate by religious players and parties already has connected theological views on economic rights to the wider moral discussion of the issues. Our present examination helps to clarify and brings to closure the case for economic rights as human rights, although, as will be made clear in Chapter Six, it cannot complete a discussion as to a complete list of valid economic rights or the absolute extent of their possible applications.[3] To ignore these materials and debaters would be to give an inaccurate and truncated picture of

urged the National Conference of Catholic Bishops to ratify the UN Covenants on civil and political rights and social and economic rights . . . The bishop's testimony, presented by Monsignor Lally at the hearings, urged ratification 'because we see in the substance of the rights enumerated in these treaties significant resonance with the enumeration of rights within the Catholic human rights tradition.'" See *Cry of the Oppressed: The History and Hope of the Human Rights Revolution* (San Francisco: Harper & Row, Pub., 1987) 61.

2 Robert Bellah, "Civil Religion in America," *Beyond Belief* (New York: Harper & Row, 1970), Chapter 9. Bellah's famous essay maintains that United States' national policy is not purely philosophical in its nature. It is always grounded in an ethos of civil religion. As Bellah points out, John F. Kennedy's inaugural address expressed confidence in the, ". . . power to abolish all forms of human poverty. . . and a . . . belief that the rights of man come not from the generosity of the state but from the hand of God." At 169.

3 Chapter Six demonstrates that economic rights require an ongoing conversation with regard to the appropriate types of rights and their appropriate implementations.

economic rights discourse.[4]
   This chapter begins with a brief survey of persons and
positions in the theological discussion of economic rights.
Following this theological survey, a brief examination of a
critical Roman Catholic economic rights debate between David
Hollenbach, S. J., and Michael Novak, will be presented. Next a
critical conversation between Nicholas Wolterstorff, professor
of philosophy at Yale University, and Richard John Neuhaus,
former Lutheran minister (now Roman Catholic), author, and
social policy strategist will be reviewed.
   The reasons for these selections are fairly simple: first, this
material continues and develops the previously discussed
debates between the two wings of Western economic rights
positions. David Hollenbach champions the economic rights
partisan position in opposition to Michael Novak who criticizes
and supports economic rights. Similarly, Nicholas Wolterstorff,
a philosopher of religion in the Reformed tradition, continues
the economic rights partisan position and is criticized for doing
so by Richard John Neuhaus. Wolterstorff continues Henry
Shue's argument from a richer point of view, with valuable
theological insights. By analyzing and evaluating this material
this chapter will further develop and critique the positions set
forth in Chapters Three and Four, without introducing new and

---

   4 John A. Coleman, S. J., asks an important question for the
justification of this chapter, namely, "Why this focus on the church as
an institutional actor in human rights advocacy, and why a concern for
the Catholic intellectual tradition on human rights?" Coleman answers
this question persuasively, stating, "Neither   governments nor
international agencies, such as the United Nations, are especially
effective advocates of human rights. Either their own self-interest, or
pressing diplomatic reasons, severely limits governmental moral
leverage on human rights questions. Transnational, nongovernmental
advocates of human rights such as Amnesty International or the
International Commission of Jurists, lack, generally, adequate resources
to organize, nurture, or protect local, indigenous human rights advocacy
in places as diverse as Lithuania or Bolivia. The churches are uniquely
on the spot to monitor human rights abuses and sustain human rights
advocacy. The Church has local, grass-roots listening posts, and often
the churches are the only possible sources of information across national
boundaries." See Coleman's influential essay, "Catholic Human Rights
Theory: Four Challenges to an Intellectual Tradition," *Journal of Law
and Religion* 2: 344.

distracting sub-arguments.

Following the examinations of these two positions, a brief statement regarding the contributions that theological explanations can make to the debate will be offered along with concluding remarks setting up the discussion in Chapter Six.

Theological Contributions to the Economic Rights Debate

The primary contribution that religion has made to rights discussion has been one of opposition. As Robert A. Traer notes, "Abba Hillel Silver writes that: 'Religion was not only tardy in championing human rights; at times it was actually retarding and reactionary'."[5] Traer maintains that the earliest contribution to rights concerns given in the Christian tradition was Tertullian's effort on behalf of religious freedom in conflict with the pre-Constantinian Roman empire.[6] This initial contribution, he maintains, was basically forgotten with the Christianization of the empire. Traer maintains that Luther was concerned with maintaining the hegemony of civil authority over the rights of people. Calvin, he maintains, was primarily concerned with the creation of a theocracy. Thus neither reformer was an active advocate of rights language and implementations.[7] In the post-Enlightenment period Traer notes that the Roman Catholic pope, Pius VI, was critical of the French Revolution's Declaration of the Rights of Man. Rights, as we have used the term, are primarily a product of legal and philosophical thought of the Enlightenment, and as such often have drawn the opposition of religious groups and leaders.

Accordingly, the Christian theological contributions to

---

5 Robert A. Traer, "Human Rights a Global Faith," 120. The original citation for Silver is, "Prophetic Religion and World Culture," in *Religious Faith and World Culture*, ed. Amandus William Loos (Freeport, New York: Books for Libraries Press, 1951; reprinted 1970), 138. In regard to Pope Pius VI, Traer notes, "It is not surprising then that Pius VI as early as the brief *Quod aliquantum* in 1791 criticized the French Revolution's Declaration of the Rights of Man for supporting freedom of opinion and communication." Ibid., 121.

6 Ibid., 120.

7 Ibid., 122. Yet Calvin, as we will demonstrate shortly, manifested a deep commitment to meeting the needs of poor people.

rights debates were not supportive until fairly recent times. Supportive statements became more frequent and intense in the post-World War II period. Since Catholics have been more prolific contributors to this discussion than Protestants, their contributions should receive our initial attention.

The modern Catholic contributions to the economic rights debate begin, in earnest, with Pope Leo XIII and his encyclical, *Rerum Novarum* in which he proposed a basic right to subsistence.[8] *Rerum Novarum* (1891) repudiated Enlightenment inspired theories on natural rights. Pope Leo XIII specifically rejected the political voluntarism of the West, which was propagated along with Deist or intuitionist theories for natural rights.[9] *Rerum Novarum* also rejected the totalitarian and

---

[8]   David Hollenbach, *Claims in Conflict* (New York: Paulist Press, 1979), 43.

[9]   Leo's encyclical "On the Modern Liberties" also raised serious questions about "first generation" rights. For an insightful review of Leo XIII, See *The Church Speaks to the Modern World: The Social Teachings of Leo XIII*, Etienne Gilson, ed. (Garden City, N.Y.: Doubleday, Image, 1954), at 15-18. Hollenbach notes in reference to Leo's rejection of Enlightenment rights that: "Thus Leo XIII's criticisms were inspired in large part by his desire to protect the Church's freedom to pursue its religious mission and by the political self-interest of the papacy. In its theoretical elaboration, however, Leo's critique was directed against all forms of democratic theory which maintain that basic values and human rights are created by human choice. It was an objection to all forms of strict moral and political voluntarism." Ibid, 44. Hollenbach is not the first Catholic to note the conflict between first generation rights and Catholic Social teachings. One of the most influential Catholics in the struggle for human rights, Jacques Maritain, thought that many of the values of the Enlightenment were incompatible with Catholic views of the state and society. For a full discussion of the conflict between traditional Catholic views (prior to Vatican II) and Enlightenment individualism and contractarianism. see Robert Carle's study, "Theological Critiques of Human Rights Theory: The Contributions of Jacques Maritain and Gustavo Gutierrez." (Ph.D. dissertation, Emory University, 1989). Michael Novak notes with regard to Leo XIII, "He roundly condemned socialism, even in its milder forms. He upheld the notion of the limited state and the critical role of private property as the protector of liberty. But he was soundly critical not only of certain practices of capitalism but of some of its philosophical bases, especially its individualism and its radical dependence on the free market." *The Spirit of Democratic Capitalism* (New York: Simon & Schuster, 1982),

humanistic claims regarding human society and government made by Marxists.[10]   Unfortunately,*Rerum Novarum* employed the both/and approach that is typical of Catholic moral teachings.[11] *Rerum Novarum* affirmed both the capitalist right to own property and the right of each person to "procure what is required in order to live."[12] Pope Leo XIII grounded his theory of subsistence rights in his understanding of human nature, and in the priority of society to the state. He maintained that, "Man precedes the State, and possesses prior to the formation of any State, the right of providing for the sustenance of his body."[13]   Pope Leo XIII's point is crucial for this discussion. His recognition that human beings and their needs

---

244.

[10] With regard to *Rerum Novarum* Thomas R. Donahue maintains, "This Encyclical greatly influenced Catholic labor leaders and provided new support for them in their opposition to Marxism and its class warfare theories."   In "From Rerum Novarum to Laborem Exercens" in *Moral Theology* 5, ed. Charles E. Curran and Richard A. McCormick (New York: Paulist Press, 1986), 387. The classic rejection of rights is that of Pope Pius IX's encyclical, *Syllabus of Errors*. Pius IX, *Syllabus of Errors, in Church and State Through the Centuries*, ed. and trans. Sidney Ehler and Hohn Morall (London: Burns and Oates, 1954), 284-85.

[11] The both/and approach is one way that newer encyclicals do not repudiate past encyclicals but instead modify the current stance by adding nuances and reinterpretations to the past encyclicals in the new encyclical.   For John Coleman's explanation of this phenomenon see Note 70 herein. Unfortunately this approach minimizes the recognition of social conflict and sometimes produces complex ambiguities.

[12] Pope Leo XIII, *Rerum Novarum*, par. 34. In *The Church Speaks to the Modern World: The Social Teachings of Leo XIII*, Etienne Gilson, ed. (Garden City, N.Y.: Doubleday, Image, 1954).   Hollenbach interprets this aspect of the encyclical in the following way: "Among the rights defended in Rerum Novarum were the right to adequate remuneration for one's labor in the form of private property.   Furthermore, The encyclical calls for the extension of actual property ownership to as great a number of persons as possible. The right to private property derives not simply from the freedom of individual persons to act in a way unimpeded by others, but also from the fact that persons necessarily depend for the preservation of their dignity upon material conditions. All have a right to have these needs fulfilled at least minimally. Thus the encyclical affirms the existence of rights to adequate food, clothing, and shelter." *Claims in Conflict*, 47, 48.

[13] *Rerum Novarum*, par. 6.

are prior to and more important than any single understanding of the State, capitalist, socialist, or communist is foundational to any understanding of Catholic human rights theory. He also wanted to resist the ideological influences of Marxism.[14] Simultaneously, he addressed some of the abuses of capitalism while not fundamentally challenging the economic structure.[15] He affirmed rights to private property *and* the rights of workers to fight for a livable wage. John Langan, S. J., a noted Catholic commentator, also sees in this encyclical the foundation for a theory of subsistence rights.[16] Thus, even as Pius IX and Leo XIII repudiated, for various reasons, aspects of liberal and socialist theories, they nevertheless called for the recognition of universal social solidarity. What Leo XIII sought to do was to set forth Catholic metaphysical presuppositions for rights theories and social arrangements that were distinct from liberal

---

14 Hollenbach writes with regard to Leo XIII and his successor that, "But like Leo XIII, Pius XI rejected the theory of class struggle adopted by Marxism-Leninism." *Claims in Conflict*, 52.

15 Hollenbach observes, "It was on the economic flank of the Church's engagement with modern society, therefore, that Leo made the most substantive advances. The positive influence toward equality exerted by his writings came chiefly from his treatment of the economic and social rights of workers." Ibid., 46. A portion of *Rerum Novarum* that reads as follows: "In any case we clearly see, and on this there is general agreement, that some opportune remedy must be found for the misery and wretchedness pressing so unjustly on the majority of the working-class . . . By Degrees it has come to pass that workingmen have been surrendered, isolated and helpless, to the hardheartedness of employers and the greed of unchecked competition." Ibid., *Rerum Novarum*, no. 3. However, Leo XIII should not be interpreted as supporting egalitarianism. Charles E. Curran notes, Leo XIII not only did not promote equality as a virtue or something to be striven for in society, but he stressed the importance of inequality . . . Leo had a view of society as a hierarchical organism in which there are different roles and functions to fulfill, but in which all will work for the common good of all." "Changing Anthropological Bases of Ethics," in *Moral Theology No. 5*, 190.

16 John Langan, S. J., "Human Rights in Roman Catholicism," *Readings in Moral Theology No. 5: Official Catholic Social Teaching*. Ed. Charles E. Curran and Richard A. McCormick, S. J., (New York: Paulist Press, 1986), 118.

or socialist thought.[17]   At the same time he wanted to
acknowledge human need and human dignity.

When the serious international debate regarding economic
rights began after WWII, Catholics were quite influential in the
shaping of this discussion. In fact, the Universal Declaration of
Human Rights was greatly influenced by two Catholics, Jacques
Maritain (one of the chief authors) and Angelo Giuseppe
Roncalli, who eventually became Pope John XXIII.[18] Although
serious consideration of economic rights may be found in Pope
Leo's encyclical, *Rerum Novarum* Pope John XXIII's encyclical,
Pacem in Terris, (1960) is the first full-fledged Catholic
endorsement of so-called economic rights.[19]

Pacem in Terris maintained that human rights were part
of the permanent structure of Catholic social teachings and

---

[17] Hollenbach maintains that Catholic suspicions of both the liberal
and socialist understandings of "human rights" remains. He notes,
"Recent Roman Catholic criticisms of liberalism and Marxism have
been directed chiefly at the way their strategic concerns tend to be
collapsed into normative theoretical descriptions of the full content of
human dignity and human rights.   When this happens strategic
morality becomes ideology--a mode of thought which narrows its
normative description of the human person in the interest of strategic
action." *Claims in Conflict*, 190. He adds that the problem usually
centers around an overly narrow (from the Catholic point of view)
understanding of "concepts of man." Ibid.

[18] Warren Holleman, "Reinhold Niebuhr on the United Nations
and Human Rights," *Soundings* 70 (Fall-Winter, 1987): 329-54.
Holleman maintains in his second endnote that, "The most prominent
Catholic intellectual of the day, Jacques Maritain, was the French
delegate to UNESCO. An Italian priest, Angelo Giuseppe Roncalli, who
later became better known as Pope John XXIII, helped write the United
Nations' Universal Declaration of Human Rights," 350.

[19] Of *Pacem in Terris* Hollenbach writes: "Pacem in Terris gives the
most complete and systematic list of these human rights in the modern
Catholic Tradition. The rights it affirms have been assembled from
those mentioned and defended in the previous documents of the
tradition. Because of its new perspective on the importance of social
institutions and organizations, the encyclical has also considerably
enlarged the domain of rights It is a domain which includes both those
rights stressed by the liberal democratic tradition and those emphasized
by socialists." *Claims in Conflict*, 66. Here Hollenbach acknowledges
that *Pacem in Terris* addresses economic rights.

were grounded in the dignity of the human person.[20] *Pacem in Terris* reads in part:

> Any human society, if it is to be well-ordered and productive, must lay down as a foundation, this principle, namely, that every human being is a person, that is, his nature is endowed with intelligence and free will. Indeed, precisely because he is a person he has rights and obligations flowing directly and simultaneously from his very nature. And as these rights and obligations are universal and inviolable so they cannot in any way be surrendered.[21]

What is important about *Pacem in Terris* is Pope John XXIII's firm grounding of all human rights in his understanding of human nature and human dignity. Rights-claimants are not always right in their demands, but they are always sacred. This high regard for human beings constitutes a higher theoretical value than Catholic ideas concerning the importance of the state or the importance of society. This foundation in human dignity is also applicable to the subset of human rights that we have called economic rights. It is this understanding of human dignity that is the basis of modern Catholic human rights teachings.[22]

---

[20] Charles E. Curran also maintains that human dignity and human rights are the theoretical bases for *Pacem in Terris*. Charles E. Curran. "Changing Anthropological Bases of Ethics, "*Readings in Moral Theology No. 5: Official Catholic Social Teaching*, 195.

[21] Ed. David M. Byers, "Pacem in Terris," *Justice in the Marketplace: Collected Statements of the Vatican and the United States Catholic Bishops on Economic Policy, 1981-1984* (Washington, D.C.: United States Catholic Conference, Inc., 1985), 152. Hereinafter referred to as *Justice*. It should also be noted, however, that some Catholics believe that the Catholic notion of the common good is more foundational to human rights than the idea of human dignity. See John Coleman, S. J., "Catholic Human Rights Theory: Four Challenges to an Intellectual Tradition," *The Journal of Law and Religion* 2, no. 2 (1984): 355.

[22] Hollenbach notes that: "The thread that ties all these documents together is their common concern for the protection of the dignity of the human person. In a speech delivered in May 1961, John XXIII stated that the entire modern tradition 'is always dominated by one basic theme--an unshakable affirmation and vigorous defense of the dignity and rights of the human person.' In John XXIII's view, human dignity is the concrete normative value which the entire tradition has attempted to defend. Respect for the dignity and worth of the person is the foundation of all

Furthermore, as we will see shortly, it is this grounding of individual human rights in a community setting that constitutes the greatest Catholic contribution to human rights.

Turning to the Protestant contributions to the economic rights debate, we find Jürgen Moltmann, a well-known German theologian and human rights commentator. Moltmann notes that the World Council of Churches was formed at about the same time as the United Nation's Universal Declaration of Human Rights.[23] The WCC contributed to the drafting of the Universal Declaration that contains economic rights. Moltmann also notes that the Commission of the Churches for International Affairs assisted in the, ". . . codification, and defense of the later human rights blueprints, especially the 1966 International Covenants, . . ."[24] Since these initial contributions, Protestant councils have been busy formalizing theological supports for economic rights and lobbying for the passage of supportive international treaties.

In summation, Protestants and Catholics both support economic rights and are likely to continue to do so.[25] Other important

---

the specific human rights and more general social ethical frameworks adopted by the encyclicals and other Church teachings. These rights and ethical frameworks have undergone a notable evolution and will continue to do so. But through this process all alterations have been governed by an attempt to remain responsive to human dignity and its concrete demands." *Claims in Conflict*, 42.

[23] Jürgen Moltmann, *On Human Dignity: Political Theology and Ethics* (Philadelphia: Fortress Press, 1984), 3.

[24] Ibid.

[25] Lowell Livezey's article is the best survey of Christian contributions to the economic rights debate. Lowell W. Livezey, "U S Religious Organizations and the International Human Rights Movement," *Human Rights Quarterly* 11, no. 1: 14-81. Livezey notes many large religious ecumenical organizations that affirm economic rights, including the National Council of Churches, the American Friends Service Committee, The United States Catholic Conference (the official political voice of Roman Catholicism in the United States), and The Union of United States Hebrew Congregations. Livezey also cites ecumenical supporters for economic rights, such as Clergy and Laity Concerned (CALC), The Coalition for a New Foreign and Military Policy, and The Washington Office on Latin America (WOLA) (implicitly). Ibid., 22, 28, 39, 40, 43, 58, 62, 66. Regarding the NCC, Livezey notes that, "By affirming the 'U. N. concept of rights,' the Council affirms that there are economic, social, and cultural rights as well as civil and political

commentators write in a world in which the Christian churches
have taken a supportive though far from uniform stance on
economic rights. Having shown the existence of theological
concerns for economic rights, we may now turn to the
Hollenbach/Novak debate.

rights, and that these rights belong to everyone in the world."
Regarding the American Friends Service Committee, "Thus, concern for
human rights is deeply rooted in the faith, history and experience of the
Religious Society of Friends: Such a broad rationale, intertwined as it is
with a broad-gauged service program, naturally supports an inclusive
concept of human rights, embracing political, civil, economic and social
rights.   Moreover, the Service Committee affirms the Universal
Declaration and the two international covenants, noting especially their
expression of the linkage of all human rights." Regarding the United
States Catholic Conference, (the official political voice of Roman
Catholicism in the United States), "The Human rights actions taken by
the USCC explicitly promote a wide range of rights--economic and social
as well as civil and political." Livezey goes on to note that, "the
Conference gives programmatic attention to economic and social rights,
explicitly identified as such, that is greater than any of the organizations
discussed so far." Regarding the Union of US Hebrew Congregations,
"Similarly, UAHC supported the right to a job (preferably to be achieved
by the expansion of the private sector) in 1977, the Hunger Relief Act in
1984, and generally legislation that makes subsistence or the means to
secure it a matter or right or entitlement. In sum, without appealing to
the United Nations or international law, or to a systematic argument for
what constitutes a right, the UAHC promotes certain economic
conditions, especially subsistence, as rights, thereby affirming that it is a
matter of duty and justice--not generosity or charity--to see that those
conditions are met." Livezey also notes ecumenical supporters for
economic rights, such as Clergy and Laity Concerned, (CALC). "In
principle, CALC affirms the complete corpus of internationally
recognized human rights, and parts of its programs and literature are
designed to explain and build support for this entire body of rights."
Regarding The Coalition for a New Foreign and Military Policy, Livezey
notes that this group published an "attractive but inexpensive
sixteen-page publication which . . . emphasized that by ratifying the
covenants the United States would be formally obligating itself to secure
for the U.S. people all the rights stated in the covenants, which would be
particularly important with respect to economic, social and cultural
rights." Lastly, regarding the Washington Office on Latin America,
(WOLA), "Although WOLA's program emphasizes violations of the
rights of the security of the person, the organization believes that these
violations arise from deprivations of both civil and political rights and
socioeconomic rights."

The Hollenbach/Novak Debate

Chapter One introduced David Hollenbach, S. J., a Catholic theologian who has restated modern Catholic socialteachings in relation to human rights discourses. His work must now receive our full attention. Hollenbach is a strong advocate for human rights in general and economic rights in particular. In his examination of a series of encyclicals, Hollenbach traces the changes in modern Catholic social teachings that we have previously alluded to that allow for human rights.[26] Chapter Four, it may be recalled, was critical of Gewirth's abilities to account for rights in a communal and social setting. As a consequence, his rights theories appeared to overemphasize individual goals and rights without commenting on the relationship of individual goals and rights to the goals and rights of the community.[27]

Hollenbach directly addresses this concern with a theory of rights located in a community setting. He first distinguishes Catholic theories of rights from libertarian schemes writing:

---

[26] *Claims in Conflict*, 89.

[27] Another Catholic scholar, John Coleman, has also expressed some doubts about Gewirth's ability to account for rights in society. Gewirth's inability to locate rights in a coherent theory of society compels Coleman to consider using Gewirth's work as a helpful approach to Catholic theories. As a critical interpretive tool to Catholic approaches, Coleman finds Gewirth valuable. Coleman has noted in an article that compares Hollenbach's approach to Gewirth's that, "Provided that this grounding by Gewirth, following the lead of the Catholic theory, entertains a sufficiently strong social understanding of human action, I would contend that it promises to be, formally and in theoretical coherence, superior to the ordinary Catholic accounts which justify rights in a norm of human dignity." "Catholic Human Rights Theory: Four Challenges to an Intellectual Tradition," *The Journal of Law and Religion* 2, no. 2 (1984): 343-66, 352. Coleman finds much that he likes in Hollenbach, but also believes that his views can be improved by a construction of a short list of rights that can be devised by the use of the approaches of Shue and Gewirth. On the other hand, Coleman believes that rights must be located in a social setting in a clearer fashion than Gewirth provides. Thus both Catholic and philosophical approaches have their strengths and weaknesses.

Catholic rights theory is far removed from individualist or libertarian social philosophy. The theory presented in the encyclicals is personalist, not individualist, and it recognizes that persons are essentially social and institution building beings. Because of this fact the personal rights which belong to every human being in an unmediated way create duties which bind other persons, society and the state. These duties are not simply interpersonal bonds such as those which exist within families and other preliminary groups. They are also social and political. Consequently the recognition of the full richness of human dignity creates a demand in the human community that the social and instrumental rights in the two outer circles of the diagram be recognized through the appropriate structures.[28]

Thus, Catholic social teachings maintain that human dignity, agency and action cannot be accounted for in theories that do not address the place of the individual in society and with society. Catholic teachings, particularly as they have been interpreted by Hollenbach, thereby make a significant contribution to the economic rights debate, as they provide a social matrix for rights recognition. Limited space prevents this study from fully discussing the social world of Catholicism and its characterization (even in the post-conciliar world) of the relationship between church and state, and between the person and his/her community. However, this brief discussion makes it clear that Catholic social teachings maintain that persons realize their humanity, including their dignity, *in community*, rather than in solitude.[29]

---

28 *Claims in Conflict*, 97. The diagram that Hollenbach is referring to is found on page 98, ibidem.

29 Even with regard to personal rights, Hollenbach asserts: "The necessity of providing for the realization of these personal rights in societal interaction and communal life gives rise to another kind of right--social rights. These social rights and Gewirth. On the other hand, Coleman believes that rights must be located in a social setting in a clearer fashion than Gewirth provides. Thus both Catholic and philosophical approaches have their strengths and weaknesses. *Claims in Conflict*, 97. The diagram that Hollenbach is referring to is found on page 98, ibidem. Even with regard to personal rights, Hollenbach asserts: "The necessity of providing for the realization of these personal rights in societal interaction and communal life gives rise to another kind of right--social rights. These of Jesus, the motifs of covenant and

Hollenbach relies upon the undifferentiated lists of human rights in *Pacem in Terris*. This reliance is problematic because *Pacem in Terris* has more than one list of possible economic rights, listing what we have called economic rights in at least two sections. Part I, section 11, entitled, "The Right to Life and a Worthy Standard of Living" reads in part:

> Beginning our discussion of the rights of man, we see that every man has the right to life, to bodily integrity, and to the means which are suitable for the proper development of life; these are primarily food, clothing, shelter, rest, medical care, and finally the necessary social services. Therefore a human being also has the right to security in cases of sickness, inability to work, widowhood, old age, unemployment, or in any other case in which he is deprived of the means of subsistence through no fault of his own.[30]

However, section 18, "Economic Rights," reads as follows, "man has a right by the natural law not only to an opportunity to work, but also to go about his work without coercion . . . and, Section 20 of *Pacem in Terris* reads:

> From the dignity of the human person, there also arises the right to carry on economic activities according to the degree of responsibility of which one is capable. Furthermore--and this must be specially emphasized--the worker has a right to a wage determined according to criteria of justice, and sufficient, therefore, in proportion to the available resources, to give the worker and his family a standard of living in keeping with the dignity of the human person. In this regard, our predecessor Pius XII said: To the personal duty to work imposed by nature, there corresponds and follows the natural right of each individual to make of his work the means to provide for his own life and the lives of his children; so fundamental is the law of nature which commands man to preserve his life.[31]

---

liberation, and the doctrine of Christian freedom have stimulated a new dynamism and critical spirit in Catholic social ethics." Ibid., 187.

[30] Pope John Paul II, "Encyclical Letter of the Supreme Pontiff John Paul II: Sollicitudo Rei Socialis," L'Osservatore Romano (English edition, 29 February 1988).

[31] Hollenbach ascribes some of the movement away from natural law as being in response to Protestant criticism that cast doubts upon the ability of human covenant and liberation, and the doctrine of Christian freedom have stimulated a new dynamism and critical spirit in Catholic social ethics." Ibid., 187.

Unfortunately, *Pacem in Terris* lacks a short list of basic rights. Its listing of many rights is unfortunate because it does not designate which rights are the most important should a conflict arise between rights. In addition, its vagueness with regard to the institutional changes that might be needed in order to implement rights is also troublesome. Regrettably, Hollenbach does not correct this vagueness. Nevertheless, despite these shortcomings, according to Hollenbach, an important break with traditional Catholic doctrine is discernible with *Pacem in Terris*. Pope John XXIII convened Vatican II with an emphasis away from Catholic natural law and traditional teachings to a more critical reinterpretation of Scripture.[32] This movement toward a more covenantal and Scriptural orientation in Catholic social teachings is continuous to the recent statement of *Sollicitudo Rei Socialis*.[33]

From Hollenbach's perspective modern Catholic social teachings moved away from the old Catholic natural law.[34] The old law was cosmologically oriented; it was that aspect of the divinely created Eternal law that was discernible to human reason, and disclosed in creation through "natural revelation." Humanity had the duty to bring its virtuous action in line with the natural and divine laws that were themselves manifestations of God's Eternal Law. However, from this

---

[32] Pope John Paul II, "Encyclical Letter of the Supreme Pontiff John Paul II: Sollicitudo Rei Socialis," L'Osservatore Romano (English edition, 29 February 1988). Hollenbach ascribes some of the movement away from natural law as being in response to Protestant criticism that cast doubts upon the ability of human reason to rightly discern natural law. John Paul II: Sollicitudo Rei Socialis," *L'Osservatore Romano* (English edition, 29 February 1988).

[33] Hollenbach ascribes some of the movement away from natural law as being in response to Protestant criticism that cast doubts upon the ability of human reason to rightly discern natural law. Revelation, in post-conciliar documents, becomes more emphasized along with the strictures of Christian doctrine. *Claims in Conflict* , 108-17.

[34] Writing in regards to pre-Vatican II natural law theory, Hollenbach offered a response to Protestant criticism that cast doubts upon the ability of human reason to rightly discern natural law. Revelation, in post-conciliar documents, becomes more emphasized along with the strictures of Christian doctrine. *Claims in Conflict*, 108-17.

perspective many of the stations in life were normatively understood to be given: people were born (supposedly) into assigned roles and were called to practice virtues applicable to those roles in that society.[35]

In contrast, the modern understanding of Catholic social teachings has taken a turn away from the social roles allegedly directed by the Divine to the needs of the anthropocentric subject. Now demands are made to insure the natural, or biological needs of humans and/or the inherent dignity of divinely created human beings in society. Human beings are now understood to be radically equal, in terms of both their spiritual worth and their social worth.[36] Slavery, and other forms of injustice and discrimination, are now understood by Catholic and Protestant alike to be unjust.

Hollenbach reinterprets the Catholic commitment to "human dignity" as independent from the actions of human agents: one does not merit human dignity. Human dignity is, for him, a doctrine, a Divine Given, and is not subject to waiver, alienation or loss due to "laziness." So, even lazy people are

---

[35] Writing in regards to pre-Vatican II natural law theory, Hollenbach observes that, "This theory was used in a way that frequently reinforced traditional ethical conclusions. For example, the right to private property, the necessity of political inequality, the illegitimacy of contraception, and the subordination of woman to man in both family and society were all justified primarily by nontheological appeals to the law of nature." *Justice, Peace and Human Rights*, 186-87.

[36] Charles Curran, "The Changing Anthropological Bases of Catholic Social Ethics," *Readings in Moral Theology No. 5: Official Catholic Social Teaching*, ed. Charles Curran and Richard A. McCormick (New York: Paulist Press, 1986), 188-218. Political equality, however, was understood, according to Hollenbach, as still under the auspices of the State to grant or withhold. With regard to Pope Leo XIII's political views Hollenbach writes: "Leo's view of the concrete implications of equal human dignity, therefore, was structured through his understanding of the means available for institutionalizing social relationships. A hierarchical understanding of social order provided the only framework within which he believed human dignity could be defended. In the economic sphere and before the law, equality received major emphasis. In Leo's treatment of social order, class, and the distribution of the benefits of higher culture, the paternalistic or hierarchical emphasis prevailed." *Claims in Conflict*, 45.

created in the image of God.[37] Accordingly, the distinction between the "deprived" and the "depraved" poor is not crucial to him.[38] Following this Catholic Social Teaching tradition he finally concludes that:

> All persons have material needs and wants which demand respect. All persons have basic rights to food, housing, health, work, etc. But in the actual pushing and shoving of economic life, the wants of some are gratified at the expense of the basic needs of others. A human rights policy, therefore must do more than abstractly proclaim the rights of all persons to have their basic needs fulfilled. It must set out to counteract the privilege of the rich whenever this denies minimal necessities to the poor. Conflict between the needs of some and the wants of others, both within nations and across national boundaries, is one of the predominant characteristics of contemporary society. An adequate human rights policy cannot avoid this conflict if it is to be responsive to the actual situation. Therefore, a choice must be made between protecting privilege and guaranteeing minimum standards of living for all.[39]

This quotation reveals Hollenbach's reliance upon the more recent Catholic social teachings that recognize substantial social conflict in modern life.[40] It also makes it clear that all

---

[37] Hollenbach should not however be interpreted as promoting a gospel of sloth. He interprets Catholic Social Teachings as demanding responsible work from all who can work. It should be noted that many of the poor work year-round. See "Economic Justice for All: Catholic Social Teaching and the U.S. Economy," *Origins* 16, no. 3 (5 June 1986) (Washington, D.C.: National Catholic News Service) (The Third Draft), note 28.

[38] The importance of this distinction has been touched upon in Chapter Three, and will be reemphasized in my discussion of Michael Novak's views.

[39] David Hollenbach, *Claims in Conflict*, 204-5.

[40] In this regard Hollenbach is giving credence to the criticisms of Protestant theologians, such as Paul Tillich and Jürgen Moltmann. Ibid., 111-13. Hollenbach writes regarding the pre-Conciliar view that, "The emphasis throughout is on organic unity, complementarity and reconciliation, rather than on conflict." Ibid., 118. With regard to post-Conciliar thought, Hollenbach writes, "When the claims of diverse groups in society conflict, the tradition increasingly grants priority to the needs of the weak over the desires and unimpeded liberty of the powerful. Christian faith and love, therefore, continually challenge,

people have equal dignity; thus the needs of some (that are necessary to allow the possibility of living a dignified life) outweigh the absolute freedom and property rights of others. This conclusion is very similar to Henry Shue's basic rights theory. Hollenbach helped to write the Catholic Bishops' Letter on the Economy. This document sets forth more fully his position on economic rights. Section seventy-eight and others outline so-called "welfare" rights that also make up an extensive list.[41] Hollenbach knows that these rights are, as we termed them in Chapter One, positive rights.[42] Yet because of his understanding of human need and human dignity, he maintains that such positive rights are morally necessary.

Hollenbach is also aware of the correlativity problem

---

transform, heal and perfect the understanding of human rights which the tradition brings to the current debate. In so doing Christian faith does not dissolve conflict by appealing to a nonexistent harmony. Rather, it brings about new understandings of the way different human rights are to be prioritized when they make competing claims. Ibid. , 132, 133.

[41] Section 79 of the Bishops' Letter lists, among other human rights, "rights to life, food, clothing, shelter, rest, medical care and basic education." This section maintains that these rights are derivable from *Pacem in Terris*

[42] Hollenbach is fully aware of some of the traditional objections to the notion of economic rights. Regarding the right to work, he writes, "Implementation of a social right such as the right to work is a considerably more complex task in our society (than implementing a negative right). An interlocking series of positive steps by the society as a whole must be taken if this right is to be secured in practice. It is a positive right, an entitlement or empowerment that demands action rather than restraint on the part of both society and the state." Yet Hollenbach also recognizes that part of the difficulty in implementing positive rights lies in the paucity of implementing institutions. He maintains that, "The institutional machinery for the protection of civil-political rights is in place in the West and therefore their implementation today is a relatively easy task compared to the implementation of socioeconomic rights. Securing the right to work is more difficult because we do not have clear and convincing ideas on how to bring them into existence in fully functional form." Despite these difficulties, Hollenbach concludes that economic rights should not be given up as conceptually incoherent; rather he demands that all parties in society, especially economic ones, continue to dialogue on the creation and implementation of appropriate institutional machinery for the implementation of economic rights.

presented by positive rights, which is the difficulty in ascertaining the duty correlative to a positive right. Nevertheless, despite his awareness of the need to limit positive rights strictly he does not do so. Gewirth and Shue attend to this problem by their creation of a short list of basic rights. They thereby present approaches Hollenbach would be wise to adapt to his approach.[43]

Another weakness in Hollenbach's approach is, as Coleman notes, his reliance upon the notion of "human dignity." Coleman believes that human dignity is a concept, which has a certain circularity that makes its foundation for rights theories doubtful.[44] What is striking, however, about Hollenbach's position, is, as Coleman notes, Hollenbach's adoption (in sections 86-89) of the preferential option for the poor.[45] The use of this principle by Hollenbach makes it clear that he recognizes a basic conflict of rights problem. He attempts to resolve this conflict in his threefold preferential option for the poor principle. Thus he attempts to resolve conflicts between conflicting rights claims with principles that function like Gewirth's principle of the criterion for degrees of necessity.[46] By doing so, he helps us to understand that on occasion interdependent rights conflict. Hollenbach's three strategic moral priorities for resolving conflicts in the application of

---

[43] Hollenbach's failure to have a short list is problematic. Essentially Hollenbach's list of economic rights is derived from *Pacem in Terris* and from the International Covenant for Social, Economic and Cultural Rights. These lists of rights are extensive and lay Hollenbach open to a claim of indeterminacy. Kirkpatrick's characterization of extensive economic rights as "desiderata" has a good deal of merit. Unlike Shue and Gewirth, Hollenbach demonstrates no approach that convincingly eliminates the problem of indeterminacy. The elimination of indeterminacy is important, however, if a consensus as to the validity of economic rights is to be achieved.

[44] For a full discussion of the problem of relying upon "human dignity" as the epistemological basis for human rights, see John Coleman's "Catholic Human Rights Theory: Four Challenges to an Intellectual Tradition," *The Journal of Law and Religion* 2, no. 2 (1984): 351.

[45] Ibid., 360.

[46] Alan Gewirth, *Reason and Morality* (Chicago: University of Chicago Press, 1978), 343-44.

economic rights serve as normative hermeneutical principles. They are: 1) The needs of the poor take priority over the wants of the rich; 2) The freedom of the dominated takes priority over the liberty of the powerful; 3) The participation of marginalized groups takes priority over the preservation of an order which excludes them.[47] Coleman criticizes Hollenbach for not making a strong case for these principles.[48] He suggests that the Catholic view of economic rights should be redrafted with the simplicity and coherence of Shue and Gewirth.[49] Thus, Hollenbach's views, though helpful, still point to a need to identify just what it is that makes certain rights "basic."

Hollenbach's attempt to distinguish the right to subsistence from less basic economic rights causes him to deviate slightly from the primary foundation of Catholic social teachings, namely, human dignity. His "preferential option for the poor" could, however, be construed as a logical requirement for the recognition of human dignity. The preferential option for the poor is a theological construct dependent upon a specific reading of the Bible. It does not appear to conflict with notions of human dignity. It is, however, a manifestation of the post-Vatican II Catholic emphasis upon new biblical hermeneutics. It is also a concept that is often associated with liberation theologians. Coleman's criticism of Hollenbach on this point focuses upon the fact that Hollenbach fails to account for his preference of this grounding for subsistence rights (the preferential option for the poor), over the prevailing Catholic norm of human dignity. Coleman correctly cautions Hollenbach for using a concept such as rights, which has evolved out of a legal and philosophical tradition that suddenly relies upon a

[47] David Hollenbach, *Claims in Conflict*, 204.

[48] Coleman writes with regard to Hollenbach's approach: "Although, intuitively, these three priority principles strongly resonate with my moral sentiments, I am unable to find in Hollenbach's work any careful argument in which to ground these human-rights priority principles. I think the difficulty in finding the argument lies in the failure of the Catholic rights theory to raise the issue of basic rights in Shue's sense." "Catholic Human Rights Theory: Four Challenges to an Intellectual Tradition," 358.

[49] Ibid., 357.

particularistic theological affirmation to lexically prioritize its rights system.[50] Coleman's observations certainly seem to be valid. Consider for example how odd Hayek's or Cranston's lexically prioritized rights for negative liberty would sound if suddenly they resorted to theological justifications. In contrast, the Catholic social teachings' traditional emphasis on human dignity is different, but quite comparable to Peter Vlastos' or Joel Feinberg's philosophical foundations based upon human dignity. Hollenbach's retreat to a particularistic reading of the Bible, necessitated by his preferential option for the poor, indicates that his rights theory may prove to be accessible for Christians only. Such a stance also raises the question as to whether traditions and accounts of human nature and human society as different as the Catholic Social Doctrine, and Gewirth's PGC are intellectually compatible.[51] As we shall discuss later on, Wolterstorff's approach, which is similar to Shue's, suggests that those two approaches are intellectually compatible.

Nevertheless, despite its flaws, Hollenbach's revisions are similar to the most recent Catholic Social Teaching, *Sollicitudo Rei Socialis* , and both appear to represent the direction in which Catholic social teachings are moving. As we shall discuss later on, *Sollicitudo Rei Socialis,* a social concern encyclical of Pope John Paul II, emphatically endorses the recognition of economic rights as a part of social justice. Our immediate attention should now be given to Hollenbach's primary rights critic Michael Novak, whose early views were briefly discussed in Chapter Three.

The Hollenbach-Novak Debate: Continued

Hollenbach published some of his views on economic rights in response to what he understood to be the contrary position of Michael Novak.[52]

---

[50] Ibid., 360.

[51] This compatibility problem will be addressed in Chapter Six.

[52] Hollenbach understands his position on economic rights as constituting one side of a debate. He believes that Michael Novak is on the other side. Hollenbach understands much of moral reasoning to occur as part of a debate. Hollenbach writes: "As [John Courtney] Murray

Novak agrees with Hollenbach that their positions have serious differences and that their conversation constitutes a debate. Novak writes:

> . . . I would like to resume an argument with David Hollenbach that began with my article in *Crisis* in October 1985, on which Hollenbach commented in *America* (30 November 1985). Hollenbach disagreed with a text of mine in which I insisted upon the essential differences between two distinct realities--between rights" to civil and political liberties, on the one hand, and the material 'goods' (such as food, shelter, medical care) necessary to life.[53]

Novak acknowledges that he agrees in some sense with Hollenbach. He writes: "Operationally, nonetheless, I come out

---

was fond of observing, however, important arguments are never finished. They always have a 'growing end.' The debate about the role of the churches in public life has been vigorous in the United States during the past few years. The question of whether religious communities should raise their voices in the public square, however, is hardly the growing end in the Catholic theological discussion today. As the council declared: 'It comes within the meaning of religious freedom that religious bodies should not be prohibited from freely undertaking to show the special value of their doctrine in what concerns the organization of society and the inspiration of the whole of human activity.' The entrance of the U.S. bishops into the public debates about abortion, U. S. defense policy, and the economy are good examples of the kind of exercise of religious freedom to which the council referred in this passage. The chief point in the argument today is not whether the voice of the bishops, for example, should be raised, but rather what should be said when it is. A case in point that is important in this context is Michael Novak's *forceful objection* to the notion that human beings have economic rights to such goods as food, housing, and employment as well as civil and political rights such as free speech and religious freedom. Novak is particularly disturbed that this idea is present in the bishops' pastoral on the economy, and he implies that the writings of certain Catholic scholars, including the present author have seriously misled the bishops into adopting this erroneous view." Ibid., 104. (Emphasis added.) Clearly Hollenbach understands Novak's comments as constituting a debate. He cites Novak's essay, "Economic Rights: the Servile State" as being an oppositional essay to his writings on economic rights.

53 The Rights and Wrongs of "Economic Rights," *This World*, 17, 17, (Spring, 87):43-52, 45.

where Hollenbach comes out."[54] Novak believes that he and Hollenbach have come to a "growing end to an argument," because he grudgingly concedes the necessity of government intervention, writing, "The primary responsibility for meeting his own/her own basic needs is invested in the individual person; secondly, in mediating human associations and social organizations; thirdly, only as a last resort and with a wary and critical eye, in the state."[55] Novak is correct: he and Hollenbach both endorse subsistence rights. They also endorse the Catholic doctrine of subsidiarity that calls for restraint on the actions of large entities before smaller ones have had a chance to act.[56] Thus neither Hollenbach nor Novak desires the State to supply basic needs summarily. What then is the importance of this debate? There is at least one important point to discuss. The point of importance is that Novak still wants to make a clear distinction between civil and political rights and any "rights" that smack of "welfare." Just before conceding that he and Hollenbach "arrived" at the same conclusion, Novak continues to dissociate the term "welfare" and the term "rights." Novak writes:

> Not only are "welfare rights" not "rights" in the full sense, and not only are they conditional (being first responsibilities, and claims upon others only under certain conditions); they are better to be described in terms of objectives, ends, goals--that is, as highly important social goals, part of the "general welfare."[57]

What Novak desires to do in this essay is to have his cake and eat it too. He wants to prioritize first generation, civil and political rights, while also embracing *Pacem in Terris* (which also embraced second generation rights). Novak seeks to accomplish this feat without employing an interdependency theory like Shue, or a dialectically necessary argument like Gewirth. Instead he seeks to make a case for the lexical

---

54 "The Rights and Wrongs of 'Economic Rights': A Debate Continued," 49.

55 Ibid.

56 Hollenbach, "The Growing End of An Argument," *America* 153, no. 16 (30 November 1985): 366.

57 Ibid.

prioritization of first generation rights by adding the intensifier "conditional" to the term welfare right. By doing so, he believes that he has made a real distinction between "welfare rights" and first generation rights.

Unfortunately, his terminology of "economic" rights is confusing: he variously calls them, among other things, welfare rights, entitlements, and goals. He further confuses the issue when he designates economic rights as being goods, as when he writes:

> In short, the true conceptual force of the argument in favor of economic rights (to income, food, shelter, a job, etc.) is not that the latter are truly "rights" inhering in the nature of human persons, but rather that they are "goods" indispensable to a full human life.[58]

What he hopes to establish with this approach is the notion that economic rights is a confusing idea. But the confusion in this matter seems to lie in how *he* describes economic rights, rather than in the terms themselves. Novak, like Coleman, is correct in challenging Hollenbach's failure to distinguish adequately between rights that are economic in nature, and rights that are basic in the sense that Shue uses the term. Yet Novak's qualifier of conditional simply further confuses the issues.[59] Thus the first point to recognize is that

---

[58] Ibid., 65.

[59] Rights are seldom claimed until a condition arises in which the object of the right is called into question. People speak freely until they are faced with the possibility of censorship. People do not claim rights to emigrate unless their intended departure is challenged. One never claims one's Fifth amendment rights until one finds oneself in a position in which one's utterances may be used to incriminate oneself. All rights therefore are invoked only when a condition necessitating their invocation arises. Human activity would be sorely complicated if people developed the habit of claiming rights before the right to an activity was challenged. In short, all rights are conditional in the sense that they are sought when their recognition is challenged and or their object appears unobtainable. Thus Novak's qualifier "conditional" adds nothing but confusion to rights discourse. Novak would be much better served attending to the task of identifying and justifying the necessary conditions for the making of a "welfare claim." As would all commentators, the present author included.

Novak has conceded the debate while at the same time he has highlighted the ambiguity in Hollenbach's rights theories.

This point can be further illustrated by turning to how Novak specifically understands economic rights. His reading of *Pacem in Terris* distinguishes between the two different sections that deal with "economic rights."[60] He interprets *Pacem in Terris* as recognizing "civil rights in economic matters," which are already recognized by the Constitution, i.e. rights to property, and the responsibilities of ownership.[61] He also recognizes his previously mentioned "conditional" right to life that he terms a welfare right. His conditional welfare right has three conditions: first, that the recipient of the benefit really needs it (a needs based assessment); second, the recipient must have tried in good faith, and without success, to obtain the benefit prior to receiving any benefits; third, that all other intervening social agencies and institutions must have also failed in good faith attempts to provide the benefits (a subsidiarity consideration). It is only after all these conditions have been met that the government is, in his opinion, obligated to step in and to provide the necessary goods and/or services. Novak's real contribution to the economic rights debate is that he demands a demonstration as to how human dignity can be continued where the provisions of basic goods are supplied. Thus he correctly points out how human dignity must have both the recognition of basic needs *and* basic responsibilities.

Novak's ultimate concession to Hollenbach would appear to be permanent in light of subsequent Catholic social teachings. In particular, *Sollicitudo Rei Socialis*, an encyclical of Pope John Paul II, appears to endorse Hollenbach's understanding of economic rights. Sollicitudo does not attribute poverty to the poor. It recognizes the principle of subsidiarity, but does not distinguish (as does Novak) between the differing economic rights listed in *Pacem in Terris*. This failure to distinguish among the economic rights is a mistake, as has been recognized by Novak and Coleman. *Sollicitudo Rei Socialis*

---

60 Novak distinguishes between section 11 of *Pacem in Terris* and sections 18-22.

61 "Economic Rights: Rethinking the Bishop's Second Draft Could Lead to Something that Endures," *National Catholic Register* (16 February 1986): 2.

does, however, emphasize the duty of the affluent (in solidarity with the poor) to utilize their goods on behalf of the poor, and insists that the wealthy and powerful must shape public policy with an inclination to help the poor.[62] One must conclude,

---

[62] In *Sollicitudo Rei Socialis*, Pope John II is most concerned with the widening gap between the world's rich and poor. The pope calls, therefore, for a definition and implementation of development that is designed to make the affluent world and the Church itself more diligent in making sure that the basic needs of the poor are met. *Sollicitudo* makes this argument while commemorating "Populorum Progressio," but does so, with *Pacem* in mind. *Sollicitudo* not only surveys Catholic social teachings, but also surveys the state of the world. It concludes that, "We are therefore faced with a serious problem of unequal distribution of the means of subsistence originally meant for everybody, and thus also an unequal distribution of the benefits deriving from them. And this happens not through the fault of the needy people and even less through a sort of inevitability dependent on natural conditions or circumstances as a whole. "Sollicitudo Rei Socialis," *Origins* 17, no. 38 (3 March 1988): 645. "Sollicitudo" does not determine precisely the cause of poverty. It also does not precisely blame any groups or forces for the presence of, and increase in, worldwide poverty. But "Sollicitudo" maintains that the affluent have contributed to the problem of increasing poverty. "Sollicitudo" notes, "Responsibility for this deterioration is due to various causes. Notable among them are undoubtedly grave instances of omissions on the part of the developing nations themselves and especially on the part of those holding economic and political power. Nor can we pretend not to see the responsibility of the developed nations, which have not always, at least in due measure, felt the duty to help countries separated from the affluent world to which they themselves belong," 646. "Sollicitudo" also recognizes, in reflecting back on "Progressio," that the gap between have and have not nations has greatly widened. What is striking about "Sollicitudo" is its clear recognition of chronic scarcity and its recognition of the moral duty of the affluent to use their assets to meet the needs of the needy *and* to fashion their policies with an eye on the effect that those policies have on the poor. Thus, "Sollicitudo" concludes that, "Therefore political leaders and citizens of rich countries considered as individuals, especially if they are Christians, have the moral obligation, according to the degree of each one's responsibility, to take into consideration in personal decisions and decisions of government this relationship of universality, this interdependence which exists between their conduct and the poverty and underdevelopment of so many millions of people . . . the duty of solidarity," 645. Furthermore, "Sollicitudo" also holds that the affluent

therefore, from any review of *Sollicitudo Rei Socialis* that, for better or worse, Catholic social teachings recognize welfare rights. Since Catholic social teachings are invariably influenced by the Vatican, *Sollicitudo Rei Socialis* should influence the economic rights debate.

Before turning from the Catholic perspective, we should note that *Sollicitudo* does imply that the poor are poor as a result of the manipulations of the wealthy. This fault finding is a theme that can be found in liberation theology and in our next commentator, Nicholas Wolterstorff.

Wolterstorff's Appropriation of Shue's Basic Rights

Nicholas Wolterstorff's real contribution to the overall economic rights debate lies in his ability to offer theological economic rights that are able to synthesize successfully the interdependency arguments of Henry Shue. Thus he is able to justify theologically a short list of economic rights. Prior to discussing the specifics of Wolterstorff's approach we should consider briefly his approach to accounting for poverty that we have characterized as being similar to *Solicitudo Rei Socialis*. Wolterstorff writes:

> In the first place, the mass poverty of the Third World is for the most part not some sort of natural condition that

---

have been seduced by their reliance upon their affluence and that this seduction is a causative factor in the phenomenon of poverty. Accordingly, *Sollicitudo* demands that, "Thus, it should be obvious that development either becomes shared in common by every part of the world or it undergoes a process of regression even in zones marked by constant progress. This tells us a great deal about the nature of authentic development: either all the nations of the world participate or it will not be true development," 648. Since *Sollicitudo*, does not blame the poor for their poverty, they are also not envisioned as leeches, innervated by having received help from the affluent. Rather the world is characterized as divided along economic lines that are deepening and worsening over time. *Sollicitudo* implicitly affirms, therefore, the economic rights previously established in encyclicals such as *Pacem in Terris* and the Universal Declaration of Rights.

exists independently of us; quite the contrary, a good deal of it is the result of the interaction of the core of the world-system with the periphery over the course of centuries. In many areas there has been a development of underdevelopment, and we in the core have played a crucial role in that development. Underdevelopment has a history, a history inseparable from ours.[63]

Whether Wolterstorff is empirically correct with regard to the primary causes of poverty is, of course, controversial. From his perspective the West should be highly motivated to assist the "Third World" economically. Thus he is morally compelled to account for a morally justifiable economic rights account.[64]

Similar to Catholic theorists, Wolterstorff employs, in his theory of economic rights, *imago Dei* language, and a notion of the Common Good. He also recognizes the relativization of property rights.[65] In addition, like José Míguez-Bonino, a Protestant liberation theologian, he embraces the partisanship of God and an option for the poor as a foundation for economic rights.[66] Third, like Joseph A. Allen, Wolterstorff grounds his conception of economic rights in the larger notion of a "covenanted community," located in a world of conflict and

---

[63] Nicholas Wolterstorff, "The Rich and the Poor," *Until Justice and Peace Embrace* (Grand Rapids: Eerdmans Pub., 1983), 86. Hereinafter referred to as *Until Justice and Peace*. See also "Christianity and Social Justice," *Christian Scholar's Review* 16, no. 3 (1987): 211-48.

[64] Wolterstorff's explanations for the causes of poverty need not be accepted to accept his economic rights theories. His poverty causation theories only add a sense of urgency to his economic rights arguments: the arguments themselves, however, are justifiable apart from his reading of economic history.

[65] The relativity of property rights is understood by some to be a traditional Catholic Social Teaching. Ignacio Ellacuria interprets Thomistic thought as maintaining that property rights were always subject to "justified" conversion by the indigent for the preservation of their lives. See his essay, "Human Rights in a Divided Society," *Human Rights in the Americas: The Struggle for Consensus*, 52-65.

[66] José Míguez-Bonino, "Religious Commitment and Human Rights: A Christian Perspective," *Understanding Human Rights: An Interdisciplinary and Interfaith Study*, ed. Alan D. Falconer (Dublin: Irish School of Ecumenics, 1980), Chapter Two.

scarcity.[67]

The importance of Wolterstorff's acknowledgment of social conflict can be seen in the criticism of a Catholic scholar, John Coleman. Coleman maintains that the Catholic worldview minimizes conflict.[68] By doing so it cripples its own social critical analysis because the world is indeed one of conflict. Wolterstorff is not saddled with a need to minimize conflict in his social theory and instead analyzes the conflict.

Wolterstorff, unlike many theologians, also demonstrates a familiarity with the technical issues in this rights discourse (taxonomy of rights problems) as well as a familiarity with the main philosophical theorists, such as Gewirth, Shue, Feinberg, and Narveson. Wolterstorff is also more aware than most theologians of the classic theoretical problems posed in this area, such as the comparison between positive rights and negative rights, and acts of omission compared to acts of malfeasance.

As previously noted, most important for our consideration is his adaptation of Henry Shue's interdependency of rights theories. By adapting Shue's arguments to a theological doctrine he is able to offer the churches an economic rights theory that is not merely moral (as is Shue's theory) but one that can also be known in relation to the ministry of the churches. Further, he is able to offer an economic rights position that has a fuller understanding of human nature, human society, and which is adaptable to a faith community without excluding alliances with other communities.

---

[67] Joseph A. Allen, *Love and Conflict* (Abingdon Press: Nashville, 1984), 42-48. See also his "Catholic and Protestant Theories of Human Rights," *Religious Studies Review* 14, no. 4 (October 1988): 347-52. (Allen's inclusive covenant is the equivalent to Wolterstorff's Calvinistic humanity, divinely created within the bonds of a universal society.) Wolterstorff's reading of economic history portrays a world of conflict over natural resources, markets, and land. These struggles constitute the primary sources of conflict.

[68] Coleman notes, "Notoriously, Catholic theology prefers both-and options to either-or decisions. It shuns conflict and avoids facing squarely the condition of sin, scarcity, and finitude which dictates at times, hard choices and trade-offs on rights. Catholic theories of society are generally conflict-free," 361.

Wolterstorff adopts Shue's basic rights approach by maintaining that certain specified rights are absolutely necessary for life and these rights are basic rights to security, freedom and sustenance.[69] He also embraces Shue's understanding of the dangerous aspects of modern life which pose certain standard threats to Shue's three quintessential values: life, security, and liberty. His response to these threats, like Shue's, declares that basic rights call into play systematic social arrangements for the prevention of the deprivations of the three basic values. What is important about Wolterstorff's work is his integration of this basic rights approach into his entire approach to Christian social ethics and moral reasoning. His economic rights theories are grounded, therefore, in a comprehensive theological worldview and a holistic ethical response. At the same time, he is able to do something that eludes Hollenbach: he is able to justify a short list of rights thus refuting any possible indeterminacy charges from economic rights skeptics. Concerning rights Wolterstorff writes that:

> A right, then, is a claim to a social arrangement that will ensure that one will not be deprived of the enjoyment of the good in question by ordinary, serious, or remediable threats. Rights always involve social structures of one sort or another. They consist in a claim on one's fellows to the effect that society be structured in such a way as to give reasonable assurance that the good in question can in fact be enjoyed. Seeing that rights are claims to guarantees against threats makes clear that rights are God's charter for the weak and defenseless ones in society. A right is the legitimate claim for protection of those too weak to help themselves. It is the legitimate claim of the defenseless against the more devastating and common of life's threats which, at that time and place, are remediable. It is the claim of the little ones in society to restraint upon economic and political and physical forces that would otherwise be too strong for them to resist.[70]

Basically, this quotation reiterates Shue's basic rights

---

[69] Wolterstorff notes regarding Shue that, "In this discussion of rights generally, and sustenance rights in particular, I am very much indebted to Henry Shue's *Basic Rights: Subsistence, Affluence, and U. S. Foreign Policy*, Ibid., 189.

[70] Ibid., 85.

arguments. Wolterstorff differs from Shue, however, in that he claims that the moral protection for those "oppressed" by the status quo issues initially as a divine initiative that must then be responded to by humanity. Humanity responds correctly when it creates the institutions and social arrangements that intervene on behalf of the "oppressed" as agents of God in the world. In this way Wolterstorff is able to state God's option for the poor in a way that is not simply reliant upon a particular reading of Scripture, or on the sheer logic of Henry Shue. In his opinion, God must intervene for the weak or tolerate their suffering passively. Wolterstorff's God avoids the radical theodicy problem posed by poverty and squalor by intervening for the oppressed. This intervention is not limited, however, to divine action: people are also under a moral obligation to intervene. The duty to intervene is divinely given **and** rational.[71] This duty to intervene is grounded in Wolterstorff's understanding of Calvinist society. His Calvinistic understanding of society is one in which the divinely created sociability of humanity is linked with a basic obligation to.intervene beneficially for others when appropriate. Thus, he adopts one of Calvin's most important social ideas; namely, his notion of "mutual communication," a system of exchange in which "each is to contribute what he or she can to the enrichment of the common life."[72] Calvin understands human beings as being "united in the bonds of mutual society, and (hence) they must mutually perform good offices for each other."[73] This Calvinist understanding of obligation grounds

---

71 The duty to intervene is a divine obligation. As such, it creates a moral obligation between the believer and God in which the believer is clearly a duty-bearer, provided he/she is able to intervene. What is not clear is whether or not the moral obligation created between God and able believers is such that the beneficiary of the duty should be called a beneficiary of a divine duty, or a rights claimant. According to modern rights/duty correlativity such a party could be called a rights-claimant.

72 Wolterstorff, *Until Justice and Peace Embrace*, 78.

73 Ibid. Mutual communication is a process where everyone is obligated and encouraged to help the other. Each person is embedded in mutuality. With regard to mutual offices, Calvin writes: "The general truth conveyed is, that the greatest stranger is our neighbor, because God has bound all men together, for the purpose of assisting each other . . . the chief design is to show that the neighborhood, which lays us under

Wolterstorff's rights doctrine. Thus Calvin and Wolterstorff have a clear theory of divine obligation that demands that everyone who can help should help.

It is in this way that Wolterstorff understands and accepts the correlativity thesis. Though Calvin did not use rights language Wolterstorff is able, appropriately, to do so.[74] Thus, he takes Shue's basic rights arguments and integrates them with his own Christian rights theories arising out of the divine duties embedded in the Reformed tradition:specifically John Calvin. Wolterstorff understands Calvin to have specifically required the rich to conduct their economic affairs in a non-oppressive fashion: this is their divinely given duty. Wolterstorff writes:

---

obligations to mutual offices of kindness, is not confined to friends or relations, but extends to the whole human race." Jean Calvin, *Commentary on a Harmony of the Evangelists, Matthew, Mark, and Luke,* trans. Rev. William Pringle (Grand Rapids, Mi.: Eerdmans, 1949) III, 61-62. With regard to a "natural mutual obligation" Calvin wrote: "For here, as in a mirror, we behold that common relationship of man, which the scribes endeavored to blot out by their wicked sophistry; and the compassion, which an enemy showed to a Jew, demonstrates that the guidance and teaching of nature are sufficient to show that man was created for the sake of men. Hence it is inferred that there is a mutual obligation between all men. Ibid. Calvin clearest statement on social obligation in society can be found in his commentary on Ezekiel. Calvin writes, "And he has given his bread to the hungry." Here the Prophet teaches what I have lately touched on, that cautious self-restraint from all injury is not sufficient, and sparing our neighbors; but that more is required, since we ought to assist them as far as we possibly can. Unless this has been added, many might object that they injured no one, never defrauded any, nor took advantage of the simple. But since God has created men in the bonds of mutual society, hence they must mutually perform good offices for each other. Here, then, it is required of the rich to succor the poor, and to offer bread to the hungry. From *Commentaries on the First Twenty Chapter of the Book of the Prophet Ezekiel,* trans. Thomas Myers (Grand Rapids, Mi.: Eerdman's, 1948) II, 224. These comments make it clear that Calvin understood human beings to be created in community.

[74] What Wolterstorff shows in his arguments is that Calvin recognized divine duties that could serve as a foundation for a modern Reformed scholar to construct an adequate rights theory, including economic rights. This is what Wolterstorff does without claiming that rights theories originated with Calvin. Ibid., 84.

It should now come as no surprise to hear Calvin thundering against the rich in his sermons. In one of them he describes certain wheat-cornering operators as "murderers, savage beasts, biting and eating up the poor, sucking in their blood," and in another he sends a warning to the rich in his own congregation: "if the poor souls that have bestowed their labor and travail and spent their sweat and blood for you be not paid their wages as they ought to be, not succored and sustained by you as they should be--if they ask vengeance against you at God's hand, who shall be your spokesman or advocate to rid you out of his hands?" It is our duty, he insists, not only to avoid the evil but to seek the good: "those who have riches, whether inherited or won by their own industry and labour, are to remember that what is left over is not meant for intemperance or luxury, but for relieving the needs of the brethren.[75]

Wolterstorff finds in Calvin's sermons and commentaries a scripturally derived option for the poor, both theologically construed and publicly announced as a historical precedent within his own Reformed history and tradition. By reviving this Calvinist activism for the poor along with Shue's basic rights theory, Wolterstorff is able to produce a simple and coherent theory for subsistence rights that is both theologically transcendent and clearly conscious of community, institutions, social solidarity, political machinery, and, most importantly, economic realities.

Wolterstorff greatest theological contribution to this discussion lies in how he develops the theological foundation for his human rights theory: Calvinistic understandings of the *imago Dei*. In his opinion, one cannot harm another human being without harming God. This axiom holds because, relying upon Calvin, he understands human beings as being the prized "earthlings" of God's Creation.[76] Human beings are,

---

75 *Until Justice and Peace Embrace*, 79. Here Wolterstorff finds Calvin making a historical determination that the wealthy of his generation are manipulating economic mechanisms so as to "deprive" the poor. The poor are characterized not as rights-claimants before a court of law, but act as supplicants before God demanding punishment (vengeance) upon rich, but duty-derelict Christians.

76 In *Justice and Peace*, 78, Wolterstorff writes that, "Fundamental to Calvin's reflections on poverty was his conviction that every human being has been made in the image of God. Thus we share with each

accordingly, for him, little "icons" of God, with whom God is well pleased. It is by this identification with God that he derives his understanding of the radical equality of human beings. Everyone is equal, for Wolterstorff, because everyone is equally created in the image of God. Thus the retarded, catatonic, or infantile, all retain an irrevocable and inalienable dignity: a dignity that is the foundational value that justifies the extension of rights to them. Accordingly, for him, economic rights are not grounded (as is true for Gewirth) in rationality, and can, with complete conceptual consistency, be extended to those who do not possess "rationality."[77] Wolterstorff is also able to escape the circularity criticisms that Coleman levels at rights theories based on human dignity.[78]

Thus, how we are treated and how we treat others is based upon *divine grace and need, not merit, rationality, or desert.* In his schema one simply cannot lounge or stand idly by while a "prize creation" of God suffers or perishes.[79] To do so not only hurts the person, but wounds and offends God. His theory is thereby grounded, not in the will of God, nor even in theories of Creation, but in an appreciation of God's joys and sorrows: the pathos of God.

---

other the most fundamental unity of nature. It is this fact--that we are each made in the image of God, mirroring him, rather than the fact that we each have some sort of inherent dignity--that is fundamental in determining what our attitude toward each other ought to be. 'We are not to consider what men deserve of themselves but to look upon the image of God in all men, to which we owe all honor and love,' Calvin declares. 'God Himself, looking on men as formed in His own image, regards them with such love and honour that He Himself feels wounded and outraged in the persons of those who are the victims of human cruelty and wickedness.' An act of injury to my fellow human being is an act of injury to God."

[77] Wolterstorff here is able to do what Okin was unable to do--to correct a weakness in Gewirth's views, by demonstrating a transcendent foundation for economic rights--one that is not primarily dependent upon a capacity for human rationality.

[78] Gewirth, John Coleman, "Catholic Human Rights Theory: Four Challenges to an Intellectual Tradition," 350-52.

[79] David B. Fletcher thoroughly discusses this lounging reference (which is, of course, a reference to Narveson's example) in full, in the helpful essay, "Must Wolterstorff Sell His House?" *Faith and Philosophy* 14, no. 2 (April 1987). Hereinafter referred to as Fletcher.

By borrowing Shue's concept of duty, which requires "haves" to arrange social institutions and systems so as to protect individuals from standard threats to the acquisition or retention of basic necessities, he is able to blunt one common philosophical criticism. This criticism (chiefly raised by Joel Feinberg) holds that each and every individual might be subject at any time (in a society that recognized and implemented economic rights) to providing individually and slavishly all the needs of the destitute.

He is also able to show from his adoption of Shue's argument why the failure to create such institutions is morally wrong, and why individual freedom (as libertarians have defined it) is not threatened, but, on the contrary, enhanced by economic rights.

Richard J. Neuhaus, former Lutheran minister (now Roman Catholic), author, and public policy theorist, poses two basic objections to Wolterstorff's views. The first objection is in regards to the extent of the right to basic goods. The second objection relates to Wolterstorff's failure to distinguish between the "depraved" and "deprived" poor. Neuhaus asserts, with regard to his first objection, that Wolterstorff's economic rights position requires him to give immediately all of his assets to the poor, writing:

> In global terms, Wolterstorff, this reviewer, and probably every reader of this journal is rich. At this very moment people are starving--in Chad, Upper Volta, and too many other places. We also know (or, if we do not know, are culpably ignorant) that we have the power to transfer, in quite direct ways, our personal wealth to starving people--all of it and right now. Is it true then that our behaviour is morally tantamount to physically assaulting the starving? I think not.[80]

This first objection is doubtful because Wolterstorff, following Shue, never suggests that "haves" are to divest themselves completely of all their worldly possessions for the benefit of the poor. Wolterstorff never claims to be interest-free; therefore Neuhaus appears to be arguing with a straw man-- his own incorrect interpretation of Wolterstorff. By limiting his theories in light of Gewirth and Shue's short lists, Wolterstorff is not obligated to act as some kind of Biblical rich

---

[80] "The Goal is not to Describe," *This World* 9 (Fall 1984): 109.

young ruler; he is not obligated to give all of his goods to the poor and to follow Jesus or St. Francis.[81] In short, his theories do not require him to be indifferent to his own goals or responsibilities.[82]

Neuhaus correctly reads Wolterstorff with regard to the second objection: Wolterstorff does extend subsistence rights to all, regardless of the "demerits" of some of the poor.[83] The distinction between the depraved and deprived should be irrelevant because Wolterstorff's position is grounded in the understanding of the human being as created in the image of God, and representative of God Himself; such a position does not explicitly entail specific duties that a "deprived" indigent

---

[81] For a full argumentation of this point see Fletcher's article previously cited. See also Wolterstorff's replies to Neuhaus in "Reply by Wolterstorff," *Reformed Journal* (December 1984): 23-29.

[82] Thus, when Neuhaus asks the rhetorical question, "Is it true then that our behavior is morally tantamount to physically assaulting the starving?" he answers, "I think not." His observation is correct in rejecting Wolterstorff's moral equivalence assertion, while missing the basic thrust of Wolterstorff's position; i.e., that to do nothing in a perceived case of evil, when intervention can bring good, and when the response required is minimal, constituting no great sacrifice on the part of the would--be intervener is morally indefensible. See Richard John Neuhaus, "The Goal is not to Describe," *This World* 9 (Fall 1984): 109.

[83] Wolterstorff himself waffles on this point. Writing in regards to subsistence claims, he observes, "we as human beings have *sustenance* rights. We have a claim on our fellow human beings to social arrangements that ensure that we will be adequately sustained in existence. No doubt this right, like others, can be forfeited; perhaps it is forfeited if a person refuses to work when decent work is available." *Justice and Peace*, 81. This position implies that God is not outraged when the "depraved" poor are left to their own depravity. This position certainly would be in line with the Protestant work-ethic, but it is not at all clear how one loses one's given status as a being created in the image of God. Does sloth so distort or efface our images that we lose our imago Dei status? This would seem odd since even criminals are treated with dignity and their punishments administered in a humane fashion. It would seem that their malfeasance would be more offensive than the sluggard's non-feasance. This logic is not, however, followed by Wolterstorff. He and Neuhaus and Novak are in basic agreement that sloth is to be responded to by non-intervention, even when intervention might not be costly or strenuous and the intervention is drastically needed.

might fail to perform, despite good faith attempts. Thus, since a deprived indigent does not earn his right to sustenance, if he/she should cease to struggle for survival by means of work, such "depravity" should not, logically speaking, bar him/her from receiving donated sustenance or basic shelter. Since his right is not based solely upon his efforts, it cannot expire, or be ignored because of a discontinuance of effort on his part. "Haves" may disapprove of the slothful indigent, but such an indigent does not automatically lose his *imago Dei* status.

This logic may be correct, but this is not the position that Wolterstorff adopts. Wolterstorff adopts a standard of minimum responsibility into his understanding of human agency. Thus, though he gives no explicit argument, Wolterstorff expects, as much as Novak or Neuhaus, that people are to be at least marginally responsible if they expect to receive aid. Thus Novak and Wolterstorff join in the traditional religious consensus in which people are discouraged from acting like the Grasshopper in Aesop's famous fable, who idled away his time, resources and opportunities.[84] In short, Neuhaus' second criticism of Wolterstorff's economic rights theories is incorrect, but illuminating because it reveals not how far Wolterstorff is from Neuhaus, but how close he is to him.

Reconsidering Wolterstorff's position helps one to see what is a very important consideration, namely, his Calvinistic understanding of the divinely created sociability of humanity and the basic need for economic justice. Thus, as has been previously mentioned, he adopts Calvin's notion of "mutual communication," a system of exchange wherein, "each is to

---

84 For example, in Catholic theories (which are also reliant upon imago Dei conceptions of human beings) people are nonetheless encouraged to produce--to exploit and subdue Creation. Hollenbach observes that, "Both Leo XIII and Murray insisted, of course, that securing economic necessities for all is not, in the first instance, the responsibility of government. Individuals, families and a variety of mediating institutions in society have an obligation to see that people do not go hungry, homeless or jobless. Nevertheless, when the problem exceeds the power of these persons and groups, government can and should intervene in ways carefully guided by political prudence. This is the meaning of the principle of subsidiary so often stated in Catholic social teaching. "The Growing End of An Argument," *America* 153, no. 16 (30 November 1985): 366.

contribute what he or she can to the enrichment of the common life."[85] Thus Calvin and Wolterstorff both demand that everyone who can help should help.

Wolterstorff's "mutual communication" theory may seem, at first, to be contradictory to his preferential option for the poor. This initial contradiction can be dispelled by a closer consideration of these doctrines. Wolterstorff's option for the poor is a declaration that God will intervene to provide justice in the gate if there is no faithful remnant to act as an agent of God. Nevertheless, wealthy Christians are divinely obliged to act as agents of God in helping the poor. If the covenantal arrangements of "mutual communication" break down, God will intervene to act as champion for the dispossessed, and will chastise the faithless rich. However, the more preferential sequence of action demands that the rich not tempt God's wrath. It is their duty to intervene as they are able. This intervention is the ideal operation of the system of mutual communication. If the covenanted community is faithful and loving, none should be poor. At the very least, the poor should be free to pursue opportunities for self-betterment, immune from the depredations of the avaricious rich.

They are also to be immune from their abandonment by the "callous" wealthy who may not be oppressing them, yet who may be derelict in their duty to intervene on their behalf.

What is striking about these ideas is that human beings are understood to be "divinely" created in society for the express purpose of pleasing God and contributing to the common good.[86] The atomistic individual, shrilly demanding his/her rights, solely for egoistic gratification, has no legitimate place in this conception. In terms of the technical language of rights, Wolterstorff is most convincing when he follows Shue's structure of basic rights closely, and shows how they are interdependent, and how they may be theologically justified. As we may recall from Chapter Four, Shue believes rights to be necessary because of basic conflicts in a world in which the powerful are able (in Shue's opinion) to defraud and oppress the

---

85 Wolterstorff, *Until Justice and Peace Embrace*, 78.

86 As Chapter Four made clear, the failure to place his rights theory in a viable theory of society constitutes the greatest weakness in Gewirth's work.

weak. Shue's argument is grounded primarily in a recognition that there are real threats in the world to rights to freedom (from oppressive political powers--which libertarian, economic rights skeptics concede) and demonstrates by analogy, which there are equally dangerous threats to the subsistence of the poor from powerful economic forces in society (which libertarian economic sceptics often deny). Wolterstorff agrees with Shue on this point, but allows for some ambivalence on the empirical cause of poverty.

Wolterstorff's position is most solidly grounded in his doctrinal confession that with regard to the distribution of basic goods, God is always on the side of the poor over and against the uncaring rich. Shue's position requires an empirical demonstration that the rich exploit the poor frequently--a question of causality, and a point always subject to empirical confirmation or contest. Though Wolterstorff shares Shue's suspicion of and antagonism toward capitalist exploitation, the persuasiveness of his economic rights position needs only his theological point to be persuasive, i.e., that the wealthy have not sufficiently intervened on behalf of the poor, to the painful detriment of the poor and God. With incontestable evidence of suffering and deprivation in a world of abundance, Wolterstorff's position (once the theological point is accepted) needs no demonstration of empirical causality (that is that the poor are poor because the wealthy manipulate exchanges solely for their own benefit). This last factor evidences a distinct advantage over many moral arguments.

Wolterstorff's theory grounds theologically Shue's understanding of rights by integrating it with his own version of Calvin's mutual communications, and a liberationist divine option for the poor. This integration of Shue, Calvin, and liberationist thought presents a powerful and coherent theory. By adopting Shue's understanding of rights as the arrangements of society designed to protect the powerless, Wolterstorff is able, unlike Hollenbach, to integrate philosophical theory, and an "option for the poor" account into one coherent, non-conflictual theological economic rights doctrine. What he also does of importance is to tie the imago Dei concept and the notion of the common good (still evident in modern Catholic social teaching approaches) to the pathos of

God. Thus, the haves of society are obligated to intervene on
behalf of the poor (in various ways, including the transferring of
their wealth). Have-nots have limited reciprocal duties only
because of their incapacity to act. Haves must be willing to
transfer their property because their property is part of the
divinely created commons dedicated to the common good.[87]
Second, in this view the poor must never be allowed to perish
(because the poor are created in the image of God--a Biblical
axiom) and such suffering pains God (the pathos of God
argument). Third, and perhaps most controversially,
Wolterstorff's liberationist God acts as a champion of the poor,
and calls believers to act as surrogate champions. He thereby
forces "haves" to abandon their neutrality, or find themselves in
the dubious position of both neglecting their duties (acts of
omission) and opposing God (an act of positive rebellion).[88]
Since Wolterstorff does not try to derive his option for the poor
from either logic or natural law reasoning, his handling of the
classic problem of the conflict of rights, in which there is a
prioritization of solidarity (for Wolterstorff solidarity means
being in actual communion with the poor in their struggles for
survival) over the maximization of liberty, remains safely
grounded in a certain interpretation of Scripture.[89]

---

[87] This obligation to assist when the commons no longer retains
raw natural resources available to the poor to convert, by means of their
labor, into useful property, echoes John Locke's understanding of moral
obligation, although I do not propose that this point was intentionally
borrowed from Locke by Wolterstorff. See Chapter One for a discussion
of Locke and property rights.

[88] Wolterstorff's position forces people to take sides. He writes,
"The poor man in Jesus' day was deprived of what was *due* him--as he
is in ours. He was deprived of his rights. He was deprived of justice . . .
In a society of both rich and poor, the recognition of poverty as a lack of
shalom involves *taking sides.*" *Until Justice and Peace Embrace*, 77.

[89] Wolterstorff relies upon a certain interpretation of Luke 1:46-53
(The Magnificat), Luke 4:16-21 (Jesus' reading of the Isaiahnic scroll), and
other passages of Luke--6:20-21 and Luke 7:18-23. What these Scriptures
do is impose duties upon their adherents. We are constrained to help
the helpless as a divine obligation. This theological solution has an
advantage over philosophical accounts in not having to demonstrate
any meta-ethical foundations. Why do we have an obligation to assist
the poor? God commands us to assist them.

His approach enables him to justify his prioritization of rights claims. Since he does not rely solely on one foundation for his theory, his interpretation of Scripture can be rejected, including his option for the poor, without necessitating the total rejection of his economic rights theory.

Particularism, the one unavoidable limitation to Wolterstorff's approach, is common to some theologies that are not primarily reliant upon human reason. His approach is grounded, in part, on a particularistic understanding of Scripture that functions "confessionally," and is, therefore, inaccessible to those who do not share his theological "faith" statements. Since, however, he does not rely solely upon a Scripturally-based option for the poor principle to ground his economic rights, his approach is not limited to an acceptance of his confession. Another way of putting this is to say that his justification of basic economic rights is not limited to just one approach. Thus an atheist supporter of economic rights might support his conclusion in favor of economic rights, while still not believing in God. Wolterstorff's accessibility and acceptability to various economic rights groups is possible because his theories are arranged primarily around the logic of Shue's interdependency argument while not being solely dependent upon it. Thus Wolterstorff's theories can be raised in churches without constructing some sort of ad hoc theological integration of Shue's secular, moral arguments. This flexibility allows Wolterstorff's views to be accessible to a wide body of economic rights supporters.

In summation, Wolterstorff's theory corrects four of Gewirth's theories' chief defects: first, he justifies the ultimate value of human beings by showing why human beings are so valuable as to be accorded rights (by way of a transcendent value-agent, God, rather than human rationality); second, he establishes the location and function of economic rights in a social matrix, with the necessary institutional supports (a siblingship of humanity, divinely created, but empirically situated in society); third, he integrates his concept of rights into a comprehensive ethical framework, which he characterizes as the common good; and lastly, he suggests a social framework for economic rights (although one that is religious and particularistic). By having an integrated theory that is not based solely in one approach, theological or philosophical, he is able to have a comprehensive theory of economic rights that could persuade and motivate ethicists, and others, of varying persuasions. Thus, by adopting Shue's basic rights approach, Wolterstorff has Shue's "short list" and his justification for it. By utilizing theological categories Wolterstorff is able to explicate economic rights in a rights-oriented world and is able to legitimate them by a transcendent God.

Wolterstorff's work has as an additional asset, his dialectical opposition to Novak. That is he contributes to what has been previously described and discussed as the Novak-Hollenbach debate. As may be recalled, Novak worries that economic rights as entitlements may encourage "servility" in the populace (particularly, the poor) and an overbearing, paternalistic, interventionist state.[90] Wolterstorff, while aware of the danger of increasing the power of the state, nevertheless looks at servility from more than one direction. He maintains that a state that enforces or condones conditions that render people unable to sustain their dignity and/or their lives is every bit as dangerous (to human dignity and human flourishing) as an overly interventionist, paternalistic state.[91] Servility is, for him, a danger that can be produced by a minimalist state as well as a totalitarian one. Thus, he recognizes the duty of the state to check both its own powers and those of powerful, overreaching economic forces within its borders (i.e., modern corporations), so that the individual is not forced to beg for individual rights as if they were privileges. His anthropology (what he believes is entailed in being human) and his demand for governmental intervention echo the actual sentiments of Dr. Martin Luther

---

[90] Novak, "Economic Rights: The Servile State," *Catholicism in Crisis* (October 1985): 8-13; "Where the Second Draft Errs," *America* 154 (18 January 1986): 23, 24; "Free Persons and the Common Good," *Crisis* (October 1986): 11-19; "The Rights and Wrongs of 'Economic Rights': A Debate Continued," *This World* 17 (Spring 1987): 43-52.

[91] Wolterstorff endorses the Kairos document that demands that the oppressed demand their justice and equal treatment. The duty to demand fair treatment and the recognition of one's dignity is a human duty, divinely given, in Wolterstorff's opinion, even to the most oppressed and deprived individual. *Christianity and Social Justice*, 216-17.

King Jr., who demanded, rather than begged for certain economic rights.[92]

Theological Contributions to the
Economic Rights Debate

There are several contributions that these theological debates make in regard to economic rights. First, an ultimate foundation is laid for economic rights in the dignity of the human being, who is created in the image of God. Thus, the retarded, the catatonic, those who may never exercise agency or rationality are nevertheless acknowledged to be fully human. Their humanity is recognized without reference to their ability to act as humans; thus Gewirth's theoretical weakness in this area is corrected. As may be recalled from Chapter Four, Gewirth attempts to account for a smaller list of generic rights for those who have, proportionately speaking, a diminished capacity for agency. This explanation seems satisfactory for those who can exercise some agency, such as the mildly retarded, or the paraplegic. Gewirth's explanation has some

---

92 King demanded that the basic rights of the poor be recognized and protected by the federal government. King understood that the "twin" of racial injustice was "economic injustice." See Ervin Smith, *The Ethics of Martin Luther King* (New York: Mellon Press, 1981), 131. Of particular note, preceding Gewirth and his notions of agency, King knew the importance of basic economic sustainability for the development of the human personality. Thus, for King, a personalist, there could be no true freedom for the human personality except through the economic means to achieve it. This maxim is analogous to Gewirth's PGC, and Wolterstorff's and Shue's views. Accordingly, King wrote that, "Negroes must therefore not only formulate a program; they must fashion new tactics which do not count on government goodwill but serve, instead, to compel unwilling authorities to yield to the mandates of justice . . . We are demanding an emergency program to provide employment for everyone in need of a job or, if a work program is impracticable, a guaranteed annual income at levels that sustain life in decent circumstances. It is now incontestable that the wealth and resources of the United States make the elimination of poverty practicable." *The Trumpet of Conscience* (New York: Harper & Row, 1968), 14. While King never explained fully his economic right theory, it is a fine example of the rejection of servility that comes from claiming one's rights.

plausibility for children, who are simply being protected until such a time as they are capable of freely exercising their agency. But it loses its plausibility for the completely and permanently incapacitated. If the exercise of agency is the basis for rights recognition, then these people should, logically speaking, not be afforded many, if any rights. For Hollenbach and Wolterstorff, however, they are fully human and thus must be accorded human rights, including rights that have a specifically economic component, such as to be provided with food, clothing, shelter and care. These theological economic rights evidence the ultimate and transcendent value accorded to human beings precisely because they are grounded in a transcendent power and source of authority. This transcendent authority qualifies current human existence while also providing a transcendent future. People must have bread and freedom, so that they can live in covenant with each other, and with God.[93]

Hollenbach's and Wolterstorff's economic rights theories are integrated into comprehensive ethical systems within history. Both theories present a transcendent value for human beings, and suggest a common destiny: people are created to live in solidarity with each other; their rights must therefore be protected in order to preserve and maintain the common good. These theories are designed for a real and living community,

---

[93] Though the inherent interdependency of rights is specifically addressed by Wolterstorff and Shue, Hollenbach is also aware of this thesis and affirms its veracity. He observes, "If the historical memory and present transnational experience of the Catholic community is in any way accurate, it would seem that the argument between those who say 'bread first' and those who say 'freedom first' has reached a dead end. People who lack bread also usually lack political freedom. And increasingly those without political freedom and access to political power seem to end up without bread. The interconnection of rights has become evident not only in theory but in practice. As J. P. Pronk, Minister for Development Cooperation from the Netherlands, puts it, 'In Latin American and elsewhere see in a dramatic way how people set about achieving social justice, how they need to exercise political freedoms to do this, and how they are oppressed and become the victims of inhuman tortures. The link between the different categories (of rights) is shown clearly not only in the preambles to treaties but also in the practical exercise of human rights.'" *Justice, Peace, and Human Rights*, 99.

beyond that of the Christian church, so that they are understandable in an international and multicultural context. According to Wolterstorff and Hollenbach, rights are for the individual, the community, and the church. Individuals, are not left alone, by these theorists, to exercise their rights solely for the purpose of their individual self-gratification. For Wolterstorff and Hollenbach, the individual is a member of a created world; of a universal community, in which the welfare of all is the concern of all. Further, these theorists posit human rights in people with no regard to the faith claims of the people. Such theories are accessible therefore, to those who do not share the Catholic or Reformed confessions. The duty to help others, though imperfect, expresses the love of God for humanity; this love is to be perfectly experienced in the next world. This vision transcends empirical reality, without abandoning that reality, or disdaining it. We are presented by these commentators with a vision of human life that transcends human life itself, without abandoning it.

Wolterstorff's theological adaptation of Henry Shue's interdependency theory succeeds in presenting a theory of society and social relations that is not foundationally reliant upon arguments regarding the nature and function of rights. Wolterstorff's incorporation of Shue's argument shows that his theory is not inherently contradictory to what is already believed by many Christians with regard to human obligations and human needs. By adopting Shue's method, Wolterstorff obtains a short list of rights sensitive to cultural differences in differing societies. Yet, by being based on basic human needs (which are constant, though differently interpreted in various societies) these rights nevertheless evidence universal qualities since basic human needs are themselves constant and universal.

These theological theories of economic rights are needed because they are able to make their claims within religious traditions and mores already in place. They are subject therefore to immediate implementation and or lobbying by religious institutions. They thereby make a more immediate claim than the claims of philosophers who are not philosopher-kings in modern society, and do not have institutions under their direct control that could implement their theories. Another way of saying this is to say that Gewirth and

Shue as academicians can be very helpful in the economic rights debate, but they do not have institutions at hand that can and do implement their theories. Academicians and other commentators must enter public debate. They must make proposals to government, the church, economic powers, and humanitarian organizations and hope that such institutions see fit to put their proposals into action.

Our review of these theological contributions to the economic rights debate reveals that the religious discussion of these issues supports rather than denies the viability and persuasiveness of economic rights. That no religious theories of economic rights encourage the Christian, or others, to be dependent upon the government, the Church, or other mediating institutions to provide for the basic needs of people should also be noted.[94] Clearly, if one understands economic rights as they have been reinterpreted similar to the Limburg principles, (i.e., economic rights consisting of the right to demand that one's government put forth its best efforts to encourage and create social arrangements that create economic production and distribution so that the poor have the minimum necessities needed for a chance at happiness in a society of equality of opportunity), then the fears that economic rights are spurious, or encourage servility would seem themselves to be spurious.[95] Novak's concession to Hollenbach that economic rights are needed (even in light of his qualifications and limitations) would seem to signal that at least in terms of the theological debate, the economic rights debate is coming to an end in an uneasy, but growing consensus. John Warwick Montgomery's endorsement of economic rights (which space limitations will not allow me to discuss), made based on a biblicist, evangelical reading of Scripture, is a clear indication

---

[94] The danger that the recognition and implementation of economic rights may unwittingly and unintentionally encourage servility from the people and totalitarian interventionism from the government is denied by most (Hollenbach, Míguez-Bonino, Wolterstorff and others) while being worried about by Michael Novak.

[95] *The Limburg Principles on the Implementation of the International Covenant on Economic, Social and Cultural Rights, Human Rights Quarterly* 9 (1987): 122-35. These principles were referred to earlier in Chapter Three, p. 143, n. 26.

that truly disparate Christian groups now also endorse economic rights.[96]

Still disputed is the actual content of the rights and their foundation. However, it is not inconceivable that in the near future, through interaction with non-governmental agencies, United Nations debates, and ecumenical debates, the basic content of economic rights may be agreed upon by consensus. It is unlikely however, that the foundation for these rights shall gain a consensus. The reason a plurality of foundations for economic rights will continue to be used lies in the nature of theological claims and rights theories. Both theological claims or doctrines and rights theories inherently present unique statements regarding human nature and human society. One may believe that the best way of defining humanity is by recognizing rationality and will (as do neo-Kantians, such as Gewirth). Or one may believe that the best image of humanity is a Catholic or Protestant understanding of the *imago Dei*. One may attempt to talk about what human society must have to be socially just. Shue takes this approach emphasizing the recognition, protection and implementation of civil and political rights, and certain economic rights. Each of these claims is unique. All of them justify economic rights. Some of the claims base themselves in particular visions of God and ultimate claims of truth. Other economic claims regarding God and ultimate truth are seen as above debate and compromise. Thus, a consensus on a single foundation for human rights is unlikely to be achieved in the future. Despite these problems, the ratification of the Covenants on Social, Economic and Cultural Rights will probably continue apace and will do so because both secular and religious non-governmental agencies believe (rightly or wrongly) that this is what is morally required of them in the modern economic world.[97] Jacques Maritain's observation that human rights would be recognized and implemented if only no one ultimate foundation for those rights were championed to the exclusion of others, still appears, from a reading of the literature, to be true (and appears to be applicable to economic rights).

---

[96] John Warwick Montgomery, *Human Rights and Human Dignity*.

[97] This is Louis Henkin's point that is fully examined in Chapter One.

Our concluding chapter will show that the call for economic rights is indirectly a critique of a society's commitment to social justice. This position has more potential for critiquing moral relationships than economic rights skepticism, which sadly, but firmly, allows one to stand idly by while some perish. Most importantly, the theological explanations for and against economic rights help us to see how economic rights may be interpreted and justified without regard to the fleeting whims of the public. Economic rights are based on economic relations, and these relations are permanent expressions of human relations in society. Such rights cannot be fully accounted for, let alone justified, or dismissed, unless they are related to broader notions of what it is to be human, and to be a member of a community. How these theological debates influenced public policy has been briefly discussed in this chapter: it will be further addressed in Chapter Six. In that chapter the clearest expression of economic rights in a non-minimalist state and what such rights would demand from a society such as ours will be formally proposed.

CHAPTER SIX

THE GROWING END TO ONE ARGUMENT: THE BEGINNING OF ANOTHER

Introduction

This study has asked whether economic rights are important moral considerations for the formation of public policy. Morally compelling arguments for economic rights that link the implementation of economic rights with the implementation of civil and political rights have been presented. Since, in American society, civil and political rights are considered a given, economic rights should be implemented if they can be shown to be inherently interdependent with the former. Chapters Four and Five demonstrated the appropriateness of this linkage by means of the interdependency arguments of Henry Shue and the dialectically necessary arguments of Alan Gewirth. Chapters Four and Five also answered the standard objections of economic rights skeptics. Chapter Five also demonstrated the value of theological contributions to the economic rights debate. The recognition of the inherent interdependency and mutual necessity of economic rights with civil and political rights has not, however, been fully accepted. It will be realized only after a lengthy period of time, and only after a great deal of struggle.

It is the purpose of this Chapter to explain further the nature of the conflictive and evolutionary rights generation process and its future implications for Western, liberal, wealthy, rights-recognizing countries. This process was given a historical exposition in Chapter One. This chapter suggests an analytical interpretation of that history by considering briefly contested political discourses. This chapter will then proceed to explain how rights discourses create, establish and change moral, economic, and political relations. The process of changing social arrangements because of rights recognition, which was discussed in Chapter Two will be more clearly articulated here, with a process of moral reasoning borrowing from the work of Adam Smith. Five major considerations of this study will then be readdressed in this chapter. The first consideration concerns the issue of indeterminacy; the fact that economic rights, by their nature, are never permanently defined. The second concern addresses three economic rights: work, education, and health. The third problem concerns the theoretical problems that continue to beset economic rights skepticism. These skepticism problems suggest the probable decline of this position. The fourth problem concerns the harmonization of differing economic rights theories. This discussion is designed to show how differing voices in support of economic rights can harmonize rather than clash. The fifth problem concerns the difficulty of coordinating the efforts of would-be-economic rights partisans. This study finally concludes with a statement suggesting the ethical superiority of economic rights recognition over economic rights skepticism.

Two articles are quite instructive in addressing our first topic: how the rights debate has evolved as it has, and what future struggles are likely to entail. Nancy Fraser's recent article gives great insight into how to analyze rights struggles, though it is explicitly written to address needs discourses.[1] David Speak's brief but insightful article also explains the moral interplay that takes place in the evolution of rights. After a

---

[1] Nancy Fraser, "Talking about Needs: Interpretive Contests as Political Conflicts in Welfare-State Societies," Ethics 99, no. 2, (January 1989), 291-313.

discussion of these two articles, we will attend to aforementioned ongoing problems.

Contested Political Discourses: Needs & Rights

Nancy Fraser, a political ethicist, is deeply concerned with how people talk about needs. She writes:

> In late-capitalist, welfare-state societies, talk about people's needs is an important species of political discourse. We argue, in the United States, for example, about whether the government ought to provide for health and day-care needs, and indeed, about whether such needs exist. And we dispute whether existing social-welfare programs really do meet the needs they purport to satisfy or whether, instead, they misconstrue those needs. We also argue about what exactly various groups of people really do need and about who should have the last word in such matters. In all of these cases, needs-talk functions as a medium for the making and contesting of political claims. It is an idiom in which political conflict is played out and through which inequalities are symbolically elaborated and challenged.[2]

What Fraser says about needs is equally true about rights. Though these two concepts are clearly distinct from each other, they generate similar discourses.[3] Fraser notes this correlation, writing:

> However, in welfare-state societies, needs-talk has been institutionalized as a major vocabulary of political discourse. It coexists, albeit often uneasily, with talk about rights and interests as the very center of political life. Indeed, this peculiar juxtaposition of a discourse about needs with discourses about rights and interests is one of the distinctive marks of late-capitalist political culture.[4]

What Fraser suggests as a superior hermeneutic is a change in focus. In describing her approach she writes:

---

2   Ibid., 291.

3   Economic rights skepticism often concerns itself with the alleged confusion of needs with rights supposedly by economic rights supporters.

4   Ibid., 291-92.

In my approach, the focus of inquiry is not needs but rather discourses about needs. The point is to shift our angle of vision on the politics of needs. Usually, the politics of needs is understood to concern the distribution of satisfactions. In my approach, by contrast, the focus is on the *politics of need interpretation.* [5]

Much of this study has similarly delved into the politics of rights interpretations: specifically economic rights interpretations. Fraser's reason for changing the focus of her inquiry is to, "bring into view the contextual and contested character of needs claims."[6] Fraser argues that thin theories of needs invite a deceptive consensus. She notes that:

> We can uncontroversially say that homeless people, like everyone in nontropical climates, need shelter in order to live. And most people will infer that governments, as guarantors of life and liberty, have a responsibility to provide for this need. However, as soon as we descend to a lesser level of generality, needs claims become far more controversial. What more 'thickly,' do homeless people need in order to be sheltered from the cold: what specific forms of provision are implied once we acknowledge their very general thin need? Do homeless people need forbearance to sleep undisturbed next to a hot air vent on a street corner? A space in a subway tunnel or a bus terminal? A bed in a temporary shelter? A permanent home? Suppose we say the latter. What kind of permanent housing do homeless people need? Rental units in high-rises in center city areas remote from good schools, discount shopping and job opportunities? Single-family homes designed for single-earner, two-parent families? And what else do homeless people need in order to have permanent homes? Rent subsidies? Income supports? Jobs? Job training and education? Day care? Finally, what is needed, at the level of housing policy, in order to insure an adequate stock of affordable housing? Tax incentives to encourage private investment in low-income housing? . . . We could continue proliferating such questions indefinitely. And we would at the same time, be proliferating controversy. That is precisely the point about needs claims. These claims tend to be nested,

---

5   Ibid.
6   Ibid.

connected to one another in ramified chains of 'in-order-to' relations. Moreover when these chains are unraveled in the course of political disputes, disagreements usually deepen rather than abate.[7]

What Fraser notes about needs and needs discourses is doubly true about rights and rights discourses. This conclusion is particularly compelling when, as with economic rights, the rights discourses are based in whole or in part on the interpretation of needs. Fraser clearly illustrates the problem that haunts economic rights theories: the issue of indeterminacy. Just as Shue argued that rights are inherently interconnected and interdependent, Fraser argues that need claims are interdependent. Fraser notes that needs theories are generated from various power groups. Each group characterizes needs in a way that favors their current social arrangements and communal meanings. Fraser sees a direct connection between needs discourses and rights discourses. If Fraser is correct, and if her focus on needs is truly analogous to rights discourse then certain aspects of the evolution of rights discourse become easier to understand. The evolutionary process described in Chapter One can be understood simply as a historical description of a political struggle over the definition and application of political and moral claims. A further consideration of Fraser's approach helps to clarify this process. Fraser is critical of thin descriptions of needs:

> I believe that thin theories of needs which do not descend into the murky depths of such networks are unable to shed much light on contemporary needs politics. Such theories assume that the politics of needs concerns only whether various predefined needs will or will not be provided for. As a result, they deflect attention from a number of important political questions. First, they take the interpretation of people's needs as simply given and unproblematic; they thus occlude the interpretive

---

7   As this study has demonstrated, gaining a consensus on even a "thin" theory of needs and any rights they might produce is considerably more difficult than Fraser realizes.   Indeed, Gewirth's and Shue's projects are designed to justify "thin" theories of needs and rights, not "thick" ones. They are convincing precisely because they do not attempt to justify either "thick" descriptions of needs, rights, or concepts of the "self."

dimension of needs politics--the fact that not just satisfactions but needs interpretations are politically contested. Second, they assume that it is unproblematic who interprets the needs in question and from what perspective and in the light of what interests; they thus occlude the fact that who gets to establish authoritative, thick definitions of people's needs is itself a political stake. Third, they take for granted that the socially authorized forms of public discourse available for interpreting people's needs are adequate and fair; they thus occlude the question whether these forms of public discourse are skewed in favor of the self-interpretations and interests of dominant social groups and, so, work to the disadvantage of subordinate or oppositional groups; they occlude, in other words, the fact that the means of public discourse themselves may be at issue in needs politics. Fourth, such theories fail to focalize the social and institutional logic of processes of need interpretation; they thus occlude such important political questions as where in society, in what institutions, are authoritative need interpretations developed, and what sorts of social relations are in force among the interlocutors or co-interpreters?[8]

Fraser hopes to address what she calls these "blind spots" by analyzing the politics of needs in three "analytically distinct but practically interrelated moments."[9] She writes:

The first [moment] is the struggle to establish or deny the political status of a given need, that is, the struggle to validate the need as a matter of legitimate political concern or to enclave it as a nonpolitical matter. The second is the struggle over the interpretation of the need, the struggle for the power to define it and, so, to determine what would satisfy it. The third moment is the struggle over the satisfaction of the need, that is, the struggle to secure or withhold the provision.[10]

If these three analytical moments are analogously applied to the economic rights debate they give us some definite ideas to where the debate has been and where it is now heading. A candidate for a first analytical moment, for economic rights, can be seen in Roosevelt's hortative support for a right to "freedom from want." A second analytical moment can be seen in the United Nations debates on first the Universal Declaration of

---

8   Ibid., 293-94.
9   Ibid.
10   Ibid., 294.

Human Rights, and subsequently, on the debates on the interpretation of the Covenant on Social, Economic and Cultural Rights. Another second analytical moment was expressed in the Carter Administration's attempts to define economic rights as well as in their hortative support for the same. This second moment does not, of course, belong solely to rights supporters.[11] Indeed, the enormous proliferation of economic rights debates in the post-Carter years is also a vital expression of second analytical moments. The third moment is now just dawning. International literature, such as the Limburg Principles, describes just what a party to the Covenant on Social, Economic, and Cultural Rights might need to do to satisfy economic rights.[12]

Similarly, the debate between Hollenbach and Novak can be interpreted as moving similarly. Thus when Novak finally concedes to Hollenbach that there are indeed economic rights, although such rights are "conditional," he is moving from a second analytical moment to the third.[13] What social arrangements are necessary for the actual satisfaction of economic rights constitutes the primary issue of the third moment. By its nature this third moment requires "thicker" descriptions of rights, and these "thicker" descriptions occasionally lead to a retreat back to the struggles of the first and second moments. As Fraser notes in terms of housing, if the description of the housing needs are not carefully circumscribed one can generate an endless proliferation of housing needs. This kind of indeterminacy is an internal one to any one need. The indeterminacy that is often related to rights is similar: it often involves a proliferation of rights to many things.

---

[11] The first moment does not belong solely to economic rights supporters: none of them do. Each moment is a contested discursive interplay. Group rights, for example, aside from genocide safeguards, have never gotten much beyond first moment discursive struggles.

[12] The Limburg Principles are, essentially a fuller explanation of the steps governments must take to "satisfy" economic rights when a full enjoyment of the right are "impracticable."

[13] Similarly Novak's early essay, "Human Rights and White Sepulchers" could be construed as a first analytical moment. In *Human Rights and U. S. Human Rights Policy*, ed. Howard J. Wiarda (Washington: American Inst. for Public Policy Research, 1982), 79.

Chapters Four and Five demonstrated moral arguments that could be used in future policy formation to bridle runaway discourse on both needs and rights. Importantly, the debate over economic rights, like other rights debates, is never-ending though the analytical moments or stages move in the direction indicated by Fraser; that is from the first to the third stages.

As a classic illustration, consider John Rawls assessment that common ground has been reached in the West regarding the issues of slavery and religious intolerance.[14] Rawls correctly maintains, that the right to be free from involuntary servitude and the right to freely practice one's religion have a permanent consensus in the West. Rawls points out that currently no one seriously argues for the previous interpretations of moral relations that legalized and supported slavery and religious intolerance. The issues are, therefore, in continuing debates to determine exactly what the rights to freedom and religion mean in terms of the *satisfaction* of the right. The continued interpretations of Sixth Amendment Rights (according to Miranda variations) and the ongoing debates on the First Amendment Rights with regard to a separation of Church and State give eloquently witness to the ongoing discussion of the satisfaction of widely accepted rights. These third moment struggles are permanent in the sense that debate with regard to actual satisfaction is inherently never-ending. Thus the actual implementation of economic rights will always be subject to continued debate and discussion. Adjustments in implementations will always be necessary.

---

14 John Rawls, "Justice as Fairness," *Philosophy & Public Affairs* 14, (Summer 1985), 223-51. Rawls writes: "We must now ask: how might political philosophy find a shared basis for settling such a fundamental question as that of the most appropriate institutional forms for liberty and equality? Of course, it is likely that the most that can be done is to narrow the range of public disagreement. Yet even firmly held convictions gradually change: religious toleration is now accepted, and arguments for persecution are no longer openly professed; similarly, slavery is rejected as inherently unjust, and however much the aftermath of slavery may persist in social practices and unavowed attitudes, no one is willing to defend it. We collect such settled convictions into a coherent conception of justice. We can regard these convictions as provisional fixed points which any conception of justice must account for if it is to be reasonable for us." At 228.

One other aspect of Fraser's insightful article needs to be considered. Fraser always assumes that needs discourses are between groups of people with some "competing need interpretations."[15] These distinct parties are often unequal in power. Fraser notes:

> From this perspective, needs-talk appears as a site of struggle where groups with unequal discursive (and nondiscursive) resources compete to establish as hegemonic their respective interpretations of legitimate social needs. Dominant groups articulate need interpretations intended to exclude, defuse, and/or coopt counter-interpretations. Subordinate or oppositional groups, on the other hand, articulate need interpretations intended to challenge, displace, and/or modify dominant ones. In both cases, the interpretations are acts and interventions.[16].

If Fraser's observations are analogized to rights discussion the very curious use of rights language by dominant groups is striking. First generation rights, as Chapter One made clear, have always been understood to be revolutionary in nature. Yet with the passage of time such rights, now positivized in Constitutions, mores and conventions, in the very civil religion of America, have become deeply accepted (perhaps more so) by the non-revolutionary people of our society. Economic rights initially flowered, in a revolutionary fashion, with socialists, primarily after the Second World War (not that there are not prior welfare liberalism antecedents). However, these second generation rights are rightly understood as challenges to the accepted first generation rights. In the United Nations a discursive struggle set in. Similarly, an interpretation of economic rights, growing out of welfare liberalism, found expression in first the Roosevelt Administration, and then in the Carter Administration. In the Carter Administration the inclusion of economic rights was understood by both supporters and skeptics as an acknowledgment of the ability of the poor to make certain moral and political claims. The thrust of the skeptics has not been that the poor could make no claims. Such a rejection of the weak would contradict the whole tradition,

---

15 Nancy Fraser, "Talking About Needs", 295.
16 Ibid., 296.

genre, and function of rights claims that have always been understood as a claim by the weak upon the "strong." Instead, skeptics rejected the claims of the poor and their spokespeople on the grounds that their new claims were incompatible, incomprehensible, or pejoristic to previously established rights whose value was considered sacrosanct. The arguments of Shue, Gewirth, Plant and others address these objections and demonstrate that though the economic rights skeptics' concerns are genuine and important, the conclusions are incorrect and misconceived. Thus the economic rights debate is growing to an end. In its place are a plethora of new questions as to what economic rights might be justified and implemented, and what such implementations will require of individuals, states and societies.

Fraser's argument posited opposing political camps in rhetorical battle over the definition, recognition and implementation of needs. No matter how opposed, such constituencies are still operating out of some shared conception of rhetorical and political claiming. What the rights discourse struggle does, as does the needs discourse struggle, is to interpret the past, the present, and, consequently, the future. Just how this process occurs can be further explained by David Speak, Associate Professor of Political Science at Georgia Southern College.[17]

The Creation of Moral Relations and Communities Through Rights Discourses

Rights discourses describe and create moral relations and communities. David Speak explains this process in an insightful essay in which he purports to, "probe some of the roots of the difficulties of reaching an agreement about rights across such cultural gaps."[18] Speak uses Adam Smith's *Theory of Moral Sentiments,* "as a tool for understanding some of the difficult questions of discussions of rights in a multicultural setting."[19]

---

17 David Speak, "Rights, Rhetoric, and Adam Smith," *Philosophical Essays of the Ideas of a Good Society: Studies in Social and Political Theory* (Lewiston: The Edwin Mellen Press, 1988), 33-44.

18 Ibid., 33.

19 Ibid.

He thereby provides insight into rights discourse between
supporters of differing "generations" of rights; possibly between
differing classes of rights, and throughout the international
arena. Speak insists that proper political rhetoric appeals to the
"truth" and to an audience.[20] The successful master of rhetoric is
somehow able to coherently address both concerns.

Speak understands rights discourse as constituting a
certain kind of moral shorthand. He maintains:

> But whatever the reason, rights claims are thus
> problematically related to truth because the claim is a
> substitution for an explicit rendering of the reasons that
> justify the particular claim, suggesting something like 'Of
> course every right thinking person agrees with this,' or
> 'You can take my word for this.' The rights claim allows
> for or encourages a shorthand argument, asserting the
> existence of justificatory reasons without spelling them
> out.[21]

Speak also maintains that rights, in the modern world, are
ways of determining and maintaining membership. Thus Speak
concludes:

> The shorthand can only be acceptable if certain shared
> assumptions or beliefs exist within a certain group. . . . The
> rights claim does not merely make reference to some
> group--it rests solidly upon particular assumptions about
> the group itself and about facts and beliefs accepted by the
> group. The rights claim is an assertion of the existence of
> certain shared though unspecified reasons.[22]

Speak characterizes rights discourse in much the same
way as Fraser characterized needs discourse. Both examples of
rhetoric arise out of definable communities that have some
shared concerns and meanings. Speak explains, however, the
dynamic dialectic that exists between rights talk and community
beliefs. Speak writes, "The existence of certain defined groups
with certain shared beliefs may give rise to rights claims. But it
may sometimes work the other way around: advancing rights

---

20 Ibid.

21 Ibid., 36.

22 Ibid. For a fuller text on the importance of shared beliefs, though
not cast in a rights analysis context, see Michael Walzer's *Spheres of
Justice*.

claims may help define certain groups and/or create shared beliefs."23 Speak importantly notes that, "Many rights claims are widely contested when initially advanced, only gaining acceptance after persistent assertion."24 Such an understanding of the evolution of rights does much to explain former President Carter's belief that the important values of civil equality, embedded in the Constitution and the Bill of Rights, were destined to gain consensus only after repeated claims by various communities.25 Thus the civil rights of African-Americans is belatedly recognized when Martin Luther King, Jr. makes the appeal in the nineteen fifties and nineteen sixties, though it had been previously, and repeatedly made by black and white abolitionists.   Though the understanding of equality of opportunity may have been inherent in the Framers' works, it is, from this perspective, only the repeated demands that finally bring down the resistance and create new shared meanings, and a *new community*. This new community then internalizes and concretizes the new understanding of rights and holds them out to be normative until new challenges arise.

Speak employs Smith's "impartial spectator" and his theory of "mutual sympathy" to further explain the process of reasoning that takes place in rights discourse.26 From Speak's

---

23   Ibid., 36.
24   Ibid.
25   See Chapter Two of this study, page 75, note 17.
26   John Rawls writes of a Smithian "impartial spectator, "Consider the following definition reminiscent of Hume and Adam Smith. Something is right, a social system say, when an ideally rational and impartial spectator would approve of it from a general point of view should he possess all the relevant knowledge of the circumstances.   A rightly ordered society is one meeting the approval of such an ideal observer." *A Theory of Justice* (Cambridge, Mass.: Belknap Press, 1971), 184. Adam Smith wrote of the impartial spectator in several ways. One way was as a conscience created by God in humanity: "But though man has, in this manner, been rendered the immediate judge of mankind, he has been rendered so only in the first instance; and an appeal lies from his sentence to a much higher tribunal, to the tribunal of their own consciences, to that of the supposed impartial and well-informed spectator, to that of the man within the breast, the great judge and arbiter of their conduct. The jurisdictions of those two tribunals are founded upon principles which, though in some respects resembling and akin, are, however, in reality different and distinct." Adam Smith, *Theory of*

standpoint rights claimants are Smithian moral agents who are sensitive to the moral approbation and disapprobation of their surrounding communities. Simultaneously, within their breasts beat the heart of the "impartial spectator" who is not bound by the mores of his parochial community. According to Speak this spectator is sensitively critical of the local rules and rights in comparison with general principles and new proposals of universal truths. Thus a rights claimant's understanding of rights and duties is formed by his community. At the same time, however, his understanding is not completely constricted to the community's current understanding of rights. Such an understanding can account for a Martin Luther King, Jr., whose understandings of rights were formed in part by first generation civil and political rights, but whose impartial spectator also demanded economic rights. The importance of these considerations is clearly explained by Speak who helps us to realize the relevance of this approach, writing:

> So where does all of this lead? What difference does it make that we can see rights as rhetorical and dependent upon sympathy as Adam Smith describes it? The goal of this exercise is to move toward a better understanding of the problem of rights in American national policy, which is to say, the problem of rights in a multi-cultural setting both within this country and in foreign relations. Sympathy, as Smith would have it, is a difficult task across cultural divides. . . . But working toward that perspectival leap is at the same time working toward the creation of community. As Smith says, affection is really just habituated sympathy. To the extent that we attempt to follow Smith's lead reaching toward some understanding of cross-cultural and international rights, we are actually creating new communities which will in turn ground greater possibilities for understanding. In creating the habit of sympathy we are as much creating truth as we are discovering it. Community may not be a prerequisite of this dialogue so much as it is a correlative activity and/or product.[27]

Economic skeptics, such as Jeanne Kirkpatrick, Michael

Moral Sentiments (Indianapolis: Liberty Classics, 1982). § III. 2.32 (Of the Sense of Duty), 130.

[27] Ibid., 41. From this perspective, the utter rejection of civil rights is now publicly condemned in most of America. This consensus can be seen as having been created, at least in part, by the struggle for and acquisition of civil rights.

Novak, and Alasdair MacIntyre are partially correct: rights language does issue out of certain communities that have a tradition of rights discourse. What they fail to consider is the other half of the dialectic. The community gives voice to certain notions of rights, but the rights and the relationships that they create act back on the community. Rights preserve the community in many ways, but they also change it. This is a process that may not be constant and fluid, but it is, nevertheless, dynamic rather than static. The new community has new relationships because of the recognition of rights and the ongoing process of talking about and arguing over the meaning of these rights. For example, while voting rights are basically settled as normative values in this country, employment rights created by judicially interpreted affirmative action are not. Affirmative action with regard to employment is in the process of discursive struggle. Presently it has opposing camps.

Speak sees the problem in most rights discourse that discussants are too sensitive to the nearby partial spectator - our family, class, nation, religion - and too insensitive to the impartial spectators who are members of our physical world, but all too often "aliens" in our moral universe. Speak maintains:

> Whether talking about the welfare rights of poor black women in Detroit or in the self-determination rights of Salvadoran peasants, our task is not to look for some idealized list of proper claims on our concern and resources. To look for a list of this sort, self-evident or written into the structure of the world is to seek a chimera. Our search must be for mutual understanding, with the goal of achieving and then habituating sympathy. This does not mean that we can treat rights as created rather than discovered, for no strategy could more radically undermine the notion of rights itself . . . . We interact to discover those commonalities about which we can create consensus. We don't create human rights--at least not exclusively. Neither do we discover them exclusively. The process of exchanging sympathetic understanding is a process which involves both the discovery and the creation of right.[28]

---

28 Ibid., 41, 42.

Fraser would add to Speak's position that the process of exchanging sympathetic understanding is not without misunderstandings and hostility. Thus from the perspectives of both Fraser and Speak it should be clear that the economic rights debate will never be absolutely settled. In particular, from Speak's position, the quest for the "ideal" list is shown to be utopian. Nevertheless, continued discourse on the types of economic rights and their application and implementation is not fruitless or misguided as long as discussants do not delusionally desire an "ideal" or "timeless" list of rights. Nevertheless, certain economic rights should be preferred to other possible candidates. Three that should be briefly considered are the rights to work, health care, and education. Our brief discussion of them indicates the direction in which the economic debate may move.

Three Crucial Economic Rights

The exact composition of economic rights is cloudy and it is likely to remain so. Economic rights are, in terms of their content, indeterminate in nature. The exact list of goods and services that are necessary to sustain human life and agency can never be precisely and timelessly defined. Thus, a concentration on basic needs is needed. At the same time, any conclusions on basic needs must be understood to be provisional. While food, clothing and shelter appear to be basic goods calling for their provision (if necessary) by haves to have nots, other goods (which Gewirth calls additive, and nonsubtractive goods) are less self-evident. Thus all of the economic rights listed in the Covenant on Social, Economic, and Cultural Rights are not likely to be recognized and implemented, and economic rights will never be uniformly implemented due to this indeterminacy in content and "parochial" applications.

As previously stated, work, education, and health care appear to be the most important of these candidates for "approved" rights.[29] Admittedly, the selection of these rights is an arbitrary choice and the relative importance of these

---

[29] These rights are beyond the even more widely recognized rights to food, shelter and clothing.

concerns is likely to vary among their proponents. Nevertheless, proposals for these rights are necessary.

It is clear from the progress of world events that a planned state has lost much of its international appeal. Thus the governmental guarantee of a "job" as such has been defined in communist states is no longer to be desired or expected. How then should rights to work be recognized?

At present Carter's approach to this problem is adequate for America's economy. In Chapter Two we demonstrated how Carter understood his governmental responsibilities to consist of encouraging the growth of jobs and production. In his view government had to be prepared to create some jobs, and job training programs.[30] In sponsoring these programs, Carter understood himself as carrying out the will of the people in removing obstacles to an equal opportunity to work. Jobs, however, were not guaranteed to any one individual: the government simply had the responsibility to take steps to increase the job pool. What this approach demands is that a calculation be made short of a zero percent as to a "tolerable" level of unemployment. Such a determination would have to be subject to a high level of debate and perhaps a national referendum. Since the monies allocated for this provision are not "handouts," but full employment allocations, the national will to accomplish this task may not be impossible to solicit. Steps like these have already been requested and justified by William J. Wilson's seminal work.[31] Obviously some forces will oppose proposals like these others will support them. Shue and Gewirth's work mount moral arguments that could appeal to the impartial spectator on both sides of this "right to work" debate.

Turning to another related "object" of a right, education, we find more theoretical difficulties. Education is a notoriously slippery concept as a feature of an economic rights theory. Certainly some education would qualify as a basic and necessary good, i.e., necessary for agency and well-being. Completely unclear is the kind of education that would qualify as a basic right. Fraser would classify this inquiry to be an issue of needs

---

[30] See Chapter Two, notes 53 and 54.

[31] W. J. Wilson, *The Truly Disadvantaged* (Chicago: University of Chicago Press 1987).

discourse. It is indeed a "needs" issue and an issue in "rights" discourse. Clearly society cannot be required to provide all of its members with the education needed to be brain surgeons. On the other hand, in an increasingly technological world, one in which employment demands ever increasing technical skills, a denial of, or lack of education can doom persons to poverty. Somewhere between these two extremes, at differing points, in differing societies, the economic right to education, appropriate to that society, may be found by its members. Hopefully it will be found with a reasonably free discussion of both sides on the issue.

Similarly health-care is equally vital, yet equally slippery. The argument for socialized medicine is not a self-evident one. While many theorists in this field believe that the health delivery system of the United States is inferior (from a distributive justice point of view, as well as in terms of effectiveness and efficiency) to the socialized systems in Canada, Great Britain and elsewhere, defenders of the present system persist. What Richard Couto makes clear in his insightful argument is that health-care is a basic need, and one that is, like fire-protection, and police-protection, not directly accessible to the individual.[32] As Couto points out, in a capitalist, free market society, the individual must purchase health care as a commodity, like a sack of flour.[33] So, if health care is treated as a commodity, like food, economic rights arguments like Gewirth's, Shue's or Wolterstorff's may be utilized for its justification. Couto's assessment of it as a basic communal service, is, however, probably a better account: health care *is* more like fire protection than a sack of flour. If even this categorization is accepted problems for basic health care advocates will persist.[34] The continued confusion will center on the level of health care needed to insure an individual, his/her human agency by means of adequate freedom and well-being. Clearly elective cosmetic

---

[32] For a full discussion of Couto see Chapter Four, page 227, note 23.

[33] See Richard Couto, "Property, Pinmakers and Physicians: Liberal Myths and America Health Care," *Soundings* 42, no. 3 (Fall 1979), 275-92.

[34] Couto's theories will also have to be put into a theological construction in a fashion similar to Wolterstorff's adaptation. The space limitations of this project do not allow me to suggest the appropriate methods for this type of integration.

surgery, for people who are not deformed or ugly, cannot be considered as dialectically necessary for human agency and action.[35] On the other hand, basic immunization for protection from preventable (but serious) diseases may be as appropriate as moral arguments for food, clothing and shelter. The continued debate on the quality and extent of health-care services will move between these two poles, vanity surgery on one hand, and basic immunization on the other. The exact content of these rights will vary from society to society depending on their culture, customs, and economic competence, and to borrow a phrase from Jürgen Habermas, depending upon their communicative competence.[36]

This discussion makes us again aware that the exact content of any economic right is not yet in sight, but is subject to continued discussion.

Economic Rights Skepticism: Time for a New Articulation?

Having failed to make a persuasive case for economic rights skepticism, skeptics should reconsider their positions. It may be prudent, even for libertarians, to assume that Henry Shue, and others are correct, unless, a critique of their theories reveals a fatal flaw in their reasoning, or serious overstatement.[37] This stance would result in giving up their skepticism. To presume otherwise, however, is to act as if Shue were incorrect, and runs the risk of creating and maintaining public policies, which may, eventually, lose both the liberal and libertarian way of life.

Skeptics should realize that the failure of economic justice

---

[35] In Gewirth's language such surgery might be an additive good, a commodity that could be purchased on the open market by "vain" people of means.

[36] Nancy Fraser's article seriously considers Jürgen Habermas' work. She is well aware of the problem of conducting needs discourses in situations in which communication is systematically distorted.

[37] Henry Shue's approach and influence are spreading. For an identical reading of Shue, see Merold Westphal, "Hegel, Human Rights, and the Hungry," *Hegel on Economics and Freedom* (Macon, Ga.: Mercer Press, 1987), Chapter 7, 210.

resulting from the rejection of economic rights may lead to the failure to protect and recognize civil and political rights. Chapter Three detailed the debate centering around Shue's theories, which we will not reexamine in depth. What should be noted, however, is the paucity of opposition to Shue. The most telling criticism offered against him is in regards to his balancing of rights. Shue as we may recall, does not have a lexical priority of liberty over equality.[38] What this criticism really objects to is Shue's refusal to endorse the minimalist state. It is only in the minimalist state that fidelity to the lexical priority of rights is absolutely necessary for rights claiming societies. Shue posits, in contrast, that certain basic rights are crucial for human life. Liberty, personal security and subsistence constitute the social goods "floor" beneath which no one is to be allowed to fall. Since Shue demands that people must also be protected from unjustified encroachments on their liberty even libertarians cannot reject him without, as a consequence, running the risk of fatally undermining their own conception of liberty. Thus the issue to be considered is whether or not the threat of the loss of absolute liberty (which could be considered a privilege) is worth the risk of the concretization of a society in which certain people are locked into a life of instability, poverty, and degrading misery. If the poor have nothing to lose, and everything to gain, why should rational haves assume that have nots are not likely, if desperate circumstances should arise, to upset the whole apple cart?[39] Accordingly, economic rights maintain a prudential

---

38 Shue does have what he calls an "almost lexical priority of basic rights recognition over non-basic rights." *Basic Rights*, 118, note 12.

39 The logic of this argument can be seen in returning to the early social contractualist thought of Thomas Hobbes. Hobbes as we may recall, posited that basic human relations in the "state of nature," were a war of all against all. Human beings entered society, not primarily, for freedom, but for security. Thus, for Hobbes, humanity in the state of nature surrendered its unconditional liberty--ostensibly, for security, guaranteed by the State under the rule of law. Why, then, should an underclass forgo the destruction or abandonment of society, if society does not at least try to guarantee a minimum of security for them including, of course, economic rights. Thus when Machan demands that Gewirth and others incorporate and integrate into their conceptions of economic rights justifiable explanations for the foundation of the State, and the justification for the State's use of coercion, he has the cart

safeguards in addition to their moral attributes.

This examination of the economic rights debate reveals that theorists have been talking past each other. The underlying issue in the debate concerns the sort of society that we should create and maintain. This issue has not been sufficiently addressed in relation to rights theories by either side. What this present work contributes to the debate is clarity: a new focus that does not end the debate, but puts the debate on the "right" track.[40] What must be recognized in an analysis of the debate is the inseparability of rights theories with arguments for social arrangements and social value theories. This recognition is applicable for all rights theories. Rights, if there are any at all, are not as H. L. A. Hart would have us believe, simply rights to "natural liberty," but rights to activities that permit and maintain human life, of which "natural liberty" is only a part. Discourses on economic rights are, in this conception of things, a manifestation of complaints of various sorts by disappointed would-be beneficiaries of neglected economic (among other types) duties. Shue's "deprived" peasants are a good example.[41] They presumably will demand the return to a previous way of life in which economic duties, carried out by a patrone, insured the possibility of success in their exercise of action and agency. They may demand new economic rights because economic conditions have changed and make the new rights necessary. Thus the peasants may demand a return to black bean production, or assistance in retooling their agriculture, or

---

before the horse. The opposite is true. Gewirth and Shue's conceptions build upon and qualify the foundations that Hobbes and Locke laid down. If the minimalist state is to be relieved of the responsibility of securing basic minimum security for its citizens (a basic premise in libertarian thought), then a new theory grounding the state must proceed from Machan and others: they cannot rely upon Hobbes, Locke, and Adam Smith. For a fuller argument on this point, see "What Does Minimal Government Minimize? ," by Elizabeth Flower and Abraham Edel, *The Personalist* 59, no. 4, (October 1978), 386.

[40] By helping theorists understand the evolutionary nature of the debate and the moral nature of the various rights theories, this work should help commentators begin to effective evaluate our society. Such an evaluation would helpfully determine what kind of society we have and what kind of society it is that we wish to create and sustain.

[41] See Chapter Four, page 224 for Shue's hypothetical starving peasant.

compensatory government subsidies for growing flowers.

A tax or tariff on the flower growers might be sufficient in meeting their economic rights, but then again, it might not. The economic rights debate came about not over a clear situation such as a child's right to be fed by its parents, but through the demands of "starving peasants"; each claiming rights to beans or bread from other independent, competent moral agents, patrones, and the government. Government has clearly violated a person's economic rights when, to paraphrase former United Nations Ambassador Andrew Young, powerful and greedy elites in government and society, do nothing to alleviate the suffering of the people when something efficacious can be done.[42] Feasibility is, therefore, a factor in assessing the performance of government; if some duty is feasible, then the failure to fulfill the duty demands further moral scrutiny. True non-feasibility, on the other hand, rather than Cranston's "impracticability" would excuse non-suffering haves (including governments) from failures to alleviate suffering.

Harmonizing Differing Concepts of Economic Rights

Chapter Four analyzed philosophical explanations of economic rights. Chapter Five examined theological theories. How do these two families of rights relate to each other?

Neither Gewirth nor Shue requires a theological

---

[42] See Chapter Two, note 64. It is in this way that economic rights take on a negative quality. It is not so much that the government must create programs to alleviate "deprivation." as they should be required, by economic rights, to prevent or compensate for private economic deprivations of "basic rights" or "paramount values." If, on the other hand, antitrust laws, or other government actions fail to prevent deprivations, or if a free market society working in conjunction with charitable organizations cannot eliminate widespread famine, or homelessness, than a government that understands the interdependency of rights must intervene to recognize and implement the rights of all of its citizens. A government that simply stands by idly when people are perishing when it could intervene successfully is not much better, morally speaking, than a governments run by greedy elites for their sole benefit.

justification for his rights theory. For Gewirth and Shue, the justifying basis for rights (the "by virtue of Y" portion) is, based on logical arguments. Shue justifies economic rights with his interrelationship of basic rights and commonly accepted civil and political rights. Gewirth stresses his dialectically necessary argument, his principle of generic consistency. Gewirth also specifically rejects rights theories that are grounded in human dignity, as many theological accounts are grounded. For Gewirth the movement in economic rights theory proceeds in the opposite direction: human beings have dignity through the action of making and recognizing human rights claims. Gewirth's rejection of theological accounts raises the specter that his theories are incompatible with theological theories. His position raises the question of whether or not theological economic rights theories can be coherent with Gewirth's PGC. From Gewirth's point of view they cannot.   From his perspective all theological economic rights theories lack a proper justifying basis. How should economic rights theories proceed? Though it is not possible from Gewirth's perspective to move from his PGC to theological theories it is possible for theologians to incorporate and "use" Gewirth's PGC and Shue's theory of basic rights. We should comment briefly on how this process of coherence might be conducted.

Chapter Five demonstrated that Wolterstorff's theories have already adopted and adapted Shue's approach.   In a similar fashion, Wolterstorff could use Gewirth's theory to demonstrate, by deductive logic, the "plausibility" of Wolterstorff's theological economic rights theory. Gewirth's PGC could be used to show that Wolterstorff's economic rights theories are not based on pure, particularist religion, but are themselves consistently rational and logical.   Thus though Gewirth would not consider the economic rights theories of Wolterstorff, Miguez-Bonino, Joseph Allen, and others, as being adequate, there is no reason theologians cannot employ his rigorous analyses in their formulations of and explanations for economic rights. That they should do so is obvious to Coleman and apparent from his research.[43] We may now conclude,

---

43 John A. Coleman, "Catholic Human Rights Theory: Four Challenges to an Intellectual Tradition," *The Journal of Law and Religion* 2, 343-66.

therefore, that the clearest and most satisfactory expression of economic rights is Wolterstorff's adaptation of Shue's basic rights approach; and it is not incompatible with Gewirth's approach to rights.

Such an expression of economic rights will be accessible to churches and other religious bodies. These theories must, however, be carefully constructed so that conversations with agnostics and atheists will not become impossible. The economic rights alliance should, accordingly, frequently employ strictly philosophical language in conversations with nonreligious people. A theological explanation would in this instance function within the church's walls in a "bilingual" manner. Rather than focusing upon doctrinal differences, economic rights proponents, churches, and international ecumenical councils, WCC, WARC, NCC, and others, would be able to focus on what Gewirth understands to be the "independent variable" in morality: human action. Religious proponents would champion basic rights as a proper response to the Command of God.[44] Or, they could also offer any of the other theological explanations that have been reviewed in Chapter Five. These theoretical foundations would also serve as their basis for supporting the necessary institutions for the concretization of such rights. In their own councils and churches the language employed and the reasons given for economic rights may be predominantly "religious." This approach may be the only way for religious enthusiasts to actively shape the habits, virtues and commitments of their respective parishioners to support economic rights. From this base of support they may then seek consensus for economic rights on a national and international basis.[45] When such groups are called to form

---

[44] Wolterstorff understands basic rights to be both logical and commanded by God. It should be conceded that Calvinists (Wolterstorff's tradition) and Thomists (Hollenbach's tradition) have little difficulty with incorporating rights theories into their respective doctrines.

[45] Max Stackhouse explains the importance of creating a public theology for the effective implementation of "human rights," "Public Theology, Human Rights and Missions," *Human rights and the Global Mission of the Church* (Cambridge, Mass.: The Boston Theological Institute, 1985), 13.

coalitions with nonreligious allies for the purpose of implementing or refining notions of economic rights, particularly when they are in third moment calculations concerning the satisfaction of rights, they may, without being self-contradictory, resort to the types of philosophical and ethical justifications that are most persuasive to nonreligious supporters. In those instances they will use their philosophical understandings of rights as stating rules for human relations. It is in this way that a social, political, and religious consensus may be established. Such an alliance might be sufficiently broad-based and persuasive as to guarantee the effective implementation of economic rights through the creation of institutions that systematically deal with economic injustices and emergencies. Economic rights can then move from hortative expressions of good will to internationally implemented rights. Such coalitions can constitute, or motivate the voting blocks that are necessary for the ratification of the U. N. Covenant on Social and Economic Rights, and other, similar, international documents.[46]

All of these arguments must, of course, reject minimalist state social arrangements. As Michael Novak's latest essays have shown, however, the theological world is moving in this direction; there appears to be, at least on the horizon, a "growing end to this argument."[47] There has been a manifestation of this phenomenon in the literature, and more importantly, a governmental manifestation of economic rights recognition and implementation.[48]

---

[46] Currently, the United Nations Covenant of Social and Economic Rights has been signed by 59 United Nation members (countries) and ratified or acceded by 90 countries. See United Nations, General Assembly, International Covenants on Human Rights: Status of the International Covenant on Civil and Political Rights and the Optional Protocol to the International Covenant on Civil and Political Rights, August 17, 1987, A/42/450.

[47] The argument over whether any economic rights are valid is growing to an end, whereas further arguments as to the contents of economic rights is just heating up.

[48] The retreat of the Reagan administration from overtly endorsing economic rights is, however, a clear demonstration that the economic rights argument is not over, but simply growing to an end.

The International Implications of
Coordinating Economic Rights

What must still be considered are the international implications of basic economic rights implementation. As Gewirth, Shue, and Wolterstorff realize, their theories of rights expand moral communities. Their positions require people to be concerned with their next door neighbor and a peasant on the other side of the world. From this perspective a starving Ethiopian has as much of a moral claim on our assistance as our hungry next door neighbor. Their positions should not be simplified, however, into personal attention to basic needs. All three theorists require the implementation of basic rights by means of systemic fulfillment: this is a very important point. From their perspectives, a sick neighbor's medical needs are usually better addressed by the creation of a national health service, in preference to the occasional personally proffered nostrum. The distance between the would be systemic rights recognizer and the desperate indigent has practical and philosophical significance. A few remarks on this issue will illustrate this point and illuminate the ramifications of this issue.

As all discussants in this area agree, economic rights must have addressees who recognize and implement such rights. They must also create systems and organizations that act on their behalf, in the modern world, to meet the duties correlative to the putative rights. The best way of understanding the assignment of these duties is to imagine the distressed rights-claimant as the epicenter of a ripple on a lake.[49] The rights-claimant is, therefore, as the epicenter of the ripple, the first addressee to the rights-claim itself. For this scenario let us assume that the rights-claimant is a small child drowning in a shallow pond. The first ring beyond the claimant-child, the first group upon whom the duty to rescue may be said to fall, is the

---

[49] My ripple analogy should be carefully distinguished from the analogy criticized by Shue in his recent article regarding duties. See Henry Shue, "Mediating Duties," *Ethics* 98, no. 4 (July 1988), 691. In Shue's epicenter, the strength of the obligations diminishes with every outward ring. In my ripple concept, the ripple simply indicates the distance of each addressee in relation to the would-be rights holder, the strength of the obligations remains the same.

child's immediate support group. Clearly, the duty to rescue the child falls most directly and immediately on its parents and guardians. In the next concentric ring are the child's friends and relatives, perhaps the child's extended family. In the next ring, we find the child's community and charitable organizations. In the next ring, we find the child's domestic government. In the next ring we find international organizations, foreign governments, and nongovernmental agencies. In the outermost rings we could imagine extraterrestrials, and angels. It should be noted in this scenario that the duty to intervene is as strong (theoretically) for people on the outermost ring as it is for people in the inner ring. What makes the duty to rescue more immediate for family and friends, is simply the issue of proximity. Society assumes that those who are the closest to people, bonded directly by blood, or ancient custom, are most likely to be near people in times of distress, to be sympathetic to their distress, to more directly share a common telos with the distressed, and to know best how to render aid in regards to efficiency and effectiveness. Assumedly, such intimates are more likely to render aid without destroying the distressed's sense of dignity. Nothing in the literature on this issue would indicate that these assumptions are incorrect. Yet though my epicenter illustration is appealing, it does not describe modern life very well.

In the modern world children are escorted to beaches in which there are lifeguard systems in place to rescue the unfortunate. If a child should be so unlucky as to wander unescorted to an unsafe beach and drowns, it is likely that some parent or guardian will have to answer to some child protective agency. Though families are closer in proximity and understanding to most individuals than are large organizations, large organizations, are, increasingly, the more common rights recognizers. Accordingly, those persons and organizations that are located in the more distant rings must develop a sensitivity to the actions of those closer to the victim. They must create, however, systems to step in and protect when intimates cannot, or will not. For example, though my spouse may be more concerned than anyone else with an invasion of our privacy, a vigilant magistrate and police force is usually a more effective protector of our rights: police also have a greater capacity to recognize security rights. Simply put, intimates are not always capable of rendering aid and may fail if they are relied upon to be the last resort for aid. Similarly, some governments are incapable of implementing economic rights on behalf of their own citizens. Where local governments are incapable, foreign governments should intervene and as we discussed in Chapter Four, such interventions are problematic.

Economic rights recognition demands, however, that everyone develop the "call" to being their sibling's helper, but this call cannot ignore the state of the modern world in which the domination of large organizations and systems is prevalent. It is only with the creation of systemic intervention that the failures of "intimates" to intervene can be minimized. A recent story tragically illustrates this point.

An outdoorsman while relaxing on a mountainside, near a beautiful but dangerous river, noticed that down below on the banks of the river people were playing, picnicking, and sleeping. The outdoorsman also noticed that one of their number had begun to wade out into the swirling water. Familiar with the treacherousness of the river's currents, the outdoorsman became mildly alarmed. He was at the same time deeply enraptured in an important philosophical conversation with a hillside companion. Nevertheless he noticed out of the corner of his eye that the wader wandered further and further out into the dangerous stream. Though they were very close to the wader and could have easily told the wader to desist, or have quickly pulled the wader to safety, no one on the wader's bank paid the slightest attention to the wader. The outdoorsman continued in his conversation until he noticed that the wader had panicked and was in the process of being swept away in the current. The wader screamed for help; his companions turned in horror finally realizing that their companion was in mortal danger and needed their help. Unfortunately, to everyone's horror, the wader was swept swiftly away: his battered, lifeless body was found several miles downstream. All efforts to save him by his close companions were too little and too late. What troubled the outdoorsman was the fact that the drowning victim's companions were not knowledgeable with regard to the inherent danger of wading in that locale. What deeply troubled the outdoorsman was the fact that he knew of the danger, being familiar with the river and the terrain, and had actually noticed another human placing himself in harm's way. Yet he had done nothing. As the article revealed, the outdoorsman felt regret, guilt, and grief for failing to intervene when he could have intervened. As he reflected upon the incident, the outdoorsman realized that he had failed to intervene because he had not wanted to discontinue his conversation. He had also assumed that someone on the bank would intervene: they were, after all, closer to the wader. Presumably he was part of their party and they should have been more concerned with his welfare. Yet despite his rationalization over the incident, the outdoorsman could not escape his feelings of grief and remorse, his sense of loss. This incident motivated the outdoorsman to write this descriptive article, and to push the proper authorities to erect warning signs along that stretch of the river.[50]

The outdoorsman discovered an important truth--though he and the victim's friends should have intervened, intimates and people in close proximity often do not intervene. A superior approach would, systematically, post warning signs and brief wildlife enthusiasts regarding the dangers in the area. Such an approach does not rely unrealistically on the vigilance and courage of oft-distracted friends and acquaintances. Since the threats in much of life are standard and systemic, the defenses and rights protection must be also. This is one of the most important points that Shue demonstrates.

This true story is illustrative of certain human truths. If we consider others to be equally human, members of our moral community, our duties toward them expand. If we fail to act, when we might have effectively acted with a minimum amount of exertion (a large posted sign would have sufficed), we will most likely feel grief and remorse should tragedy occur.[51] Too often human life is organized so that people cannot see that they are morally related in a common humanity. When tragedy occurs the pain of grief is localized because of artificially created

---

[50] By pressuring local government to erect warning signs the outdoorsman met his duty to others along the river not by acting personally as a lifeguard, but by helping to create a security system.

[51] The systemic posting of signs could be paid for out of taxes and would be cheaper, no doubt, than a lifeguard system for the river, or a search party devoted to recovering drowning victims.

barriers. However, in a global village world, artificial barriers are being removed. In the increasing exposure of modern mass culture and communications the "free but starving peasant" is now America's homeless. They are unwilling to expire anonymously in some obscurely situated shack: the "homeless" now erect shanty towns in front of the White House. They want a systemic recognition of their housing rights, not just a handout. Their presence is now noted by international human rights agencies. The economic rights position suggested herein forces us to address such people as moral members of our community; as our moral if not our economic peers. Such recognition may call for the creation of a new international economic order although this work cannot address this question. What is clear, even at this point, is that the system of economic rights already in force, that is, those rights already recognized by the various international and domestic covenants for economic rights has to be carefully scrutinized for its effectiveness. Perhaps new agencies must be created to implement the "new" economic rights. Finally, formal justifications for economic rights should be continuously discussed. To do less is to let aid linger as a quasi-charitable endeavor; an ideal that requires not our best systemic efforts, but only our best individual intentions.

In the interim economic rights will continue to be recognized and implemented internationally and domestically. Without a clearly recognized and publicly justified expression, the domestic implementation will lack the force and persuasiveness that it needs for maximized effectiveness. Churches, nonprofit organizations and others should continue to lobby governments to fully endorse and implement basic rights. Our attention should now turn to final arguments for the moral superiority of economic rights recognition.

The Moral Advantages of Economic Rights:
God Bless the Child that's Got its Own.

A coherent justified, economic rights theory allows us to address a number of economic problems confidently. We can give money to starving nations and our perishing fellow citizens because their humanity is precious to us (for a variety of reasons) and not because of a passing whim, or purely in furtherance of our current "national interests." Social arrangements that recognize economic rights are, admittedly, inherently paternalistic, but this quality is also inherent in the protection and recognition of any rights, of any type.[52] Economic rights recognize the right to own property, *and* subsistence rights that provide "property" to those who cannot help themselves. A coherent theory of economic rights enables us to systemically recognize and address people who cannot help themselves. Taxes can be used, without equivocation, to meet vital needs that various individuals and groups are not able to meet. To avoid dependency and servility, entitlements can be attached to systems of "workfare" or "skills acquisition." Furthermore, while poverty may not be eliminated with the recognition of economic rights, the feelings of degradation that often accompanies the distribution of welfare entitlements should be. A few remarks about feelings of degradation in relation to economic rights are now in order.

When a police officer or a firefighter rescues a person from a dangerous situation the beneficiary of their services is, in a best case scenario, grateful. The rescued person may contribute to fraternal police organizations or he may raise money for bulletproof vests for police forces too modest to afford the same. In a similar way, a rescued person may contribute to a fire department. Neither the police nor the rescued person feels obligated in a strict sense of the word. People are grateful for police and fire protection, but they expect it. It is their "right." If they subsequently buy tickets to a policemen's ball that act is considered to be a gratuitous act. People feel this way because our society has established these services, charged taxes for them, and provided them as a "right" to everyone. The poor, who may pay no taxes at all, and who on a strict quid pro quo basis has not paid for these services, nevertheless expect them as their "rights." People of means agree with them on this point: enjoyment of these services is an acknowledged aspect of

---

52 For a full explanation of the inherent chauvinistic qualities of rights implementation, see H. J. McCloskey, "The Moralism and Paternalism Inherent in Enforcing Respect for Human Rights," *Laws, Rights and the Welfare State*, ed. C. J. G. Sampford and D. J. Galligan (London: Croom Helm, Ltd. 1986): 150.

membership in our society. In a worst case scenario the jaundiced public takes the services for granted, not even offering a word of thanks. Welfare workers and other social workers, and the poor and marginalized people that they help could experience welfare entitlement services as most of us experience police and fire protection. That it should not be degrading to demand one's right to receiving help from society, in meeting one's vital needs, is the basic thrust of Shue's work. Such a feeling does not currently exist on the American scene. In America it is not uncommon to be ashamed to receive "welfare," even when one is only temporarily indigent, or is alternatively, a permanent member of the "working poor." While Novak's dedication to "rugged individualism" cannot be suggested as contributing to the cause of the shame that many feel in getting help, it is self-evident that his approach is not designed to eliminate such feelings. Economic rights as strict moral rights (though limited in scope and application) would seem to be more conducive for creating the ethos and moral consensus needed for minimizing the feelings of shame often attendant with receiving welfare entitlements.[53]

Some may feel that this elimination of shame is not to be socially desired. It could be argued that if this impediment to receiving aid is removed, irresponsible demands would be encouraged. This work cannot go into a discussion of the sociopsychological issues that answering this question might entail. It would seem to be apparent, however, that to be poor, and to have to be ashamed of being poor, is an unnecessary

---

[53] Novak's theories emphasize the moral and legal duty to work and the enormous opportunities that American democratic capitalism presents. "Losers" in this brave new world have, seemingly, weaker excuses than the poor in previous generations and in other countries. As a consequence they may feel more embarrassed about receiving the dole. In addition, this country has a basic more of individualistic assertiveness and suspicion of the poor. For a full description of this tradition see Alan Keith-Lucas's work. *The Poor You Have With You Always: Concepts of Aid to the Poor in the Western World from Biblical Times to the Present* (St. Davids, Pa.: North American Association of Christians in Social Work, 1989).

double burden.[54] While it may not be possible to eliminate poverty, it should not be necessary to encourage or tolerate public shaming. All of these remarks have been necessary to explain why economic rights might be preferable for a society such as ours. One other major point should be noted prior to concluding this examination.

A theory of justified economic rights compels more than certain social arrangements; such a theory inherently demands a continual evaluation of economic relationships and economic justice. Just as a commitment to the Bill of Rights demands that citizens be eternally vigilant regarding their civil liberties, an explicit commitment to economic rights commits our society (especially the State) to continuously examine its level of commutative and distributive justice. If the failure to assist the perishing poor is a strict moral and legal failure, on the parts of competent haves, and if the government's failure to put forth its best efforts (subject to considerations of subsidiarity and feasibility) to alleviate needless suffering is a positive political and moral failure, then institutions and practices that are designed to monitor and prevent such occurrences become mandatory. If affluent nations truly embrace economic rights and desire to retain their moral integrity, they must be actively concerned with the effectiveness of their social institutions in regards to their interaction with the poor, domestic and international. Moreover, a viable theory of economic rights need not discourage the continued support of private charities and philanthropies though such organizations may no longer be taken for granted as being effective. Mechanisms for discovering and measuring poverty, which are already in place, will, of necessity, have to be periodically evaluated and changed.[55] To do less would not simply be ungenerous: to do less would constitute a dereliction of duty.

---

[54] Even Adam Smith (hardly an egalitarian) recognized the enormous affront to dignity that the poor have to endure. Smith writes that: "The poor man, on the contrary, is ashamed of his poverty. He feels that it either places him out of the sight of mankind, or, that if they take any notice of him, they have, however, scarce any fellow-feeling with the misery and distress which he suffers." *The Theory of Moral Sentiments*, 51.

[55] One such device is, of course, the standard unemployment index.

This approach is better designed to discover why the poor are poor because it keeps their welfare on view. In contrast, economic rights skeptics do not address the causes of poverty adequately: this lack of perspective is their greatest weakness. Skeptics believe that they are merely obligated to monitor the State's involvement so that the State does not become intrusive. They do not believe that they <u>have</u> to act to feed the "free, but starving poor." It is for this reason that economic rights skepticism is less useful to ethical analysis, and "ethical" policy formation. The skeptic's theories do not require haves to ask certain questions and they do not require haves to take certain steps. Economic rights skepticism, like Hart's and Cranston's are able to function smoothly as theories even when outrageous scarcity, and concomitant suffering abound. This lack of perspicacity makes these approaches less valuable to the process of ethical reflection and moral reasoning. They are also "suspect" as theories because they may nurture haphazard, nonsystematic approaches to discovering and responding to poverty. They may also encourage versions of rights in complete opposition to the traditional understanding of rights that is "revolutionary" in nature.[56] By doing so, rights may help powerful economic elites to retain tyrannical power without explanation or accounting. In societies in which economic rights are forbidden problems in helping the poor may be obfuscated. For example, charities, which by necessity must proliferate where economic rights are barred and concern for the poor is prevalent, may or may not adequately address the needs of the poor. Clearly charities are seldom as tightly regulated, or as systematically operated, as public institutions. If and when they become corrupt, inefficient, or ineffective, there is no one outside individual who can compel their reform, or accountability.

Moreover, if relating to the poor is strictly an imperfect moral obligation, or a voluntary charitable act, a moral agent's time and attention may be wooed away easily to other "charitable" causes. "Saving the whales" may be as "good" a cause as saving starving people. Animals may have rights, and

---

[56] Chapter One explains how rights have traditionally been understood as being revolutionary.

certainly have more than an aesthetic, or instrumental value, but such charitable endeavors do not appear to have a "paramount" value superior to the salvation, and/or preservation of human life.

It should also be acknowledged that the economic rights skeptic is less likely to get the cooperation and support of the poor in addressing the problems of poverty. The beneficiary of "charity" is seldom as active and competent a moral agent as a holder of rights whose rights are in jeopardy. The old adage, "Beggars can't be choosers," is true, at least from a psychological point of view. Neither the charitable donor, nor the mendicant really expects the mendicant to comment critically upon the quality of the charity provided. Rights-holders, in contrast, though not the sole judges as to the satisfaction of their rights claims, are expected, nonetheless, to be able to continue to demand their rights. They are capable thereby of demanding further moral scrutiny and review of their claims and the satisfaction of those claims from other members of society. Rights-holders are always more dignified than beggars, and this consideration is of no small import.[57] Nevertheless, a real commitment to economic rights must be limited to "basic rights." Claims beyond basic rights threaten to enmesh society in an endless process of claiming, implementation, and review. It is for this reason that Shue's short list is so very important.

This study has been an investigation into the ongoing economic rights debate. The insights gleaned from a review of the literature on the debate should assist nongovernment organizations, governments, and others in their formal investigations of economic rights, and in further justifications of the concept of economic rights. This study should also assist us all in declaring and implementing programs and systems that show how we ought to live with each other in a conjoined moral and economic community. No view on economic rights can be considered to be self-evident; this contribution must be considered therefore as being propositional and provisional. Yet if we are to have rights to life, liberty and the genuine

---

[57] By far the best discussion of the relationship between dignity and rights is a recent article by Michael J. Meyer, "Dignity, Rights and Self-Control," *Ethics* 99, no. 3 (21 April 1989), 520-35.

pursuit of happiness, certain economic rights will now have to be explicitly, publicly, and widely recognized. Lastly, while the divinely blessed child that's got its own is indeed fortunate, the society that leaves the survival of a child to the unpredictability of divine interventions appears to be uncommonly naive, incompetent, unstable, and immoral. It is unlikely that it will be concomitantly blessed.

SELECTED BIBLIOGRAPHY

Ake, Claude. "The African Context of Human Rights." *Africa Today* 1st/2nd Quarters (1987): 5-12.

Allen, Joseph L. *Love and Conflict*. Nashville: Abingdon Press, 1984.

_____. "Catholic and Protestant Theories of Human Rights," *Religious Studies Review* 14, no 4. (October 1988): 347-352.

Allen, Michael Leroy. "The Human Rights Policy of Jimmy Carter: Foundations for Understanding." Ph.D. diss., The Southern Baptist Theological Seminary, 1984.

Alston, Phillip, and Tomasevski, K. *Human Rights and The Basic Needs Strategy for Development*. London: Anti-Slavery Society, 1979.

_____. *The Right to Food: International Studies in Human Rights*. London: Anti-Slavery Society, 1984.

Arblaster, Anthony. *The Rise and Decline of Western Liberalism*. Oxford: Basil Blackwood Pub., 1984.

318

Archer, Peter. "Action by Unofficial Organizations on Human Rights." *The International Protection of Human Rights.* Ed. Evan Luard. New York: Praeger, 1967.

Bauer, Lord P. T. *Equality, the Third World, and Economic Decision.* Cambridge: Harvard University Press, 1981.

Bay, Christian. "A Human Rights Approach to Transnational Politics." *Universal Human Rights* 1, no. 1 (January-March 1979): 19-42.

_____. "On Needs and Rights Beyond Liberalism: A Rejoinder to Flathman." *Political Theory* 8, no. 3 (August 1980): 331.

_____. *Strategies of Political Emancipation.* Notre Dame: Notre Dame Press, 1981.

_____. "Self-Respect as a Human Right: Thoughts on the Dialectic of Wants and Needs in the Struggle for Human Community." *Human Rights Quarterly* 9 (1982): 53-75.

Bedau, Hugo A. *Justice and Equality.* Englewood Cliffs: Prentice-Hall, Inc., 1971.

Bellah, Robert et als. "Civil Religion in America." *Beyond Belief.* New York: Harper & Row, 1976.

_____. *Habits of the Heart.* Berkeley: University of California Press 1985.

Bentham, Jeremy. "Anarchical Fallacies." *Human Rights.* ed. A. I. Melden. Wadsworth: Belmont, Calif. 1970: 30, 31.

Berger, Peter. "Are Human Rights Universal?" *Commentary* 64, no. 3 (September 1977): 60-63.

Berlin, Isaiah. *Four Essays on Liberty.* London: Oxford University Press, 1969.

Bluestone, Barry. "Capitalism and Poverty in America: A Discussion." *Monthly Review* 24, no. 2 (June 1972): 65-77, 71.

Bock, Paul. *In Search of a Responsible World Society: The Social Teachings of the World Council of Churches.* Philadelphia: The Westminster Press, 1974.

Browning, Edgar K. "How Much More Equality Can We Afford?" *Public Interest* 43 (Spring 1976): 90-110.

Brzezinski, Zbigniev. *Power and Principle: Memoirs of the National Security Advisor, 1877-1981.* New York: Farrar, Straus, and Giroux, 1983.

Burke, Edmund. *Reflections on the French Revolution and Other Essays.* London: J. M. Dent and Sons, Ltd., 1910.

Burke. W. Scott. "In the American Tradition Rights." *The Center Magazine*, (July/August 1984), 40.

Byers, David M, ed. "Pacem in Terris." *Justice in the Marketplace: Collected Statements of the Vatican and the United States Catholic Bishops on Economic Policy, 1981-1984.* Washington D. C. : United States Catholic Conference, Inc., 1985: 152.

Campbell, Tom. *The Left and Rights: A Conceptual Analysis of the Idea of Socialist Rights.* London: Routledge & Kegan Paul plc, 1983.

Carle, Robert. "Theological Critiques of Human Rights Theory: The Contributions of Jacques Maritain and Gustavo Gutierrez." Ph.D. dissertation, Emory University, 1989.

Carter, Jimmy. *A Government as Good as Its People.* New York: Simon & Schuster, 1977.

_____. "State of the Union Address." (20 January 1981): 2995.

_____. *The International Bill of Human Rights*. United Nations Publication, foreword. Glen Ellyn: Entwhistle Books, 1981.

_____. *Keeping the Faith*. New York: Bantam Books, 1982.

Carter, Marshall and Marenin, Otwin. "Human Rights in the Nigerian Context: A Case Study and Discussion of the Nigerian Police. *"Universal Human Rights* 1, no. 2 (April-June 1979): 43-61.

Cecil, Andrew R. "Economic Freedom: The Rights and Responsibilities of the Entrepreneur in Our Mixed Economy." *Our Freedoms and Responsibilities*. ed. Jerre S. Williams, et al. Dallas: University of Texas Press, 1985.

Cicero. *The Republic*, III, 23. Loeb Classical Library. Cambridge: Harvard Press, 1970.

Clark, William. *New York Times* (5 November 1081).

Claude, Richard P. *Comparative Human Rights*. Baltimore: Johns Hopkins University Press, 1976.

Coleman, John. "Catholic Human Rights Theory: Four Challenges to an Intellectual Tradition." *Journal of Law and Religion* 2: 344.

_____. "Human Rights in Roman Catholicism," *Readings in Moral Theology No. 5: Official Catholic Social Teaching*. Ed. Charles E. Curran and Richard A. McCormick. New York: Paulist Press, 1986.

Cooper, John Wesley. "The Political Theologies of Jacques Maritain and Reinhold Niebuhr." Ph.D. diss., Syracuse University, 1982.

Couto, Richard. "Property, Pinmakers, and Physicians: Liberal Myths and American Health Care. *Soundings* 62, no. 3 (Fall 1979): 275-292.

Crahan, Margaret E. ed. *Human Rights and Basic Needs in the Americas.* Washington, D.C.: Georgetown University Press, 1982.

Cranston, Maurice. "On Human Rights." *Daedalus* 112, no 4. (Fall, 1983): 1-18.

_____. *What Are Human Rights?* New York: Basic Books, Inc., Pub., 1962.

_____. "Human Rights, Real and Supposed." *Political Theory and the Rights of Man.* ed. D. D. Raphael. Bloomington: Indiana University Press, 1967.

Curran, Charles. "The Changing Anthropological Bases of Catholic Social Ethics," *Readings in Moral Theology No. 5: Official Catholic Social Teaching* New York: Paulist Press, 1986.

Dankwa, E. V. O., and Cees Flinterman, Cees "Commentary by the Rapporteurs On the Nature and Scope of States Parties' Obligations." *Human Rights Quarterly* 9, no 2. (1987): 136-146.

Decter, Midge. "Understanding Human Rights." *Vital Speeches of the Day* (10 October 1987): 139-142.

Den Uyl, Douglas J. and Machan Tibor. "Gewirth and the Supportive State." *Positive and Negative Duties.* ed. Eric Mack. New Orleans: Tulane University Press, 1985.

Derian, Patricia. "Human Rights in American Foreign Policy." *The Notre Dame Lawyer* 55 (December, 1979): 270.

_____. "Overhaul U. S. Policy on Human Rights?" *U. S. News and World Report* (2 March 1981): 49.

Dishman, Robert. *Burke and Paine.* New York: Charles Scribner & Sons, 1981.

Donnelly, Jack. "Recent Trends in UN Human Rights Activity:

Description and Polemic." *International Organization* 35, no. 4 (Autumn 1981): 633.

_____. *The Concept of Human Rights.* London: Croom Helm, 1985.

_____. and Howard Rhoda E., "Assessing National Human Rights Performance: A Theoretical Framework." *Human Rights Quarterly* 10 (1988).

Drinan, Robert F. *Cry of the Oppressed: The History and Hope of the Human Rights Revolution.* San Francisco: Harper & Row, 1987.

Dworkin, Ronald. *Taking Rights Seriously.* Cambridge: Harvard University Press, 1977.

Ellacuria, Ignacio. "Human Rights for a Divided Society." *Human Rights in the Americas: The Struggle for Consensus.*

Farley, Noel. "Human Rights in the Contemporary World: Some Notes from an Economist." *Human Rights in Religious Traditions.* ed. Arlene Swidler. New York: Pilgrim Press, 1982.

Feinberg, Joel. "The Nature and Value of Rights." *Journal of Value Inquiry* 4 (1970): 243-257.

_____. *Social Philosophy.* Englewood Cliffs, NJ: Prentice-Hall, 1973.

_____. *Rights, Justice, and the Bounds of Liberty.* Princeton: Princeton University Press, 1980.

Figueres, Jose. "Some Economic Foundations of Human Rights." *The Human Rights Reader* ed. Walter Laqueur and Barry Rubin. Philadelphia: Temple University Press, 1979.

Flathman, Richard E. "Rights, Needs, and Liberalism: A Comment on Bay." *Political Theory* 8, no. 3 (August 1980): 319-330.

323

Fletcher, David B. "Is There A Right To Health Care." *Christian Scholar Review* 16, no. 3: 283-299.

_____. "Must Wolterstorff Sell His House?" *Faith and Philosophy* 4, (April 1987): 187.

Forell, George W., and Lazareth, William H. ed. *Human Rights: Rhetoric or Reality?* Philadelphia: Fortress Press, 1978.

Forsythe, David B. "Congress and Human Rights in U.S. Foreign Policy: The Fate of General Litigation." *Human Rights Quarterly* 9 (1987): 382-404.

_____. *Human Rights and U. S. Foreign Policy: Congress Reconsidered.* Gainsville, Fla.: University of Florida Press, 1987: 10-13.

Franck, Thomas M. *Human Rights in Third World Perspective.* Dobbs Ferry, NY: Oceana Pub., 1983.

Frankel, Charles. *Human Rights and Foreign Policy.* Headline Series No. 241. New York: Foreign Policy Association, 1978.

Frankena, W. K. "The Concept of Universal Human Rights." *Science, Language, and Human Rights.* Philadelphia: University of Pennsylvania Press, 1952: 189-207.

Fraser, Nancy. "Talking About Needs: Interpretive Contests as Political Conflicts in Welfare-State Societies," *Ethics* 99, no. 2 (January 1989), 291-313.

Friedman, Milton. *The Essence of Friedman.* Stanford: The Hoover Institution Press, 1987.

Gauraudy, Roger. *From Anathema to Dialogue.* New York: Vintage, 1968.

Gewirth, Alan. *Reason and Morality.* Chicago: University of Chicago, 1978.

324

_____. *Human Rights: Essays on Justification and Applications.* Chicago: University of Chicago Press, 1982.

_____. "Economic Rights." *Poverty, Justice And the Law: New Essays on Needs, Rights, and Obligations.* Boston: University Press, 1986.

_____. "The Epistemology of Human Rights." *Human Rights* ed. Ellen F. Paul, Fred D. Miller and Jeffery Paul. Oxford: Basis Blackwell, 1986.

_____. "Private Philanthropy and Positive Rights." *Social Philosophy and Policy* 4, no. 2 (1987): 55-78.

_____. "Human Rights and Conceptions of the Self." *Philosophia* 18 (July 1988): 129-149.

Gilder, George F. *Wealth & Poverty.* London: Buchan & Enright, 1982.

Good, Martha H. "Freedom From Want: The Failure of United States Courts to Protect Subsistence Rights." *Human Rights Quarterly* 6 (August 1984): 335-365.

Green, T. H. "Liberal Legislation and Freedom of Contract." *The Political Theory of T. H. Green.* ed. John R. Rodman. New York: Appleton-Century-Crofts, 1964.

Gunnemann, Jon P. "Human Rights and Modernity: The Truth of the Fiction of Individual Rights." An unpublished paper.

Gutierrez, Gustavo. *The Power of the Poor in History.* Maryknoll: Orbis Books, 1984.

Hardin, Garrett. "The Tragedy of the Commons." *Science* 162, no. 3859 (13 December 1968): 1243-1248.

_____. "Living on a Lifeboat." *BioScience* 24, no. 10 (October 1974): 561-568.

Harrington, Michael. "The Future of Poverty: Faith and Economics-A New Numbers Game." *Commonweal* 111, (November 1984): 625.

Hart, H. L. A. "Are There Any Natural Rights?" *Philosophical Review* 64 (1955): 175-191.

Hassan, Riffat. "On Human Rights and the Qur'anic Perspective." *Human Rights in Religious Traditions.* ed. Arlene Swidler. New York: Pilgrim Press, 1982.

Hayek, F. A. "Liberty and Liberties," *The Constitution of Liberty.* Chicago: University of Chicago Press, 1960.

_____. *Law, Legislation and Liberty: The Mirage of Social Justice.* Chicago: University of Chicago Press, 1976.

Henkin, Louis. "International Human Rights as Rights." *Human Rights.* ed. J. R. Pennock and J. W. Chapman. Nomos, XXIII Yearbook of the Society for American Political & Legal Philosophy. New York: University Press 1981: 257-280.

_____. "Economic Social Rights as 'Rights': A United States Perspective." *Human Rights Law Journal* 2, nos. 3-4 (1981), 223-36.

Hennelly, Alfred, and Langan, John ed. *Human Rights in the Americas: The Struggle for Consensus.* Washington D. C.: Georgetown University Press, 1982.

Hevener, Natalie K., ed. *The Dynamics of Human Rights in U.S. Foreign Policy.* New Brunswick: Transaction Books, 1984.

Himes, Kenneth Robert. "Freedom and Self-Realization: Toward A Theology of Human Rights." Ph.D. diss., University of Chicago, 1987.

Hobbes, Thomas. *Leviathan.* Baltimore, Maryland: Penguin 1971: Chap. 14.

Hohfeld, Wesley. *Fundamental Legal Conceptions.* New Haven: Yale University Press, 1919.

Holcombe, Arthur. *Human Rights in the Modern World.* New York: New York University Press, 1948.

Holman, Frank. "International Proposals Affecting So-Called Human Rights" *Law and Contemporary Problems* 14 (Summer, 1949) 481.

Holleman, Warren Lee. *The Human Rights Movement: Western Values and Theological Perspectives.* New York: Praeger, 1987.

_____. "Reinhold Niebuhr on the United Nations and Human Rights" *Soundings* 70 (Fall-Winter 1987): 329-354.

Hollenbach, David. *Claims In Conflict.* New York: Paulist Press, 1979.

_____. "The Growing End of an Argument." *America* 153, no. 16 (30 November 1985): 363-366.

_____. *Justice, Peace, and Human Rights.* New York: Crossroad Pub., 1988.

Horne, Thomas A. "The Poor Have a Claim Founded in the Law of Nature: William Paley and the Rights of the Poor." *Journal of the History of Philosophy* 23, no. 1 (Jan. 1985): 51-71.

Howard, Rhoda. "The Full-Belly Thesis: Should Economic Rights Take Priority Over Civil and Political Rights? Sub-Saharan Africa." *Human Rights Quarterly* 9: 467-470.

Ierley, Merritt. *With Charity for All.* New York: Praeger Pub., 1985.

Inada, Kenneth K. "The Buddhist Perspective On Human Rights." ed. Arlene Swidler. *Human Rights in Religious*

Traditions. New York: Pilgrim Press 1982: 51.

Jacoby, Tamar. "The Reagan Turnaround on Human Rights" *Foreign Affairs* 64, nos. 4, 5 (Summer 1986).

Jefferson, Thomas. *The Declaration of Independence.* 1776.

Joblin, Joseph. "The Role of human, economic and social rights in the advent of a new society." *Labor and Society* 2, no. 4 (October 1977).

John Paul II. "Sollicitudo Rei Socialis." *Origins* 17 no. 38 (3 March 1988).

John XXIII, Pope. *Pacem in Terris/Peace on Earth.* New York: America Press, 1963.

Kamenka, Eugene. "The Anatomy of an Idea." *Human Rights.* New York: St. Martin's Press 1978: 1-12.

Kant, Immanuel. *Foundations of the Metaphysics of Morals.* Indianapolis: Bobbs-Merrill, 1981.

Keith-Lucas, Alan. *The Poor You Have With You Always: Concepts of Aid to the Poor in the Western World from Biblical Times to the Present.* St. Davids, Pa.: North American Association of Christians in Social Work, 1989.

King, Martin L. *Where Do We Go from Here: Chaos or Community?* New York: Harper & Row, 1967.

_____. *The Trumpet of Conscience.* New York: Harper & Row, 1968.

Kirkpatrick, Jean. "Dictatorships and Double Standards." *Human Rights U.S. Human Rights Policy.* ed. Howard J. Wiarda. Washington: American Enterprise Institute, 1982.

_____. "Establishing a Viable Human Rights Policy" *World Affairs* 143, no. 4. (Spring 1981): 323-335.

Kleinig, John. "Human Rights, Legal Rights and Social Change." New York: St. Martin's Press, 1978.

Kondziela, Joachim. "Citoyen Freedom and Bourgeois Freedom: Religion and the Dialectics of Human Rights." *Soundings* (1987): 172-172.

Kowalczyk, Stanislaw. "The Possibilities of Christian-Marxist Dialogue on Human Rights." *Soundings* LXVII, no 2 (Summer 1984).

Kuhn, James W. "Conflicts Between Rights: Substance and Sophistry." *Christianity and Crisis* (15 January 1979): 328-334.

Kuttner, Robert. *The Economic Illusion: False Choices Between Prosperity and Social Justice*. Boston: Houghton Mifflin Co., 1984.

Langan, John. "Human Rights in Roman Catholicism," *Readings in Moral Theology No. 5: Official Catholic Social Teaching*. ed. Charles E. Curran and Richard A. McCormick. New York: Paulist Press, 1986.

Lappe, Frances Moore, and Collins, Joseph. *Food First: Beyond the Myth of Scarcity*. Boston: Houghton Mifflin Co., 1977.

_____. "Democracy and Dogma in the Fight Against Hunger." *The Christian Century* 103, no. 38 (10 December 1986): 1115-1117.

Laqueur, Walter. "Third World Fantasies." *Commentary* (February 1977): 550-56.

_____. "The Issue of Human Rights." *Commentary* 63, no. 5 (May 1977): 30.

_____. and Rubin, Barry, ed. *The Human Rights Reader*. Philadelphia: University Press, 1979.

329

Lazreg, Marnia. "Human Rights, State and Ideology." *Human Rights: Cultural and Ideological Perspectives.* ed. Adamantia Pollis and Peter Schwab. New York: Praeger Publishers, 1979.

Ledogar, Robert J. *Hungry for Profits: U. S. Food and Drug Multinationals in Latin America.* New York: IDOC, 1976.

Lefever, Ernest. "The Rights Standard." *New York Times* (24 January 1977): 24.

_____. "The Trivialization of Human Rights." *Policy Review* (Winter 1978): 11.

_____. "Human Rights and U. S. Foreign Policy." *Vital Speeches of the Day* 48 (15 March 1982): 343-348

Leo XIII, Pope. *Rerum Novarum.* 1891.

Lillich, Richard. *U.S. Ratification of the Human Rights Treaties: With or Without Reservation?* Charlottesville: University Press of Virginia, 1981.

"The Limburg Principles on the Implementation of the International Covenant on Economic, Social and Cultural Rights." *Human Rights Quarterly* 9 (May 1987): 122-135.

Lindbeck, George. *The Nature of Doctrine.* Philadelphia: Westminster Press, 1984.

Lincoln, Abraham. "First Inaugural Address." (March 4, 1861). *Lincoln's Stories and Speeches.* ed. Edward F. Allen. New York: Books, Inc., 1920.

Livezey, Lowell W. "U. S. Religious Organizations and the International Human Rights Movement," *Human Rights Quarterly* 11, no. 1: 14-81.

Locke, John. *Two Treatises on Government.* ed. Peter Laslett. Cambridge, England: University Press, 1960.

330

_____. *Letter on Toleration 1689*. New York: Liberal Arts Press, 1950.

Lucas, George R., Jr. *Poverty, Justice, and the Law: New Essays on Needs, Rights, and Obligations*. Lanham: University Press of America, 1986.

Lyons, David. "Human Rights and the General Welfare." *Philosophy and Public Affairs* 6 (Winter 1977): 113-129.

_____. *Rights*. Belmont: Wadsworth Press, 1979.

Machan, Tibor, R. *Human Rights and Human Liberties*. Chicago: Nelson Hall, 1975.

_____. "Are There Any Human Rights?" *The Personalist* 59, no. 2 (April 1978): 165.

_____. "Some Recent Work In Human Rights Theory." *American Philosophical Quarterly* 17, no. 2 (April 1980): 103-115.

_____. "Moral Myths and Basic Positive Rights." *Positive and Negative Duties*. ed. Eric Mack. New Orleans: Tulane University Press, 1985.

MacCormick, Neil. "Childrens' Rights: A Test-Case for Theories of Right." *Legal Right and Social Democracy*. Oxford: Clarendon, 1982.

Macpherson, C. B. *The Rise and Fall of Economic Justice and Other Papers*. New York: Oxford University Press, 1985.

Machan, Tibor. "Are There Any Human Rights?" *The Personalist* 59, no. 2 (April 1978): 169.

MacIntyre, Alasdair. *After Virtue*. South Bend: University of Notre Dame, 1981.

Mack, Eric, ed. *Positive and Negative Duties*. New Orleans:

Tulane University Press, 1985.

Mackie, J. L. "Can There Be A Rights-Based Moral Theory?" *MidWest Studies In Philosophy* 3 (1978): 350-359.

Magnet, Myron. "The Rich and the Poor: Are the Haves Responsible for the Disquieting Plight of the Have-Nots?" *Fortune* 117 (6 June 1988): 206-20.

Makkai, Laszlo. "The Development of Human Rights in Hungary from the Reformation to the Present." *Soundings* LXVII, no 2 (Summer 1984).

Malik, Charles. "Human Rights and the United Nations," *United Nations Bulletin* 13 (1 September 1952): 253.

Malthus, Thomas. *Essay on the Principle of Population.* Homewood, Illinois: Richard D. Irwin, Pub., 1963.

Martin, Rex, and Nickel, James "A Bibliography on the Nature and Foundations of Rights, 1947-1977." *Political Theory* 6:3 (August 1978): 395-413. Annotated.

Marx, Karl. "On the Jewish Question." ed. Frederick Engels, *Collected Works* III (London, 1975), 162.

McCloskey, H. J., "Rights," *Philosophy Quarterly* 15 (1965): 118.

McCulloch, Lawrence, Thomas Fenton, and Toland, Gene "The Myth of Capitalism." *Moral Issues and Christian Response.* eds. Paul Jersild and Dale A. Johnson. New York: Holt, Rinehart and Winston, 1983.

McMahan, Jeff. *Reagan and the World.* London: Pluto Press, 1984.

Melden, A. I. *Human Rights.* Belmont: Wadsworth Pub. Co., 1970.

Michael, Wes. "Jimmy Carter, Jacques Ellul, and human rights."

Sojourners 6, no. 6 (June 1977).

Miguez-Bonino, José. "Theology and Human Rights." An unpublished, private paper.

_____. "Religious Commitment and Human Rights: A Christian Perspective" *Understanding Human Rights: An Interdisciplinary and Interfaith Study.* ed. Alan D. Falconer. Dublin: Irish School of Ecumenics, 1980.

Miller, Allen O., ed. "A Christian Declaration on Human Rights." *Theological Studies of the World Alliance of Reformed Churches.* Grand Rapids: Eerdmans Pub. Co., 1977: Chap. 4.

Mitra, Kana. "Human Rights in Hinduism." *Human Rights in Religious Traditions.* ed. Arlene Swidler. New York: Pilgrim Press, 1982.

Moltmann, Jürgen. *On Human Dignity: Political Theology and Ethics.* Translated by M. Douglas Meeks. Philadelphia: Fortress Press, 1984.

Montgomery, John Warwick. *Human Rights & Human Dignity.* Grand Rapids, Michigan: Zondervan Pub., 1986.

Morgenthau, Hans. "Political Theory of Foreign Aid." *American Foreign Policy in International Perspective.* Englewood Cliffs: Prentice-Hall, 1971.

Mott, Stephen Charles. "The Contribution of the Bible to Human Rights." *Human Rights and the Global Mission of the Church.* Cambridge: Boston Theological Institute, 1983.

Mower, Glenn. *International Cooperation for Social Justice.* Westport: Greenwood Press, 1985.

Muravchik, Joshua. *The Uncertain Crusade: Jimmy Carter and the Dilemma of Human Rights Policy.* Lanham: Hamilton Press, 1986.

Murray, Charles. *Losing Ground: American Social Policy, 1950-1980*. New York: Basic Books, 1984.

_____. *In Pursuit of Happiness and Good Government*. New York: Simon and Schuster, 1988.

Nagami, Isamu. "Cultural Gaps: Why Do We Misunderstand?" *Liberation and Ethics*. ed. Charles Amjad-Ali. Chicago: Center for the Scientific Study of Religion, 1985.

Nanda, Ved P. *Global Human Rights: Public Policies, Comparative Measures, and NGO Strategies*. Boulder: Westview Press, 1981.

Narveson, Jan. "Negative and Positive Rights in Gewirth's Reason and Morality." *Gewirth's Ethical Rationalism*. ed. Edward Regis, Jr. Chicago: University of Chicago Press, 1984.

_____. "Positive/Negative: Why Bother?" *Positive and Negative Duties*, ed. Eric Mack. New Orleans, La.: Tulane University 1986, 56.

Neal, Marie, A. *The Just Demands of the Poor*. Paulist Press: 1986.

Neuhaus, Richard John. "The Goal Is Not To Describe." *This World* 9 (Fall 1984): 105-110.

_____. "Beyond the Bounds?" *The Reformed Journal* (February 1985): 6.

New York Times. "Malcolm X Bids Africans Take Negro Issue to U.N." (18 July 1964): 2.

_____. "Malcolm X Seeks U.N. Negro Debate." (13 August 1964): 22.

_____. "From Micah to the New Beginning." (21 January 1977).

334

_____. "Plea by King's Father Add Touch of Revivalism to the Day." Funeral service by Methodist Bishop Cannon and Reverend Martin Luther King, Sr. (21 January 1977).

_____. A Human Rights Memo by Deputy Secretary of State, William Clark (5 November 1981).

Nickel, James. *Making Sense of Human Rights.* Berkeley: University of California Press, 1987.

Niebuhr, Reinhold. "Preface" to Maurice Cranston. *What Are Human Rights?* New York: Basic Books, 1962.

Nielson, Kai. "Scepticism and Human Rights." *The Monist* 52 (October 1981): 573-594.

Nietzsche, Friedrich. *The Gay Science.* Kauffman, 1974, section 335.

Novak, Michael. *The March of Defeat: Morality and Foreign Policy.* Washington, D.C.: Georgetown Press, 1978.

_____. "Human Rights and Whited Sepulchres." ed. Howard J. Wiarda. *Human Rights and U. S. Human Rights Policy.* Washington: American Institute for Public Policy Research, 1982.

_____. *Toward the Future Catholic Social Thought and the U. S. Economy:A Lay Letter.* New York, New York: Lay Commission on Catholic Social Teaching and the U.S. Economy, 1984.

_____. "Economic Rights: The Servile State." *Catholicism in Crisis* (October 1985).

_____. "Where the Second Draft Errs." *America* 154 , no. 2 (18 January 1986): 23-24.

_____. "Economic Rights: Rethinking the Bishop's Second Draft Could Lead to Something that Endures." *National*

Catholic Register (16 February 1986): 2.

_____. "Free Persons and the Common Good." *Crisis* (October 1986), 19.

_____. "Attacking Problems Money Can't Solve" *New York Times* (22 March 1987), sec. F, p. 2.

_____. "The Rights and Wrongs of 'Economic Rights': A Debate Continued." *This World* 17, no. 17 (Spring 1987).

_____. "Truth About Poverty." *Forbes* (11 December 1989):82.

Nozick, Robert. *Anarchy, State and Utopia*. Oxford, 1974.

O'Grady, Ron. *Bread and Freedom*. Geneva: World Council of Churches, 1979.

Okin, Susan Moller. "Liberty and Welfare: Some Issues in Human Rights Theory." *Nomos*. 23, ed. Pennock and Chapman. New York: New York University Press, 1981.

O'Manique, John O. "The Ethics of Survival." *Philosophy Forum* 15 (1977): 225-243.

Orwell, George. *1984*. New York: Harcourt, Brace & Jovanovich, 1982.

Orwin, Clifford, and Thomas L. Pangle, Thomas L. "Restoring the Human Rights Tradition." *This World* 3 (Fall, 1982): 22.

Pacini, David. *The Cunning of Modern Religious Thought*. Philadelphia: Fortress Press, 1987.

Paine, Thomas. *Agrarian Justice*. Philadelphia: Folwell, 1797.

Paul, Ellen Frankel; Miller, Jr., Fred D., and Paul, Jeffrey, eds. *Human Rights*. Oxford: Basil Blackwood Pub., 1984.

Pope John Paul II. "Encyclical Letter of the Supreme Pontiff John Paul II: Sollicitudo Rei Socialis." *L'Osservatore Romano*. (English edition, February 29, 1988).

Peffer, Rodney. "A Defense of Rights to Well-Being." *Philosophy and Public Affairs* 8 no. 1 (Fall 1978): 65-87.

Pennock, J. Roland, and Chapman, John W. *Human Rights Nomos XXIII Yearbook of the Society for American Political & Legal Philosophy*. New York: New York University Press, 1981.

Petro, Nicolai. N. *The Predicament of Human Rights: The Carter and Reagan Policies*. Lanham, Maryland: University of America Press, 1983.

Piscatori, James P. "Human Rights In Indian Political Culture." *The Moral Imperatives of Human Rights*. ed. Kenneth W. Thompson. University Press of America, 1980.

Plant, Raymond. "Needs, Agency and Rights." *Law, Rights and the Welfare State*. ed. C. J. G. Sampford and D. J. Galligan. London: Croom Helm, 1986.

Polis, Adamantia, and Peter Schwab. "Human Rights: A Western Construct With Limited Applicability." *Human Rights-Cultural and Ideological Perspectives*. New York: Praeger Press, 1979.

Pratt, Virginia. *The Influence of Domestic Controversy on American Participation in the U. N. Commission on Human Rights*. New York: Garland Publishing Co., 1986.

Ramsey, Paul. *Christian Ethics and the Sit-In*. New York: Association Press, 1961.

Rawls, John. *A Theory of Justice*. Cambridge: Belknap Press, 1971.

Raphael, D. D. *Political Theory and the Rights of Man*. ed. D. D. Raphael. Bloomington: Indiana University Press, 1967.

Regis, Edward Jr. *Gewirth's Ethical Rationalism: Critical Essays with a Reply by Alan Gewirth*. Chicago: University of Chicago, 1984.

Renteln, Alison Dunden. "A Conceptual Analysis of International Human Rights." Ph.D. dissertation, Berkeley: University of California, 1987.

Ricard, John. "Hunger: A Moral Issue." *Origins* 17, no. 39 (10 March 1988).

Ritchie, David. *Natural Rights*. Woodport: Hyperion Press, 1952.

Roosevelt, Franklin Delano. "The Four Freedoms." *U. S. Office of War Information* (1942): 3-15.

_____. *The Public Papers and Addresses of F. D. R.* New York: Harper & Row, 1942.

_____. "Economic Rights." *The Human Rights Reader.* ed. Walter Laqueur and Barry Rubin. Philadelphia: Temple University Press, 1979.

Rosenbaum, Alan S. *The Philosophy of Human Rights: International Perspectives*. Westport: Greenwood Press, 1980.

Sadurski, Wojciech. "Economic Rights and Basic Needs." *Law, Rights and the Welfare State.* ed. Charles Sampford and D. J. Galligan. London: Croom Helm, 1986.

Sampford, Charles, and Galligan, D. J., eds. *Law, Rights, and the Welfare State*. London: Croom Helm, 1986.

Sandel, Michael J. *Liberalism and the Limits of Justice*. Cambridge: University Press, 1982.

Scanlon, Thomas. "Nozick on Rights, Liberty, and Property." *Philosophy and Public Affairs* 8: 3.

338

Scheuermann, James. "Gewirth's Concept of Prudential Rights." *The Philosophical Quarterly* 37, no. 148: 291.

Schlesinger, Arthur. "Human Rights and the American Tradition." *Foreign Affairs* 57, no. 3: 511.

_____. "The Great Carter Mystery." *The New Republic* 182, (12 April 1980), cover page.

Schultz, George. *Human Rights and the Moral Dimensions of U.S. Foreign Policy.* Peoria, Ill. (22 February 1984).

Schwelb, Egon. *Human Rights and the International Community.* Chicago: Quadrangle Books, 1964.

Sellers, James. "Human Rights and the American Tradition of Justice." *Soundings* 42, no. 3 (Fall 1979): 226.

Sen, Amartya. *On Ethics and Economics.* Oxford: Basil Blackwell, Pub. 1987.

Shepherd, George. "Transnational Development of Human Rights: The Third World Crucible." *Global Human Rights: Public Policies, Comparative Measures, and NGO Strategies.* ed. Ved P. Nanda, James R. Scaritt and George W. Shepherd, Jr. Boulder: Westview Press, 1981.

Shearmur, Jeremy. "The Right to Subsistence in a 'Lockean' State of Nature." *The Southern Journal of Philosophy* XXVII, no. 4, (1989): 561-68.

Shue, Henry. *Basic Rights: Subsistence, Affluence, and U.S. Foreign Policy.* Princeton: Princeton University Press, 1981.

_____. "Mediating Duties." *Ethics* 98, no.4 (July 1988): 678-704.

Singer, Peter. "Famine, Affluence, and Morality." *Philosophy and Public Affairs* 1, no. 3 (Spring 1972): 229-243.

Smith, Adam. *Lectures on Jurisprudence.* ed. R. L. Meek, D. D. Raphael and P. G. Stein. Oxford: Oxford University, 1977.

_____. *Theory of Moral Sentiments.* Indianapolis: Liberty Classics, 1982.

Smith, Ervin. *The Ethics of Martin Luther King.* New York: Mellon Press, 1981.

Sowell, Thomas. *Civil Rights: Rhetoric or Reality?"* New York: William Morrow, 1984.

Stackhouse, Max. *Creeds, Society, and Human Rights: A Study In Three Cultures.* Grand Rapids: Eerdmans, 1984.

Starke, J. G. "Human Rights and International Law." *Human Rights.* ed. Eugene Kamenka and Alice Erh-Soon Tay. New York: St. Martin's Press, 1978.

Stout, Jeffery. *Ethics after Babel: The Language of Morals and Their Discontents.* Boston: Beacon Press, 1990.

Streeten, Paul. "Basic Needs and Human Rights." *World Development* 8 (1980): 107-111.

Sweeny, Vernon E. "A Note on Classical Economics." *Social Science* 52, no 2 (Spring 1977): 90-93.

Swidler, Arlene, ed. *Human Rights in Religious Traditions.* New York: Pilgrim Press, 1982.

Szabo, Stephen F. "Contemporary French Orientations Toward Economic and Political Dimensions of Human Rights." *Universal Human Rights* 1, no. 3 (July-September 1979): 51-76.

Tay, Alice Erh-Soon. "Marxism, socialism and human rights," *Human Rights.* New York: St. Martin's Press, 1978.

Thielicke, Helmut. *Theological Ethics, II, Politics.* Philadelphia:

340

Fortress Press, 1969.

Thomas, J. Mark. "Myth and Mythos of Meritocracy." *The Ecumenist* 26, no. 1 (November-December, 1987).

Traer, Robert. *Being Human . . . Becoming Human.* Garden City: Doubleday & Co., 1984.

_____. "Human Rights: A Global Faith." Ph.D. diss., Graduate Theological Union, 1988.

_____. "Religious Communities in the Struggle for Human Rights." *The Christian Century* (28 September 1988): 835-838.

Upton, Hugh. "Rights and Duties: A Reply to Gewirth" *Mind* (1986): 329-344.

United Nations Publication. *The International Bill of Human Rights.* Forward by Jimmy Carter. Glen Ellyn: Entwhistle Books, 1981.

U. S. Catholic Bishops. "Economic Justice for All: Catholic Social Teaching and the U.S. Economy." *Origins* 16, no. 3 (5 June 1986): 33-76.

U.S. News. "Moral Policeman to the World." 82: 17-21.

U. S. News and World Report. "Overhaul U. S. Policy on Human Rights?" Debate by Patricia Derian in her rebuttal to Kirkpatrick's criticisms (2 March 1981).

Vance, Cyrus. *Hard Choices.* New York: Simon and Schuster, 1983.

_____. "The Human Rights Imperative." *Foreign Policy* 63, (Summer 1986): 4-8.

Van De Veer, Donald. "A Right To Be Saved From Starvation?" *The Personalist* 60, no. 2 (16 April 1979): 2.

_____. "Are Human Rights Alienable?" *Philosophical Studies* 37 (1980): 165-176.

Van Dyke, Vernon. *Human Rights, Ethnicity and Discrimination*. Westport: Greenwood Press, 1985.

VanElderen, Marlin. "No Crossed Arms." *One World* 128 (September 1987): 11-14.

Vasak, Karel. *The International Dimensions of Human Rights*. Westport, Connecticut: Greenwood Press, 1982.

Velasquez, Manuel, and Rostankowski, Cynthia, ed. *Ethics, Theory and Practice*. Englewood Cliffs: Prentice Hall, 1985.

Vogelgesang, Sandy. *American Dream? Global Nightmare: The Dilemma of U. S. Human Rights Policy*. New York: W. W. Norton & Co., 1980.

Waldron, Jeremy. "Welfare and the Images of Charity." *The Philosophical Quarterly* 36, no. 145 (October 1986) 463-482.

_____. *Nonsense on Stilts: Bentham, Burke and Marx on the Rights of Man*. London: Methuen and Co., 1987.

Wall Street Journal. "The Reagan Approach to Human Rights Policy." Editorial by Michael Novak. (28 April 1981).

Walzer, Michael. *Just and Unjust Wars: A Moral Argument with Historical Illustrations*. New York: Basic Books, 1977.

_____. *Spheres of Justice: A Defense of Pluralism and Equality*. New York: Basic Books, 1983.

Wein, Sheldon. *Spheres of Justice: A Defense of Pluralism and Equality*. New York: Basic Books, 1983.

_____. "Rights and Needs." *Dialogue* (Canadian) 26 (Spring 1987): 55.

_____. "Libertarianism and Welfare Rights." *Philosophical Essays on the Ideas of a Good Society*. ed. Yeager Hudson and Creighton Peden Lewiston: Edwin Mellen Press 1988.

_____. Weingartner, Erich. *Human Rights on the Ecumenical Agenda*. Geneva: Commission of the Churches on International Affairs-World Council of Churches, 1983.

Weissbrodt, David. "The Role of International Non-Government Organizations in the Implementation of Human Rights." *Texas International Law Journal* 2 (1977): 293-320.

Wellman, Carl. *A Theory of Rights*. Totowa, NJ: Rowman and Allanheld Pub., 1985: 9.

White, Alan. *Rights*. Oxford: Clarendon, 1984.

Winch, Donald. *Adam Smith's Politics*. Cambridge: Cambridge University Press, 1978.

Willard, L. Duane. "Needs and Rights." *Dialogue* (Canadian) 26 (Spring 1987): 42.

_____. *Virginia Journal of International Law* 22, no. 1 (1981): 1-89.

Wilson, William J. *The Truly Disadvantaged*. Chicago: University of Chicago Press, 1987.

_____. "The Charge of the Little Platoons." *New York Times Review of Books* (23 October 1988): 12.

Wogaman, J. Philip. *Christians and the Great Economic Debate*. London: SCM Press, 1977.

_____. *Economics and Ethics: A Christian Inquiry*. Philadelphia: Fortress Press, 1986.

Wolterstorff, Nicholas. *Until Justice and Peace Embrace.* Grand Rapids: Eerdmans Pub. Co., 1983.

_____. "Christianity and Social Justice." *Christian Scholar's Review* 16, no. 3 (1987): 211-248.

Wood, David. "Nozick's Justification of the Minimal State." *Ethics* 88, no. 3 (April, 1978): 260.

X, Malcolm. "A Letter To Cairo." *By Any Means Necessary.* New York: Pathfinder Press, 1970.

_____. "Appeal to African Heads of State." *Malcolm X Speaks: Selected Speeches and Statements.* ed. George Breitman. New York: Grove Press, 1965.

_____. and Haley, Alex. *The Autobiography of Malcolm X.* New York: Grove Press, 1965.

Young, T. R. "The Sociology of Human Rights." *Humanity in Society* 5, no. 4 (November, 1981): 353-369.

GOVERNMENT SOURCES CONSULTED

Carter, Jimmy. *Papers, 1977,* 1328.

_____. "Inaugural Address." *Department of State Bulletin.* (20 January 1977).

_____. "President Carter Signs Covenants on Human Rights," *Department of State Bulletin* 77, no. 2001 (31 October 1977): 586, 587.

_____. "Interview With the President," *Weekly Compilation of Presidential Documents,* (19 December 1977).

_____. "Human Rights Day and Week," *Department of State Bulletin* 78, no. 2010, 38.

_____. "Message from the President of the United States, Transmitting His Recommendations for Welfare Reform: A Message Referred to the Committees on Ways and Means, Education and Labor, and Agriculture." *House Document No. 96-131.* Washington D. C.: GPO, 1979.

_____. "International Development: A Message from The President of the United States, Transmitting: A Report on

Steps He has Taken and Proposes to Take to Strengthen The Coordination Of U.S. Economic Policies Affecting Developing Countries, Pursuant to Section 303 of Public Law 95-424," *House Document No. 96-70,* Washington, D. C.: GPO (8 March 1979).

Christopher, Warren. "Human Rights: An Important Concern of U.S. Policy." *Department of State Bulletin* 76, no. 1970, (28, March 1977): 290-91.

_____. "Four Treaties on Human Rights," *GPO Policy* 112, Washington, D. C. (14 November 1979): 2.

_____. "The Diplomacy of Human Rights: The First Year." Speech made before the American Bar Association. Bureau of Public Affairs, Office of Public Communication. Washington, D.C. (13 February 1978): 4.

Derian, Patricia. "Human Rights: A World Perspective." *Current Policy Statement* No. 42. Washington, D. C. (November 1978), 2.

Reagan, Ronald. *Department of State Bulletin* 81.

Roosevelt, Franklin Delano. "The Four Freedoms." *U. S. Office of War Information* (1942): 3-15.

Schultz, George. *Human Rights and the Moral Dimensions of U.S. Foreign Policy.* Peoria, Ill (22 February 1984).

Vance, Cyrus. "Secretary Testifies on Administration's Approach to Foreign Assistance." *Department of State Bulletin* 76, no 1968 (14 March 1977).

_____. "Foreign Assistance Authorization, Hearings before the Committee On Foreign Relations and the Subcommittee On Foreign Assistance, Ninety-Fifth Congress." *Washington, D. C.: GPO* (23, 24, 25 March 1977).

_____. "Human Rights and Foreign Policy." Law Day Address at the University of Georgia. *Department of State*

Bulletin 76 , no. 1978 (30 April 1977): 505.

_____. *Department of State Bulletin 76, no. 1978, 508.*

_____. *Department of State Bulletin 77.*

_____. "Secretary Testifies on Administration's Approach to Foreign Assistance." *Department of State Bulletin* 76, no. 1968, 236.

_____. "Secretary Testifies on Administration's Approach to Foreign Assistance." *Department of State Bulletin* 76, no. 1968, (14 March 1977): 237.

Young, Andrew. "The Challenge to the Economic & Social Council: Advancing the Quality of Life in All Its Aspects." *Department of State Bulletin 76* (16 May 1977): 496.

_____. "A New Unity and a New Hope in the Western Hemisphere: Economic Growth with Social Justice." *Department of State Bulletin 76, no. 1979* (30 May 1977): 576.

_____. "Human Rights." *Department of State Bulletin* 79, no. 2023 (February 1979): 59, 60.

INDEX

352

353